THE
PROMISE
OF THE
CITY

THE PROMISE OF THE CITY

Adventures in learning cities and higher education

DAVID WILMOTH

LANEWAY PRESS

First published in October 2021
by Laneway Press
Abbotsford Convent
St Heliers Street
Abbotsford Victoria 3067
Australia
www.lanewaypress.com.au
info@lanewaypress.com.au
Instagram: @lanewaypress

A catalogue record for this book is available from the National Library of Australia

All '$' signs are for Australian dollars unless otherwise indicated.

Unless otherwise indicated, all photographs are by the author. All reasonable efforts were taken to obtain copyright material reproduced in this book, but in some cases copyright could not be traced. The author welcomes information in this regard.

Cover design and layout: Luke Harris, Working Type Studio

ISBN: 978-0-6450070-3-9 (hardback)
978-0-6450070-4-6 (ebook)

For Patrick Troy

CONTENTS

INVITATION TO ADVENTURE

This book began its life as a collection of adventures and misadventures in urban policy, university development, and intercultural learning in Australia and around the world. I started writing with an urge to set down key events of my working life; this included some important periods of history in major institutions not before recorded. But as I reviewed the stories, it became clear there was much more to tell—my development as a professional and as a person, the roots of my values and why, as an urban planner, activist, technocrat, university leader and consultant, some of my work came to fruition and other work failed or just faded away. For much of my career I was out my depth. I took risks, learned by doing, and was helped by friends, family and mentors along the way.

The events recounted in this book are all set in vital periods of change from the 1960s to the present day. They help us see, through my eyes and my reflections, my scrapes and near misses, the enormous social and economic changes to Australia and other countries over that time, the rise and fall of neo-liberal practices in public policy, the globalisation of economies, and the underside of the modern capitalist state.

One's values form in practice and it is not always easy to identify their origins. I grew up in Queensland as a typical baby boomer with little direction but a feeling the world was at my feet. A year at a US boarding school gave me independence and self-assurance, but it exposed me to the deep inequalities in urban life there. An unexpected dose of culture shock and friendships with people from other countries made me yearn for better understanding across borders and stoked an interest in international affairs. A university education in urban geography and economics then strengthened my desire to understand how cities change. I wanted to get to the bottom of what had to be done to make them fairer. Around me, the war in Vietnam and the suppression of dissent in the streets of Brisbane politicised this desire, though I was not sure whether this should be through reform or radical change. I was not alone in these thoughts. The movements of the 1960s inspired a whole generation to question the decisions of our leaders.

I had a chance in Sydney of the 1970s to develop my ideas further at university and put them into practice through professional experience in planning firms and joining urban social movements of the time. The period consolidated my values, and I jumped at the opportunity to work with the Whitlam government in Canberra, and Tom Uren's new department, where social justice was driving urban and regional policies and programs. It was heady work, wielding influence way beyond my earlier expectations. But the limits put around the changes we wanted, by politics and the immovability of the structure of state, were hard to take. Sadly, much of the work of that government did not survive.

I left government after the 'constitutional coup' of 1975 to drift across Asia in a half-formed spiritual quest, then I spent the next six years in California, studying at the University of California at Berkeley. Reviewing my Australian experience in the time available at Berkeley, I thought about what it would take to be a more effective agent of change, so I joined a New Left group to test out the path of radical action.

My understanding of the need for fundamental change towards greater equality and more equal distribution of power grew during the California years, and my resolve hardened. I re-entered government in Sydney with technocratic optimism as an expert and policy executive for nearly six years during the turbulent 1980s, leading metropolitan planning and putting into place the systems for good urban growth management. This approach kept me away from statutory urban planning as far as possible. I was led by what I saw as the need for whole-of-government commitment to strategic planning and good urban management, using financial and other instruments way outside the planner's normal toolkit.

But here, too, time saw the innovations my colleagues and I made withered by neglect and political amnesia. Returning to my understanding of the role of the capitalist state, I was starting to see that a key path to reform and radical change should be on good governance, the framework around how we make decisions, whether that governance is of metropolitan areas or, as corporate governance, within organisations. I was tired of coming up against the inertia of the state in which policymakers are situated. Virtually all my friends from Berkeley were pursuing intellectual careers, shaping critical ideas. Perhaps I could push my ideas through a more academic channel too.

I was thus attracted to Melbourne into a deanship in 1988 and then other senior jobs as a university leader. Unprepared for university management at first, I ended up working at RMIT for 17 years during historic change to the sector. This period saw mass access to higher education, institutional mergers, building the framework of a new university, going through a crisis of governance, leading explosive growth in international programs and internationalisation, and starting up successful and unsuccessful offshore campuses. Starting up RMIT Vietnam was a most rewarding experience.

During much of the work I was again out of my depth, but so were many of my colleagues. The commitment to practical education of the 'working man's college'—as RMIT was traditionally known—attracted me. Its commitment to internationalisation and multicultural engagement sustained me. Working in the education sector in other countries opened my eyes to the transformation that higher education can bring to societies. I agreed with the aspiration that one of the most important ways to overcome poverty is through education.

I left RMIT in 2005 to work on advising and managing international projects where cities and education come together. I enjoyed helping others start new campuses, develop education hubs and other ventures in many countries. I was not always prepared for the task, nor the adventures I was drawn into along the way. The classic frustration of being a consultant without executive power to implement recommendations dogged me too. Whether as a practitioner of urban policy or a leader in a university, I was always drawn to the latest methods of leadership and management. I saw myself serving up policy solutions and the technocratic means to enable leaders and mass movements to address equity, efficiency and social inclusion. On reflection, I see that some results lasted and some did not.

Honestly though, how much change can one keen professional make, even with executive authority? The question tests the power of agency and the limits of collaborative leadership. In my dissertation work at Berkeley, I started out with a fascination with the structure of the modern state, especially the 'local state' where much of the power to manage cities lies. That includes the states in Australia. Political movements, bureaucratic reform and individual leadership always come face-to-face with the seeming impossibility of changing some things. The experience of national urban policy in the Whitlam government and the US Carter administration shows that amply.

Yes, there are always limits, as I was to learn. But look closer. Nothing in governance is immutable. Regimes, constitutions, laws and practices are all socially constructed and they do not only change as a result of abstract structural forces. The state is not just a reflection of the economy and an enabler of its mode of production. It is also a mesh of contested arenas. One actor's 'not possible' can be another's opportunity. There's plenty of room for manoeuvre, and my great mentors showed me how, with vision and drive, that could be done. I wanted to be like them—brave and strong, willing to take things apart when necessary. Change is never smooth— growth and development often come through 'creative destruction'.[1]

For a time, I was fascinated with urban communications and the idea of harnessing the exploding power of technology to the betterment of cities. It was a small field of work then, huge now. It had the potential to be a career relevant for what has come about, but I am glad I didn't follow it. Policy and action trumped research and technology among my priorities during the Whitlam government. The spatial inequalities across cities, a concern of mine right through my career, stay as stark as ever. Even deeper structural inequalities in wealth and real income are laid bare in societies around the world.

It is as if I have returned to the place of the formation of my values in the 1970s, and have come to understand it for the first time.

The two major threads of my life have always been intertwined—strategic urban planning and education leadership—with education a key part of urban development. The cities and towns in which most universities are embedded provided a rich learning environment. I saw the potential of consciously planned education hubs and technology precincts. This work aligned strongly with my values, as wider access and opportunity for learning is a key pathway to a more equitable society.

The stories in this book indirectly document part of the greater societal changes of the last half-century: the long post-war boom coming to an end; government 'reinvented' by neo-liberal practices of privatisation, corporatisation and public–private partnerships; cities transformed by technology and marred by neglect and bad decisions; the old prescriptive urban planning going 'strategic' and then losing its way; universities radically restructured and internationalised; a world failing to learn across time and cultures. Much of what has been wrought by neo-liberalism has to be undone before we can progress. Reinvigorating government and empowering civil society are necessary for a more humane capitalism and a more collective economy.

Being the technocrat, knowing what should be done isn't enough. Fortune does favour the prepared mind, the person with a plan, but it also smiles on those with an appetite for risk and a good degree of determination.

And so I extend an invitation to adventure to you, the reader, in the hope that you'll join me as we explore these changing times and the ongoing promise of the city.

ONE

QUEENSLAND ROOTS AND BRANCHING OUT

The older kids in Beaton Street wouldn't let me play with them. Miffed, I rounded up the younger set and we went under a house. Queensland houses then were built high on flood-resistant stilts, with the resulting space on the ground often becoming an inverted attic. We pulled together boxes and other props and went on an imaginary train trip around Mackay. The big kids came back and joined in playing with us too; the more the merrier as far as I was concerned.

That wasn't my earliest memory, but I remember I always wanted to break out, even from my earliest days cooped up in a playpen. My first playpen was actually in Bundaberg, Queensland. I was born in November 1946, an early baby boomer. My mother, Norma (née Ferrier), came from a grazing family near Roma. She was generous, caring and chaotic. My father, Geoff, returned from the Second World War, was the city engineer of Bundaberg. He grew up in Horsham, Victoria, the son of a solicitor and three-time mayor of Horsham. Coming north after graduation to find a civil engineering job during the Great Depression, he met and married Norma in Roma. Shortly thereafter he enlisted in the Australian Infantry Force (AIF) and went to the war. It was nearly four years before they reunited. They wasted no time in starting a family upon my father's return; after me, they had four daughters in eight years. We had a large group of relatives and friends, and a full social life as a family.

Sometimes stern, remote and absorbed in work, my father had a sense of fun about him and, especially in those early years, was a doting father. We moved to Mackay in 1948 and later Toowoomba in 1954. Geoff did not hold back on his ambition for me. I was given 'engineering' toys—Meccano, Bayco (a house building set), Hornby trains and so on. Sunday family drives would include visiting project sites for Toowoomba's infrastructure and conducting searches for new dams. My mother and others in the community later rued that Perseverance Dam, which my father started and saw to operation, was not named after him.

Toowoomba was a city small enough for me to imagine, as a child, the range of professions I could follow. Charles Barton, Queensland's coordinator-general, in charge of infrastructure and regional development for the state, was a close friend of my parents and godfather to my sister Bessie. Dad and Charlie talked about development projects when we visited each other. My father wanted me to be a scientist, sadly then a more glamourous calling than it is today. Perhaps, post-COVID-19, science might rise again as an attractive career. I was scrabbling towards geology as I liked collecting rocks and semi-precious stones, some of them from the council quarry nearby which was under Dad's responsibility. He didn't know I used to jump the fence and go fossicking there, a place of occasional gelignite blasts. When I shared this passion for geology with my US pen pal, he called me a 'rockhound'.

School at Toowoomba East State School was a typical set of ups and downs. My home life was mostly unsupervised. My father was too busy with work and my mother was spread too thin across five children. The long walk to and from school let me wander around the eastern side of Toowoomba, and on weekends I could hike 'down the range' (part of the Great Dividing Range), and sometimes camp overnight at the Seven Mile Caves. There, I learned to fill empty old bullet shells with match-heads and hit them with a hammer to make a big 'bang'. It felt good to make a noise.

I fiddled ineptly with science and technology, breaking rules as I went. I made a chemistry set mostly of household chemicals, and I melted lead from stray roof-nails in my mother's saucepans. I built a multi-storey treehouse in the bunya pines, and made lethal shanghais with strong wire and aeroplane rubber, grateful for the tools in Dad's shed, his retreat. With these I would exact schoolyard revenge on the bums of school bullies, for which I copped more than one beating as they laid in wait for me on the walk home. Though they didn't start by bullying me, they were picking on weaker kids and I was determined not to let them get away with their behaviour.

I found that the world could be unfair. I was knocked out in the first round of the state-wide finals of *The Telegraph* spelling bee with the rare word *pibroch*, in a competition saddened by the death by road crash of the newspaper driver coming up to Toowoomba to collect me.

I also found that the system can be gamed, as when I used a thesaurus to substitute hard words for easy ones in school essays. One of which, about an 'erudite old owl', was read, to my embarrassment, to the visiting school inspector.

I was disillusioned at school and bored by the stuffy norms of the conservative social environment. As I grew older, I wanted to make my own way. At family gatherings we didn't talk about topics that interested me; perhaps I was a little arrogant, and I was certainly rude on such occasions. Though relatives and family friends were kind to me, I wanted to break out somehow. I read a lot, despite my mother saying 'get off your bed and go out and play with the other kids'. I became interested in jazz and wanted to become a beatnik—without knowing much about the beat generation—and to be a big city cool guy.

I was privileged, to be sure, known as the son of the prominent city engineer. I was even picked on in class by a teacher for that. But the reality of poverty came home to me over a week on a farm in Cambooya (about 30 minutes from Toowoomba) with a friend's grandparents. We lived on their dirt floors and bathed in a tin tub in shared water. I felt pity and injustice, but at eight years old I had no idea these disadvantages were part of a wider societal pattern that I was yet to discover.

With my friends in Toowoomba we formed a little gang called 'Droop'.

We dared each other to do silly stunts like midnight swims in the Fairholme pool at a girls' boarding school, and even dressing up as a girl to go to that school one morning, only to be chased away by a teacher. I liked rabble-rousing, and as a schoolboy I had little purpose in life.

After primary school my father sent me off to boarding school in Brisbane at 'Churchie' (Church of England Grammar School), much against my will. He thought it would open up more educational opportunities and he nudged me towards science. I sorely missed my Toowoomba friends and my freedom. Against school rules I broke out and roamed around Brisbane, using the trams years before the car lobby had them ripped up. I loved geography—getting to know a little of the big world out there—and English, the latter because Gavin 'Bomber' Vance was an exceptional teacher. He was rotund, fierce, clouded in pipe smoke, and a Jungian in his approach to life and literature. His sex-drenched archetypes were eye-opening to me.

Unfortunately, he was also my boarding housemaster. He caned ('socked') me so many times I had the status of scoring the highest number of canings in my year across the school. How shocking to find out only now that he is the subject of post-mortem allegations of gang-raping a Churchie student.[1]

I am not sure whether a streak of defiance in my makeup was a cause or result of that punishment. I seemed to want to break all the rules—destroy them—but I had little idea of what the alternative values should be. Here was a young man of 17, without direction, naïve about politics, unformed but for the example and direction of my father and the generosity of my mother, but feeling that the environment in which I was growing up, supportive though it might be, was not enough. It was too stuffy for new ideas, and could be very unfair.

An adventure of a lifetime

A year as an exchange student to the USA in 1964–65, the middle of my senior year, changed all that. It gave me an opportunity to start again in a rich learning environment, make new friends and independently explore US cities. There were challenges: unexpected culture shock, some loneliness, the normal frustrations of adolescence. More important, though, I learnt self-reliance, some understanding of wealth, race and inequality, and got an insight into different cultures. I also started to see the need for basic change to modern society, mostly in the realm of politics.

It started when I found out about the American Field Service (AFS) and applied for a scholarship. It would mean losing a year at school, but I was offered a place and accepted. I was thrilled as it was my first overseas trip. I was sure I could handle it; after all, I thought, brimming with confidence, the USA was just like Australia, only better, and I could do anything there.

Five of us Queenslanders set out for the crossing, leaving Sydney in a Boeing 707. We then joined a bunch of over-excited 17-year-old teens from around Australia. Was I in heaven? Looking out the window, I thought so: the clouds were so beautiful I shot two rolls of film on them—just clouds and blue skies. I still remember the stopovers in Nandi and Honolulu, where I had the wrong visa and was nearly left behind. This didn't matter to me in my state of elation, nor even that I had no host family assigned to me at that stage.

For some time, I had been admitted to a boarding school in Wallingford, Connecticut: the Choate School. It was an elite prep school that prepared students for college. However, I did not know where I would spend the summer before school began. En route to the airport out from San Francisco came the news: I would be living with the Iglehart family, consisting of Bob, Jane and four boys. John would be my roommate at Choate, and Steve, Ken, and Whit were his brothers. But something was odd. They all lived in a boarding school, another one, a *girls'* boarding school. This would be interesting ...

I took another flight where Jane Iglehart said to take the limo from Idlewild airport (since renamed JFK) in New York. She would meet me in New Haven, near Westover, which was the name of the girls' school and of its village. And a limo it was, stretched like on TV, impressive indeed for this provincial boy. I was feeling a little out of my depth already. Jane was an elegant, educated New Englander, daughter of a banking family, the Whitcombs. Bob was more reserved, dignified by thoughtful puffing of the pipe, and he had a dry and rather literary sense of humour. Together they gave me a generous welcome, as did the skeleton summer staff of the school.

I was in transition. John was still away at summer camp, and the other boys were moving round, so I had plenty of time to myself. The village of Westover, a classic postcard New England village dressed up for late summer, was gorgeous, and the woods around it were penetrated by long trails. This was pure running country, and by the barns and little lakes I ran and ran, compensating even then for the first pangs of disorientation. I had an affinity for running, and remembering the exhilaration of my early morning runs up 'Big Burleigh' hill on the Gold Coast while at the National Fitness Camp some years earlier, I quickly came to love long-distance running again. I ran every day of that summer.

With John's return from camp came the first taste of unexpected culture shock: my awkwardness at parties John invited me to, and the outspokenness of new friends around me relative to my quietness. ('Modesty is a virtue', the Choate yearbook later said of me, something that hadn't been part of my self-image.)

It was also a step up in sophistication, where a girl who had just performed in Sibelius' first symphony asked me what I thought of it. 'Pretty good', I blurted out, trying to be cool. I found the Iglehart family more formal than my background prepared me for, the rules unstated (I quickly learned not to hang my clothes outside the window to dry—how common!) But they looked after me well.

Westover, I came to learn, was one of the best ladies' prep schools in the country. Kindly, Bob and Jane timed their summer college visits to enable me to come along. They were promoting Westover to good universities for women, including an early trip to Barnard College (affiliated with Columbia University), in Harlem, New York City. This was the summer of 1964, hot and angry, hydrants and hoses. People banged on our big car as we drove slowly through the crowded streets. We may not have been in danger, but Bob and Jane certainly felt the potential as Bob gritted his teeth and kept driving.

This was a dramatic introduction to life in the inner-city, to the roots of the urban riots I had seen on television in Australia. These images stayed with me. We stayed overnight, with Bob and Jane showing me around and talking about race and poverty in New York City. This was a different *West Side Story* from the musical I had memorised at school in Brisbane and with my friends turned into a farce. Here, instead, was the reality around me.

But during this summer transition I was impatient to move on to Choate itself. I finally arrived there in late September. It seemed more like a suburb of Wallingford, spilling out into the countryside, than a school with a fence around it as I knew in Brisbane. I was ready to be impressed—any place that had an indoor running track, 13 squash courts and an 18-hole golf course next door sounded pretty good to me.

The curriculum was collegiate, with electives, small classes, and in the advanced classes which I took—physics and chemistry—reliance was emphasised on self-directed learning. Conservatively, I chose these subjects to align with exam requirements back in Brisbane, given that, on my return, I would only have three months to prepare for the 'do or die' Queensland Senior Public Examination in November. I wasted some of the educational opportunities, cheekily choosing a test of the temperature at which water boiled as my advanced physics project, and making touch powder that blew up on the floor of the chemistry lab when fellow students walked on it. I was not handling my freedom to learn very well.

I was overwhelmed by the richness of the campus, the old buildings, the libraries, the arrangements for learning, and the care of young men. More than that, people my age talked about ideas, made music, did interesting things, and came from all over. This was all so new to me. We had the run of the town—I enjoyed literally running around it, my passion for running unabated—as well as eating apple pie with a regular group at the local 'greasy spoon' and exploring the back streets of this old manufacturing town, not itself so picturesque.

As a result of all that training during the summer holidays (I must have been the only one from school who did), I became a champion runner, even setting records at Choate and the Hotchkiss School, another nearby prep school. The regional standards were clearly not high. Whatever else, this little bit of stardom meant that I was generally well known around the school, and it was easy to make friends when I chose.

Yet, I still carried that feeling of disorientation. The landscape and school activities brought out the photographer in me, which was a solace for the dark feelings that had stayed around. I thought I knew the USA through films and books and wouldn't have difficulty adapting, but I did. More and more I wanted independence, but I was overpowered by the size and complexity of the region around me. The seasons affected my moods; this was new too. I'd never experienced such radical shifts in the weather. The brilliant cool fall, cross-country season and busy; the deep snow of winter that stretched too long through slushy weeks; the green explosion of spring, in the landscape and among the Choaties; and the quiet return of summer. The Red Cross arranged for every foreigner in Wallingford to send home a Christmas message, recorded on 45 rpm vinyl. I can still listen to my uncertain young voice describing school in mid-winter, but expressing none of my feelings.

My housing situation at the school didn't change things. John Iglehart and I shared an upstairs room in Pitman House—known to us as 'the Pit'—with Burr Johnson, my English teacher as the house master, along with his family, including his young children. This is how the house system at Choate worked; our education was intended to be family-based. All the same, I had difficulty adapting to some things.

One was the honour system, under which it was up to each of us to keep the school principles. For a 17-year-old, freshly released from boarding school in Brisbane, this was an invitation to trouble. I had been peer-trained to treat every rule as if it had to be broken. I didn't change my ways at first. My desire for independence and liking for adventure put me at risk.

With Tuck Norton, a Choate graduate from the year before waiting to take up an exchange year in England, we would slip out of Wallingford and drive to bars and freshman 'rushes' (mixer parties) at nearby Yale University in New Haven. Tragically, he took his own life not long after, and though I met in condolence with his parents, I was never aware of his depression.

Sometimes I would go alone into New Haven. It was there I saw my first ever political demonstration, a forlorn group on a frozen street with placards against the growing war in Vietnam. They grew suspicious as I took photographs, and asked me where I was from. It was flattering to be mistaken for a police spy. But the scene of perfectly respectable-looking people protesting on the street about an issue on which I was little aware made a deep impression on me. Feeling against the war was rising in the community, but at Choate the anger and frustration was slow to filter through. I thought later of some of the 'bull sessions' we had; late-night talks about the war and the civil rights movement, among other topics, that would come to embroil many of those friends soon after.

However, the school was not cut off from the outside world. I met Adlai Stevenson, a distinguished statesman and Democrat presidential candidate (and alumnus), in a group to discuss foreign policy, but I was so overawed with the great man I don't recall what we talked about. I do remember what Jimmy Breslin talked about, the journalist famous for interviewing young black men on the street while the moon landing was being telecast ('Why go to the moon when we haven't fixed our cities?'). This echoed my visit to Harlem and raised broader societal issues that I'd seldom considered.

Boarders in the top quintile of academic results at Choate were allowed unlimited weekend leave, and being so close to New York City I wanted to go back there. My grades let me do that. I stayed at AFS headquarters on East 43rd Street, accepted weekend invitations from fellow Choaties, slept in a beatnik flophouse (the 'International Student Hospice' on the Lower East Side for US$2/night), and on a couple of occasions imposed myself on dates' families for the night ('Oh no, it's past midnight, the AFS dorm has closed!')

The free time was a wonderful way for a teenager to explore Gotham—the different districts, the parties, the bars, the subways. At the 1964 World Trade Fair, among other memorable pavilions, I saw the unsettling GM Futurama exhibit, a vision of a giant road-building machine chewing up jungles in under-developed countries and shitting out freeways. It struck a chord.

This was the city-killing modernity loved by Robert Moses, the untouchable 'master builder' and powerbroker of New York's development, whose power was only just starting to wane at the time.[2] Against him was Jane Jacobs, the inspirational opponent of 'urban renewal' and celebrant of neighbourhoods and their participatory planning, whose power was waxing.[3] I didn't know about either of them at the time, but I was learning about New York and I didn't like all that I saw. The seeds of my views on urban politics were planted.

I built a good mental picture of Manhattan. There I bought a decent SLR camera, only to have it stolen from under my nose at Grand Central Station while I was on the phone. I was still the innocent abroad on things like that. Still, I'd shot a few good rolls of film that I'd saved. The school put me into a state inter-scholastic photography competition in which, to my surprise, I won a gold key for a photograph of a skyscraper.

Because the New York, New Haven and Hartford train service to Wallingford (sadly, now deceased) started from Grand Central Station, the Roughrider Room and the Oyster Bar were frequent venues to drink and eat before departure. The Sunday night trip back to school, and not only our school, was a party event, as crowds of lubricated prep school returnees mixed together. One time I had to create a tourniquet with my tie to stop the blood squirting out of the arm of a friend who cut his artery punching a train window. He recovered and thanked me profusely, but I couldn't help thinking I'd been part of some F. Scott Fitzgerald novel (I was reading him at the time) about doomed rich young men living recklessly in the city. I later faced an embarrassing disciplinary matter for my behaviour on a train too, for absent-mindedly leaving a signed school library copy of Robert Frost's poems on the seat.

As the months raced on, an administrative issue sought to dampen my hopes. It was clear to me there was a misunderstanding about whether the Igleharts were to be my 'parents' for the full year, or merely my summer hosts. Given the experience of staying with friends in the city, I preferred the latter interpretation, and so I negotiated with AFS a tactical separation under which my weekend and holiday times were my own. To their credit, the Igleharts were always there for me, including at the end of the year.

This decision opened the way to holidays at will, not just weekends in the city. The most ambitious of these holiday ventures was a spring road trip to Florida with two British schoolmates, driven by another Brit, a biology teacher. With his modest car loaded up with purloined school cans of Nutrament, a sports drink tasty only in small quantities and definitely not a staple diet for long trips, we headed for the sunshine. This was spring 1965. Unaware of paranoid connections in the minds of local highway patrol officers between northern numberplates and northern participation in the civil rights movement then on the march, we copped an unwarranted traffic violation and any number of unfriendly remarks. One exception was at a dumpy motel in Baton Rouge, where a local offered unwanted support: 'So, you are from Arrstralia. They-at must be a great place, ah hear yew have no nigras thar'.

Ouch.

This was a spur to learn more about the civil rights movement, and back at school I studied the 'underground railway', an organised movement to enable escaped slaves from the south to move to the north undercover, replete with adventure.

The travelling highlight of the year, though, was the AFS bus trip organised at the end of the stay. Students farewelled their communities, and, loosely chaperoned, travelled around together, staying with families at other places. At Poughkeepsie and West Point earlier in the year I became infatuated with a Swedish AFS girl, and for this bus trip I really wanted to be on her bus, even though it started from Fairfield, Connecticut, some way from Westover. At my request, to get a taste of high school life, I had earlier spent a week near there, at Newport High, swapping school and family with Shinichi Kitajima, a Japanese AFS student later to distinguish himself as a senior ambassador. At the end of the year, so keen was I to get started, I mistakenly asked the Igleharts to take me there to the bus pickup point a full week before the trip was due to start. The appointed place was empty.

Diary management was not my strong point.

I apologised meekly to the Igleharts for the mistake and returned to spend a quiet week with them before departure. This was probably just as well, given the pace of the three weeks that followed. And the Swedish girl was indeed on the same bus, but we became 'just friends'.

The purpose of these events was to give AFS students a taste of other communities before their departure, and vice-versa, so we travelled around the northeast and converged with other buses in Washington DC. The main event there was a big gathering at the White House for a speech from President Lyndon Johnson (known more colloquially as LBJ) and to meet First Lady Lady Bird Johnson. In the seething mass of AFS-ers we tried to find friends to farewell, including our indulgent 'Bus 62' chaperones.

As for the Igleharts, I stayed in contact, with Bob and Jane visiting my family and me in Australia. The couple later moved to run a school in Zimbabwe after an unhappy departure from Westover, and concerns about Bob's alleged misconduct at Choate coming to light after his death.[4] John moved permanently to Switzerland where he practices as a lawyer and we meet whenever I am in Geneva, which is not often now.

All too soon after the Washington excitement we were back in Australia as AFS returnees, and I was back at Churchie, hermit-like, preparing for November exams (which I managed to pass well enough to get a commonwealth scholarship to university).

However, there was some unfinished business on my return: reconciliation with my headmaster and learning about how to face up to personal responsibility.

The lesson came from an unlikely chain of events. I wrote a piece in the *Choate News* unfavourably comparing Churchie with Choate— honour code versus rules, open access versus fences, higher standard of education, no school uniforms. My mother, helpfully so she thought, gave the article to Roland Hill, a reporter and ex-schoolfriend from the *Toowoomba Chronicle*, who printed it in its entirety. Harry Roberts (aka 'Boofhead'), headmaster of Churchie, read the story with dismay. I wrote to him trying to make amends. There followed an adult correspondence between us, comparing the different school models and what ideas might be worth bringing back to Australia. But he was defensive of what money there would be to implement some of them: 'Here in Australia we don't value Education (or the Schoolmaster) at anything like that price'.

On my return, he invited me to give a talk at Churchie's assembly. The episode taught me to be sure to write for everyone, not just targeted readers, and made me think more seriously about different approaches to school education. From the guilt and embarrassment I learnt some discretion, a value I tried to keep. Perhaps, as I reflect, practicing it too much in my career.

This was not the only lesson. Like so many AFS year program students, and with a wonderful year at Choate, I returned a different person. I was certainly more confident and self-reliant, having made a new start, surviving a year with a generous serving of independence in a pivotal stage of US history, and by now a reasonable public speaker. I grew a new interest in cities and regions, and, for the first time, something of an understanding of racial inequality, American warmongering, and the need for change. One may think a privileged and predominantly white prep school might shield a vulnerable young man from the conflicts building up in American society, but this freedom to travel around, especially in New York City, and experiencing small but influential encounters in the south, combined with the curriculum, the school's visitors, and much learning from my peers—sometimes in opposition to their views—served to open my mind and nudged my thinking towards the necessity for political action.

Without doubt, I was touched by periods of loneliness, but I had time to think about big issues; generally with a wider view of what life can hold. Having rejected Christianity as a boy, I was touched by a sermon at Choate from a black pastor whose only act was to look at us and say, 'Who are you?' over and over again.

After my return, I spouted my teenage view of morality one night in the back seat of a car with AFS returnees Tricia Caswell (who appears again in the narrative before you) and Greg Winterflood, to make one's inner life and outward actions self-consistent.

I was sure I would get back to the US one day, but little could I know

I would later live there. My interest in urban affairs was just forming. So much was ahead.

Opportunities in Queensland

The next four years of university studies, first love, and the beginning of professional work established my personal and professional directions. The AFS year away had nudged me away from geology to more people-focused interests, in particular the wellbeing of people in big cities. I studied economics and geography, worked with an urban planning firm, married Jill Lang, and we prepared to move to Sydney together.

In the Australian summer of my return, at age 19, I started at the University of Queensland, living in St John's College. Despite being an Anglican college on a secular university campus, it was a wild place. The campus was at St Lucia in Brisbane, not far from the city centre. Late at night, senior collegians would drive 'freshers', many of whom had been drinking too much, out to the far suburbs and leave them to get back to campus clad in nothing but an academic gown. This happened to me more than once. It was not the worst of 'fresherisation', which could brutalise young men, and some years later when I was president of the students' club we banned the practice. It bore the marks of wartime military initiation, right down to the songs we had to sing. As usual, reaction followed reform, and our successors the following year put some of the odious scheme back.

Leadership is not forever. I may have been elected as president because I put on a good memorial lecture series the year before that included Charlie Barton, my father's friend, and Stan Seers, a university academic and plausible flying saucers expert. I played no competitive sports, but I built street credibility among my fellow students by breaking into the kitchen at night with them for midnight snacks. They didn't know I broke into the nearby Women's College too, and not for food.

The task of being president was time-consuming and interfered with my studies. The college warden was well enough disposed to me, but our relations were adversarial on account of the student issues I had to defend. I enjoyed this little taste of leadership, and understood any policies made might not be lasting. My relations with 'the next boss up', the archbishop, were not so good because I stood him up for dinner as a result of a timetable conflict. As for me, though not religious, I enjoyed contemplation at the quiet late night compline services in the chapel.

My desire for better intercultural understanding, after my exchange experience, led me to sign up for anthropology. Through ethnography, I learned how cultures and world views could be so very different. As a child I often fantasised about what it would be like to be another person, but keeping a little bit of myself in there to observe. I sometimes still imagine what it is like to wake up as a different person. In the anthropology course I could put my mind inside other world views, imagining what it would be like to be them.

My AFS year kindled an interest in international relations and I joined the Australian Institute of International Affairs while a student. At that time some of the good graduates, especially from history, went on to the Australian Department of Foreign Affairs to be diplomats. I couldn't imagine ever having to defend Australia's aggression in Vietnam, as my post-US views had become more informed and more in opposition, so I took no interest in taking a diplomatic path. With no credible national interest at stake, Australia was going 'all the way with LBJ', attacking what started as a nationalist movement in another country, not a communist threat, and conscripting many of my contemporaries to military service. I escaped call up in the conscription ballot, nervously scanning for my birthdate on the designated day through the college breakfast newspaper and not finding it. My relief was palpable, but I felt angry that my country was doing this to its young men, let alone what they were doing to the people of Vietnam.

As with other cities around the world, the 1960s in Brisbane were tumultuous, on and off campus. The war in Vietnam was only one issue. Others were the right to protest (tightly restricted under the Bjelke-Peterson Queensland government) and educational inequality. My activism while a student, tame though it was, appalled my father. He saw me on television doorknocking about how bad the state education system was, and in *The Courier Mail* for being arrested for disorderly conduct. The latter was more hijinks than political protest, I have to admit. He came down to Brisbane and threatened to take me out of university but then backed off, possibly because I had a commonwealth scholarship. It wasn't a bitter argument; my parents were kind to me, even on other, less honourable, transgressions. He did not see that we were on the streets because we felt powerless to bring improvements to society, some of which he might have supported, and the state government was acting to restrict even the right to protest.

My friends and I, including Jill Lang, my girlfriend, were angry about these backward politics, and I wanted a career that would help reduce inequality. My studies in urban geography and economics seemed to be a good avenue both for reform and for employment. And I was pleased to be working in an area adjacent to that of my father, who perhaps indirectly influenced my choice. He had been chair of the Queensland division of the Australian Institute of Urban Studies. I just wish he had lived long enough to see me become the NSW chair in later years.

Geography took me to tourism. During the next university summer holidays, 1966–67, I worked as a yardman at Hayman Island near the Great Barrier Reef, overlapping my time there with Jill, and doing the lowliest jobs: cleaning bathrooms, carting crates, monitoring the weather station data, and breaking the smelly crust on the Imhoff septic tanks. Life in the staff quarters was rough and casual. I would wake up, pull on my shorts, go down to the jetty, jump in for a swim and then, barefoot, help unload a ship.

I was intrigued by the infrastructure and logistics of this remote resort. I observed how they got water, their supplies, urgent health services, and how they managed visitors. Back in Brisbane I pulled together notes on the experience and published a paper on Hayman Island in *Capricornia*, the geography department journal.[5] Then, thinking that the resorts on the Whitsunday Islands might be an enjoyable working environment (to describe such beauty mildly), I contacted the regional chamber of commerce and they offered me unlimited accommodation and travel (with Roylen Cruises) around the resorts for research. Alas, being away from Brisbane for much of the honours year, 1969, seemed too difficult for a thesis, so I took on a different topic, still related to tourism, but this time with an urban theme. I chose to study the retail structure of the Gold Coast.

Buoyed by some understanding of this simple north–south urban string of pearls, I talked a group of friends onto a hired bus and off we went interviewing shoppers on their travel and shopping behaviour.

'Are you a visitor or resident?'

'Which were the last four shops you visited here this morning?'

'What is your street address on the Gold Coast?'

And so on. Part of the fun was having Russell Handyside, a gleefully mischievous engineering student from college, crunch the gravity model data on a deck of punch cards, through a *real computer*. How far we have come since then ...

It went well enough (tourists tend more than locals to bypass local retail centres for larger more distant ones), and I was encouraged to present the findings at a symposium in Melbourne at a landmark conference organised by Nick Clark, son of the great economist Colin Clark. It featured the work of rising star John Paterson, who presented an analysis of the economic drivers of cities in Australia.[6] Paterson continued as a thinker and policy analyst for many years, and we became friends. He easily whipped me at *Go*. Later he became a controversial department head in water, health and other fields, and we regularly lunched in Melbourne until his death in 2003.

Looking for work next summer more in line with my urban economics interests, I made contact with a practice called Clarke Gazzard and Partners in Sydney, and was surprised to get an enthusiastic invitation to work there during the summer of 1968–69. George Clarke was the co-founder, a larger than life architect-planner driven to modernise and promote better city planning not only through practice but through brazen promotion of his ideas. He had led a blue ribbon group on metropolitan planning and intergovernmental relations in 1967, calling for commonwealth 'interest, participation, leadership and finance' in the cities, something about which I had not thought much before.[7]

Work at Clarke Gazzard was exciting: real issues, smart colleagues, the big city all around me. It was a taste of what professional work to come might be like. Staying in a little harbour-side flat in Wallaringa Mansions at Neutral Bay with Jill, who came down from Brisbane with me, I would ferry to work at 117 Harrington Street around the Sydney Opera House, still under construction at that time, and join workmates for coffee, standing on the sawdust-strewn George Street floor of Andronicus Brothers, or having drinks in the numerous old pubs in the area.

It was a good match, and George and I wanted it to continue.

When back at university during the 1969 school year, I did a little work for Clarke Gazzard in Brisbane on regional shopping centre location, memorably flying around Brisbane in a chartered plane spotting potential sites for Myer, a department store chain. Of course, the analysis was more than that. For the following summer, 1969–70, he asked me to work on the Gold Coast.

The main work was helping Andy Stenders, a British architect-planner, and others in the office, prepare the Gold Coast strategic plan and its associated action plans.[8] The strategic plan set the pattern of development of the Gold Coast for decades to come, connecting and fattening up the linear string of villages and towns into the hinterland.

George asked me to review a site in the Paradise Point action plan area near the Southport Spit for the Lewis Real Estate company, a big property developer. It was beautiful coastal wet heathland, but it was subject to a sand mining lease application. At that time, sand miners were destroying coastal dunes by mining rutile, ilmenite, zircon and other minerals, and leaving behind unstable sandy deserts along the coast. I photographed and mapped the ecology of the site and read up on these types of paperbark (*Eucalyptus maculata*) ecosystems.

In Brisbane, in the state archives, I dug up an old geological survey that assessed the mineral deposits of the area as poor quality. Our client won the case against the mining lease application in part on this evidence and on my documentation of the quality of the environment. We recommended conservation protection over the best lands, and development over the other, modified lands. In the years that followed I was afraid that I had worked to save this beautiful part of the coast only to give it up to land development—the destruction that goes before urban growth. So not long ago, with trepidation, I checked the pattern of urban development and was delighted to see that the lands have been preserved as Pine Ridge Conservation Park to this day.[9]

Life as a student in Queensland and my work there in urban geography and planning were coming to an end. I had lots of early experience, good contacts, and some idea of a career ahead in the urban sector, ready for bigger and more responsible tasks. I was teamed up happily with Jill in both work and love, but both of us were dissatisfied with the glaring inequalities we saw around us—blind redevelopment, displacement of poor communities, haphazard growth, environmental destruction—and the parlous state of politics in Queensland. She was more consolidated in her anti-poverty values than me. I wanted to understand how cities worked and to change them for the better. We had optimism too, both for solutions to problems through activism and reform, and for our careers, which seemed to be opening up. Jill wanted more involvement in social planning; I wanted to mix economics and urban planning.

However, Queensland was not going to be the state where that happened.

TWO

URBAN LIFE IN SYDNEY

Living, studying and working in Sydney from 1971–73 launched my life as an independent adult. I was enjoying married life, finding scholarly direction, working productively, making new friends and getting involved in the urban social movements of the day.

It made sense for Jill and me to move to Sydney in 1970 after we graduated and married. We had been together since our early days at university and we were inseparable. She grew up in Kingaroy where her parents ran a well-established hardware store, and she had boarded at Brisbane Girls' Grammar School before studying arts with a sociology major at the same university as me. We met when she lived at the Women's College and had much in common, including views on politics.

In Sydney, Jill worked with Jim Colman's planning practice on projects like an open space survey in western Sydney and a stocktake of social infrastructure there. Jim was a widely practiced planning consultant and became a friend. Jill and I both enrolled for the master of town and country planning at the University of Sydney, with her starting a year later than me. We rented a terrace house in Glebe near the university, living for a time among near-feral cats, and another time next to a friendly dope dealer.

The early 1970s saw historic change in Australian urban affairs and we tried to be part of it. My views on urban policy were shaping up.

I thought the planning profession was overburdened with the fixed zoning of statutory planning, and the roles of planners little more than para-professional land use regulators. To me, with my geography and economics background, the 'light on the hill' was more comprehensive planning that encompassed housing, economic development and services, all led by strategic—not statutory—plans that reflected people's aspirations. Only that way, I thought, could we get to more radical change and address inequality.

If planning was just what town planners did back then, then I was anti-planning. Worse, town planners were trying to professionalise, to limit the preparation of urban plans only to certified planners. As with other guild-like practices, I thought this was a 'conspiracy against the laity'. Perhaps coming to these views was connected to my youthful restlessness.

Hugh Stretton's self-published *Ideas for Australian Cities* and David Harvey's *Social Justice and the City* were influential books at the time, in their different ways supporting my direction. Stretton's talk at a Canberra conference was inspiring. Momentum for federal involvement in the cities was building up.[1]

At the university, we became friends with like-minded students, particularly Jeremy Dawkins and Graham Sansom, with whom over the years we did, and still do, much together. Jeremy went on to be city planner for Fremantle in Western Australia; later he was planning commissioner for the state. Graham became the CEO of the Australian Local Government Association, the head of the centre for local government at the University of Technology Sydney, and leader of a commission of review for local government in NSW.

The Department of Town and Country Planning at the University of Sydney was led by Professor Denis Winston, a distinguished architect and planner influential over the County of Cumberland Planning Scheme and its successor, the Sydney Region Outline Plan. He happened to be on the same National Capital Planning Committee for Canberra as my father, who was by then prominent in the civil engineering profession. My father had been appointed for his local government experience. We found the department old-fashioned and stuffy, and agitated for change. To his credit John Toon, a lecturer and the editor of the *Royal Australian Planning Institute Journal*, handed over to three of us students— Jeremy, Graham and me—a special issue on planning education, and we had a field day. We did give the planning school directors around the country their voices, but we dubbed them 'the heads' tales', and sandwiched the article between a collection of critical writings.[2] Tony Powell later called it 'the most significant issue in the Journal's publishing history'.[3]

Actually, our master's course was quite multi-disciplinary with an eclectic parade of guest lecturers, though not much from the development industry, which planners tended to see as 'the enemy'. The projects were interesting. They took us into different parts of Sydney, including the 'slum clearance' of Redfern and the distant suburban Hills District of northwest Sydney, where the planning solution of our fellow students from Hong Kong was, of course, to build high-rises.

I was less interested in what planners did than in how cities worked and how they changed. The department had a good collection of old urban books. Still interested in New York City, I took out from its locked case the yellowed 1927 volume that presented the New York Plan Association's economic analysis of the city.[4] The authors claimed the raison d'être for the dense city centre was 'knowledge in a hurry'. Communications, yes, but above all, face-to-face contact. This was compelling.

Urban communications

A research thesis was an important part of the master's degree. During the process of plan-making for the City of Sydney in 1970, described in the coming pages, I followed 'knowledge in a hurry': communication linkages as an organising principle for cities, and a determinant of office location in particular. I was able to get detailed telephone traffic data to play with. I wondered if the data were surrogates for people's linkages between places, or do they go the other way, with telecommunication a substitute for travel? This work led to my choice of thesis topic.

I dug around technical publications like RAND (a government-funded research company), reports and the proceedings of the Institute of Electrical and Electronic Engineers, and found eye-opening accounts of technologies under development to make the future 'information utility'. The technological explosion we are familiar with today was well under way before 1970, even 'intersex' and 'cybersex'. That was Japanese work envisaging the use of equipment similar to that used by Masters and Johnson's work on human sexual response, to enable (respectively) couples to couple remotely, or individuals to interact with programmed intelligent responses already recorded.[5]

The shape of today's digital infrastructure and the virtual realm was mapped out then with an extraordinary accuracy not acknowledged today (the 'Picturephone' excepted—it failed the network test through drawing too few early subscribers to attract enough later subscribers).

Starting on the basis that the core purpose of clustering in cities is for contact, that the city itself is a huge engine for communication, I explored communication linkages, a key factor in location decisions. I found that the technologies ahead would likely lead to more dense cities as routine activities were able to be moved from central city offices in favour of intense, and more densely developed, face-to-face business districts. This approach was contrary to general thinking that telecommuting would cause cities to spread, insofar as people thought about that topic at all.

Post-COVID-19, that work should be revisited again, as teleworking has finally taken hold and advanced economy cities will change forever. I also found that understanding the flows of information was the lesser part of forecasting urban impact. The indirect impacts, through changes in people's everyday activities, the nature of work, personal values and the structure of institutions, would be more profound, if very difficult to predict. The 'digital divide' was not a term in use then, but I was apprehensive about the impact of the technologies I saw coming on equity and participation—core values that drove my work.

In fact, hardly anyone in the urban sector thought about the potentially enormous impact on cities, with the notable exceptions of Ronald Abler, a geographer at Pennsylvania State University, and Richard Meier, a theorist in the College of Environmental Design at the University of California at Berkeley.[6] Correspondence with Meier about using information network analysis to understand city structure was useful to my thinking about possible doctoral work, and led to his encouragement for me to study at the University of California. I applied to Berkeley and was pleased to be offered a place, a story picked up in chapter five.

My thesis created interest, and I found myself writing and speaking on the topic.[7] Against advice from everyone close to me, I kept old boxes of documents, including the master's thesis papers, hoping one day to return to the field. And return I did. In 2003, more than 30 years later, I committed myself to write a paper for the State of Australian Cities conference on the topic.[8] Of course, I found a vastly expanded field of study covering the transformation of society and cities we now see so well, but I persevered with warming the embers of my old work. It was satisfying to read online reviews praising the paper.

By the time I finished the original work in 1973, my interests in urban communications had to be shelved, along with study at Berkeley. Work in the Whitlam government, a once-in-a-lifetime opportunity, would take their place.

And while in Sydney my head was in the technology clouds, my boots were firmly in protest demonstrations.

Urban activism

Jill and I tagged along with the political movements of the day, joining the anti-war moratoria, memorable marches around the town hall, and other events as the movement went from strength to strength. We went to the infamous rugby test against South Africa to protest against apartheid, but we did not join the incursion on the pitch. All the same, my overcoat, a family gift for my AFS visit to the US, was burnt up by a flare.

Jill and I became minor activists in a number of urban social movements. We joined opposition to the plans of the Rocks Redevelopment Authority (led by the villainous Colonel McGee, backed by the corrupt Premier Robert Askin, and contested in the streets by the brave Nita McCrea of the Rocks Resident Group and the Builders' Labourers Federation Green Bans led by Jack Mundey). The movement was ultimately successful, preventing redevelopment and enabling some of the local housing to stay in working class hands, as documented by Jim Coleman, among others, in his book on Jack Mundey. [9]

We offered to help the Aboriginal housing movement in Redfern, originally connected through Colin James, an inspiring thinker and activist. A modest architect, Col made a lifelong commitment to remedy the shocking housing conditions that Indigenous people faced. Jill and I had been disconcerted at the living conditions and restraints on finance and movement that we saw put on Aboriginal people at the Cherbourg reserve near Kingaroy where her father, a one-time good boxer, kindly helped out with sports training. At our house, by then in Annandale, we spent some Saturday afternoons drinking wine and talking action with people like Bob Maza, Lester and Gerry Bostok, and Gordon Briscoe. We joined demonstrations at the Aboriginal Tent Embassy in Canberra and gatherings in defiance of 'Australia Day' in Hyde Park.

Much of this was just turning up. But Jill and I did some planning work with the Aboriginal Legal Service in Redfern, a community-based service for Aboriginal people formed by white lawyers and black activists to respond to police harassment in the area over squatting, vagrancy, and a number of vaguely defined and inflated offences. Unable to gain legal access to housing and facing antagonistic local council and state government, Aboriginal residents of the area were seeking to acquire vacant properties and refurbish them. This would need funding, and Gordon Briscoe and others proposed an Aboriginal Development Cooperative as a vehicle for housing development. After Charles Perkins was taken ill, a prospective candidate for the Australia Party in the federal seat of the Northern Territory for the 1972 election, Gordon went up to campaign there and left the Aboriginal Legal Service. He dropped the registration of the cooperative on my lap and I became its unlikely founding secretary, presenting the application to the state government. He reasoned I would know the ins and outs of registration and could help make the case for funding. I did not feel well equipped for the task, being a *gubbah*, a non-Aboriginal, with little detailed knowledge of the movement.

Anyway, events overtook us. Without our being involved at all, a number of aggressive arrests and jailings brought community housing needs to a head. The Aboriginal Housing Committee turned this into direct action and a hard-fought campaign by Aboriginal people themselves. Eventually, over local and state government opposition, foot-dragging by key property owners, and racist opposition from many local non-Aboriginal people, a change of government brought commonwealth funding commitment to this opportunity for Aboriginal self-determination.

The housing development that resulted is famous in Sydney's—and indeed Australia's—urban history. I was relieved to pull back from work that was to be fully controlled by the Aboriginal residents themselves, as I was sure any more involvement would not be acceptable to the radical activists now in the lead. Jill, as a social planner building up professional experience, had a better understanding of these urban social movements than I did.

Still, participating in those movements gave me a better understanding of urban issues from those people affected by the 'slum clearance' and redevelopment that came from urban plans, and the depth of racism that was front and centre in issues of Aboriginal housing, and also clear in the war in Vietnam.

Helping to make a plan for Sydney

I stayed part-time with Urban Systems Corporation through 1971, the new name for Clarke Gazzard. George Clarke's dream was realised. He won the tender for the City of Sydney strategic plan (despite having had a role in preparing the brief) and I had a role in making the plan. I was proud to be involved, if only part-time during my studies. I worked with Darrel Conybeare (an urbane and imaginative designer who coordinated the plan document), Peter Casey (a high-energy pencil-licking transport planner), Sonya Lyneham (a charming, savvy urban planner) and Gavan McDonnel (a learned, smooth economist). Mike Llewelyn-Smith, a fellow student, was also involved. This was long before he went on to be chief planner for the Cities of Sydney and Adelaide and CEO of the City of Adelaide, and to write an engaging memoir of the period.[10]

Elizabeth Farrelly calls this and the larger group, for Sydney, 'a rare convergence of creative minds'.[11]

George was all over the work; in this and other projects he was an irrepressible mentor and showman, pushing me to do things out of my grasp and letting me wing it. He showed me how to extract maximum mileage from imperfect data favouring an argument, and sometimes exaggerating my skills to clients. But I didn't mind too much—I learnt a lot on the job. In the words of Jim Colman (Jill's then employer), George had 'a towering ego, boundless energy, prodigious curiosity, ferocious intellect and a passion for urban planning'.[12] I was able to do some simple modelling and my scenarios were published as appendices to the plan. The capacity of the CBD was a core issue. The plan took a booster approach to the city's economy.

Work was fast-moving, a bit chaotic, but George was absolutely the editor, controlling the sections and structure. With fast turnaround you would get George's changes to drafts, but he was open to initiatives. At one point, I wrote a note about the organisation of data in the office, 'Is it a system or cistern?', and as a result found myself assigned to its reorganisation. He would monitor the media quickly too, and in detail, so I would spend time answering questions from the press or making statements for them.

The plan was big news when it was published in 1971, and to this day, some 50 years later, it is seen as a milestone on the way from prescriptive urban planning to strategic planning.[13] Gone was the static zoning map as the only core document, though as a statutory document the previous City of Sydney Planning Scheme did live on. The new strategic plan was very clearly presented. It had many of the goals I sought built in, including affordable housing and heritage protection.

It was a milestone in my thinking, too, putting into practice the kind of strategic planning I wanted.

But despite being a landmark in strategic city planning for Australia, it is difficult to measure what changes came from it. At the local level, the clear delineation of areas with adopted action plans did help keep inner Sydney from becoming worse than it might have become. But as Mike

Llewelyn-Smith points out, the plan as a whole could not be enforced formally because the state 'through its agencies the SPA (State Planning Authority) and HOBAC (Height of Buildings Advisory Committee), continued to have effective control of the city through the statutory plan'.[14] In other words, in some respects the statutory planners had their way.

The success of the strategic plan led to other projects for Urban Systems and their research subsidiary Urbsearch, some of which I worked on, including action plans for city centre precincts in Sydney. By 1972, my courses complete and thesis finished, I worked with the firm full-time. I was trusted as a project manager, so I ran a population forecasting study for Coffs Harbour council on the NSW coast and a housing demand study for medium density housing for Lake Macquarie council, south of Newcastle.

I felt on top of the world. I was flying around, talking to clients, and presenting my work. Early in 1973 I moved to Adelaide for a few weeks to help set up operations for the City of Adelaide Strategic Plan, just as the new Whitlam government was getting started.

In his typical style, George lined up a meeting in a big town hall room between the above mentioned Hugh Stretton, an Adelaide resident, and myself. A professor of history by discipline, but a polymath across the social sciences in practice, he was one of the leading thinkers on urban affairs. We sat down with a small audience of city employees and members of the planning team. With no agenda, George said, 'You two talk'. Then he left the room. In the presence of greatness, I mumbled on, but recovered my composure and we soon got into a good conversation on what people wanted from inner Adelaide.

I moved back to Sydney once we appointed a project director in Adelaide, and started to lose touch with George after I then moved to Canberra, as discussed in the coming pages. At its peak, Urban Systems employed around 80 people, but the company was unable to do much work for the new Labor government and their numbers dropped. George asked me to see if I could put commonwealth urban work his way, but at that stage I couldn't. I was mindful of what Hugh Stretton said of the ALP cities policy, that there would be critical personnel problems in starting up a new commonwealth urban capacity, as 'only George Clarke's organisation can do these sorts of studies'.[15]

Nevertheless, George and I stayed friends over the years. He visited me twice when I lived in Berkeley, once going bird-watching in San Francisco Bay's wetlands, and I saw him on my return to Sydney after my return to Australia in 1982 when he was active with the Paddington Society. When he died in 2005 I felt very sad, in part because I hadn't thanked him enough for his crazy mentorship of this young urban planner. We must remember to thank our mentors fulsomely while they are living.

Lessons for an urban learner

These years made an urban planner, but perhaps not the common variety. My interest in economics and geography and my disdain for quasi-legal statutory planning led me more to strategic planning and urban research than mainstream planning. It was clear to me, from the unsolved problems with which Jill and I engaged, that good urban plans or regulations would not solve them. We needed social and political change. Not small reforms but a structural shift led by a better understanding of the underlying drivers of change to cities and the patterns of settlement for those who live in them with such uneven chances in life.

Living in Sydney was wonderful, an exciting mix of new places and causes. My friends and I felt part of a new wave, the world at our feet, a fairer society ahead. Jobs were plenty, a stark contrast to opportunities for young professionals today. Like them, though, we could see no straight careers before us. In our case, we felt we could weave our paths wherever dreams and opportunities took us.

For me, interest in work was double-sided: infatuation with the issues mixed with early-onset workaholism. Success on the job and with studies just make me work harder. Apart from sometimes visiting my family in Toowoomba, I saw my father occasionally when he came to Sydney for professional meetings and committees or was buying equipment for Toowoomba City Council. Once, when he asked me to join him on his only night available, we went to the all-male review nightclub Les Girls in King's Cross with his accompanying aldermen (who claimed they had to go to Sydney to inspect the tractors council was buying). He was embarrassed. 'The Cross' was swamped at that time with US service people taking R & R from the Vietnam war.

His last visit was more sombre. Carrying lung cancer, probably caused by smoking begun on his doctor's advice during the Second World War, he passed through Sydney with my mother to and from a painful New Zealand holiday that my sisters and I had arranged. It was not a wise gift. We innocently thought that an overseas holiday might relieve their suffering. Dad's condition worsened during the holiday, but I left it too late to see him again in Toowoomba before he died.

How I wish I'd learned to sort out my life's priorities better.

Soon after, I left Sydney too.

THREE

THE SHORT FLOWERING OF
NATIONAL URBAN POLICY

From early 1973 to late 1975 I worked for Minister Tom Uren's
Department of Urban and Regional Development in the Whitlam
Labor government. It was transformative for urban affairs as well
as for Jill and me personally. I was responsible for much of the government's strategy for urban and regional development. I was also partial
to regional policy, the new cities program and metropolitan strategies,
sometimes from the vantage of high policy, sometimes from very hands-
on interventions. It was as if everything I had done in my life prepared
me for this time, but it was an intense period. Eventually I tired out,
and by the time the government was dismissed, Jill and I had agreed
to separate too.

The cities and towns of Australia were showing the strains of fast
urban growth over the 1950s and 1960s: unserviced urban land,
unplanned sprawl, lagged infrastructure, housing without sewerage,
land price spirals, long delays in the supply of human services and road
transport, urban freeways in the wrong place, and very little new investment in public transport.[1]

Worse than all this, social disparities in access to employment and
services were growing and very obvious to the public. The metropolitan
areas, especially, but not only, Sydney and Melbourne, were marked by

wide gaps in opportunities and amenities between areas where rich and poor lived.

That much had already become clear to me over the time in Sydney. I shared these concerns with many other professionals working in the urban sector. It was structural; the unfairly structured cities reflected the political economy of post-war Australia. We knew there was no easy fix. The lazy conservative national governments—Menzies and his minnow successors—and corrupt state administrations, such as the Askin government in NSW and the Bjelke-Petersen government in Queensland, represented the 'big end of town' and ignored environmental and urban equity issues.

Migration was also diversifying the makeup of the cities. The 'White Australia' policy was repealed in 1966, but racism was still pervasive, especially as far as Indigenous people's rights to the city were concerned. Aboriginal people were pressed into enclaves like Redfern in Sydney, but chose to live there too as a meeting place.

Jill's and my urban sector friends knew we had to work hard to change the way the economy worked, and the way cities developed and changed. Palliative redistribution by normal government programs was not enough. We had become radicalised during the rise of urban policy in Labor's opposition program, and now they were in government.

Gough Whitlam was reforming the Labor Party and became leader in 1967. As Pat Troy points out, though Whitlam was no socialist, his urban policies were in the 'mainstream of Fabian socialism', and lined up with mine.[2] We meet Pat many times in the narrative to come. He was the most influential person behind the ALP's urban policy. By the time of the 1972 election campaign, Whitlam had electrified the debate in a way I found appealing:

> We will involve the national government in a massive effort to rebuild our existing cities and to build new ones. A deep and direct national involvement in Australia's cities will be the great thrust of our government. It's not just because 85% of our people live in cities and towns, but because in modern Australia social

inequality is fixed upon families by the place in which they are forced to live even more than by what they are able to earn.[3]

Tom Uren, the Labor Party's cities spokesman from 1969 until then, spoke passionately and well on the theme. He had a real talent for putting complex issues in simple terms. A leader of the Labor left and some-time prize boxer, tall, loud, and prone to hugging people, Tom could be pugnacious in meetings and this was sometimes effective in cabinet. But he was also a good negotiator with managerial experience.[4] Jill and I had gone to listen to him in 1970, liked him, and followed the debate past the election in 1972.

The Labor Party built political appeal for their platform to solve urban problems, especially in fast-suburbanising electorates. A combination of improved services and changes to the way urban decisions were to be made appealed to Jill and me, addressing issues we saw on the ground. The programs included targeted 'area assistance programs' and were wrapped up in a national urban and regional strategy that included a new cities program.

Neither Jill nor I joined the Labor Party. We thought radical change in Aboriginal affairs and the environment, for example, was best advanced by direct popular movements. Much as we liked the party's urban policies as they were forming, we disagreed with other policies, and didn't like the idea of sitting in tedious branch meetings. The urban policies were different. Here we were professionals in the field and would be open to opportunities to contribute, though at that time we had little idea of what we might do.

In the related area of regional policy, decentralisation of the population had been a government mantra for decades, with 'selective decentrali-sation' its modern version. A joint commonwealth–state committee went on for eight years, finally reporting in 1972.[5] The Labor opposi-tion was scathing about the delay, with Tom Uren saying that inaction on decentralisation 'has been notorious' and that the 'major enemy of decentralisation has been the Commonwealth Government'.[6] Among the committee's otherwise tame recommendations was the development of a limited number of decentralised growth centres to be chosen from aspiring host towns and cities.

The McMahon government recognised the groundswell and established a National Urban and Regional Development Authority (NURDA) in October 1972, in part to neutralise the appeal of Labor policies. It was to advise government on a program of building new cities to attract households and establishments away from 'overgrown' metropolitan areas, and to structure expansion in some areas into 'system cities', government-initiated metropolitan satellite cities.[7] But as prime minister (PM) McMahon said in his second reading speech on the legislation, 'It is not the Government's intention that the Authority should produce by that time [30 June 1973] a definitive statement on a national urban and regional development strategy'.[8]

It was all too late. The ALP swept to power in November 1972, ending 23 years of opposition, and the urban and regional development platform became government policy. On one of those 'where were you when …?' evenings to remember, Jill and I were at Jim Colman's place for an election party. It was an historic moment. In his Lane Cove backyard on a warm night, we drank wine and checked in with the news. It was clear early that Labor had won. This was cause for much celebration. Our hopes for urban reform were sky-high, but even on that night Jill and I had no thoughts that we would play some part in it.

We knew Pat Troy a little from the 1970 Canberra Urban Forum, an urban research seminar at the Australian National University. We had a long lunch at Tony and Gay Bilson's legendary Labor watering-hole, Bon Gout restaurant, on Elizabeth Street in Sydney. Pat was well known as the ideas man behind Labor's urban policy. The son of Paddy Troy, a famous communist waterside worker, and scion of a rambunctious Fremantle family, Pat was brilliant, energetic, funny and, above all, driven to make Australian cities fairer places.

With Tom's support, Pat approached Jill first—headhunted her, as he knew her work—and she moved to Canberra to join the Department of Urban and Regional Development to work on forming an area improvement plan. I said I would follow and soon did, also invited by Pat. We rented a house in Turner, a walk away from Civic, Canberra's downtown. It was a lovely old brick house with a garden. We hosted many a lunch and party there and brought up cats.

It was also the start of an intense period of my life.

A newborn DURD

The new Department of Urban and Regional Development was built from the ground up; it inherited no predecessor departments or agencies. This was possibly the first full departmental example of this since federation. Pat's and Clem Lloyd's book documents it in detail.[9] The ideas for a new department, recounted by Whitlam, covered the platform taken to the election, including development of a national strategy for cities and regions.[10]

A review of the machinery of government set up by Whitlam soon after taking office recommended a department of cities, but this title was unpopular with non-metropolitan members of the Labor caucus. Instead, it became known as the Department of Urban and Regional Development (DURD).[11]

The advantages of a clean sheet and an influx of enthusiastic young professionals, along with a few more seasoned contract executives, were offset by delays and opposition from the commonwealth public service: the Treasury, which resisted a new economic department of potentially equivalent status, and the Public Service Board (PSB), for which DURD was too big a change in standard administrative procedures.

Robert Lansdown, a suave and experienced deputy commissioner of the National Capital Development Commission (NCDC), became department head rather than Pat Troy, who turned down the position. Pat kept his academic post part-time at the Australian National University and acted as deputy secretary for the duration of DURD. He continued to build the department with Lansdown's consent and to be the minister's closest adviser on key decisions. On the whole, the three worked well together, balancing very different but complementary skills and temperaments.[12]

Tom Uren did not become minister for urban and regional development until after the two-week Whitlam–Barnard duumvirate, but even during that time he started holding meetings about continuation of the growth centres, while Whitlam alluded to his urban and regional promises in a letter to state premiers as early as 16 December 1972. At its creation, the urban and regional development portfolio had no provenance other than the NCDC and NURDA. It did not include environment, housing, transport or capital territories, as Whitlam had intended before the election.[13] But it was a key portfolio, nonetheless.

The minister's office focused in the early days on the formation of the department. Jill and I found it easy to mix with the staff there, and our daily work in the early days was very fluid as programs and organisations had not been fully set up. We kept a little flat in Sydney while we made the transition, thinking we would return on weekends, but work in Canberra became all-encompassing.

Tom Uren and Pat Troy wanted to waste no time in putting programs in place, drafting legislation and making more senior appointments. They started negotiations with the states for land commissions, growth centres (with the first meeting of Whitlam and Uren with NSW and Victorian premiers on 25 January 1973 agreeing on joint action), and the sewerage backlog program (no pun intended) inside the first month. They reached agreement on Albury–Wodonga's growth centre development in the second month.[14] To some in the states it looked like a speeding train coming at them. As Lloyd and Troy say, DURD's founders had to find a balance between getting programs running and building a capacity for long-term planning.[15]

Pat Troy, the minister and their senior advisers—not to mention this junior adviser—took a jaundiced view of established urban planners and the state planning systems. The attitude of Norman Fisher, a division head in the new department, was typical: 'Not only do I doubt if the existing town planning courses will produce our needs, but also I doubt if any proposal emanating from academic Town Planning Departments or based on Town Planning Departments would meet our needs'.[16] The ambition of DURD's founders was to make headway on economic, financial and social fronts, reducing inequality and using new instruments across government to reform urban development fundamentally.

I liked that.

Setting up the department's establishment took more than six months. There was no prior authoritative statement of functions other than election commitments. NURDA was established and its functions had to be reconciled with those of a new department one way or the other, and the Public Service Board, an independent authority, fought the departmental proposals most of the way.[17] Finally, the department's functions were agreed. They included the development of a national urban and regional development strategy.[18] While living with a compromise on its scope—housing and environment were excluded, as noted earlier—it did get PM support for DURD's status to be a senior department, equivalent, in principle at least, to Treasury and the Department of Prime Minister and Cabinet.[19]

The structure for the third division of mid-level officers (myself included) was approved earlier during these negotiations, with an unprecedented flexible 'pool' arrangement. No mid-level officer was permanently attached to a division or branch. As part of the pool we could be readily assigned to work on projects or programs in different parts of the department. This was anathema to the traditional stability that the Public Service Board sought, but I liked it a lot as it appealed to my modernising instincts.

The long delays in approving an establishment required early appointment of senior consultants, which, not surprisingly, brought more reluctance from traditional public service quarters. The PM was concerned that the seniority of the DURD positions might allow poaching from other senior departments, and early appointees to DURD did come with Treasury experience. But most came from outside active commonwealth service, notably Michael Keating (a brilliant and assertive economist with strong ideas who was substantively appointed later and ran the urban resources planning division) and Peter Till (a British economist from the OECD who ran the resource allocation division as a consultant from March). From that same month, Henry Wardlaw (a distinguished urban and transport planner who had much to do with Singapore's early development) ran the urban and regional development division, and Tony Powell, a planner from NCDC and visiting lecturer to Jill's and my planning courses at the University of Sydney, ran the division I was assigned to, urban and regional strategy. Both Henry and Tony were on consultant contracts.

From mid-1973 the other senior positions were filled with full-time or part-time senior bureaucrats and professionals, including Bill Butler (coordination division) and Norman Fisher (infrastructure division). Pat Troy was substantively head of the land division but acted as deputy secretary for the duration of DURD. There were no senior female appointments. In this respect, despite its founders' progressive politics and the strength of the women's movement at the time, DURD broke no mould.

The intended policy instruments, such as urban and regional budgets, needed whole-of-government consideration. Up to then, most forms of direct federal intervention had been prevented by the states' constitutional powers, express and reserve. But section 96 of the Australian constitution allows the commonwealth to grant financial assistance to any state on such terms and conditions as it thinks fit. The founding group of DURD saw conditional financial assistance to the states as a key instrument to make big changes in the structures, instruments and processes of government.

But the new department could not succeed without the cooperation of other ministries. A standing interdepartmental committee on urban and regional development (SIDCURD) was formed as a clearing house for government issues and cabinet submissions, authorised by the PM on 17 February 1973. Lloyd and Troy remind us of DURD's reluctance to use standing interdepartmental committees for policy development, as distinct from administrative purposes, given their potential to waste the time of an understaffed department, but that '[o]f necessity, DURD descended into this maelstrom.'[20] According to one source, 'SIDCURD was treated as a forum for other departments and authorities to discover what DURD was doing, with DURD getting little in return.'[21]

Interdepartmental conflict didn't stop respect and good personal relations forming, nor occasionally some fun. My diary records a 'Treasury counterpart lunch' on 4 October 1974. Paul Barratt, on the Treasury side of the table, became a respected antagonist and, much later, after a career that included a spectacular rise to and fall from the position of secretary of defence, a friend. On the DURD side of the table, Peter Till, brilliant and abrasive, became well known for his demeanour at meetings. John Mant told it well:

> When Peter Till came amongst us at the embryonic DURD in early 1973, we wondered yet again what Pat Troy had done to us. This wild man, with a broken face and broken teeth, a kind of untidy Einstein hair-do, and innumerable red shirts which, as the afternoon wore on, he would peel off one by one before the eyes of astounded FAS's [First Assistant Secretaries] from outside, still dressed in their Menzies whites and darks.[22]

Peter was the only man on record to have ridden his bike through Parliament House.[23] Jill and I saw a lot of him, with Peter spending afternoons with us in our backyard. When he passed away in 1976 he still had my father's watch, a keepsake which I had lent him.

At last, after six months of bureaucratic battles and delays in appointing key people, the department was up and operating. In the early days, however, I was one of very few people working in my intended division, national urban and regional strategy.

A division with no staff

The department attracted people with commitment to the values of the new government, equity and territorial justice, and to the department's fresh start. With mostly empty divisions, we junior and mid-level staff had to organise ourselves for much of the work, especially on cross-department issues. We met weekly in an effort to communicate and coordinate across the divisions and form department-wide policies and positions where they did not yet exist, and to field staff representatives for senior appointments and committees, 'unheard of' then in the commonwealth public service.[24] It was messy, but so keen were we that nothing would stop us. We jocularly called the informal staff coordination group the *Staff Soviet*.

Communication in and out of the department was very open, a very different feel from the secure government offices of today. Many of us turned up for Friday night drinks at the pub or in Parliament House (the old one), and there was easy access to ministers and their officers. I organised a DURD 'open day' during which activists, hiring buses from the cities, went through the staid-looking DURD offices to find out what was going on and offer their help.[25] On the whole the visitors were welcomed, and I was aware of no complaints from more traditional bureaucrats. Even the private sector had easy and informal access. I recall driving Vic Jennings (of AV Jennings, the big housing development company) to the airport after a meeting in Jill's and my clapped-out Volkswagen. It was a sign of the informality, the openness, and on so many little things, the disorganisation of the department.

When Richard Acland, a journalist with the *Financial Review*, asked to talk to me about what DURD was doing, I was happy to oblige, thinking he might write something about a new approach to national urban policy, and feeling important. The next morning, I was appalled to see a front page story headlining 'staff soviets' forming in the public service:

> So enshrined is the worker participation concept becoming in the department that quite a number of Third and Fourth Division officials are refusing to sign time books and attendance sheets, and insist on appearing at the office in somewhat more casual garb than the traditional grey suit.
>
> The Public Service Board is threatening to tighten up the enforcement of the regulations should the situation 'deteriorate' any further.
>
> However, the most radical aspect of the management of the department is the team or task force structure as opposed to the usual linear organisation.
>
> ... the bulk of the staff of the department have been products of the universities, graduating in the late 1960s, when student

democracy and student power were becoming more and more a fact of life for university administrators.

They are people who to some extent expect a say in the running of things.[26]

Some of the article was inaccurate, but this was it, I thought, as I waited at the secretary's door on arrival at work that morning, the end of my not-so-brilliant career in the commonwealth public service. But Bob Lansdown showed me mercy.

'It's not a big issue', he said, 'these things happen; just be more discreet with the press in future'.

I survived. I lost a little of my naiveté that day, and learned to be cautious with my words with the media, even friendly ones.

I should have learnt from the *Toowoomba Chronicle* episode years before ...

One of the sober responsibilities of the department was 'developing and implementing a national urban strategy', but the urban and regional strategy division was perhaps less popular among those wanting more front line action, big infrastructure spending, or high-stakes economic influence at the centre of government. To me, though, the area looked like it could be the high ground, a chance to form Australia's best ever national urban policy, and through it improve, if indirectly and over the longer term, the lives of many.

Without a substantive head of division, a number of temporary and part-time division heads were found, starting with Tony Powell. Tony came from Bob Lansdown's old agency, the National Capital Development Commission (NCDC). Working with Tony felt close to home as my father had been on the National Capital Planning Committee, their high-level advisory board during Tony's time there, and they knew each other. Unfortunately, my father died that year, 1973, but while sick he passed on to me some fascinating internal reports about the future of Canberra. Later, when I was involved for NSW in negotiations to change the ACT–NSW border to cope with the Queanbeyan anomaly (a less-planned overspill city on the edge of Canberra), they gave me some context.

Then followed Professor Malcolm Logan, head of the geography department at Monash University. Mal headed the division not much more than a day a week, but we saw each other socially as he'd hired me as his tutor in geography at the University of Sydney. We got along very well, sharing common spatial approaches to urban policy and an understanding of the slow-changing but dynamic national settlement system, on which we published together. We worked together a number of times over the years, once when Tom Roper, the Victorian education minister, appointed me to review a Monash University campus decision when Mal was vice-chancellor, and once, less in harmony, on a very fast train project where our governments took different positions on the Sydney–Melbourne route that helped crash the proposal: we, NSW, the inland route, versus the findings of Mal's Victorian review panel for an alternative coastal route.[27]

Anyway, under Tony, Mal and Pat Troy's watchful eyes the strategy division staffed up with convivial people I thought very smart, coming from a range of disciplines: Andrew Strickland, a sociologist, Rob Purdon, a geographer-planner friend from Sydney days, Peter Coaldrake, a graduate entrant who later went on to senior Queensland government and vice-chancellor roles, and others. Much later—too late—in March 1975 I was delighted when Ray Bunker, once my lecturer, was finally appointed out of the University of Sydney as the first substantive head of the division.

Making national urban strategy

Many ingredients

Our main job was to form a national urban and regional strategy. At the beginning of the government, our minister Tom Uren wrote to the prime minister, Gough Whitlam, to confirm, among other things, the mandate to form this strategy:

> I have been looking at the arrangements to give practical effect
> to the Government's objectives in old cities as well as in new.
> In taking a national view of the problems of the cities, we will

want to develop an overall strategy which can serve as a guideline in forming associated policies and as a basis on which our
Departments and agencies can work. It will take time to produce
this though we can obviously make progressive statements about
it and there will be many opportunities for public debate.[28]

National urban policy was not a small field. The government had a
political commitment to it, the ALP platform set out its themes, and the
Cities Commission was already working on it. As my colleagues rushed to
put the new programs into practice, they wanted a clearer policy framework. Is it already in place through the election mandate? How should
the different promises fit together? What higher goals should be served?

I thought that national urban policy should be different from just
the announcements and commitments, more than the sum of the parts.
It needed to be an articulated strategy that brought them together, and
more rationally, but went well beyond too, to express an evidence-based
strategy for settlement in the country and to redistribute resources more
fairly across regions. Why couldn't advanced capitalist countries benefit
from a capability for national planning?

At the time of the minister's letter above, NURDA was working out
what national urban strategy would mean for them, if they survived,
alongside this new 'department of urban affairs'. In April 1973 NURDA
became the Cities Commission, a statutory authority in Tom Uren's
ministry, charged with conducting studies of regional areas. Its other
mandates were to play a leading role in the establishment of new cities,
act as a professional consultant to DURD in physical planning exercises,
and be available to provide advice and information to state and local
government. Their work on national urban strategy continued to provide
context for these roles. The commission's role focused on the new cities
program, but it could develop broad strategy around that, including 'the
implementation of those Australian government policies which set out
consciously to influence the future location of population'.[29]

I was very happy with this. With DURD responsibility set out for
'issues of broad strategy or policy across the whole field of urban and

regional development', our strategy team started to prepare an interim statement over the months that followed. We soon agreed the tasks were to weave the existing policies and commitments together into a coherent narrative, to rationalise and improve them where possible, and to create an updated framework with a clear long-term vision.

Once again, this was new territory for me, but I persuaded myself that most of my colleagues were in the same boat. Anyway, being in the deep end was exciting. The work was in part abstract, in contrast with my earlier consultant experience. It drew on my research interest, though information gathering in these pre-internet days could be slow. There was time to think about who would be key stakeholders in forming national urban policy and I set about making new contacts.

By this time, I had good working relations with Lyndsay Neilson and Ian Morrison of the Cities Commission, who cooperated with the DURD strategy division on our task of forming policy. Later, Lyndsay was to join the division. In 1973 John Paterson wrote a framework report on national urban policy for the Cities Commission which was also useful for us as we took over the policy responsibility.[30] It saw Australia's system of cities driven more by investment and economic development trends than by policy intent.

However, incompatibilities of work style elsewhere in the department between commission transferees and new recruits created tension, and confusion still remained about the commission and department's respective functions, including overlapping dealings with the states. These problems stayed right through to June 1975, when the minister's frustration finally saw the commission abolished in favour of a new Bureau of Cities. It never really got started before the change of government in November 1975.[31]

At least the Cities Commission was interested in learning from international experience, as was I. For most of my DURD colleagues, this was esoteric stuff. The Urban Research Unit at the ANU, to which DURD was joined at the hip through Pat Troy, provided a good seminar forum for testing our ideas. A string of visiting scholars and practitioners all helped to widen our understanding of national urban policy issues.[32]

The latter included Lois Dean who came from the US Department of Housing and Urban Development and talked about US national policy.

Above all, for me, William Alonso, from the University of California Berkeley knew what it was about. In his view, 'implicit' urban policy was the main game: you have a national urban policy in practice whether you like it or not, made up of a host of policies and programs that have effects on cities, intended and unintended.[33] The task was to identify these policy instruments, understand their consequence, modify them and make them drivers of a more explicit policy. They could be housing, immigration, foreign investment, tax policy, capital projects, machinery of government, intergovernmental financial relations, the location of government employment, government procurement, health and human services policies. All were implicit urban policies and grist to the strategy mill. This lined up absolutely with my view of national planning.

Most of our interdepartmental colleagues did not see it this way. For them, despite DURD's mandate, urban policy was not much more than what state governments, planning departments and development authorities did, with local government tacked on. We in the department struggled to counter these backward views, as we saw them. DURD sought to commit the whole of government to the task of doing three main things: reducing inequality in regions and cities and in patterns and processes of urban development, coping with the stresses of rapid urban growth, and widening the tools we use to do those things. I was fully signed on.

Hence the program to form a whole-of-government urban and regional budget among the annual budget papers. Its aims were to collate the impacts of all government activities as a basis for channelling the implicit urban and regional policies embedded in all levels and parts of government, especially the regional distribution of expenditure, 'an admirable and essential first step to clearer thinking about the spatial impacts of urban policy'.[34] This included use of the Commonwealth Grants Commission to redistribute finance to local governments in need, active use of section 96 of the constitution to make conditional payments to the states for urban and regional purposes, and a set of other fiscal policies.

This strategy was well outside what we learnt in planning school.

Once again, I was gloriously out of my depth. I was simply learning on the job, but I was not the only one in that situation in DURD. This time the stakes were higher than before. Finding the ingredients for national urban and regional policy was exciting intellectually; the hard part would be bringing them together and putting them into action.

Framing the strategy

The work to form—or recast—a strategy got under way early in 1973.

I saw two possible frameworks for bringing the parts together. One, a more sophisticated national settlement strategy seeking to guide the patterns of urban and regional development through direct and indirect instruments, including economic and financial means, along the lines of Alonso's and Paterson's advice. A second option appeared to me to be a national land use plan with some flexibility that set development into sustainable patterns through regional and urban plans (essentially those of the states, with the Australian government as partner).

On the latter, the Department of Environment made a move to set up national land use planning, with some support from DURD's own urban environment branch. However, DURD's leadership resisted that initiative, as it would conflict with clear state powers for most land use planning. Moreover, the way it was expressed tended towards a static macro-zoning approach inconsistent with the more flexible strategic planning that I had learnt as a student.[35] I now saw that this would be a step back to the kind of planning we were trying to get past, and bring certain failure in an area where the states' powers were supreme.

So, our preference in the division was for the first option, a long-term national strategy that would transform cities and regions through better governance, innovative policy instruments and reformed planning and development processes.

Our early work reviewed the many government objectives and commitments to urban and regional development. It was clear to me that when put together some of them were inconsistent. Further, when taken as a whole, they would be difficult to meet. We built a work program around strengthening the justification for a national urban strategy.

After all, it was Australia's first time to bring together settlement policy, regional policy, employment location policy, transportation, the urban and regional budget, and the capacity of the bureaucracy to carry out the policy objectives. We wrote and commissioned a series of strategy background papers.

At the same time as preparing an overall strategy statement, those of us in the strategy division tried to support and align the different programs of the department, and in some cases other departments. We often found ourselves responding to requests for feedback and contributions. As Tom Uren (who would have read his Barry Commoner) would often say: 'everything is connected to everything else'.[36] And, further, *everything* the department communicated seemed to be related to urban and regional policy, for which we spent much time meeting-sitting and draft-reading. I found Tony Powell, as division head, helpful sorting out priorities, in part because he was already engaged in public discussion. Ever the realist, he cautioned us:

> I think it would be a mistake for us to think that the nation shares our concerns and our values. There are many who are doubtless sympathetic but few who are—to use a fashionable term—committed. I suspect that in the main most of us are selfish and short-sighted, otherwise the problems we are now grappling with would not have arisen in the first place.[37]

I agreed with his view but kept charging ahead. By August 1973, the team I led had sketched a first internal report. For background it covered the idea of a national urban and regional strategy, the experience of other countries and the dynamics of the Australian settlement system. The heart of the strategy was a rationalised statement of policies and programs. We outlined the government machinery necessary for implementation, including reformed intergovernmental and interdepartmental relations. I was relieved to get something together but knew it was far from acceptable.

Alonso reviewed the draft and wrote that it was sensible, with useful lists of programs and problems. But he had criticisms: for him, it was blank on overarching policy. He advised us to take an historical view of the evolution of Australian cities and regions, linking policies to examples of national development to help gain bureaucratic and political acceptance. As a response we stretched as far as the Snowy Mountains hydro-electricity scheme, the Ord River irrigation scheme for Australia's north, the national pipeline grid (for which minister Rex Connor's disastrous efforts to find finance later contributed to the government's downfall) and other contributions to national spatial development.

One particular focus he recommended was to link with political themes and symbols acceptable to both major parties to help a national urban policy to survive. As an example, he suggested an emphasis on growth. He recommended that we raise an awareness that Australia did not, at that time, share the worst problems of many other countries. He reminded us that Australia had no severely depressed areas, no separatist tendencies, no French 'desert' (neglect of any area outside Paris). He also advised that we take exceptional care with the 'rational' approach which he thought was embodied in my draft. It would be easier, he cautioned, to get agreement on actions rather than specific goals.

Bob Lansdown agreed with him. Perhaps both of them saw the plan-making team as being a little naïve in our belief in the persuasive power of a rational argument. Lansdown expressed concern at what he saw as our 'blind assumption' that democratic governments can get goals and objectives agreed upon, and commented that Australia didn't share the US penchant for rhetorical preambles. He preferred a more modest statement about national urban strategy, to be followed up later with a more detailed plan. I still wanted to keep a strong rationale for a national strategy, and make the case with some bravado, but of course I toned it down on my boss' advice.

Alonso was also concerned that the report over-emphasised the 'residential' quality of life; land, housing and services, rather than the productive capacity of cities. Pat Troy and Peter Till didn't accept Alonso's point. They argued that consumption and production are part of the same political economy. For them, modern socialism had expanded its appreciation of consumption to join its longer-standing focus on production. I agreed with Alonso, but much of the economic sector, say, industry policy, was at the margins of our mandate.

Alonso was also critical that the drafts he had seen ignored the role of women in Australian cities and regions. By this time, there was a wide debate in Australia and internationally about what was then called 'women and environments', culminating in the UN Habitat Forum conference in Vancouver in 1976, anchored by elderly feminist Margaret Mead. That discourse was already well developed by 1973, but the drafts proceeded with little more than an aim to remove sex discrimination in urban development.

By early 1974, the work had progressed further, but there were unanswered questions and the strategy team still had to map out some of the decisions needed to implement them. The minister tried unsuccessfully to list the topic for a special premiers' conference.[38]

Our work was getting a higher profile in government and ministers' statements, but I felt it needed more traction. We workshopped our ideas at a policy weekend with Tom Uren, policy doorkeepers like Peter Wilenski and Jim Spigelman from the PM's office, and our own minister's staff. These ideas covered the issues identified earlier: the rationale for national urban policy, regionalisation, settlement strategy, employment location, transport, and the urban and regional budget. The capacity of the bureaucracy to carry out the policy objectives was important, given interdepartmental pushback against DURD's rising power.

The senior advisers supported our direction, but they sought a more sophisticated version of what we were doing. Dutifully, we went on to sketch out the geographic shape of a national settlement strategy, based on economic development, access to services, protection of the environment and resources, and conservation of energy and the national heritage. We set out the pattern of settlements and the stewardship of land use (short of drawing a detailed map), to structure the emerging conurbations around Brisbane, Sydney and Melbourne, slow the growth of Sydney and Melbourne and moderate the growth of other large cities, back the new satellite 'system cities' around them, push ahead with the regional growth centres and promote the growth of existing provincial cities, prevent urban sprawl and concentrate selected sub-regional commercial centres in the metropolitan areas.[39]

While they were not published at the time, these remained our guidelines for action. Later we used them to review draft Loan Council capital projects and guide spatial aspects of the national budget. The list of policy guidelines seemed long, but this time we linked geographic priorities better to the overall strategy.[40] This allowed us to make more focused expressions of strategy, with Bob Lansdown looking over our shoulders to be 'sensible'. We were ready to produce a clear public statement of intent and give sharper guidelines to the program areas.

I realised that forming policy was highly transactional, consulting with many people and making the case not only on rational grounds but on a political and emotional basis. I had to get out of my evidence-based mindset. This was an important lesson and was about to become more important still.

Headwinds

The political climate was changing unfavourably for the government. Framing the strategy, I sensed a narrowing of our freedom to propose anything not already committed—and that was the feeling across the whole Whitlam government. The senate blocked key bills, threatened to block supply, and rejected important draft referenda, including a proposal to recognise local government on the Loan Council. An election was coming.

Whitlam called a double dissolution and set elections for 18 May 1974.

The department rushed out our interim statement on national urban policy in low-key format before the government went into a 'caretaker' period.[41] This gave me some relief; the ball was rolling. I'd passed the first big test. The statement was about all we could do under the time pressure. It offered little new policy content. It set out a strategy consisting of the department's understanding of national goals and urban and regional objectives to be achieved within the Australian pattern of settlement and within metropolitan areas. It set out a program of action for policy integration, programs operating on a regional basis, programs relating to single sectors, and information programs.[42]

All this effort had little impact. The statement had to be cautious, purged of anything controversial, with the humble aim of 'stimulating discussion within DURD and in the broader academic and professional community'.[43] The election was the news, not our strategy. It had little media coverage and only indirect influence on policymaking. At least its versions stayed on for later reviewers of DURD to be 'the most coherent versions of the policy guidelines of the new department available', but for reasons of work not yet done and an uncharacteristic departmental bias towards caution, it didn't hold some of the strategy we wanted to build.[44]

At least the government won the election, if with a reduced majority, and there was more time to develop policy and express it in a revised statement. But the economic outlook was deteriorating and budget preparation became the key policy arena. Treasury pressed departments to cut back their budgets, and the strategy division, like other parts of the department, worked on the tolerance to DURD programs of cuts of 5, 10 and 15 percent. If we had to, the division could carry the cuts, but DURD economists took a more aggressive line, expressing concern about the 'real' economy and advocating stimulus, despite high inflation.

Thus Tom Uren defended an expansionary budget bid for 1974/75, arguing the merits of the programs and the need to mobilise real resources to take up the forecast slack in capacity, despite strains already showing in the building and construction industry. In the minister's scripted words:

> Inflation is unlikely to be reduced and may easily increase. At the same time, on present policies, I would expect aggregate output for the economy (excluding farms) to increase at considerably less than capacity rates … In my opinion the expected slowdown of the economy creates the opportunity for us as a Government to pursue more effectively our urban and regional development programs in the year ahead.[45]

Treasury argued ineffectively for a strong deflationary shock and

DURD's Michael Keating found holes in the budget draft that had devastating consequences. Thus, at least for that year, DURD had a major influence over the whole budget, which followed the department's expansionary line for the government.

I was pleased, at least for the department. The budget funded growth in DURD's new programs, which were still ramping up. The approach was indeed to take up slack in the economy, construction resources permitting, as the economy entered a downturn. However, that budget turned out badly because the downturn was unexpectedly strong, and the Australian economy went into recession.

Under Mal Logan's leadership, the overall strategy work continued through late 1974. He directed my team to give priority to advise on restructuring the Australian urban system, though he admitted 'we have very limited understanding of how socio-economic objectives can be translated into spatial terms'.[46] The team was well prepared to communicate the current overall strategy and develop the pre-election statement to a new and higher stage, so as ultimately to give comprehensive context to the minister and DURD program leaders on such matters as how to restructure the metropolitan areas, influence patterns of transport and communications, change the distribution of employment, and be strategic about land acquisition policies. I was also speaking around the states at conferences and business gatherings; this gave me a good feel for the pulse of urban policy nationally, but the feedback offered little change in the work's direction.

Despite more engagement with key players, the strategy formation still had a research flavour, and I started to envy our departmental colleagues, some of whom were whizzing around in government VIP jets to high-level negotiations. It was clear they could not wait for the next strategy statement; they were frantically implementing their own programs and typically wanted policy advice on particular matters on the spot. Spending more time with other teams in specific program and policy arenas seemed a more effective way to embed the strategy, at least within the department, and to those areas of action we now turn.

Tweaking the new cities program

The growth centres program emerged from a long and inconclusive policy debate about selective decentralisation and more recent state initiatives to kick-start growth in regional centres. It was the flagship of Labor's urban and regional programs. The original aim was to divert about ten percent of population growth into growth centres from the metropolitan cities.[47] While at first glance that seemed a reasonable aim, it implied a big diversion of population growth.

The Cities Commission built on NURDA work and some commitments to produce its first five-year report by June 1973. DURD budgeted $33m for the 1973–74 financial year.[48] The first list comprised regional cities and near-metropolitan sub-regional growth centres, or 'system cities': Albury–Wodonga, Bathurst–Orange, Holsworthy–Campbelltown, Gosford–Wyong, Townsville, Rockhampton–Gladstone, the Moreton Region, Geelong and southeast Melbourne, Monarto (a South Australian new town proposal), the northwest corridor of Perth (Salvado) and the Tamar region in Tasmania. All of these promising sites were subject to further investigations and negotiations. The program also folded in Canberra, for whose urban development the minister was responsible. Canberra was regarded as 'by far the most important centre'. Cabinet officially recognised Canberra as a regional growth centre in September 1974.[49]

The rationale for the growth centres program included population redistribution away from the core metropolitan areas and development of the chosen regions. Its planning and much of its implementation were clearly the main purpose of the Cities Commission. Apart from providing a wider framework, the DURD strategy division had little direct influence on the program, other than some joint planning, and sharing data and analyses of national population distribution and regional economic development. We wove the growth centres program into regional policy as an advanced element of what might become a national system of designated regional centres.

When demographers did the population numbers they realised that big numbers would have to move to the new cities to make a difference, nine more Canberras according to Max Neutze.[50] 'Unlikely', said many policy analysts. The population numbers were too big, and the motivations to move too little. A vein of scepticism flowed through the debate in the wake of Bill Alonso's landmark article 'What are new towns for?'.[51] Despite inflated public expectations, it soon became clear that even the most ambitious version of the regional growth centres program would make little difference to population distribution. It was not going to decant many people and jobs from the metropolitan regions.

I was one of the staff who had to grapple with this problem. In our communications, including from Cities Commission colleagues, we tried to soften expectations that this program would make a real difference in decentralising the metropolitan populations. Instead, we tried to direct the rationale for the program more towards trialling the best of the new policies. For example there were opportunities to experiment with land commission intervention in the land market for price stabilisation, to work with new development corporations, and to use modified land tenures, as recommended by the Else–Mitchell inquiry, to create more attractive cities.[52] The political rhetoric associated growth centres with 'alternative lifestyles' before that term became a codeword for the counterculture. I wasn't sure this was the right way to put it. To be more honest, the rationale was to be a test for putting the new urban programs and policies into place in areas where they could be accelerated.

While we policy people sought to shift the rationale, other parts of DURD were heavily involved in its implementation, particularly Peter Till's division, which busied itself negotiating agreements with the states and setting up the development corporations.

The first priority was Albury–Wodonga. That was a sensible choice as its cross-border location more clearly justified the federal initiative. It drew the majority of growth centres funding. New South Wales nominated Bathurst–Orange as a regional growth centre in October 1972 before Labor was elected federally, and on Cities Commission advice DURD adopted it too, with funding mostly for land acquisition once the Bathurst–Orange Development Corporation was established in 1974. South Australia also established the Monarto Development

Corporation in 1972 and the Cities Commission and DURD picked this up as well. None of the other regional growth centres came into development through the protracted negotiations and non-negotiations with the other states. Blocked discussions with Queensland and Western Australia were classic cases of 'non-decision-making'.[53]

For the 'system cities' only the southwest of Sydney, NSW's Macarthur initiative, was funded through the program. Efforts to support Gosford–Wyong, Geelong, southeast Melbourne, northern Perth, southern Brisbane and Townsville's growth did not succeed. In the 1975–76 budget estimates the minister reported good progress, with prospective support for urban expansion and redevelopment in all the active states under the more comprehensive 'umbrella agreements'. It is a pity the growth centres program did not expand into that last year of the government.

In summary, the growth centres policy was established well before our national urban strategy was formed, and at best I was able to help shape a change in its rationale. The success of the new cities program, such as it was, relied more on the urban planning and implementation efforts of others. This was not the case with regional policy, where the strategy team had a decisive role.

Shaping regional policy

The Labor government's regionalisation policy

Over time, Australian regional policy has meant different things. Among these have been national development for post-war reconstruction, various state versions of regional planning and decentralisation, and regional economic adjustment programs at commonwealth and state levels.

A particular form of regionalisation was at the heart of the new Labor government's strategies. Gough Whitlam, a constitutional lawyer, painted a vision of an Australian governance system with a working 'fourth tier', made up of a set of regional organisations capable of high-level planning, intergovernmental and inter-agency coordination, and reformed fiscal and financial arrangements to reduce inequalities of service provision and promote economic opportunity.

Whitlam put the ideal case forward, arguing that if Australian governance were created from a clean slate, there would be only two tiers, national government and a set of regional governments:

> Vested interests and legal complexities should not discourage or deter us from attempts to modernise and rationalise our inherited structure. If we were devising a new structure for representative government for our continent we would have neither so few State Governments nor so many local authorities.[54]

The states and most local government associations were uncomfortable with this vision, to say the least. For them, it had the potential to undermine their powers. Conservatives saw it as an existential threat to the Australian federal separation of powers. At first, the prime minister did little to placate the sceptics about the possibility of replacing the states in a unitary constitution made up of only a unicameral national government, an assembly for each of the metropolitan areas, and a few score regional assemblies elsewhere.

Of course, the reality was more complex. Regional policy was no clean slate. Ambiguities about the government's long-term intentions kept getting in the way of making practical policies on regionalisation, as Michael Wood, one of my DURD strategy divisional colleagues explained:

> The ALP's policies amounted to reform of the federal system and implied ... the enforced atrophy of the State governments by using the financial power of federal grants to raise the prestige and influence of local authorities whose amalgamation into regions was to be encouraged through financial inducements. Labor's policies for urban and regional development emerged as a vehicle for significant and unprecedented political and administrative reform.[55]

Members of the government sometimes did not help either. There was an unfortunate moment when Senator Wheeldon (WA) said 'it was the Federal Government's policy that State Governments should be abolished'.[56]

The spectre of constitutional restructure haunted regional policy long after Labor came to power and made more moderate statements about it. It continued on after the government lost referendum bills to empower local government by representation on the Loan Council and in any future constitutional conventions, and to enable the Australian government to provide direct financial assistance to local government. Regional policy was probably the most important area of my work, and with my economic geography background and familiarity with NSW regional policy I felt well prepared for it.

Regional policy writ large

The Department of Urban and Regional Development was established in part to create a wider regional planning system for Australia, in a way, to resume post-war resettlement planning in a modern form. We aimed to harness mechanisms like the urban and regional budget, and the various urban development programs, not only for a national settlement strategy but to pave the way for a more powerful capacity for regional planning. At the very least, DURD's aims appealed to me: coordinating the regional boundaries and centres for delivery of all levels of government services, and relocating government employment to these centres. The area improvement program was another means of effecting this coordination at the regional level.

A large share of my time (which had expanded to take up most of my waking time, and I was not alone in that), as well as the time of others like Rob Purdon (in Canberra a squash partner, and geographer-planner friend from my University of Sydney days) was to help DURD give shape to the vision of regionalisation as expressed in the Labor Party platform and election promises. It had to be broken down into recognisable and implementable parts. The most prominent part of our early work came from the mooted extension of the Commonwealth Grants Commission, driven by fiscal equalisation practices still unique among OECD countries. The aim was to provide financial assistance to local governments, individually and in regional groupings, for which legislation, but thankfully not a referendum, would be necessary.[57]

Common regional boundaries and a set of regional organisations had wider possibilities:

+ Commonly accepted regions for Australia that would strengthen statistical collection and regional planning
+ Regional groupings of local governments necessary to broaden the base of government and give more recognition to local government[58]
+ Competent regional organisations to enable other agencies (including those of the Australian government) to tackle deficiencies in urban and regional development, especially to ameliorate interregional inequities
+ Economies of scale in public administration built up as more and more activities of government engaged at that level, and
+ Finally, and much dreamed-of at the time by DURD staff, strong regional organisations with commonly accepted boundaries that would make continuing horizontal and vertical coordination of Australia's complex government system more likely.[59]

A new level of government was not on our practical agenda, as I kept saying:

> It has been suggested that regional groupings constitute an emergent fourth tier of government. It is important to realise that none of these [DURD and rest of government] programs individually nor all taken together, amount to a form of government; there is no legislative assembly, no direct electoral process, no independent money raising power, and no independent executive.[60]

The more limited aims were radical enough. Even the Australian government agencies did not combine their approaches, with departmental regional development programs going their own way and no overriding policy other than ambiguous political statements. There were at least 38 definitions of regions for government purposes at the time.[61]

The PM wrote a letter to all ministers, aiming to tidy it up:

> I am particularly concerned ... to achieve our goal of balancing the functions and finances of the Australian Government, States, regional and local authorities to ensure that resources are adequately developed and services adequately provided. We should, I believe, aim at having an appropriate Australia-wide grouping of regions and centres which all programs should be expected to adopt unless there are strong reasons for not doing so.[62]

While this directive was powerful, horizontal coordination of the government's regional presence nevertheless stayed a continuing struggle not just for the government but for me in my work ahead.

The department's commitment to regionalisation also had to deal with the states' detailed and changing arrangements. The aim was to help integrate them too, with an eye to the various resource reallocation possibilities that might exist among regions in public administration and economic development. We wanted common administrative boundaries and centres, the location of Australian government employment in support of regional policy, and the coordination of programs, whatever their level of government responsibility, operating on a regional basis.

Whether coordinating Australian government regional activities or reconciling state regional activities, the establishment of regional organisations and common regional boundaries would enable wider regional planning to occur. The Australian government would thereby relate directly to organisations with more significant coverage of development issues than the fragmented pattern of small local governments.

Above all, the rationale was to reduce regional disparities in services, and ultimately to redistribute economic opportunity. This aligned strongly with my values. We might have to upset some arrangements to get a better system in place—a little destruction can be a creative thing. Given well-documented inequalities in the big cities, territorial justice (and population equivalence for funding) required sub-metropolitan regional organisations and thus boundaries for them. This task also fell to the strategy division, particularly me.

Interim regional boundaries

The Commonwealth Grants Commission Bill was an early priority in 1973. The mechanism was to form regional groupings of local governments, fund them to form program and project plans, and enable the Commonwealth Grants Commission to make recommendations to government to fund the new bodies directly. The prospect of funding was an incentive for regional organisations of councils (ROCs) to form; indeed, the Grants Commission took the view that only constituted ROCs should be eligible for funding. In the meantime, someone had to define the regional boundaries, and that was us in the division. The work was urgent, and even though state-designated regions were a starting point for non-metropolitan regions, a good evidence base was needed.

We had to recommend regional boundaries that were generally built up from local government areas, including within the metropolitan areas of Sydney and Melbourne, to be based on good evidence. We would consider current practice as well, and aim for some population equivalence. Given the limited time available, we could do no more than delineate interim regional boundaries. They would need to be adjusted through further research, negotiation with state and local governments and review of first round practice.

My research interest in communications was by now shared with others in the department, so we took part in long-term government telecommunications planning and a commission of enquiry into the Australian Post Office. These interests helped get regional boundary work done from network analysis of telephone traffic in non-metropolitan areas to define functional regions based on connectivity as a surrogate for social and business interaction.[63] In other words, they could uncover the pattern of social and business connections that make up communities. Though this work was groundbreaking, the results were not too different from the regions used by the states. This was surprising to me, but reassuring. I would not have to argue for rejection of state regional boundaries.

The departmental leadership tried to influence telecommunications policy as we saw it as critical urban and regional infrastructure, and recognised my expertise in this area. So I wrote draft submissions and appeared before the commission with Bob Lansdown to argue for rate concessions and advanced services for growth centres, to have regard for the location of government employment policy, to set unit fee areas without disadvantaging outer suburban areas, and to take account of urban and regional impacts when introducing new technology, especially as the 'information utility' became a reality.[64] The 1970s mostly predated the internet, but work on my master's thesis showed that the shape of the system was already quite clearly mapped out in the eyes of the experts, if not the public.[65] I briefed the minister on the review before cabinet.

The submission I drafted must not have been very clear, because after the meeting Bob Lansdown discreetly asked me to explain what the minister said in cabinet. That was because the cabinet secretary writing the minutes had rung him to say he didn't understand the idea of an information utility.

So much for telephone traffic regions for this round. At least the role of communications in urban policy was becoming established.

What would ecological regions look like? Surely, they would be very different. Among ecologists, there was growing interest in 'cities as life systems'; the modified systems of materials and energy flows in cities. This was a topic of great interest to me too. I'd taught a course on it to engineers at the University of NSW, systems thinking was a key part of my master's thesis, and the Ecological Society of Australia was championing it.[66] Across the country, river catchment-based planning was gaining favour for resources planning. We commissioned Commonwealth Scientific and Industrial Research Organisation (CSIRO) experts in this area to delimit biophysical regions for the country. There might even be a connection with patterns of Indigenous occupation of the continent, the longest continuing culture on earth. The work was finished well after the first round of regions was defined, but we were confident that the results could help in later modifications, and beyond regional policy.

The CSIRO produced advice and later a full report and an unprecedented set of maps, a modern biophysical regionalisation of Australia.[67] They have been used for many purposes since, and have been updated in more electronic forms. I saw some potential then for an approach to national land use planning if it were to get up.[68] I was happy with this project because it was my own initiative. But it didn't fit the imperatives of the day, nor my own view about the main arena for national settlement strategy. I was afraid it might lead to unrealistically prescriptive hope in land use planning among policy proponents outside the urban sector who thought that drawing up land use plans could magically result in decisions that implemented them. Nevertheless, I was proud to promote a contemporary look at this continent's ecosystems set out on a set of maps.

Within the larger metropolitan areas, the government was determined to create sub-metropolitan regions to address social and economic inequalities. At the time 'factor analysis' was the rage, and Monash University's geography department won the job to do the research over Flinders University. The analysis was based on census data, with regions assembled step-wise from smaller areas based on their similarity from multifactor correlations of data. We adjusted the results for population equivalence and topography, and the work became the basis for metropolitan regions in Sydney and Melbourne. This was a very pleasing result.

A round of discussions with the states and local government followed in a climate of hostility to the Australian government's previously mentioned aims and the use of the Grants Commission to create regional organisations. Even the local government associations formally opposed the policy, with the exception of those in New South Wales and Tasmania. Different people from the department, including myself, discussed the regional boundaries with state planning and regional development agency staff, who bristled with opposition to virtually anything other than their current non-metropolitan boundaries. They needn't have worried. The final 68 regional delineations were close to the state's own regions, at least for non-metropolitan areas.

The *Regions* report to accompany the May 1973 bill was a top priority and its production generated a flurry of activity in the department. We had to pull together different lines of work. Some of it was unfinished, and we had to make sure there were no mistakes.[69] The schedule of the government printer was too long for us to get the report printed in time.

And the document was too big for the department to print in one go. So, we spent a harrowing morning at the photocopier, producing and stapling reports as the Bill was physically being tabled in parliament, rushing the documents to Parliament House in couriers as each batch was finished.

We made it!

Exhausted but delighted, we were finally able to rest. In our modest view, it was a landmark in Australian regional policy. The Commonwealth Grants Commission Act 1973 was proclaimed on 23 June 1973.

Regional policy widens

As mentioned, the Grants Commission took a more conservative view than the department hoped, recognising only incorporated ROCs. The obstructive states could thus refuse their incorporation, treating the ROCs merely as 'post boxes' for the purposes of the program, and solely for assistance with services and amenities, and not for planning—which was, of course, our wider objective.

The Grants Commission criteria for grants of financial assistance were based on inter-state fiscal equalisation criteria, calculations of the revenue differential between a 'standard' rate and the local authority's taxable capacity, plus the expenditure differential needed to enable it to provide a 'standard' range of services and amenities. This was the approach that served Australia well in reducing inter-state fiscal disparities. The Grants Commission, with DURD support, invited authorities to consider documenting the special needs of citizens arising from 'welfare problems deriving from high population density and/or a predominance of low income groups', high rates of growth, and high costs associated with distance or the strains from mining or industrial developments on council capacities.[70]

We were gratified that Whitlam's wider original aims for the ROCs were not lost, as they began their work. He explained it this way:

> Regional bodies or organisations should be given a responsibility
> for … services wherever possible, noting that this responsibility
> may range from direct involvement in decision-making through

to consultation; public participation in planning and decision making for, and implementation of, programs should be
encouraged and assisted; State and local Government should be
encouraged to delegate to regional bodies more responsibility
for those State and local government programs which are most
appropriately delivered at the regional level, and to foster public
participation.[71]

Meanwhile, in Canberra, efforts to coordinate the regional effects of
government programs were still facing what seemed like endless setbacks.
After the policy weekend described above, Bill Butler, head of DURD's
coordination division, drafted a backchannel letter for Whitlam, who
signed it to all ministers on 14 November 1973 to have the standing
interdepartmental committee on urban and regional development do
a 'thorough-going review' of departmental regional programs to ensure
coordination.[72] Butler sought to ensure that the formation of working
parties and task forces in urban and regional development were constituted under that committee as much as possible, including a working
party on regional activities, and tried to prevent it being a talk-shop for
complex policy issues.

The committee set up the working party on regional activities in
November 1973 to report on the forms of regional administration
established by federal, state and local governments and to recommend
common regional boundaries and the preferred locations of regional
administrative units. This initiative had the potential to open the way
to use the interim regional boundaries defined earlier in the year and to
link the location of Australian government employment to urban and
regional strategies. Information collection and negotiations followed
with many agencies of government. DURD itself used the new regional
boundaries and ROCs, particularly for the area improvement program.
This was progress.

But with typical department and agency foot-dragging (including
Treasury being 'traditionally unhelpful'), the information gathering first
phase exceeded the February 1974 deadline.[73] DURD staff used an April

draft bilaterally with agencies to try to achieve more inclusion, and allowed exemptions and deferrals for the Australian Post Office, Commonwealth Bureau of Roads, and Department of Housing and Construction. I was spared doing the nitty-gritty work on this. A team in another division led by Chris O'Connell, an erstwhile prominent student politician, was responsible for servicing the committee. However, I shared the frustration. We seemed to be losing momentum and facing too many exemptions.

Meanwhile, the government's response to economic stagnation brought another regional program into being, the regional employment development scheme, approved in August 1974. At least our minister was on the supervising cabinet committee. It took until September–October 1974 for a final draft from the working party to circulate, by which time three other parallel developments occurred. Regional policymaking was getting complicated.

The first was an updated set of regional boundaries. The 1974 statement of urban and regional development programs (that I led) anticipated revised regional boundaries to serve these wider purposes. Preparation of 'long-term' regional boundaries for the 1974–75 Grants Commission process was designed to be more suitable for integrating the many other programs operating on a regional basis. Criteria were better spelt out—functional linkages, socio-economic homogeneity, expressions of communities of interest, topography where significant, population equivalence where other criteria were not determining, and major developments likely to affect future local government.[74] Some local government areas split by state planning regions or census districts were recombined, some states had modified regional boundaries since the last set of boundaries. Many local governments made representations, some of which were accepted. Finally, Adelaide and Perth were subdivided, once the results of further factorial ecology studies were completed.

The second development was an effort to combine the main strands of regionalisation policy. This was a task led by the strategy division more directly. In DURD, we believed that common governmental regional boundaries and local grant mechanisms alone did not measure up to our vision of an ideal policy on regionalism.

After the policy weekend in February 1974, we in the regional policy team persuaded Bob Lansdown, the departmental secretary, that regional policy needed a stronger government-wide commitment. This was because, in our experience, it continued to be contested or ignored by departments and agencies. On 3 April 1974, Lansdown asked Tony Powell, head of the strategy division, to help out:

> It is increasingly evident that there is a need for Cabinet to consider an Australian Government policy on regionalism. I would like you to co-ordinate the preparation of a draft Cabinet Submission ... The submission should face up to the issue of the fourth tier of Government and ask the Cabinet to give some thought to the long-term aims of regional policy.[75]

There followed a surge of work within the department, heavily involving Rob Purdon and me. I was badly overloaded. I recall being frustrated by Pat Troy's request for me to lead yet another exploratory seminar, this time on regional policy, at the ANU, where he kept a joint appointment. It conflicted with my need to deliver on this cabinet opportunity. The growth centres and the area improvement program for disadvantaged regions, on which Jill was working, were priorities for the advance of regionalism. One core idea was to build on the mechanisms of the area improvement program, expand them to more regions, and then, around each regional organisation, bring about horizontal coordination with other Australian government regional programs and vertical coordination to encompass, as far as possible, state and local government regional initiatives and regional planning.

The draft DURD cabinet submission on an 'integrated regional action program' that followed drew strong criticism before the May 1974 meeting of the main committee. For the Special Ministry of State, and on the basis of discussion with the Priority Review Staff, John Enfield said:

> ... we are concerned at the extent to which particular proposals advanced in your draft Submission would carry the Government

forward towards the development of systems of government and to far-reaching financial commitments without fundamental policy questions being addressed in advance.[76]

It seemed to us that many of our government colleagues did not understand the government's commitment and the prime minister's vision. We asked ourselves how to get the wider policy and program adopted. It could go through an interdepartmental committee process or go more directly to cabinet. At first, the department sought to use the interdepartmental machinery in place.

Then a third arena opened up. Public confusion over different Australian government boundaries continued, even with an *entente cordiale* on the regional councils for social development. Following complaints in the media and around the cabinet table on 11 June 1974, this third line of work outside the main committee was opened up, the creation of an interdepartmental committee on overlap in Australian government grants to local bodies. It was also chaired and serviced by DURD.

This work, too, ground down in disputes over efforts to set the wider policy context for the removal of overlap, and in particular the emerging form of DURD's integrated regional action program, the proposed coordination mechanism for all relevant Australian government programs in designated regions.[77] Treasury was not at first on the 'overlap' committee, and vigorously opposed its formation in detail and in principle because its officers still saw themselves as the controllers of all resource allocation. They were against mechanisms for specific purpose grants to regions, ostensibly because they might become a method of pork-barrelling.[78] At least the DURD proposal for an expanded area improvement program was accepted by the budget cabinet that year.[79]

Treasury sought a different mechanism to eliminate overlaps in grants of administrative assistance to regional organisations. If you can't control one committee, start another one. Indeed, Treasury sought to eliminate such grant programs altogether and curb DURD's power of coordination of other departments. This view was at odds with government and ALP undertakings on which the programs were based.

The final 'overlap committee' report in March 1975, recommending rationalisation of overlaps and revision of functional responsibilities among the overlap culprits, carried a DURD minority clause upholding comprehensive regional coordination and budgeting processes as a better means to working with overlap than reversion to the actions of each agency.[80]

We spent a lot of time in interdepartmental meetings during this time, sometimes in large numbers. Though everyone thought they had a purpose, it was inefficient. Once or twice Mike Keating, in his inimitable style, said to us around the table, 'You, you and you, out!' This work was also taking a long time, and Whitlam found the resistance to integrating regional programs even more frustrating.

So, what did he do?

He set up *another* ad hoc committee (this time of ministers), the Australia–state regional relations committee of cabinet, with oversight of resolving overlaps and conflicts in this area. That more senior committee and its supporting group of officers came back to a more comprehensive view of regional policy in its 3 June 1975 report, supporting the DURD view and rebuffing Treasury.[81]

I had little to do directly with these machinations but contributed advice along the way. I found the interdepartmental arena tiresome. I didn't question my purpose for being in DURD, but bureaucratic coordination was not the style of work I liked. I much preferred the more free-wheeling ways of operating like it had been in Sydney. But I knew this was a price I had to pay for the privilege of being in DURD.

The department lost some battles in this alphabet soup but came out in front in the war to widen the scope of regional policy. Its map for regionalisation was laid out:

- Retention of the ALP's vision (not for a regional tier of government any time soon)
- Authorised federal regional boundaries that mostly fitted those of the states
- The capacity for urban and regional budgets to have a stronger regional dimension, and

- A growing number of regional organisations of councils, many to be capable of drawing in extended powers as conditions might permit.

Overall, the DURD strategy team did a good job defining regional boundaries and shaping a more coherent regional policy out of the confusing set of mixed parts that made up the government's mandate. We also had some success in shifting gear to chase regional policy's more ambitious aims, learn from the states' pushback, and adapt to political changes.

By contrast, the federal government's more coherent policies on metropolitan areas were late to get started.

A new federal voice on metropolitan strategies

The creation of sub-metropolitan regions and the reduction of intra-metropolitan place-based inequality were two distinctive features of the government's regionalisation policy. Whitlam's oft-quoted words rang in our ears:

> Increasingly, a citizen's real standard of living, the health of himself [sic] and his family, his children's opportunities for education and self-improvement, his access to employment opportunities, his ability to enjoy the nation's resources for recreation or culture, his ability to participate in the decisions and actions of the community are determined not by his income, not by the hours he works, but by where he lives.[82]

We were going further, aiming to bring Australian government resources to the better planning of metropolitan regions, and coordinating Australian government activities in that task. Almost every DURD program—the urban and regional budget, land commissions, sewerage backlog remediation, area improvement program, inner-city projects, transport interventions, environment and heritage programs, the system cities of the growth centres program—aimed to improve the metropolitan areas. Systematic division work on metropolitan strategies began in mid-1974, late because of more urgent tasks like forming regional policy. However, across the department engagement with the states on metropolitan planning and program, and policy interventions in planning and development began early.

As the division staffed up, the metropolitan branch was my designated home, insofar as any branches were home in DURD's 'pool' staff structure. But that latent organisational structure never came into being, given the fluid nature of the work. Forming a federal view on the metropolitan areas was contentious, as we'd seen from delineation of their regions. Thus, I was delighted when Ray Bunker joined us as the first full-time head of division, even if it was late in the day. Metropolitan planning was his primary field.[83] By then, in March 1975, the 'umbrella' agreements with the states were on the table, most particularly with South Australia, which Ray has documented.[84] Members of the strategy division had decent working relationships with the various states' metropolitan planners.

As most DURD people didn't have nuanced views about what should be done with the states and local governments about metropolitan development, we produced a series of working papers to provide that oversight. There was plenty of material on the topic as we had been working on it off and on for some time, reflecting our involvement with program areas to inject strategy thinking on the run on the inner urban projects, CBDs, office construction, freeways, equity, access to service, urban land, Australian government employment location, public transport and others.

The strategy division also spent time on submissions to enquiries under way that we believed needed to have urban and regional strategy, such as the Borrie population enquiry.[85] This continued my view that engagement in projects and submissions was 'strategy in action', with two-way enrichment. We worked loyally on these initiatives, but, in truth, we lost time by spreading ourselves so thin.

The aims of metropolitan strategy were set from the policy weekend in 1974: to redistribute resources and services and job opportunities within metropolitan areas to favour disadvantaged areas, to develop sub-metropolitan centres to reduce the dominance of the central area and help redistribution, and to promote activities in and around the metropolitan centres, including housing for low income groups.

The priority areas for action on policy were on regionalisation, the location of Australian government employment, on which cabinet and a dedicated interdepartmental committee took particular interest, and building more friendly working relationships with the state metropolitan planners and capital city lord mayors.

Overall, metropolitan strategies never took off, though they could have been an important part of national urban strategy. The first full version of a metropolitan strategy—for Sydney—was circulated in DURD in January 1975.[86] We published the last version of the full metropolitan strategy as a working paper in November 1975, just before the end of the government.[87]

Relocating Australian government employment

The location of Australian government employment was an obvious direct instrument of federal policy to help restructure the metropolitan areas and boost key non-metropolitan regional centres. Rob Purdon and I, as students, weighed in before we knew we would work together at DURD, with a submission to the parliamentary standing committee on public works that the commonwealth should consider the metropolitan consequences of its own activities, adopt a consistent policy of office location and locate the proposed commonwealth office complex at Parramatta rather than Woolloomooloo.[88]

In the early DURD days location strategies at play were decades long transfers to Canberra (which were put on hold from July 1973), moves from Canberra and other places to the growth centres, dispersal from CBDs to sub-metropolitan regional centres, and the regionalisation of administration and service delivery discussed earlier.[89] It was the subject of election promises, including for Parramatta.

We began work early through an ad hoc interdepartmental committee on Australian government office accommodation. In December 1973 cabinet approved office provision for 2500 employees on a acquired site in Parramatta and 2000 at Campbelltown, and also chose, in principle, sites at Ringwood in Melbourne, Albury–Wodonga, Geelong and Bathurst–Orange.

The background study estimated that about 10,500 Australian government employees in Sydney and 20,400 in Melbourne could be relocated from inner-city areas, including, for Melbourne, about 5700 relocatable to regional growth centres.[90] Cabinet also established a standing interdepartmental committee on the location of Australian government employment, with detailed terms of reference, to be chaired by the Public Service Board.[91]

With this work in progress, the strategy division, particularly Peter Coaldrake, then developed location criteria and a nomination of locations. That involved consultations with the states. The guidelines were endorsed by cabinet in April 1975, requiring that any location decision would have to come before the relevant interdepartmental committee.[92]

The specific moves to Albury–Wodonga, Bathurst–Orange and Geelong needed more consultation before we could make recommendations. Nevertheless, we were successful in having them accepted. Interdepartmental objections slowed that work, but it was made easier from June 1975 when DURD took over acquisition, leasing and disposal responsibilities from the Department of Property and Services. Then, because of the risks arising from these responsibilities being separate from the control, use and management of property, all of that department's property functions were transferred as well. This reorganisation swelled the number of staff in DURD by an order of magnitude. It did not change the working arrangements for most parts of the department, but it certainly made the strategy division's work on the location of government employment easier.

Meanwhile, on 30 June 1975, true to his promise, the prime minister opened a Parramatta government office building for 5000 tax office employees, with many more moves planned to come. We were aware of the informal resistance from Canberra-based public servants to moves out of Canberra to such places as Parramatta, Dandenong, Albury–Wodonga,

Bathurst–Orange and Geelong, building up in the last months of the government, as well as formal bureaucratic opposition.[93]

Against these, the full program of relocation hardly started before the government changed. The succeeding Fraser government decided not to proceed with most of the transfers 'on the basis of cost and priority', and decided that any policies to foster growth centres would 'not include transfers of staff from Canberra'. That was a pity. I strongly believed that the Whitlam government moves were well worked through and based on good evidence. They would have added momentum to the development of regional centres without much, or any, loss of efficiency.

With hindsight, I can now see that the initiative was much better thought through than the various commonwealth pork-barrel moves to relocate Canberra agencies to regional centres in the following years. In a post-COVID-19 environment, improving the location of government service centres and employment has become even more important.

Overheated capital city CBDs

The leadership of DURD saw over-developed central business districts (CBDs) as part of the problem we had to address. Decanting government employment could not be our only strategy. Through over-concentration, big city CBDs were harming equitable employment distribution, reducing opportunities to strengthen sub-regional centres, displacing housing for low income people, threatening environmental and heritage assets and sucking scarce real resources into an office boom that could better go into housing.

Something had to be done. From December 1973, the capital city lord mayors formed a secretariat of town clerks and officers which met regularly with DURD. In these forums we explored where the capital cities fitted into DURD's emerging metropolitan strategies and the research questions that I drafted that might form the basis of joint work. The lord mayors and their officials were attracted to the low risk tasks of joint research and benchmarking city performance. My earlier work on the City of Sydney strategic plan came in handy here as I had first-hand experience of what research on inner cities was relevant to policy.

The division, via Rob Purdon, led a cross-departmental team to draft positions on each metropolitan CBD, starting with Sydney and Melbourne. At the same time, we were preparing the metropolis-wide position papers. Tom Uren's frequent media comments about overbuilt CBDs clearly irked the lord mayors, who by June 1975 must have been complaining to the PM, who said:

> I understand that my colleague, Mr Tom Uren, the Minister for Urban and Regional Development, has made some remarks about the role of the central business districts of Australian cities in the context of the whole city. It is certainly my experience, for all his talk about gentleness, that Tom Uren can be blunt when he is talking about something which greatly concerns him.
>
> My government's programs and policies cannot be viewed in isolation, along with the major decisions which you take, they should be developed within a strategic framework in which they and other initiatives in urban and regional development throughout Australia are seen as part of a coordinated whole.[94]

This was a rebuke to Tom. He didn't back off, though, as DURD's key role in national economic policy during the recession that followed the 1974 budget was designed in part to stimulate housing and move investment away from CBD office blocks. With my knowledge of Sydney's CBD office market dating from the City of Sydney strategic plan, I advised Peter Till and Michael Keating on this issue.

This was strategy in action, everything that I had hoped for in this role. Sure, it cost time to divert from policy formulation, but working with program people on the ground helped inform them, too, of national urban policy. By then, mid-1975, the combination of policy work and involvement in front line action covered most elements of metropolitan policy: CBDs, sub-regional centres, area improvement, inner-city community protection projects, sub-metropolitan growth centres, airport location and major transport projects. The metropolitan strategy team had formed a federal government level vision for Australia's capital cities. It is a great pity that this momentum was lost.

Helping stop an inner-city expressway

During this time, 1974–75, the states were modifying their metropolitan transport plans, but some still pressed ahead with inner-city expressway construction. The minister and DURD were very concerned about that. Our narrative here doesn't have much about the transport program of DURD, but it promoted and funded urban public transport projects and had a very real interest in integrated transport/land use planning. Community groups pressed DURD to do more to stop inner-city expressways, but we agreed in DURD that interventions like this had to be systematic.

This approach became much more practical for Sydney's Glebe Estate. The NSW government had an advanced plan to cut the western distributor through Glebe, directly threatening the estate, an old church-owned community of generally low income households that DURD had acquired to protect and upgrade as a model project. There was wide agreement across Tom Uren's office and DURD that the expressway had to be stopped. Tom spoke out about it and got support from the rest of the federal government to stop it by any legal means.

The DURD transport branch people had some meetings with the NSW Department of Main Roads and the State Planning Authority, but the minister thought transport people alone might get too comfortable talking to their counterparts, and he asked Pat Troy to take someone like me along as part of a stronger team to bring the crisis to a conclusion. The meetings were icy but not acrimonious. Threats to deny funds were made. The stoppage was won.

The work was enjoyable, especially with Pat's ebullience and drive, and it didn't take too much time off my strategy work that was already under way. Forays like these were a welcome change from more abstract policy work, and enriched our production of the metropolitan strategies.

Sydney's second airport crashes

Another foray into strategy in action was Sydney's second airport site selection, a rare arena, for DURD, of undisputed federal responsibility. But it was far from being without conflict. The government inherited a 1972 cost-benefit study of alternative sites for a second Sydney airport by R. Travers Morgan and Partners, a British firm, and a joint federal–state committee to consider recommendations that included environmental impact.[95] The government preferred Richmond and Somersby as its first two priorities, followed by Duffy's Forest and Wattamolla. I did some work on the site selection issues, and Des Hoban from the transport branch and I accompanied Pat Troy (who had previously worked in the NSW State Planning Authority) to a meeting with the ever-dapper Graham Crockett and others in the NSW government on 21 June 1973. There was some tension in the air, but it was a friendly enough meeting. Graham offered a preference for Long Point, not far from the Holsworthy option.

At the same time, the Australian government was then also considering an extension to Kingsford-Smith Airport, Sydney's main airport. That was eventually recommended by the minister for transport to cabinet on 27 August, but cabinet knocked it back in favour of nominating a second airport site. The next day, completely out of the blue, that minister, Charlie Jones, announced a site hardly considered at all: Galston.

Galston was in a fairly well-heeled and conservative voting electorate. There were immediate demonstrations, as I suppose there would be for any airport site decision. What was worse, Minister Jones' press release wrongly stated that the choice was on DURD's recommendation. Des Hoban, a long-standing friend who had carriage of the project in DURD, was incandescent with rage. In a memo on 31 August, he wrote that 'DURD's professionalism is seriously and unnecessarily eroded when it is misrepresented as having recommended a course of action which is publicly taken to be political whimsy'.[96] Minister Jones did not correct his statement and continued to cop anger for the choice from all sides. By 10 May of the following year, the government retracted the decision.

The other options bumped along in and out of controversy for another 13 years until the Hawke government announced Badgerys Creek in February 1986. By chance, I was then working with the NSW Department of Environment and Planning and responsible for metropolitan planning, and with Bob Meyer (who has had a long and distinguished career in this area), we fed the data to the state transport study group (the staff of which were happy to hide behind our employment and population distribution forecasts and not make a call on it themselves) that helped lead the state to endorse the site. Controversial as it still is, especially over seemingly corrupt land purchase deals, the airport construction is under way. Such long delays are normal around the world for new metropolitan airports. The Western Sydney International (Nancy Bird Walton) Airport will start operating in 2026.

Airport funding in commonwealth budgets is clearly an example of an 'implicit' urban policy instrument, a means of pursuing goals for urban and regional development, and the national settlement system. As well as getting involved in particular projects, as described above, I was keen to put the overall national urban and regional strategy to the test and intervene in the budget's spatial priorities, in line with the successful urban regional budget program of DURD's.

The 1975–76 budget

By 1975 economic conditions deteriorated further as Australia, along with other countries, suffered continuing 'stagflation' (economic stagnation combined with high inflation). This section is about how Ray Bunker, the new head of the strategy division, and I reviewed the draft 1975–76 budget to reflect our strategy. First, though, a small diversion shows the temper of the times.

Tensions were showing between factions in the parliamentary Labor Party. Tom Uren asked a sympathetic colleague and me to spend some unauthorised days off-line documenting Whitlam's errors in leadership, especially his caving in to US security demands and failure to support East Timor during Indonesia's invasion. The issue haunted Australia for decades later, and caused Tom to say that '[a]ll Australians carry some guilt for what has happened to the people of East Timor. I certainly feel that guilt'.[97] These left–right tensions played out in economic policy too, as the leader of the left, Jim Cairns, was treasurer.

It was a delight to be asked by Tom to do some clandestine political work, and I was happy to add to my record of rule breaking because I was disgusted at Australia's acquiescence to Indonesia's invasion. I was not burdened by the public service ethic of independence, but on reflection, seeing the widespread politicisation of senior levels of the public service, I doubt that I would do it again.

Meanwhile, returning to legitimate work, the 1975–76 budget round was building up for another Treasury vs. DURD fight. Tom was the leader of the left by then and deputy leader of the ALP. The expenditure review committee of cabinet was looking for dramatic cuts in budget and forward estimates, but once again, notwithstanding a looming budget deficit, DURD took an expansionary stance on its own programs, as most of them were still in their early years of development. Again, the aim was to take up the slack in the private sector by expanding the public sector.

This time, the urban and regional strategy was developed enough for us to make a wider contribution. The department put Loan Council proposed capital works expenditures through a triage from the point of view of the urban and regional strategy (for example, protect from cuts, neutral/more information needed, and let it be cut), especially protecting proposals in the growth centres, protecting projects in area improvement program regions where they would be supportive of the program, protecting the new proposed regional administrative centres, and restraining growth in CBDs and inner-city areas unless otherwise warranted.

Ray Bunker and I did the same when the full budget was circulated to cabinet (my moth-eaten numbered copy is stamped 'copy 1'). We holed up in a Sydney hotel for a weekend with a 'security cleared' secretary and against the clock put every detail through the strategy filter. We felt important.

Our work had some effect on priorities, such as recommending the Brisbane airport expansion over Sydney, but it was not really on the front line of budget policy. We really needed to focus on a more definitive statement of strategy that government could endorse and could be used by others in such priority decisions.

Altogether, the national urban strategy shifted metropolitan structures directly only in minor ways, but in association with program interventions the strategy team made more of an impact. Engagement with states and local government, and setting signals for the private sector in this area of policy, needed to be nuanced and patiently pursued over a longer time than we had. The end stage of the government was under way.

The end of the dream

By late 1975, I was run down from work, separating from Jill, and generally not in good shape. It wasn't only the pace of work, but I had doubts about whether we would ever get out a full version of the strategy, and how effective it might be if we did. Diving into areas of action to align the programs and projects delayed work on policy formation and added to my fatigue. I wasn't keeping fit, and the mix of policy and politics came with a lot of drinking. High levels of stress were my constant partner.

I felt I needed a break, a decent break, but as I was living separately from Jill in a house in Yarralumla owned by Michael and Kerrie Eyers (Michael being DURD's lead officer on the land commission program), she and I were not seeing each other enough to work out whether we had a future or not, and I didn't have the presence of mind to seek counselling. I was confused.

I decided to make a major change in my life and take up the place I had deferred in the PhD program at Berkeley. I planned to start in September the following year. Though I was still interested in communications and urban growth, I was preoccupied with national urban policy and wanted to reflect on the experience and deepen my understanding of the field, hopefully working with Bill Alonso there and possibly comparing Australian and US experience with national urban policy.

Like many in the 1970s, I'd become interested in Marxism and Buddhism, contradictory currents of thought that both attracted wide interest as disillusioned radicals went hard left or out of politics altogether into matters spiritual. With the pace of work so intense, there was next to no time for me to explore these at any length. The ethos of DURD, and particularly that of Pat Troy, my constant mentor, was democratic socialism. What did Marxism say about this, and what would a Marxist interpretation of the deeper structure in which I was working look like?

I also wanted to explore more of Asia and spend time in a Buddhist setting (my only exposure to Asia had been an eye-opening holiday in Indonesia in 1973, where I was overpowered by being alone in Borobudur, the great Buddhist ruin, before dawn). I felt that simple Buddhism, not needing a faith in a god, might be worth exploring. I made some travel plans well in advance of starting at Berkeley and got approval for extended leave without pay, starting December 1975.

As I made plans for the next stage of my life, a political crisis, centred on the senate's denial of supply, was engulfing the government. I learned from John Mant, principal private secretary to the prime minister, who frequently visited the house in Yarralumla, that a strategic and security crisis was also playing out between the Australian and US intelligence services. An unmarked car with driver was parked outside the house for long periods, probably from an intelligence service, given John's key role. The climate was tense across government as the senate's denial of supply continued without resolution.

As the morning of 11 November 1975 began, I knew nothing of what was happening nearby at government house, nor around parliament, as I drove by on the way to work. A crowd was gathering on the steps of Parliament House. I turned on the car radio.

During the rest of that day at work we were glued to the television and the radio, following the truly unprecedented events that unfolded very quickly. The Whitlam government had been dismissed by the governor-general, without advice from the government as required by law. The governor-general's approval of a double-dissolution of parliament to follow appalled and angered most of my colleagues, and stoked fears of a possible conservative government abolishing DURD and winding back its programs. Those colleagues thought my taking leave showed great prescience, but it really was just a coincidence.

I am still angry, at the time of writing some 45 years later, about this 'constitutional coup'. I continue to follow the never-ending case, including evidence of Buckingham Palace's complicity shown in recently released documents.[98]

Gough Whitlam's and Tom Uren's big memorial services in and around Sydney's grand town hall were memorable occasions that recalled these events. Tom's service in February 2015 was a reunion of friends from the DURD days, and as John Mant, Tom's chief of staff before becoming principal private secretary to Whitlam, was a City of Sydney councillor and had a room next to the town hall in the building, we gathered in his room for drinks and reminiscences. We shared a mixture of sorrow for Tom, pride for our role in his historic ministry, and anger at how the lessons of DURD were being forgotten even within the ALP. My thoughts also went back to 11 November 1975.

A caretaker coalition government took office immediately, and an election was called for 13 December 1975. Thankfully, the caretaker conservative government allowed a raft of imminent DURD agreements with the states to be signed during the period.[99]

After I left Canberra to travel through Asia en route to Berkeley, the coalition won the election and Malcolm Fraser became prime minister. As noted, my leaving showed no particular political foresight. Though excited by what lay ahead, especially at Berkeley, I felt a little guilty leaving my DURD friends to struggle for the survival of its programs.

During this period and soon after, Pat Troy and others in the department showed great loyalty to Michael Eyers and me. We were awarded generous scholarships for overseas study. Michael went to the London School of Economics and I took up my place at Berkeley. The awards came with an implied moral obligation to return to the commonwealth public service, and I was happy to accept that.

The Fraser government set about slashing expenditure and public service numbers. I was absorbed in life in California by that time, and study at Berkeley, and didn't follow Australian politics very closely. I was therefore surprised to get a telegram instructing me to report for duty back at the Department of Environment, Housing and Community

Development, DURD's successor, early in September 1978. On further investigation I found that, despite the call to duty, the government, through the dreaded *Commonwealth Employees (Employment Provisions) Act of 1977*, was wanting to reduce the workforce, so the right thing to do was to resign. Vivian Lin, my American fiancée by then, bravely accompanied me back to wintry Canberra for six weeks or so, living in a cold tin shed Jill Lang kindly arranged. The bonfire to burn my hoarded papers from the DURD era took all night.

It felt good.

The legacy remains

The days of DURD and their legacy have been widely reviewed, with analysts concluding variously that the policies and programs of the time were a courageous surge with a few ripples remaining; or that they were never likely to succeed because of structural conditions in the political economy; or that they were ill-conceived in the first place.[100] I think the legacy is beyond any of these, through its programs, its policies and ideas, its people and the institutions that survived and followed. But to paraphrase Mandy Rice-Davies from the British Profumo affair, I would say that, wouldn't I? DURD was very important to me. I had been able to work to my absolute limit to make Australian cities and regions fairer and more efficient, a dream I had held for years and which now seemed dead.

Surprisingly, though, key programs of DURD did survive the early months of the new government. I missed all this, as I was, blessedly, out of the country. Senator Ivan Greenwood, the minister for environment, housing and community development, took a reasonable approach and continued most of the programs, seeking to bring his harder-line colleagues around to his view.

But by July 1976 he had to resign through ill health and his ministerial successor and the prime minister Malcolm Fraser set about dismantling the programs and the commonwealth–state and other arrangements that went with them. Pat Troy's explanation for this is revealing:

I felt at the time that one of the pressures on the Coalition was that they could not afford many of the Government's policies and programs to continue for much longer. From their point of view there was a real danger that the processes and programs of the government would become embedded and be seen by the population as the correct way to approach and order public life. I felt this was certainly true of urban and regional development.[101]

Labor had only three years in power, and so many of the longer-term changes sought through policies, programs, institutions and practices did not survive or barely got started, including the full national urban and regional strategy. We members of the strategy team independently published a version of the strategy anyway, as it was in November 1975 at the change of government.[102] This was not an act of defiance—it was to set the record straight. It must have been an awful time for my DURD colleagues to have to weather the transition after November 1975.

The arena faded away until Labor returned in 1983. Though the Hawke and Keating governments distanced themselves from what they implied was an over-reach by the Whitlam government, some ex-DURD people led the new policies. Brian Howe, Hawke government deputy prime minister, minister for housing and regional development, and responsible for the Better Cities Program, had been a community activist engaging with DURD (his Fitzroy Ecumenical Centre was a source of good urban ideas and actions). Lyndsay Neilson, policy leader in the Cities Commission and member of DURD after the Cities Commission wound up in 1975, became his deputy secretary. Lyndsay also later became director-general of planning and infrastructure for Victoria.

The wider DURD diaspora was important, not only through appointments, but also through policy reviews and advice. Pat Troy stayed influential through publishing, consulting and personal persuasion long after DURD's demise, though this waned after a while with his disillusionment over Labor retreats from real public housing and other deviations from what he saw as the light on the hill. His 1980 review of the Sydney land market set the framework for the urban development program in NSW, with DURD-like coordination machinery and urban and regional budget possibilities (more on this shortly).[103] Pat's passing, in 2018, when we were working on a book together about the history of urban policy in Australia, marked the end of his remarkable leadership.

John Mant reviewed and reformed state planning systems around the country with some of the DURD ideas in mind. Michael Keating became secretary of the Department of Prime Minister and Cabinet, carrying the experience, if not most of the policies, over into practice. Michael Eyers, who had been responsible for DURD's land commission programs, became director of housing in NSW, one of the executives who delivered the Olympic Games, and was active in other NSW policy areas. Jill Lang and Murray Geddes went on to be leading forces in social planning, with Jill leading the Queensland Council of Social Services and active nationally on anti-poverty campaigns. John Paterson continued the approaches he took advising DURD and the Cities Commission into running planning, infrastructure and health agencies in NSW and Victoria. My move to the NSW government in 1983 was another small example, and there are many others.

Reviews of DURD's legacy usually start with its incontestable results on the ground: elimination of much of the sewerage backlog; the acquisition and protection of Woolloomooloo, the Glebe Estate and the Redfern Aboriginal housing development in Sydney, and Emerald Hill in Melbourne; the many projects of the area improvement program; the further development of the growth centres program (though Albury–Wodonga and Macarthur in south-west Sydney were the only growth centres that had time to get on with some real city building).[104] The other growth centres, still in phases of negotiation, planning or start-up, were wound back, with Bathurst–Orange lands sold off and the development authority abolished in the 1980s, the 'embattled survivor' Albury–Wodonga lasting until 1995, and the quixotic South Australian growth centre of Monarto reverting to a zoo, albeit a good one, and rural activities.[105]

Some other institutions did survive into the long term, depending in part on the condition of state acceptance and cooperation at the time, as well as on what the states did to the new institutions and their assets afterwards. During 1975 DURD had moved towards 'umbrella' urban and regional development agreements with the states, to bring all the relevant DURD programs, and potentially other federal programs, into a coordinated framework with corresponding state programs and potentially link them to regionalisation policy.

South Australia under premier Don Dunstan was the most advanced, but even here the agreement did not survive, and most of the DURD legacy was abandoned as conservative governments came into power in Canberra and then in Adelaide. Lionel Orchard argues that the very enthusiasm of South Australia's cooperation with the Whitlam government contributed to the programs' fate when the state government changed.[106] The South Australian land commission was downgraded to an urban lands trust in 1981, holding a land bank but not developing it. The great achievement of establishing state land commissions was washed away elsewhere or watered down by diminution of their mandates, disposal of their holdings, and undue extraction of dividends from the development that continued, rather than pursuit of the land and housing affordability aims of the original program.[107]

The survival of some of the regional organisations of councils is an interesting legacy. Ian McPhail describes the positive state of play in 1975 at a meeting of ROC chairs in the government's last year: '[M]ost councils had evolved from hostility to forced cooperation to the development of cooperative arrangements which in many cases were to persist after the change of Government and the withdrawal of Commonwealth support'.[108]

Despite discontinuation of direct funding through the Commonwealth Grants Commission (which became income tax revenue sharing grants under the Fraser government's 'new federalism' and then financial assistance grants after Peter Self's local government review in 1984), and without in some regions the area improvement program (which by the end of DURD had grown to cover 13 regions and in budget estimates 19 regions), to this day some of the same ROCs still operate. They have changed names in some cases—such as in western Sydney, Illawarra and Hunter regions—surviving off constituent council funding and good grant-getting.[109] Across Australia the model, which has now become voluntary, has spread, with 17 in NSW and 18 in Queensland, the hold out state against DURD in the 1970s. The regional boundaries have in many cases changed as well, as over time they should, but the idea of intra-metropolitan regional groupings of councils (now 'districts' in NSW for planning purposes) has become firmly established.

The will for national engagement in urban and regional development with the determination of the Whitlam government has long gone, possibly not to return in force again. But the policy ideas of those in and around DURD have an enduring legacy, if nowhere near sole provenance. They include:

+ Whole-of-government attention to urban and regional affairs (including the use of Alonso's 'implicit' instruments like the location of government employment)
+ A more holistic view of what makes good urban and regional development (Tom Uren's 'everything is connected to everything else')
+ Federal and state recognition of the interconnectedness of investment decisions
+ Acceptance of the economic roles of cities and the importance in government budgets and infrastructure priorities of expenditures for cities
+ A more sophisticated view of territorial justice and the entrenchment of forces opposing redistribution
+ A deeper understanding of the intergovernmental character of city planning and development
+ Continued acceptance of the merits of regional cooperation, especially among local councils; and, in these days where even the coalition government has a minister for population, cities and urban infrastructure, and
+ Recognition across a wider political spectrum of the need for national urban policy.[110]

The three intensive years of the Whitlam government changed Australia forever in so many ways. They certainly changed the lives of most of us who worked in DURD. It was a memorable experiment with long-lasting but under-acknowledged improvements to Australian urban and regional life.

Remarkably, a national settlement strategy has come back onto the agenda for coalition governments in recent years, as well as an urban policy of sorts offering 'city deals' to some state and local governments. In 2018 a parliamentary committee recommended a national plan of settlement.[111]

The bushfires, floods and pandemic of 2020 and 2021, along with the onset of the climate emergency, brought a succession of new ideas for national urban and regional policy. My hope is that the best of these ideas find their way again into policy, and that the policymakers find their way to acknowledge the contribution, still relevant, that DURD made.

Growing up fast

In three short years I was thoroughly 'blooded' as an urban professional. Spending so much time close to power and people driven to change also gave me some courage and determination. Resistance to change and the brick walls of constitutional structures and politics were stark evidence of the limits of reform.

Blooded, yes, but burned out too. Tired, frustrated at work, separated at home. How can one rise from the ashes and renew?

I asked many questions after these times. Were the barriers just contingencies against which we had too little time and power to move? Or were they structural, built into the capitalist state? Did we lack patience in our frenetic drive to do so much at once, where wiser heads and hearts might have laid longer-lasting foundations? Should I have bided my time, surviving fatigue and frayed relationships, and stayed not only with Jill if possible, but the rest of my neglected family and my non-DURD friends? How can driven professionals keep centred and sustain their energy and direction? How can one be successful in the bureaucracy without an armoured and well-fed ego? Can anyone possibly have a spiritual life among all this?

Through the following chapters I looked for some of these answers, as I had none when I left Canberra.

FOUR

DRIFTING IN ASIA

After my farewells I left Sydney for Bangkok on 3 December 1975. For the next 10 months I would make my way to Berkeley the long way for the doctoral program. I had little idea at first of what I would do, other than visit friends and explore different countries en route. Perhaps come to understand some of the cities on the way and their planning. It was a period of drift for me, and I experienced a number of narrow escapes from disaster, including one rather harrowing one from a serial killer. I learned little professionally during this time, but immersion in the cities and towns of south Asia, and their religions, brought me lessons of its own.

Introduction to the road

In Thailand I was surely a tourist, apart from a visit to ESCAP headquarters (the Economic and Social Commission for Asia and the Pacific), and meeting up with friends from the planning world. In Canberra I had met planners from Thailand on a training program for the Australian Development Assistance Agency, created by the Whitlam government, who told me a little about the planning of Bangkok. It wasn't until I confronted the traffic jams and walked through streets that had been inundated by rain for two weeks that the enormity of the city's metropolitan planning problems hit me. I noted in my diary that at first the city seems to have no order, land uses all mixed up, the old and new, no city centre. But after a while, or more specifically after learning the bus system, the different districts begin to take on identities of their own.

Walking on a wet road by the opening of the 1975 Southeast Asia Peninsular Games, I saw pigeons and balloons go up and heard loud bangs. I thought they might have been fireworks or military salutes, but they were petrol bombs between rival youth groups that injured four people.[1]

A low-budget four-day walking tour of the northern 'Hill Tribes' (including the Karen, Hmong and Lisu tribes) out of the remote town of Fang (up-market tours didn't go near it) added to this impression of lawlessness. I noticed a new plate glass windowed gun shop in an otherwise dilapidated town, the ease with which tourists could try out opium, and more. I visited a 'Kuomintang' village, settled with refugees from communist China funded by the US CIA during the war in Vietnam, which had just ended. Smuggled goods were for sale wherever I went. Some of these were jewels, which leads us to a close encounter with a jewel trader who was making havoc in Thailand.

An escape

I left Bangkok on the morning of Christmas eve, 1975, with an Australian travelling companion on flight TG311 to Kathmandu. The passenger next to me kindly invited me to swap his window seat in order to see the Himalaya, a magnificent procession of icy peaks to the north. It was a perfectly clear day. Alain Gautier was the jewel trader, on his way to Nepal to buy turquoise and other valuables brought down from the mountains and over the passes from Tibet.

The plane's descent into Kathmandu Valley, with its toy villages and ordered green paddies, was magical. I was grateful for my charming new friend. On arrival we wound our way through the airport, seeing piles of thangkas, Tibetan Buddhist devotional paintings, being stamped en masse for export. This was the first of many times I saw the plunder of treasures from Nepal and Tibet.

Alain was travelling with his wife Monique and he asked my companion and me to dinner at the Oberoi Hotel that night. That didn't quite fit my view of how to spend time in this ancient city, but she and I readily agreed. We were staying in far more humble premises. His driver, Ajay, later picked us up at the set time. Alain and his wife were there to greet us.

The venue lived down to our expectations: a lacklustre western hotel, a band playing bad country and western music, and, to cap it off, a dowdy casino. We ate from an ostentatious but second-rate buffet. Most of the guests and all of the other gamblers seemed to be visiting Indians. Alain insisted I take his US$50 note and try my luck. My diary notes that

> here he was, betting $50 a time, while some of the others around the roulette were shaking with fear over bets of a few rupees … The American tourists were drunk, the Indian and Nepalese were quietly sitting at tables trying to look like they were having a good time, tapping on the table, drinking brandy.

I was starting to feel uncomfortable. Alain was big-noting himself—literally—and we were the object of attention from hotel staff and others standing around. Alain asked us to his hotel room for a nightcap, room 415, and I was glad to accept just to get out of there.

While room service staff brought coffee, Alain showed us what looked like elaborate recording equipment which he said he used in negotiations to buy jewels. He would leave a bug under the table before leaving the sellers to discuss price and listen to what they said.

Clearly, I thought, here was a shady character, possibly a small-time crook.

I was interested in the changing geopolitical situation in Nepal, and we talked about the new road built, with Chinese aid, up to the China border. At least he was well-informed, I remember thinking. We stayed talking and drinking, whisky I think, until 3 am.

As Ajay waited to take me and my companion back to the hotel, Alain asked if we would like to drive up that road to see it the next day.

We declined.

We were in an amazing historical city and we hadn't even started looking around. Besides, I didn't like him now, friendly though he seemed at first. He insisted, and said he would send Ajay around the morning anyway, just in case we changed our minds.

We declined again.

The next morning, Christmas day, Ajay called from the front of the hotel and yet again we declined. My travelling partner was not well, perhaps it was something she had had the night before. Ajay went away without us, but he came the next morning yet again. This was weird, but he didn't contact us after that and we had nothing to do with the three again.

My diary of 24 December 1975, written innocent of the truth about Alain, says: 'After seeing the poverty and simplicity of life in Nepal, the night out was obscene! After that night, Alain's schemes became more and more mysterious and we eventually lost track of him.'

Or so I thought.

The next year, when I was teaching at San Francisco State University (SFSU) part-time while studying at the University of California at Berkeley, I was having dinner with Dick LeGates, the urban studies program head at SFSU. He described a book he was reading about a notorious psychopathic serial killer in Asia called Charles Sobhraj.[2]

I borrowed it that night and, to my horror, there was a photograph of Alain!

A cold chill went over me as I ran through my memories of that time and flicked through the book. There was a whole section about that very night at the casino! He was wanted for the murder of an American–Canadian couple whose bodies had been found four days before. After strangling and burning the hapless couple, he flew to Bangkok. Then, on my flight, audaciously, he had returned to Nepal. Many of those people standing round at the casino that night were police, but they did not have evidence to arrest him.

As I read on through the book, my horror worsened. The grotesque murder was along the China road. Had I accepted the offer of an outing up the road, I could have—probably would have—been his next victim.

The driver who came around to our hotel, Ajay Chowdhury, later mysteriously disappeared. Estimates of Sobhraj's murders range between 12 and 24. He had a vendetta against westerners on the 'hippy trail'. He would drug them so they were sick, entice them to join his entourage while they took his medication to 'get better', take their passports, and in some cases get rid of them. He must have thought with my long hair, which I had even in DURD, that I was a prospect.

Years later, inexplicably, he returned to Nepal and was arrested.

When I heard about the arrest and then his 2004 appeal against his conviction, I thought about going public and giving evidence, but I was a little concerned for my safety if he were to go on the revenge trail. He was a master escape artist, having escaped using drugging and bribery from jail many times. One of these, in India, was deliberate. He wanted to be rearrested and prolong his jail time there so as to exceed the extradition time limit to Thailand, which, unlike India, had the death penalty. Even in Kathmandu, he had been photographed having coffee out of jail in the street, and in 2004, the year I considered giving evidence, guards foiled yet another escape attempt.[3]

I talked it through with the late Richard Neville, who with his wife Julie Clarke had also written a book about Sobhraj.[4] Richard encouraged me to go to the police. So in February 2005, from the St Kilda police station in Melbourne where a friendly detective translated my plain English into turgid police-speak, they prepared my evidence and sent it remotely to Interpol. New evidence is allowed in such appeals in Nepal. I was the only non-police witness to his presence in the country at the time, and I still had the boarding pass, stamped passport and diary notes, written innocent of my knowledge of his crimes, to prove it.[5]

This evidence was crucial in overturning the appeal. Indeed, through me Dick's book played a role too. Sobhraj's lawyer, Isabelle Coutant-Peyre, notorious for her defence of terrorist 'Carlos the Jackal', claimed Sobhraj never was there and that I was lying—the book I cited didn't even have photographs. 'It's a crude fraud', said Sobhraj, protesting he was never in the country.[6] But Hermann Knippenberg, the brave Dutch ex-diplomat who did more than anyone to chase him down, pointed out to me, from seclusion in New Zealand, it was the Asian edition that Coutant-Peyre was referring to. The US edition I read *did* have photographs.

Thankfully Sobhraj is still in jail, convicted of yet more murders in Nepal. I still keep in touch with the little group of survivors and witnesses, along with the prosecutor in Kathmandu, who signs his emails piously with *Hare Krishna*, and with whom, improbably, I am working on a possible new eco-resort in the Kathmandu valley. I found myself fielding media interest, and interviewed for newspapers and films about Sobhraj.[7] Interest is likely to continue, as BBC One opened its 2021 season with *The Serpent*, a miniseries about Sobhraj, which over 30 million people in the UK have already viewed.

Engaging with the real Nepal

Those were just three days of eight weeks in Nepal, despite their impact. And at the time, I was innocent of how they would affect me later. I continued my journey and made friends and grew to understand this extraordinary kingdom better. I stayed in Kathmandu, trekked up to see Mount Everest and up along other routes, slept in villagers' houses and camped at the Annapurna base camp.

I became friendly with a young man in Kathmandu named Keshav and his older friend Joshi, who ran a small shoe factory. I was interested to taste *chang*, a local beer brewed from millet or rice, and they obligingly made me some. Some of Keshav's friends were engaged to marry, and February being the last auspicious month for some time in which to tie the knot, Keshav proudly brought me an invitation to attend the arranged wedding of two of his friends, brothers, in the ancient Shakya caste of the Newari community. It is from this clan that Kathmandu's *Kumari* or 'living goddess' is chosen, a young girl who has never shed blood and is secluded in a temple and worshipped until puberty, as the manifestation of divine female energy. I saw her once, big-eyed, looking scared.

I felt honoured to be invited, and the families made me welcome. The wedding was a three-day affair, involving processions through the city, a marching band, and dinners every night. I was the only person there with a camera, so with the hosts' encouragement I became the wedding photographer. The scenes were spectacular, with happiness all round, except on the faces of the brides, who had to feign glumness in view of their imminent loss of virginity and domicile.

When in London later, I prepared two photograph albums and mailed them to Nepal. I didn't hear back, but I understood that communications can sometimes be difficult. The years passed with no word. It became clear the photos never arrived. In 2005, while looking in my records for evidence in the Sobhraj case, I came across the old wedding invitation, and idly searched on the internet to see if there was any trace of the couples. None. But my curiosity was piqued, and I spent some of the next few days looking for ways to locate them. I spread emails to all the people who I thought might be them, or know them. Imagine my pleasure when I opened an email, not from one of the couples, but from a son, issue from the marriage. He attached a scanned simple letter from one of my original friends: 'Thank you very much for your writing after such a long time. I got real surprize'. This time I sent the photographs by parallel means—postage of new albums, email, CD-ROMs. Twenty-nine years after their wedding, the photographs arrived!

When settled I got out my professional self, tidying up one day and paying a visit to the Kathmandu Valley Development Authority where I had a contact from the DURD days. They had the daunting task of promoting social and economic development while protecting the world heritage and environmental values of the country's most important valley. The meeting was polite and uneventful. With my long hair I don't think I looked the part. My interests in planning were slipping away for the time being, but I didn't mind. Urban policy could come later. Here I wanted to understand, as best I could, a very different culture, and to make a clean break from the DURD years.

Forming a group of friends gave me a little insight into Nepalese society, a beguiling mix of modernity and tradition. This was no more starkly evident than around a religious circle I joined. Joshi, mentioned in the previous pages, was a devotee of a medium. After some days, he gained permission from the rest of the circle to allow Jim Carmody and myself to join them. Jim was a New Zealand-born academic psychologist, well along the eastern spiritual path, and a new friend of mine.

We went to a simple house and gathered our chairs around a shy young woman no older than 16, sitting in silence for what seemed a long time. Then she changed dramatically, shaking and rolling her eyes. She manifested four or five very different deities. It was as if she was gone, replaced in voice and demeanour by entirely different people. Some of the circle made requests of particular presences, especially of Kali, destroyer of evil, a powerful goddess popular in Kathmandu. Afterwards, Joshi said most requests were about health or financial success. The only recognisable presence to me was the Buddha, who filled the room with a palpable tranquillity. It really was as if she were possessed, but I found it hard to believe, and still do even now. After almost an hour, she slumped, exhausted, herself again. These episodes were not voluntary, and she was clearly not well. My secular self was shocked by the event, even more so that one of those asking the gods for intervention was the director of Kathmandu's main hospital. Spiritual life and mundane life in Nepal seemed inseparable. Mysteries surrounded me.

On one trek, from the thin air of the Annapurna base camp, I had to rush down to Pokhara, its service town, scrambling along valleys to rescue a hallucinating Japanese fellow trekker. Otherwise, the treks were welcome quiet relief from the intensity of Kathmandu, with the mountains of Everest and Annapurna bringing a power and beauty of their own.

Having seen transient Tibetan Buddhism and its exploitation in the city, I was moved by a full moon festival at Langtang, hosted in long settled Tibetan villages, and hearing their monks' deep chants resounding across the valleys, long and glorious as the sun set. Interesting though the rich art and lore of the religion was, it seemed to me overladen, as most religions are, with the metaphysical and social crust of centuries.

Journey to the heart

Jim and I decided to head south to learn a purer, simpler form of Buddhism, Vipassana, the practice of Theravada Buddhists from

Burma and Sri Lanka, loosely translated as 'insight'. The great teacher, S. N. Goenka, offered non-sectarian courses to westerners at Igatpuri in Maharashtra state, India. The trouble was that he was sick, and we would have to wait. Nonetheless, in late February we left Nepal and headed that way. My diary notes:

> … eating a breakfast comprising fine day-old dry chicken sand-wiches, German beer, and cabbage, cheese, carrot, brown bread and orange brought onto the plane. This mixed-up breakfast circled around inside as the plane circled out of the Kathmandu Valley under the snowy mountains; soon giving way to brown Indian plains and a dusty landing at Patna.

I had started my journey into India. It would take me three months, but I never got to Igatpuri. My identity as an urban planner was fading with each new discovery, but as a traveller I learnt a lot about India's amazing cities, in which daily life was even more intense than Kathmandu.

They didn't come more intense than Varanasi, Jim's and my first stop. A muddy mix of the sacred and profane, the city lived up to its reputation. My diary notes that our hotel was in a maze of lanes with

> thousands of vendors providing strange and wonderful goods and services to residents and pilgrims who walk, or are carried, dead or alive, through to the ghats on Benares River, the holiest in India. Dasaswamedh Ghat was nearby, where Brahma sacrificed ten horses and where everyone goes and anything goes. Further along, burning ghats, and Scindia Ghat with its monument sinking into the river. Holy water, washed, drunk, body parts floating by, vultures, filthy mud. No dunking for me thank you, though some western travellers did like to try.
>
> The sellers of chai and pan, thandai (a sweet milk drink), bindi, saris and trinkets provide aids and impediments to spiritual enlightenment. For us, more visitors than pilgrim, temptation trumped religious expression, in the form of bhang (cannabis)

lassi, taken by pilgrims before their puja, their rituals (hence, perhaps the trippy iconography of the temples?) and served from box-sized, intricate shops or stoops. No enlightenment for me, but fits of laughter, craving for food, music and more.

Highlights for me were immersion in a Carnatic music festival and a visit to a surprisingly accurate fortune-teller (as the years to come showed). In a coffee shop I asked a solo western woman how long she had been in India. She said three years.

'What have you been doing?'

'Watching my breath.'

This was where I was headed. It was time to move on to Bodh Gaya, place of the Buddha's enlightenment. Jim was staying on in Varanasi and we did not meet again until I lived in California. He went on to be a professor at the University of Massachusetts, teaching, among other topics, mindfulness.

Before Bodh Gaya, though, I went to Gaya itself, a city in Bihar, one of India's poorest states. The day a new travelling friend and I arrived we met a local judge, who invited us to his court the following day. I seemed to be getting into the practice of having adventures with people I met. His court was in session and we watched a murder case conducted in English though the defendant couldn't understand a word of the language. Our kind host, embarrassingly for us, took a recess when he saw us and invited us back into his chamber for tea, and there he invited us to dinner at his home that night. Predictably, his house reflected his relative prosperity. Unpredictably, it was built on a large grain storehouse, unconscionable during the famine that was under way and with obviously malnourished people on the streets. It got worse. With the meal prepared by his wife, whom we never met, he made a move on my female travel partner. We hurried back to the hotel. This was not an auspicious stop on the path to enlightenment.

Bodh Gaya was much better. It was a loose collection of temples from every Buddhist tradition spread across a dusty plain and set around a successor to the original Bodhi Tree, under which Gautam Buddha attained enlightenment. At the Burmese temple I found a teacher willing to show me Vipassana meditation practice, and took it seriously, watching my thoughts and feelings fly away as I let them go and became more centred. Twice a day I would also join the Zen temple, with more disciplined sitting (yes, our backs straightened with light slaps of the stick). Though Zen practice can attain insight suddenly, as one gives up fruitless cycles of clinging to the desire to stop clinging, at my beginning phase the quiet sitting of Vipassana and Zen practices reinforced each other.[8]

The weeks passed this way and Goenka-ji was still sick. It was apparent I would have to take the full Vipassana course another time. The Zen master asked if I would join his temple community and live there, but at the time, all too typically, I was unwilling to vow to chastity. The pre-monsoon heat was building up insufferably, and it was time to move on.

My adventures continued with yoga at Rishikesh, intense urban living in old Delhi, robbery of my money on the train, amoebic dysentery in Bombay (from which a detailed description of my stools, typed up carefully in red and black, serves as souvenir), dreamy overnight ferry rides down to Goa and Cochin sleeping hard on the deck, and a relaxing month in Kerala.

There, in Trivandrum, my faith in the goodness of human nature was reinforced. Late one afternoon, I found that my wallet, passport and air tickets were all gone. This was May 1976, in the middle of prime minister Indira Gandhi's Emergency, a period of suspension of congress and civil liberties. It would be impossible to move anywhere without documents. With dread, I retraced all my steps, but none of the venues knew anything. The last stop was the post office, site of the first chore of my day. There, upstairs in the postmaster's office, surrounded by a crowd of people, were all three lost objects. Not a rupee had been taken from the wallet, though it held enough for months of living for the average person. It is a commonplace to say that India 'gets you', that you cannot avoid going into a deep love-hate relationship with the country. To these feelings for me was added an unusual respect for much of its officialdom.

My spiritual journey was then placed on hold as time started to catch up with me. A few weeks in Sri Lanka, much of it immersed in its rich

Buddhist traditions and places, did not change that. I flew to London to see friends, some of whom make appearances in these chapters, including Michael Eyers, Leonie Sandercock, and a British friend from Choate. The milieu in Europe was of course very different, and it took some time adjusting. While I was on the road my friend Peter Till died, and so I spent weeks walking in the Auvergne and staying in Paris with Isabelle Olivier, his partner during most of the DURD years, both of us grieving him but enjoying the time together.

In London and Paris my interests ran to left-wing political movements and their various meetings, rather than urban affairs, save for a memorable meal with John Mant and other urban sector friends at La Tour d'Argent, the famous Parisian restaurant, courtesy of the South Australian taxpayer (John was travelling with a state minister at the time, and so we 'had to talk shop' while dining).

In my mind there was still confusion between the seemingly polar opposites of my quest—politics and spirit—insofar as I was on a quest at all. Sure, both Buddhism and Marxism are doctrines of constant change, whether through impermanence or dialectical change. They were mixed in my mind in odd ways. One sign of that is my well-thumbed copy of *Das Kapital*, carried through south Asia, its margins marked with thoughts about capitalism and its blank pages covered with my dreams and recollections on the way, a kind of subconscious monitoring of how I was travelling. Clearly there was much further to go.

There was no way out of it. I had to go to Berkeley.

FIVE

CALIFORNIAN POLITICS AND US NATIONAL URBAN POLICY

The years in California from 1976–82 marked a turning point in my life: exploration of new directions, study and research with great people, more understanding of the USA and its local cultures and politics, lifelong friendships, love and marriage. The country was well into the 1970s oil-shock recession and there was an atmosphere of economic and social crisis even in the affluent San Francisco region. The state and its cities were in fiscal disarray, heading towards Proposition 13, the cap on property taxing that made matters much worse. The student movements of the 1960s and early 1970s had broken up into fragments warring about ideology and ways ahead. I wanted to be involved.

The San Francisco Bay Area was seeing a flowering of new forms of spirituality, New Left politics and emboldened gay and feminist movements. Here, too, I wanted to be involved. I wanted my AFS-era California dreaming to become a reality. I thought I might be there for just a few years but stayed longer. Looking back, my education was as much through the friends I made as through the university's course or the zeitgeist of the area.

Diving into US urban policy

Travel to San Francisco in September 1976 from Paris went well enough;

at least the strangers along the check-in queue were willing to put through as their own most of my 13 pieces of luggage. But my arrival in Berkeley was less auspicious. I went around to Bill Alonso's house with two fresh camemberts only to find it shut up. He had moved to Harvard. It was my fault for being out of touch. I could possibly have followed him there, but I really wanted to settle into the East Bay and find another supervisor at the university. Thinking of the Free Speech movement and People's Park of the 1960s, I was disappointed to see from my seedy hotel on Telegraph Avenue ('Freak Street') the general degradation of the area: homeless people, signs of a hard drugs scene. I quickly found a shared house and moved off the street.

The Department of City and Regional Planning at the University of California was, by contrast, wonderful. It was a line-up of well-known and younger rising faculty eager to talk of my study plans. Before research, there was coursework to be undertaken, so I settled into the routine. My approach was off-hand, I didn't take the work seriously, and I had to repeat urban economics, even though I topped the class when I applied myself. I took the attitude that Berkeley was just a base for wider learning. It wasn't helped by my forming a graduate student association with a newsletter not long after my arrival, running unfriendly articles like 'Is the department on the skids?'. I must have been trying on a 'bad boy' radical persona, and paid for this by having to take a course in French, as a second language was a prerequisite for which I was not up to scratch. At least I was awarded an untied university fellowship, in the ignoble science of eugenics no less!

My mind was set on a dissertation on national urban policy, but I was not sure what the exact topic would be. I tried out different ideas on different faculty, big names with good ideas. Richard Meier was still there and open to cooperation on communications if I were to rethink that as a topic. I eliminated Australian urban and regional policy as a subject, though it would have helped my reflection on the DURD years, mainly because I was not there, and for a similar reason a comparative study would be difficult. So, it had to be something about US national urban policy, preferably something current. It seemed to me that successful national urban policy had much to do with institutional and political processes, not just policy merit, so policy formation would need to be part of the work.

Ann Markusen seemed the best fit for my field and she was very open to working together. She had a strong presence in regional economic development and national urban policy, feminism and cities, and urban political economy.[1] And she was great to work with: open, energetic, scholarly, challenging, and friendly. The thesis committee consisted of Manuel Castells, a newly arrived star working on the US economic crisis, local urban social movements and the technology-led transformation of the San Francisco Bay Area, Richard Walker, a Marxist urban and economic geographer building a big reputation, and Bob Alford, a well-known political scientist from the University of California, Santa Cruz.[2] My defence of the proposal, held in a grand room high in Wurster Hall, the campus' monument to brutalist architecture, had a moment of levity. Across the floor, in the middle of the formal grilling, loped a Californian surfie, a skateboard under his arm, looking for access to the roof.

I decided on the formation of the Carter administration's urban policy as a topic, because it seemed more interesting to be looking at contemporary processes. Looking back, I concede it wasn't one of those transformational periods of history where everyone—or even perhaps anyone—would want to read my thesis. I think sometimes, though without regret, of what an alternative career might have been if I had kept on with communication technology and urban development. Apart from Ann Markusen, with whom I later co-published, few of the faculty or my fellow students at the time seemed involved with national urban policy directly.[3] And Washington DC seemed far away. So, for a time, despite plenty of support on offer, it looked a reasonably lonely road ahead.

As I settled in, this changed. I became friendly with a remarkable group of fellow students and faculty who shared New Left critiques of the US political economy and urban and regional development issues. The country was coming out of the same 1973–75 recession that had hit Australia, but for many cities, economic and social conditions were at crisis point, and urban social movements were on the rise. The US had a much weaker horizontal fiscal equalisation framework than Australia. That meant there was a pattern of rich cities and poor cities that accentuated other social and economic inequalities. I learned more about such matters of public finance from Richard Musgrave, a guru of the field, who was visiting Berkeley.

My friends wanted to understand the underlying trends of the urban fiscal crisis, each in their own way, but sharing a political-economic critique. A lot of theoretical work was under way around this issue, including on theories of the state. The San Francisco Bay Area had a concentration of prominent left scholars in that field gathered as a collective around the journal *Kapitalistate*.[4] I joined them informally through Alan Wolfe, an influential political scientist who became a friend, and I contributed a couple of papers to their journal.[5]

There was a celebrated controversy in the collective about how self-consciously elites ruled. One camp, branded as 'instrumentalists', saw ruling classes exercise their power self-consciously. It included John Mollenkopf and the more noted Ralph Miliband in Britain. In the other camp the 'structuralists' argued that the occupants of institutional positions of power were less consciously (or with Marcuse, unconsciously) acting to reproduce the power structure embedded in the late capitalist mode of production. This included Nicos Poulantzas and pre-Berkeley Manuel Castells, broadly followers of Louis Althusser.[6]

What did the work of all these people mean for national urban policy? I asked myself, could I use the 'Kapstate' group and the interesting academics at Berkeley better to understand national urban policy formation?

As I was turning to thesis work, the Carter administration was about to release its 1978 annual statement of national urban policy, a requirement of the federal government since 1970. A group of us got it early and wrote a searching critique, hoping somehow to have influence.[7] We held a weekend workshop in a community hall that was open to the public on the issues. Representatives from the California office of the Department of Housing and Urban Development (HUD) came along; they seemed bemused at the concentrated work on an issue that seemed remote, even for them. Certainly, they had nothing to contribute and made no substantive responses.

Thus was the 'national urban policy collective' (NUPC) born. It went on to hold other events of a political character and many small scholarly meetings, critiquing each other's work outside the university confines. Created through common interests that had a bearing on national urban policy, it became an arena for a group of friends and colleagues to do a lot else together. The friendships were very important to me, a freer-wheeling group than my DURD friendships. Marc Weiss and Erica Schoenberger have written up this movement well, taking the story forward to when it became the 'western urban and regional collective' with wider interests to encompass inclusiveness, sustainability and innovation, and linking it to recognition of the late and great Peter Hall's contribution.[8] Marc and Ann Markusen married, and I was privileged to be at the birth of their son David, stuffing up the photos by failing to synchronise the shutter on my new camera.

I became friendly with Chester Hartman, who was an influential planner and activist for accessible housing and an opponent of the ways in which urban renewal was grabbing land in San Francisco. He had a good book out at the time.[9] Chester was coordinator of the Planners' Network, an informal national organisation of progressive urban planners that had its birth in a walkout from an American Institute of Planners conference some years before. The network operated through a good long newsletter and occasional national events, including a 1979 conference at Cornell University that we helped organise and from which a book was published.[10] Chester was moving to Washington DC to take up a lead national advocacy role in housing and urban renewal. He asked us if we could run the newsletter while he was away, with Ann as the editor. The NUPC team contributed a lot, and I was happy to do my part editing and compiling. Everyone chipped in.

One feature of production was that some contributors around the country sent in material electronically, through what we now call email. I wanted to produce my dissertation myself through the sluggish 300 bps terminals in the department. Of course, around me, Berkeley was on the cusp of inventing the internet. I recall typing my thesis text into the faster terminals of the computer department lab in Evans Hall when fellow users hacked my terminal and popped up messages on my screen. Scary, then, but impressive. The Planners' Network still carries on the good fight and it is good that our Berkeley group helped them survive.[11]

Now that I had friends with linked interests, including a supervisor, I had a lot of work to do on the dissertation. Not much of interest to national policy formation was on the west coast, so I had to spend a lot of time in Washington DC. Cheap unlimited open tickets (each for a fixed period) from World Airways, a budget carrier, helped.[12] Lois Dean, a national urban policy manager from HUD, who had come to DURD as an expert visitor, was helpful in inserting me into her department for information and interviews.

Open access to government documents, US-style, was a revelation for me, coming from an environment of confidentiality in the Australian government, even within DURD. The method in HUD was to take a shopping trolley to the working shelves and files of the department, fill it, go to the photocopy room, and spend whatever time was needed copying. Nobody asked me what I was doing. US Americans, in their eternal optimism, and unlike Australians, think the government is owned by the people. At the time, this attitude to information, including copies of handwritten presidential notes, was a great benefit to my work.

The White House planned a conference on urban and regional development and, with support from the Australian embassy after I made contact, I went along. The sessions were useful but better still were the rooms piled high with reports from government departments, states, interest groups, think tanks; all there for the taking. Grist to my mill.

During these visits, I organised interviews and followed new trails. I knew what areas within national urban policy I wanted to cover—the urban development bank proposal and community development block grants to cities in particular. However, despite having done the theory reading, I wasn't sure how it would fit together or what the 'big question' would be. There was much more happening in urban policy than I thought, and I enjoyed digging in. It was very different from Australia.

The history of US urban policy has a lot more richness than is generally known outside that country, and even ideas from the period of the Carter administration, not renowned for its innovative domestic policy, resonate today.

The first cluster of proposals in the 1978 statement aimed at improving government activities. The urban policy landscape was complex, much more so than in Australia, with many intergovernmental programs. In Australia, with a small number of sub-national governments, things can be crafted each to suit, and face-to-face meetings held effectively. In the US, with so many states, more complex formulae are needed. In Washington DC, as if to perpetuate the urban and regional policy group that drafted the statement, the president proposed an inter-agency coordination council to coordinate and resolve conflicts.

An 'urban impact statement' was mandated for every agency in its budget and legislative submissions. As it turned out, the only urban impact statement ever made under this policy, which was never legislated in Congress, was prepared by the Berkeley group. Michael Teitz, a senior faculty member, passed the opportunity along to my friend Marc Weiss and it was successful, preventing federal funding and development consent for a shopping mall that would have killed a long string of small businesses that were supported by other federal grants.[13]

The location of federal employment (shades of the equivalent earlier policy in Australia) was part of this first cluster. The General Services Administration, responsible for the location of federal employment, was required to give priority to distressed downtown areas, including investment into them (unlike in Australia where for reasons of different patterns of disadvantage DURD sought to relocate employment *from* inner urban areas). The same requirement was made of government procurement, but with a wider geographic definition of distress, and incentives were to be offered to states for plans to address the underlying issues of regional distress. These disparities were much sharper than I knew in Australia, and I thought this a good policy.

The second cluster was fiscal assistance to local governments with high unemployment or slow growth, replacing emergency counter-cyclical efforts. Although horizontal fiscal equalisation was not the target, this was broadly comparable to Australia's Grants Commission process.

The third cluster was to promote employment and economic development in cities through a national development bank (known as 'Urbank'), the centrepiece of the urban policy. Its aim was 'to provide a number of financing tools to encourage businesses to remain, expand, or locate in economically depressed urban and rural areas and to increase lending in such distressed areas'.[14] Its forebears were the Roosevelt-era Reconstruction Finance Corporation, international development banks and a string of earlier US proposals. President Carter promised the national development bank to a group of mayors, but the idea was vaguely formed, dubbed 'a unicorn' and 'a catchy title in search of a program'.[15]

When shaped up by executive agencies, it became a package of loan guarantees for private capital investments, interest rate subsidies on long-term debt, grants towards capital cost, taxable development bonds and a liquidity facility to buy loans—all of these targeted on areas of high unemployment, low population growth, slow per capita income growth and other indicators of severe poverty or local fiscal distress. Congressional committees and reluctant lawmakers took a long time to consider the bill, and it missed the 95th congressional deadline.

After the mid-term elections, the economic outlook darkened and conservative forces strengthened, making the bill something of a liability in the build-up to the 1980 elections. It failed to be agreed before the 'lame duck' sittings, and so died. I spent much of my time investigating this interesting but ill-fated proposal, and believe it is still relevant today. Urbank was successfully accompanied by a more conventional counter-cyclical labour-intensive public works scheme and employment tax credits.

The fourth part of the national urban policy was for community and human development through a new urban volunteer corps. The policy package as a whole was generally well received by its stakeholders, but less so by Congress, which enacted only 10 of the 20 bills arising from the urban policy statement, including failure to approve tax credits for investments in distressed areas.

This made a good story and I had a big collection of material.

What to make of it?

The first pass through was to explain the formation of policy in economic, political, institutional and ideological terms. The economy was in some crisis throughout the period, and problems of capital accumulation dominated the aims of policy, narrowed its scope but brought some innovation. So, policy wasn't structurally determined, even if one were to hold, from a Marxist perspective, as I did, that the institutional, political and ideological forces were, in turn, determined by the political economy. There were many contingencies; there was still wide scope for policy choice, for agency. The political forces could be well explained through pluralist or instrumentalist theories of the state, and the institutional forces through elite theory. Echoing Anthony Giddens, I concluded that

> Conditions of accumulation do not mystically set constraints on action; they are interpreted by people in their practice. Of course, people may decide incorrectly, suffer the consequences and be judged by posterity, but the broader economic, social, political and ideological conditions that are often called 'structural' become constraints and opportunities only through historical interpretation of events as they occur. We do make history hemmed in by the constraints of past events, but even the most apparently immutable structures were once socially constructed.[16]

Looking back, I am satisfied with the choice of dissertation topic, though a 'hotter' topic may have seen my ideas disseminated wider and brought me more recognition. But of its conclusions I would change little today. I have been enriched as an activist, policy adviser and executive by having a decent understanding of the limits of agency, but I also understood how the very structures of our state and society can change.

Fanning out

Life back at Berkeley was busy and engaging, but I wanted more of the 'real' Bay Area, so I moved to an Oakland shared house with non-students. Oakland was next door to Berkeley but very different. Famous for Gertrude Stein's accolade—'the trouble with Oakland is that when you get there there's no there there'—in reality, it was very interesting with a predominantly black downtown, a patchwork of discrete and relatively segregated neighbourhoods (our housing association still had racially restrictive and anti-Semitic covenants on the books, as I found out when I went to a meeting for our Vernon Street housemates), and very lively local politics, including the headquarters of the Black Panther Party. At UC Berkeley, I became friends with Ed Blakely, an academic who later ran for mayor, and learned more about Oakland city politics from him. And through Dan Lindheim, a fellow student and local political activist, I got to know Ron Dellums a bit, the most progressive Democrat in Congress. Dan worked for him in Washington DC, which was helpful for my thesis work as I was able to visit his office. More generally, I found it easy to make key contacts and get into arenas often closed. In part I thank the audacity I learnt finding my way around America during my AFS year of 1964–65, and confidence working in Sydney and Canberra. For any reader shy of being turned down, there really is little harm in asking. Just prepare first.

Apart from Berkeley and Oakland, San Francisco drew me in too. I consciously reached out to meet progressive urban sector people on my arrival to the Bay Area, including in San Francisco, and indicated I'd be interested in work outside the confines of Berkeley. I did some consulting work for the San Francisco Arts Commission on their role in the city charter. At the invitation of Richard Le Gates and Deborah LeVeen, friendly urbanists keen on practical engagement in city issues, I started to teach courses on urban studies and on 'alternative urban futures' at San Francisco State University. The university was part of a state-wide system separate from the UC system; it was much more in the thick of urban local politics and culture, and well-known for its radical academics, ethnic diversity and legendary demonstrations.

For my predecessor, the latter course was about the green counterculture; for me, it was more about urban futurology and technological forecasting. The author of a forecasting text I used, Erich Jantsch, came to live in Berkeley, and we became friends over the last months of his life.[17]

My technocratic self was reasserting itself—perhaps I was helping put the hippie movement to bed and replacing it with managerialism.

Making revolution in the East Bay

California is not the first place that comes to mind when thinking of socialist revolution. The same global economic crisis that hit Australia during DURD's time was still hitting US cities hard, and there in the US, city governments had more vital responsibilities. A book by Roger Alcaly and David Mermelstein on the urban fiscal crisis was influential at the time, and I wrote an extended paper on the topic.[18] The issues weren't just economic and social. They were to do with the nature of the local state and how power was concentrated and exercised, whether by the self-conscious formation of elites or by the structure of the political economy, the way it just was.

Jim Schoch, an ex-Students for a Democratic Society (a just defunct anti-war group) and continuing activist, liked it and asked me to speak at the San Francisco Liberation School, an open learning centre. I didn't know at the time that the Liberation School was born out of the Women's Movement, a breakaway from the 'patriarchal' Bay Area School.[19] That speech went well and led to me teaching there on the topic, unpaid of course. Would I also teach a course on the history of California? Why not another jump into the deep end? I knew nothing, so I had to read a lot at short notice.

It was thrilling. The students didn't seem to mind my starting point of ignorance, and I saw parallels with Australian history that I didn't know about: gold rushes around the same time with immigration of the Chinese and their oppression, people coming and going between Australia and California, some of them becoming prominent. I was delighted to meet a more recent Australian renegade, Harry Bridges, a famous communist longshoreman and leader of the 1934 great general strike, perhaps an equivalent to Pat Troy's Fremantle waterside worker father, Paddy Troy. Bridges was in his 90s and still active, though union control of San Francisco's waterfront and its union hiring hall had long since been squashed.

The Liberation School was a part of the Northern Californian Alliance (NCA), founded in 1976, the year of my arrival. Before long, I was invited to join its East Bay base committee. It is hard to summarise the New Left political movements of the time because there were so many organisations and schisms, but basically, after the anti-war and civil rights movements of the 1960s, the mostly white New Left took two tracks. One was a democratic socialist movement through the Students of Democratic Society into the New America Movement, associated with Tom Hayden and Jane Fonda. The other was a group of communist parties and Marxist–Leninist pre-party formations, of which NCA was one.[20]

Why join the NCA? In part, curiosity. I was hardly part of the working class, but as a free-floating 'intellectual' with interests in urban political economy and the theory of the state I was of some interest to them. It would be interesting to see democratic centralism, Leninist-style, in action, and see if it made sense. In part, my sense of injustice and how power was formed and exercised in cities was hardening. And the university would be no use—my Berkeley faculty adviser said that the university didn't offer courses on Leninism. He seemed surprised at my question.

The Northern California Alliance had an urban strategy too, 'that the Alliance orient its work in the coming period around the urban crisis in San Francisco and Oakland, with the struggle against racism to be kept at the centre of all our activities'.[21] It had to be my primary political organisation; no other socialist or communist organisation membership was allowed. The main reason for my joining was that NCA offered a structured engagement with local radical politics. I willingly went along as I had no other political affiliation.

And structured it was. The NCA was highly disciplined, with theoretical training required of everyone and thorough discussion of any proposed action, a common practice with other pre-party formations as well. This was quite defensible. It sought to be 'a revolutionary movement rooted in the working class and representing all of its sectors, especially Third World peoples and women', the beginnings of a mass movement towards party formation. To these ends the NCA worked with the Union of Democratic Filipinos (KDP) and the Third World Women's

Alliance.[22] The KDP activists were impressive, and leaders of the three organisations came out of secrecy and formed a 'rectification' movement as a model for new party formation (dubbed the *Line of March* for the theoretical journal of the same name). They disassociated themselves from the Communist Party USA, which still grotesquely defended the Soviet Union, and other socialist left movements like the clubs forming around *The Guardian* newspaper.

In our work in Oakland, the Black Panther Party was also involved. They had once been important in the area, one of the best known urban revolutionary groups in the country. But by 1977 they were a waning force, resorting to acts of violence (Oakland happened to have about twice the murder rate of San Francisco, though, of course, that was not the doing of the Panthers), and were leaderless, with Huey Newton 'in exile' in Cuba, avoiding another murder charge.

The people of the East Bay chapter of NCA were a pleasant and lively group, white and Latino, with mostly ordinary jobs, true to their ideology. Every issue was open to struggle, including people's most intimate relationships (excruciating to take part in at times), with a search even on such personal matters for what was the primary contradiction among any set of linked issues, such as the use of dialectical materialism.[23] From resolution of any contradiction, a synthesis is formed, and as events move on, new contradictions arise, and so on. In this way, history is made and can be understood that way.

Our study sessions were serious. Lester, a member, got as a group birthday gift the collected works of V. I. Lenin and seemed very pleased with the gift. But action was serious, too. We organised or joined demonstrations on a number of issues with the wider movement, distributed *Common Sense*, the newspaper, and took on other activities according to the issues.

In the East Bay during 1977 and 1978, the NCA focused on two issues. The first was police repression, an issue that went to the heart of racism and black and Chicano unemployment. We joined and helped organise marches and rallies with the Panthers and the Huey P. Newton Justice Committee, among others. Part of the purpose of this priority was to build a more multiracial base to the fledgling mass movement. Over the bay, the San Francisco group included the rising gay movement as part of their base-building.

I was assigned to a second issue, also aimed at building a multiracial mass movement, agitating around the Bakke case, a local issue, as Berkeley was home to the University of California (UC) system headquarters. The *Regents of the University of California v. Allan Bakke* was a national case that had, and even today still has, national consequences. As *The Atlantic* magazine headlined it, the issue before the court was 'who gets ahead in America'.[24]

Allan P. Bakke, a former US Marine Corps officer, was rejected for admission twice by the University of California Davis medical school, and he brought suit in a state court alleging that a quota of 16 percent for qualified racial minorities had caused him, a white, to be disqualified, and that this form of affirmative action was unconstitutional according to the equal protection clause of the 14th amendment. The case had huge implications for affirmative action programs across the country, a legacy of the civil rights movement, and whether race could be considered at all in university entry and other rights. The California Supreme Court upheld the claim and struck down the university's affirmative action program as violating the rights of white applicants. The case went to the US Supreme Court when we were campaigning.

We feared a further loss would authorise a resurgence of white racism, and it would certainly set back opportunities for racial minorities and women. We and others took to the streets in noisy but peaceful demonstrations, and held forums to spread word of the issue. Around Berkeley, many people would know about the case, but for working class areas like in Emeryville, an adjacent industrial suburb since gentrified, we thought the working class of whatever race would benefit from seeing where their class interests lay in this case. I spent afternoons handing out letters setting out the case at factory gates at shift changes, a hard job trying to talk around tired workers on their way home about an issue they thought was not very relevant to their lives. For us, there was no direct lobbying to anyone (after all, it was a court case), just building consciousness of the importance of the case and an anti-racism movement. The movement did have strength. The 'rectification' core involving NCA took the lead in forming the National Committee to Overturn the Bakke Decision, which allied with reformists to organise a 20,000-person demonstration in Washington DC.[25] I didn't go, but I felt I had contributed a little to the movement. It was quite unlike my Australian experience.

The landmark case was decided by a majority of the court in June 1978 after it had been badly split on the issues—nine justices issued six opinions. It upheld affirmative action under the constitution and the Civil Rights Act of 1964 to the great relief of NCA and progressives across the country. But it ruled that setting quotas like those of UC Davis went too far, and they specifically were struck down. Bakke was admitted. In 1996, California, by citizen's initiative (not by legislation), banned the use of race in admissions to public education, as did the UC system. Affirmative action and the means of getting diversity in public institutions are still big issues in the US, but 'positive discrimination' has mostly turned to 'blind' admissions. There are certainly problems with using admission quotas, as I learned later in universities, but this retreat from affirmative action is a retreat from social justice.

My work at UC Berkeley was getting more demanding, including teaching there, and I was worried about slow progress on the thesis research. My comrades from NCA didn't mix very well with my friends at the university, on those occasions when they did meet. Internal struggle within NCA was getting tedious, as divisions got sharper and position papers got longer, particularly between the 'transformation' caucus, seeking to resolve issues through principled 'two-line struggle', and the 'real issues' caucus, willing to allow like-minded members to form tendencies to develop positions. I drifted away. The NCA folded by 1979, a product of these divisions.

Those years were a time when the US would have benefited from a stronger left, built in and around the social movements growing in reaction to the recession, and threats to civil rights won in the 1960s and early 1970s. The prospects of a mass movement led by a disciplined party were remote, but the activists I worked with in NCA knew that, and gains on the way were worthwhile, if not building a revolutionary movement. The leadership stayed active in other ways. The reliability of a more disciplined group saw actions and results that might not have been achieved with only a loose New Left form of organisation. I give NCA credit for that. The constant internal struggle and time spent on strategy sapped energy for community and political action. Overall, the movement endured a long period of political backtracking and retreat into the margins.

Until now, perhaps. The new rise of democratic socialists around the Democratic campaigns in 2016 and 2020, the resurgence of intelligent and explicit socialist movements and thinking, and the re-energised women's and anti-racism movements give me hope at least for progressive reform in opposition to the reactionary current day movements in US politics. Notwithstanding the richness of Marxist and New Left thinking in academe at the time, my work with the NCA showed me a different side of the Bay Area and gave me a different set of activist friends, for which I am grateful.

Another political group took my interest, the Australia Support Network, a bunch of leftist Australian expatriates Peter Hayes and I brought together, mostly in the East Bay, for reasons of conviviality and occasional political action. Peter was at UC Berkeley, too, deeply involved in how resource and energy politics affected the strategic and security interests of countries in the Pacific. He would go on to found the Nautilus Foundation, still in Berkeley, a research and action organisation with radical politics, but respected then, and still now, by the Pentagon, for the foundation's analysis and contacts. Indeed, for President Clinton, Nautilus opened doors in North Korea, holding retreats about security scenarios with leaders there; an audacious project.

Tall and tousle-haired, Peter was a master of media politics, a founder in Australia of Friends of the Earth. Among the demonstrations he organised was one against the Portland aluminium smelter in Victoria, for which he invited a Native American drumming group to make the very small group of demonstrators turning up look and sound, for Australian television, much bigger and louder than it was. Another member was Jeannie Lewis, an Australian singing star, finding her way from Berkeley to a huge following in central and south America, and affiliated with the wonderful La Peña cultural centre down the road from where I then lived in Berkeley. My task was to cheer wildly at her performances to get the crowd going, but that didn't take much. The City of Berkeley also had strong connections in central and Caribbean America, as I was about to find out.

A look at Cuba

For the summer of 1977, I had two choices. I was invited to work, unpaid, in the urban sector group of the OECD, but living in Paris seemed expensive, so I chose to join a tour of Cuba. When else would I be able to do that? The Carter administration had softened the bans on US citizens travelling to Cuba, though we still had to fly through Montreal as there were no direct flights. The group was organised by the travel arm of the Communist Party USA (CPUSA), but the Cubans sought to treat it as just another one of the 'rum and beaches' tours that they offered to Russian and eastern European holiday-makers. After some negotiation, we managed to get a more political itinerary, but I didn't mind the remaining nightclub and beach visits at all. Apart from Havana, we visited the new city of Alamar, a smaller new community at Jibacoa, and had a decent stay at Santiago de Cuba, a city important to the Cuban revolution for independence.

The group divided up interests so that we could brief one another as we went. I covered housing and the urban sector. Our return created a lot of interest for speaking, and I published a little piece in a UC Berkeley newsletter, as Cuba had been officially out of bounds for US Americans up to that point.[26]

Some things were impressive. Literacy was almost universal, primary health and education were at good levels by Latin American standards. In urban and regional planning, it was difficult in a two-week visit to see how Cuba was going.[27] The strategy was to hold back the growth of cities, Havana in particular, and build new settlements to decentralise population and production, more than any other Latin American country.[28] Government financial impoverishment and some conservation efforts, especially in later years, also explain Havana's colonial charm, at least to outsiders' eyes. The new settlements we saw were modern and well serviced. Massive land reforms were necessary after the revolution to redistribute land—80 percent, said our hosts—previously owned by foreigners.

The structure of governance was interesting too. The ruling communist party of Cuba was much as we expected. Mass organisations were important, 'peoples' power', and we saw a number of CDRs, neighbourhood Committees to Defend the Revolution. They seemed something of a double-edged sword, good for local service delivery and solidarity, so that everyone's wellbeing is known, but young people we talked to found it too intrusive. Though our group was sympathetic to the Cuban revolution, we were very critical about human rights, especially the jailing of dissident writers and the suppression of gay people. We went to Santiago de Cuba, a home of the Cuban revolution, and looked across the water of Guantanamo Bay at the US enclave.

Information within the group was not very good, but it seemed *Carnaval* was the next night. Vivian Lin, a fellow traveller, and I thought we'd go out into the streets that night anyway, and enjoyed all the dancing and crowds. If this was the night before, how much more fun would *Carnaval* be? It turned out that *was Carnaval*; we got the night wrong. We should have checked the itinerary more carefully. The tour leaders from the CPUSA were generally not very helpful, and true to form, tried to steal for themselves a pile of *Carnaval* posters meant for each of us. So much for their socialism.

But the mishap with the dates was fortuitous for me. I enjoyed being with Vivian. Later, after Vivian came to Berkeley from the east coast, we got together and formed a group household in Oakland.

The visit to Cuba left me angry at the long-standing and brutal US embargo on Cuba's economic and social development, sympathetic to the country's efforts towards self-determination, and sad at how US opposition to what started as a nationalist revolution pushed them towards USSR-style communism and penury for over a generation. But in retrospect the trip was the right decision for the summer, compared with the OECD in Paris. For one thing, I might not have met Vivian.

Adventures and escapes

Back in Berkeley there were other adventures and some near escapes. After Christmas lunch in 1980, a couple of friends and I went for a walk in the lovely hills behind the campus, only to be interrupted by a loud-speaker from a distance telling us to get out of there. It turned out we were on private water catchment land. I couldn't believe this was serious, so in high spirits I decided to give chase. My friends left the area, but I ran across the hills and up gullies with the uniformed guards chasing me, an exciting game of hide-and-seek. I felt like I was in a cross-country race again, perhaps not so fit this time. Surely, on Christmas day, they could see the fun. They couldn't. They had my name from my nervous friends and were broadcasting threats. Not knowing if they were armed, after a good half hour, I walked out of the woods, sweating but laughing. They didn't see the joke but let me off with a warning; my friends couldn't believe I'd been so silly.

Another time I was driving around Berkeley and I picked up a hitch-hiker. I did this on principle, as I'd benefited myself from the kindness of drivers in different countries. This was different. My passenger pulled out a big knife, in a kind of reversal of the *Crocodile Dundee* trope. It was his ostentatious—and threatening—way of asking if I wanted to buy some cocaine, which the knife was supposedly to cut. I had little choice, so after the transaction I let him off, relieved to get away. Of course, the knife was enough to convince me to try it out. After that I went to get some more, at one of Malvina Reynolds' 'little boxes, on the hillside' in Daly City. This was no local dealer, but a wholesale house with gun-toting guards waiting for a new shipment and a sales hatch served by a woman with most of the insides of her nose snorted away. I hate to think of what the penalty for being caught would have been. Close shave or not, this stopped my experimentation.

However, the closest shave I had was in the mountains. From time to time in winter, I'd drive up to the Sierras and enjoy a day or two of skiing.

This time I went up with Wendy Sarkissian, an urban sector Canadian friend I'd come to know from Australia. After Reno, we went to Squaw Valley, a big ski resort once host to the Winter Olympics. It was a good day's skiing, quite windy. In fact, a blizzard was moving in and the lift announced the last ride on the gondola. Greedy to fit one more run in, I went up. Wendy stayed below.

The wind rose and the gondola swayed wildly; only a few of us got off to ski down, the others stayed on to go down safely. I skied down alone in the windy white-out, a bit scared but exhilarated. Those staying in the gondola were not so lucky. It swung so widely that it came off the ropes, whip-cracking down and tragically killing seven people and injuring others. I didn't know about my near miss until after Wendy and I left the resort.

In the 1970s I was one of many interested both in political action and spiritual enlightenment. In less dangerous times, I'd given myself the opportunity to explore my interest in Marx. After eight months wandering in south Asia and more than a month practicing meditation seriously, where was my friend the Buddha now? My spiritual guide from travels together in Nepal and India, Jim Carmody, was by now something of a recluse, but he hosted me on a number of weekends in his forest hut in northern California. I was continuing the mediation practice I learned in India from the month in both the Burmese and Zen temples.

The highlight for me was a 10-day Vipassana course in total silence behind Santa Barbara with Jack Kornfield, clearing away, minute by minute, the thoughts, feelings and obstructions that arose as I sat there. It is highly recommended as a way of spring cleaning the mind and taming the hungry ego! I came out a changed person, centred and clear-headed. That was in 1977, and I was soon to return to Australian shores.

Growing with the flow

When I returned to Australia I had more or less met my aims in going to California: rest and recovery, a deeper understanding of national urban policy, a test of radical politics, realisation of my AFS dream to return and live in the USA, and an extraordinary network of new friends.

I learnt a great deal, not least through studies, research and association with those friends.

I brought an undeveloped interest in Marxism with me. I soon found myself practicing the politics through the Northern California Alliance and other groups, but I edged back towards democratic socialism, unhappy with the sectarianism of the radical left and wiser about the power of political agency.

I didn't bring about much political change while I was there. I can't blame that alone on the difficulty of making change 'in the belly of the beast'. But unlike the liberalism and conservatism that currently contend so viciously in the US, Marxism does give us an understanding of how changes in society, changes in us, are indissoluble from the political economy, and how the modern state has come about and evolves.

I also brought an interest in spiritual practices with me, alongside unchanging disdain for institutional religion. The Vipassana practices and yoga I learned in India and California opened my heart a little, and certainly cleared my mind. The core practices of Buddhism really aren't a religion at all, just good psychology, but there too, many of them have been crusted over with too much unnecessary ritual. I remembered the Lawrences' definition of religion from my undergraduate anthropology days: 'the putative extension of men's [sic] social relationships into the non-empirical realm of the cosmos'.[29] That seems to fit. Religions are socially constructed, though transcendence through and above day-to-day experience is at the heart of being human.

But I should not overstate my experience. I let my new-gained mindfulness gradually slip away in California and on return to Australia.

In truth, all my California years continued that long period of drift. I spent more years there than planned, a loose grip on my formal learning at Berkeley, much of it wasted time. They were, however, the culmination of my teenage dream to return, and they became a time of unexpected love and marriage.

Yes, in 1979, Vivian and I married. We did it at the Oakland courthouse for a US$8 fee, rushing from the airport before our earlier Wassermann (syphilis) test results needed for a clean bill for marriage expired. A cast of extras, diverted from the TV while waiting for jury duty, cheered us on.

By 1982, I felt it was time to leave California. John Paterson was encouraging me to join the NSW Department of Environment and Planning in Sydney and it was a good opportunity. I'd kept in touch with him over these years. He followed closely the revolution in economic thought under way at Chicago and Berkeley—the use of rational choice theory in urban and environmental economics—and sought my help, unsuccessfully, in getting a job at Berkeley. Vivian was willing to come to Australia, if not perhaps enthusiastically. For her it would be a big change in her life.

With my PhD thesis not quite finished, I enrolled in a post-graduate course at the University of NSW solely to get access to their computing system, which housed my thesis word processing program, Berkeley UNIX version 7. It was satisfying to finish the dissertation and publish much of it, though not in a widely read journal. The process of writing had been good for me, the dissertation defence successful, and the reception among other readers complimentary about its thoroughness, systematic reasoning and irrefutable findings. But the results on their own did not make a splash outside my own circle. It was about a presidency quickly, if wrongly, forgotten for its domestic policy, and a topic, national urban policy, swept away by the gale of neo-liberal policy that followed. The Carter Library sent me a kind letter from Jimmy Carter, but they didn't want to publish it as a book.

After six months in Singapore and Malaysia working on her dissertation on electronics industry workers, Vivian was willing to give life in Australia a go and came to join me. So began a new chapter.

THE ROUGH AND TUMBLE OF SYDNEY'S PLANNING

R e-entry into Sydney from February 1982 was enjoyable, though without Vivian initially, as she was still doing her research in Malaysia. The job, head of the central policy division (CPD) of the NSW Department of Environment and Planning (DEP), seemed well suited for me, though there had been other possibilities. I felt there was full scope for me professionally and personally. Though I was back in government, it was a Labor government with ambitions that seemed to align with my values. It was time to put into practice what I had learned about work and about life, if not the balance between the two.

When Vivian arrived, she landed on her feet with a senior public health job in the NSW state government. Entry into my department was another matter. John Paterson was deputy director and I started working with him while running a division. This was the John Paterson who had given DURD some of its intellectual underpinning, brilliant and at times scathing. Richard Smyth was director of the department, deeply involved in political and bureaucratic manoeuvring in promotion and defence of the department. Pat Troy was occasional adviser to the government on planning and administrative matters and I continued to see him too, especially on land policy and urban development.

I was responsible for metropolitan planning, the urban development program, state-wide strategic planning issues (to the extent that they were ever addressed) and a host of policy matters. John was developing a macro-strategy for the Sydney–Hunter–Illawarra regions, something along the lines of the County of Cumberland plan, in reaction to the vagueness of the Sydney region outline plan that had succeeded it. At the same time, the CPD, with Bob Meyer as the team leader, was moving towards a metropolitan strategy for Sydney itself, borne out of earlier 'long-term options' work on where and how Sydney could expand. The methodologies of John Paterson and Bob Meyer were different and had to be reconciled.

My appointment over an acting incumbent, Robyn Read, created some friction with her supporters in the division, but in any case, the division needed some reorganisation. The changes I made were not universally well-received, but that is usually the case with any organisational change. The schism stayed an issue in the division, and I was not fully able to bring full harmony again.

My days of freedom were over. I was back in the fray.

Resources infrastructure

John was in the thick of forming state policy for infrastructure finance requirements and development contributions policy for resource developments for the NSW Wran government, especially new coalmines in the upper Hunter Valley. It was a difficult time for policy. By mid-1982 the resources boom based on coal and other exports and mineral processing such as aluminium smelting was coming to an end, with state finances threatened, and the state budget being drained by 'the backwash from the turbulence encountered by the resources boom in NSW'.[1] The government was in a double-bind with the big projects; it had to raise revenue from resource developers to pay for infrastructure and services needed by the mines, ports and smelters, and it needed to ease the state burden on resource development companies to retain investment and encourage more if possible. In July 1982 the government put a freeze on royalties and a ceiling on social infrastructure levies attached to new coal industry developments.

What should this ceiling be? That was the job of the division. Based on the work of David Roman, a hyper-energetic rock'n'roller economist in the division, and Dr Glen Searle, a smart, modest scholarly analyst, cabinet adopted a policy of requiring all projects to provide their own industrial infrastructure (taking away pressure from the state to provide it), pay for all the social infrastructure arising from the population increases generated by new projects, and pay only up to capped amounts of $1500 per direct project employee for local council general funds and $2000 as an interest-free loan for local water and sewerage investments. Should the government keep a lid on this decision even from its own ministers, and apply it quietly?

Gerald Gleeson, the all-powerful secretary of the Department of Premier and Cabinet, advised the premier, 'You may have doubts about sending this [cabinet committee decision] but Depts. need to know.'[2] The premier, Neville Wran, wrote 'no'. Around it went, and then of course to the media. Lithgow, Singleton and Muswellbrook and other project-hosting councils were livid about the state 'robbing' them of their negotiating power, but in truth it was the beginning of the end of an era. Development contributions in the future would still be contested, but with few new projects swamping localities with unfunded needs, they became part of the normal business of services financing.

John Paterson soon left DEP to run the Hunter District Water Board, audaciously and with an economic rationalism rare then for the utilities sector. I stayed involved in the region, more to do with economic planning and promotion than funding infrastructure. I went onto the Hunter Development Board to represent DEP's interests as the boom faded, enjoying my Aeropelican flights over the beautiful landscapes north of Sydney. It was a new government–private sector hybrid body to promote investment in the region beyond resources. Wine was one such industry. At the time the Australian wine industry was hit by an Austrian wine contamination scandal, in which anti-freeze was added to wine by unscrupulous producers there, deterring international buyers who didn't know the country difference between Australia and Austria. Murray Tyrrell, a celebrated winemaker, was on the board, and we led a campaign trying to promote the top end of the wine market. It wasn't helped by Austrade, Australia's trade promotion body, promoting cheap bulk wines to Japan.

My role on the board was to liaise with the different parties and to promote better regional planning for this rich and diverse region. It wasn't otherwise much connected to the bread-and-butter of my department, land use planning and development control. My duties lay more in Sydney, this time with affordable housing.

The urban consolidation wars

Apart from resource development infrastructure, the early months in DEP from mid-1982 were dominated by urban consolidation, the government's effort to bring about higher housing and population densities, mainly in the Sydney region. Some of the controversy it generated was inadvertently of my own making through disclosure of a cabinet decision. But much happened before we got to that point.

Unusual growth constraints on Sydney—for a big metropolitan region—gave rise to a debate on how to increase housing density in the built-up areas.[3] Costs of urban expansion were biting government budgets and balance sheets, and after the boom in multi-unit housing construction between 1968 and 1974 that industry stayed flat. Local governments mouthed 'in principle' support for urban consolidation, but most councils opposed it in their localities or went slow in relaxing zoning provisions and development standards. The legacy of the boom in ugly red brick walk-up flats ('six-packs') in middle and inner suburbs was still fresh in councillors' minds. Many of the buildings still mar Sydney's urban landscape today, though they often provide affordable housing. The evidence base for urban consolidation was not strong, but anecdotes and development industry tales were persuasive, more about the high costs of low-density development than what savings from urban consolidation might actually be.

So the Wran government cabinet agreed on an urban consolidation policy, and in October 1981, before I came, the minister for planning and environment, Eric Bedford, set it out. He defined urban consolidation as 'a change within the existing area resulting in an increase of dwellings, population or both'.[4] This later changed to 'increasing the density of dwellings or population, or both'.[5] In other words, the focus on existing areas was dropped. The minister said, 'I would even extend this concept to include … situations where innovative urban designs lead to more compact, less wasteful expansion on the outskirts', an important nuance because urban consolidation planning provisions applied mostly to new developments, and most of them were indeed in outer areas.[6]

In other words, the concept was to seek an increase in density wherever it was possible, not to make the centre more compact. There was no preferred spatial pattern of higher density as cities elsewhere sought, other than a preference for increasing density in accessible areas. This later changed back as the state specified medium-density housing unit targets by council area, and expressed preferences for denser development around sub-regional centres. The aims of urban consolidation shifted to include reduction of the cost of housing (or at least rates of its increase), contain the costs of urban expansion, and meet changes in underlying housing demand as households got older in average age of occupant, and smaller.

The policy area was highly political even within the Labor government. The Left sought to open up the traditionally low densities of Australian housing to multi-unit housing development so as to be more like comparable cities overseas. The Labor Right, including my planning minister Bedford, tended to oppose aggressive measures to open up suburbs to higher densities and favoured trying by moderate means to persuade local governments, rather than to override them. After all, it would be the planning minister having to do most of any overriding, responsible for the *Environmental Planning and Assessment Act of 1979* (EP&A Act), still then in its early years of use.

He had made early progress with a number of new policies and plans. In June 1981, DEP started a six-month program of consultation with local councils to report back to the housing committee of cabinet (HCC), identifying areas suitable for medium-density housing.[7] The minister spoke publicly in favour, as noted above, and the local consultations had good media support.[8] But some members of the HCC—particularly

Frank Walker (minister for housing, including Landcom, the land commission established in DURD's wake) and Jack Ferguson, deputy premier and minister for public works—wanted more action, including stronger use of the EP&A Act's planning instruments. Ferguson in full flight at cabinet meetings was a sight to see: standing, growling, gesticulating, threatening, persuading.

However, the consultations dragged on and many councils opposed the policy or did not cooperate. They had been acting for some time to protect the amenity of their areas, as they saw it, by reducing areas available for medium-density housing, lowering permitted densities, increasing required distances between buildings, and prohibiting or minimising bed-sitter and one-bedroom flats. It amounted to social exclusion.[9] There was an equity argument for urban consolidation, an issue that my friend and sounding board Leonie Sandercock, then at Macquarie University, took up.[10] Protective resident action groups criss-crossed Sydney and elsewhere. Naturally, the land development and housing industries wanted action on urban consolidation.

When the second stage of consultations, this time with elected local officials, was approved by the HCC at its February 1982 meeting, the committee pressed DEP to take a firm stand in consultations with councils unwilling to respond, which might include preparing a regional environmental plan (REP) to increase opportunities for medium-density housing.

Still impatient by the time of its 21 July meeting, when I started attending, Walker and Ferguson prevailed on the HCC to adopt a target of 12,000 'other' (i.e. multi-unit) dwellings per year, and directed DEP to specify the areas with potential for rezoning for this housing to be built. Then they put in the boot: DEP was to 'prepare a draft state environmental planning policy permitting town houses, villa houses and semi-detached houses up to two stories in *all* residential zones of the state [my italics] for the committee's consideration by 31st August 1982'. This was a big defeat for DEP's moderate line, and the planning minister and the department were certain to take most of the flak.

On return I quickly drafted a note to the departmental executive and the strategy team, describing the decision and how it might be implemented. This was not wise. My division, as noted above, was in a stressful position, reorganising after my arrival, and not all staff were on side with me. The department's executive had been worried about what was happening with urban consolidation policy for some time. Next day, a leaked version of that memo, including the cabinet committee decision I'd reproduced, made its appearance in local councillors' letterboxes across the state and in much of the media.[11] I was mortified.

There was an immediate negative reaction directed at the minister, coordinated by Ted Mack, mayor of North Sydney. Many letters from councils started with something like this: 'A document has come into the possession of this Council which Council believes gives great concern in regard to the Department of Environment and Planning's policies for the State'.[12] Frank Walker, chair of the HCC, rubbed it in, expressing concern that details of the committee appeared in the *Sydney Morning Herald* the morning after the original scheduled date.

I wasn't blamed as people knew someone else leaked the document, but my written report of a cabinet meeting in a contested environment showed up my inexperience working at the cabinet level.

The minister duly circulated the draft state environmental planning policy (SEPP) for medium-density housing to implement the decision and once again started consultation with local governments, this time in hostile circumstances.[13] A state-wide campaign against the SEPP was under way, including in state parliament. Under pressure, the draft policy was modified to extend the time for response and to invite local council alternatives, including their own targets.[14]

In December 1982 an interdepartmental urban consolidation committee was re-established to discuss policy and try to coordinate the conflicting views of the relevant agencies. By then Robyn Read, who had been acting as head of the central policy division up until when I came in at mid-year, headed up a new land coordination unit in the housing minister's portfolio. Its aim was to keep the pressure on the other land and housing supply agencies to perform, including on her old department; us. She promoted the metropolitan-wide search to identify particular development opportunities in parallel with the blanket SEPP, starting with Landcom in February when she was acting head of CPD.[15] This was a good idea.

The housing committee of cabinet saw the firestorm they had lit and agreed to exclude all non-metropolitan areas from the SEPP (leaving in Sydney, Hunter and Illawarra regions), unless otherwise requested by a council, there were areas of special environmental significance, or there were local areas where councils' own initiatives, as invited, would meet the state's objectives. However, DEP was not yet in the clear. The HCC required it to set medium-density housing targets for local government areas through the urban consolidation committee, which DEP chaired but on which it did not have the numbers around the table.

Trying to recover the broader agenda, my department formed a full-time team and my division brought the various initiatives into a coherent program, like the successful urban development program, including monitoring of development towards the targets. That was reported to the urban consolidation committee in March 1983. I started presenting this program with colleagues in professional and community settings to get some headway in public opinion.[16] We started work on a policy publication and hired consultants to test the evidence base for urban consolidation, which to date relied not on financial savings and development stimulus but on the high costs of urban expansion.[17]

But for the HCC, some of whose members distrusted DEP resolve, even that program was not enough. When the report on local consultations came back from DEP in July 1983, the HCC finally agreed to withdraw the original SEPP (medium-density housing), but by majority vote the committee required the metropolitan target of 12,000 multi-unit housing commencements, and subsidiary local targets, be locked into a statutory instrument, another SEPP on targets for medium-density housing. Something of an obsession about setting targets had set in, as if, in a flat housing market, opening up more land and easing restrictions could reach the government's targets.

Losing in the HCC once more hit minister Bedford hard. He was normally a mild-mannered man. He took the July decisions, along with

Family in Mackay, 1950
At back, from left: Margaret,
Norma, Geoff and Mary Ann
Wilmoth; author at front

Dad and the author
on the beach, Mackay,
1948

The author, 1955

From left: The author, Dad, Margaret and Mary Ann

Queensland AFS-ers, 1964
From left: Greg Winterflood, Pauline McGregor, Kerry Clarke, Judy Stephenson
and the author

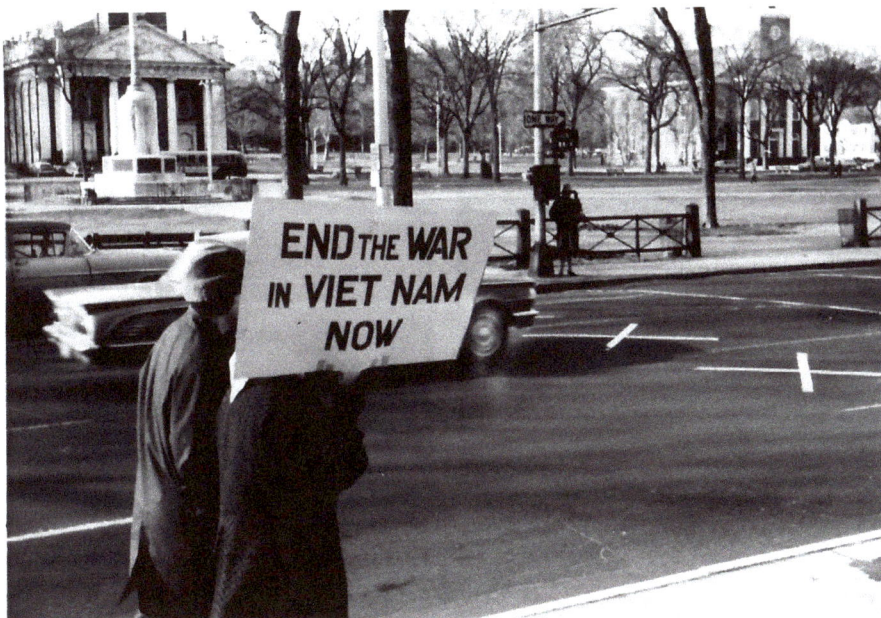

Anti-war demonstration, New Haven, 1964

July 4th patriotism at Livonia, Michigan, 1965

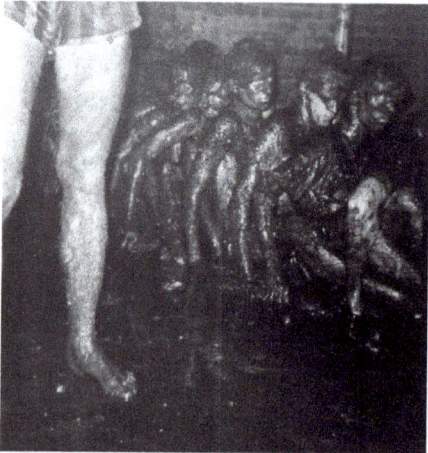

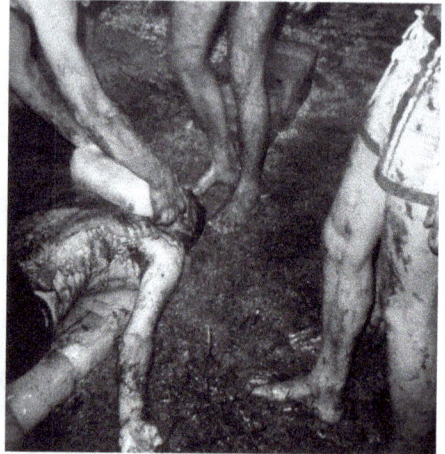

Freshers under assault, St John's College Brisbane, 1966

Clearing the garbage on Hayman Island, 1966

Vietnam war moratorium demonstration, Sydney Town Hall, 1970

Anti-apartheid demonstration, Springboks–Wallabies rugby test,
Sydney Cricket Ground, 1971

Aboriginal Tent Embassy, Canberra, 1972
Elizabeth Dalley facing camera

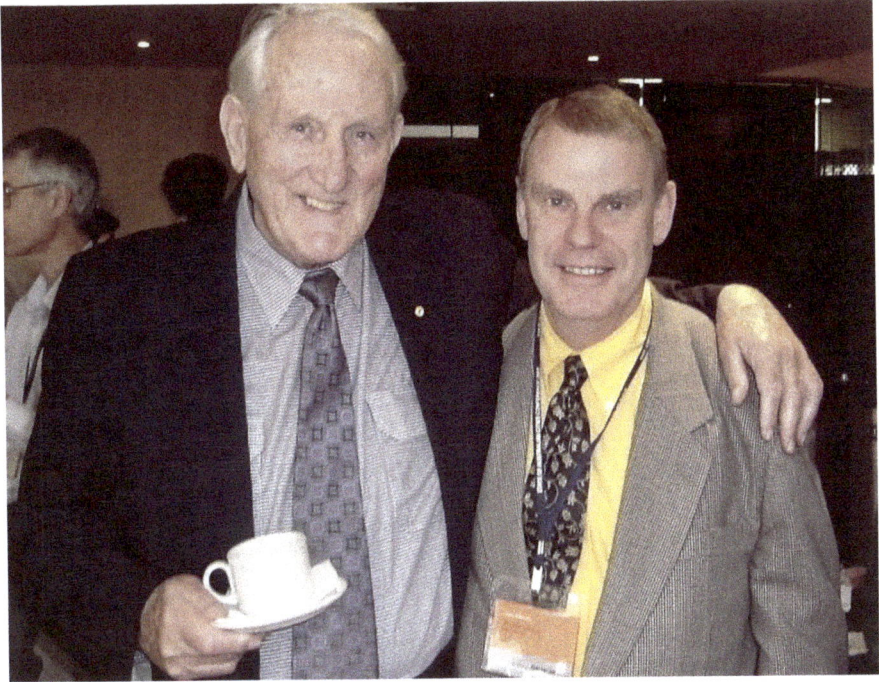

The author with Tom Uren at State of the Cities conference, Parramatta, December 2003

*The author, Patrick Troy, a conference host and
Hein Struben at karaoke in Japan, 1989*

Peter Till, wearing his trademark red skivvy, with Jill Lang and the author in our backyard in Turner, ACT, 1974

Ex-DURD people and friends after Tom Uren's memorial service, 4 February 2015 Back from left: David Chesterman, Germanus Pause, Cathi Moore, unidentified, unidentified, Jill Lang, Michael Eyers; front from centre: Diane Talty, John Mant (in whose Sydney Town Hall office we were), and unidentified

With friend Keshav, drinking chang, Kathmandu, 1976

Wedding procession, Kathmandu, 1976
Note Jim Carmody centre of crowd

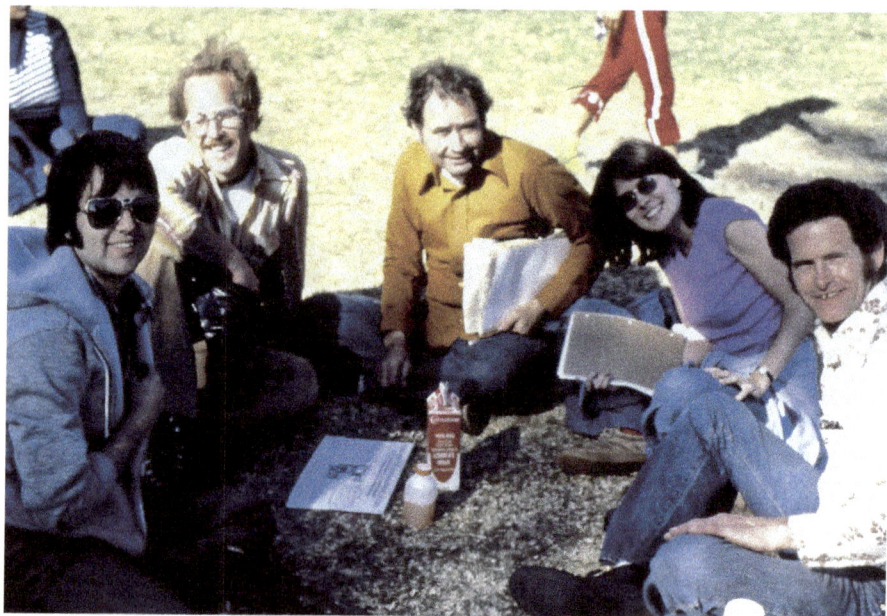

Members of the East Bay Chapter, Northern California Alliance

Northern California Alliance demonstration, Oakland, 1977

Reunion with friends from California days while at the UN World Urban Forum,
Vancouver, 2006
From left: John Friedmann, Leonie Sandercock, Wendy Sarkissian, Janice Perlman

NSW Department of Environment and Planning executive group, 1987
From left: Neville Apitz, Les McGowan, Gabrielle Kibble (Deputy Director),
John Roseth, Jim Waugh, unidentified, Sam Haddad (partly obscured), Sue Holliday,
Richard Smyth (Director), Elaine Stewart, the author

AIUS China delegation, 1984
From left: Bid Wardlaw, Henry Wardlaw, Jeremy Dawkins, Lyndsay Neilson,
Jane Neilson, Blair Badcock, Vivian Lin, David Chesterman, Michael Bennett, Marie
Heaney, Cris Cifuentes, Guangdong official, Di Talty (looking away)

Down-home briefing on Xiamen urban plan, 1984
From left, seated: Xiamen official, David Chesterman, Marie Heaney,
Jeremy Dawkins; on the floor: John Toon, Zhu Xiao Jian, our guide, Vivian Lin

The author with Hu Qili, wife Hao Keming and daughter Hu Lan at Zhongnanhai (Party headquarters, Beijing) shortly before Tiananmen incident, 1989

*NSW government planner exchangees, 1986
From left: Gillian Reffell, Yang Gang, Planning Minister Bob Carr, Deng Yuyou, David Kanaley*

In the faculty, 1989
From left: Chris Ryan, director of the Key Centre for Urban Design,
Leon van Schaik, Head of the Department of Architecture, the author

The 'three monkeys', ca. 1995
From left: Ruth Dunkin, Deputy Vice-Chancellor of Teaching and Learning,
David Beanland, Vice-Chancellor, the author

RMIT deans, 1989
Back from left: Leon van Schaik, the author,
Peter Done (applied science); front from left: David Pugh (research),
John Milton-Smith (business), Michael Ramsden (applied social sciences
and communications), Rod Clarke (art), Bill Carroll (engineering)

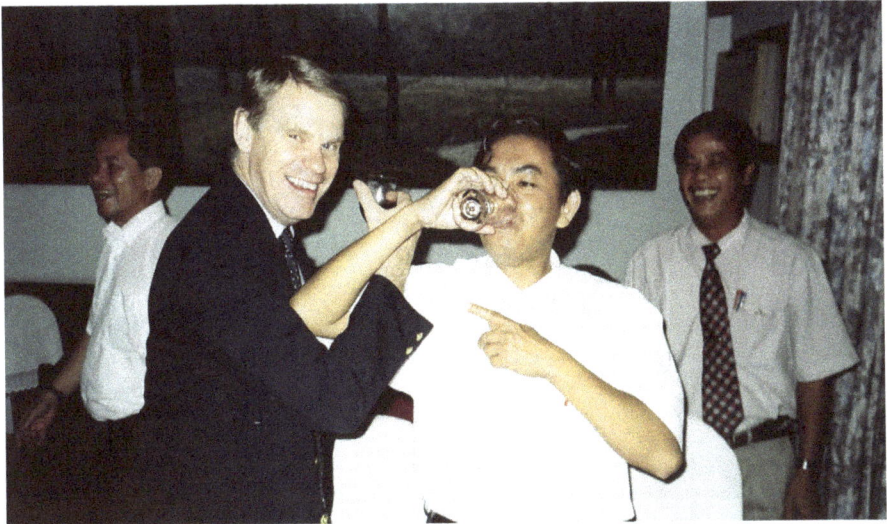

The hazards of doing international business:
RMIT-Vinatex agreement signing, Vietnam, 2002

With PM Paul Keating, Inaugural Australian Export Award for Education, 1998

Display model of RMIT Penang campus, 1996
Central four persons, from left: Tunku Dato' Dr Ismail Jewa, Professor David Beanland,
Tan Sri Dr Koh Tsu Koon, Dato' John Fong

his minority report, to the more senior policy and priorities committee of cabinet, where his right wing faction of the party had the numbers, and got withdrawal of the original SEPP endorsed. In October, Bedford finally had the decision on the replacement SEPP overturned too, to be replaced with the non-statutory urban consolidation program, a more moderate multi-pronged approach setting local development targets with more geographic and design sensitivities.[18]

There was some clear water ahead. Meanwhile, though, more and more local councils were seeking exemptions from dual occupancy provisions and the NSW Land and Environment Court upheld some council appeals against inappropriate higher densities. Plausible but superficial international comparative research that linked high urban density with energy saving and the efficient use of existing urban infrastructure was shown up as poorly based.

Denser new development in NSW too often meant denser outer suburbs and not urban infill, because that's where new houses were being built. The consequence of mandated small maximum residential lot sizes are there for all to see in Sydney's suburbs today; big houses (I dare not call them 'McMansions') squeezed together. The vision of more efficient use of the urban capital stock and savings to the public works program had a continuing appeal in the economic agencies of government. However, political infighting had given urban consolidation a bad name, even among its former supporters, as a half thought through means of saving urban infrastructure costs.

By this time Pat Troy had become a scathing opponent of urban consolidation, NSW-style. As he saw it, from his research on housing density and utility costs, the policy had no evidence base, and indeed the evidence pointed the other way: '... the simplistic initiatives designed to produce *consolidation* are more likely to intensify environmental stresses rather than ameliorate them'.[19] Among other things, Pat thought it would destroy the Australian backyard, a traditional refuge of the working class.

Our work, including my own research, was showing there was indeed an evidence basis for urban consolidation, but it was overstated and miscast by NSW government statements. Pat was not at all happy with me, but he reserved his rancour for Peter Newton, a Western Australian academic who used comprehensive but sweeping international correlations of urban density with wellbeing.[20] The argument between these two went on for decades, indeed it continued up to Pat's untimely death in 2018.

In any case, the government's rationale for urban consolidation policy shifted, from saving infrastructure costs to promoting housing variety, better urban design, and a mix of lifestyles. A new design manual for medium density housing showed how it could be done. State adoption of non-binding local government targets for multi-unit housing brought an effort to find infill development sites in built up areas, through the development of surplus government sites and Landcom and public housing programs, to support infill and sub-regional centres. But even by the end of the 1980s, urban consolidation policy had not brought a significant change in Sydney's housing structure.

In hindsight, housing density plans have mattered less than the local area housing target-setters wanted. To twist an old saying — the planning dogs barked in the night, but the development caravan moved on.[21] Market-led urban consolidation, as we defined it, has now become the reality in greater Sydney, with dwellings other than houses running around 60 percent of approvals, driven by foreign investment—at least until the pandemic-induced recession—and significant changes to housing preferences and household structure.[22] Was this really the denser Sydney we wanted then? Broadly, yes. What was the metropolitan plan around it?

Making the metropolitan plan

The mandate for metropolitan planning in NSW came from the government's recognition of the need for a new framework for urban expansion. The designated land release areas set by the Troy review and embodied in the urban development program were going beyond the open-ended corridors of the Sydney region outline plan of 1968 (SROP), with quite different economic, financial and demographic conditions now in play.[23] Medium-term expansion options and a site for Sydney's second airport needed to be decided upon.

That Sydney is unusually hemmed in by sea and national parks, an encircling vulnerable river system, good agricultural land, flood liability and other shortages of developable land, all contributed to a sense of urgency over spiralling land prices and delays and confusion over implementation arrangements for SROP. John Paterson's urban policy review encompassing the whole Newcastle–Sydney–Wollongong conurbation would have set the regional framework, but something more specific was needed.[24]

In my division Bob Meyer knew potential urban areas well and led the work on long- and medium-term options, along with Brian Riera and Christina DeMarco, the latter going on later to lead British Colombia's role in Vancouver's metropolitan planning. She and Peter Spearritt wrote a good book on Sydney's metropolitan development.[25] This long-term and medium-term strategy work was overseen by the department's executive and by ministers on the housing committee of cabinet, supported by other agencies on the urban development committee (UDC), each agency seeking answers to metropolitan priority and location questions, especially the transport agencies. Later, the work was supported by local governments wanting an overview, and by industry associations wanting more certainty in development markets. But the origins of metropolitan strategy lay more in the department's background work, the committee rooms of government and the state Labor government's agenda for reform.

A formal review of the Sydney region outline plan in 1980 kicked off that work on long-term options and by the end of 1981 it was ready to report to the HCC, which then in February 1982 endorsed a further work program and asked for it to present two options with different second Sydney airport locations, Scheyville and Badgerys Creek.[26] A population of 4.75 million was assumed (then likely to be reached by 2015), along with assumptions of population density (ironically, by government analysts sceptical about its own urban consolidation targets) and population, workforce and employment distribution forecasts, transport assumptions and developable urban land estimates. In May it endorsed structure plans for the northwest and Bringelly sectors to be incorporated into the metropolitan structure plan.

By September the UDC's transport strategy advisory committee produced its 'first cut' of a Sydney urban expansion study, serviced by my divisional team and the state transport study group, an inter-agency team made up of full-time secondees.[27] The report discussed at length the corridor options and used the long-term urban land use options for employment distribution forecasts provided by the metropolitan strategy team. There was still a good database left from the 1974 Sydney area transportation study.[28] The DEP—mostly my division—was to produce issue papers on different elements of the strategy such as sub-centres and office location and the rural–urban fringe. There was a lot of work to do in a short time, so 'educated guesses' were acceptable.

New to the work, I worried about the westward-only thrust, as most people wanted to live in the east even though the development options there were limited.[29] Moreover, western development contributed less-dispersible air pollution into the Sydney basin and more water runoff pollution into the Hawkesbury–Nepean river system that encircled it. Dick Smyth, DEP director, agreed, and we looked harder in the east, but the yield was small, with some gains in options for Gosford–Wyong limited by subsidence from old coal mines.

The second progress report to HCC in November followed the directions of the 'first cut'. Within the department the designation of sub-regional centres in Sydney also created a sharp but productive debate with the regional managers, for example with Sue Holliday arguing for Blacktown.

During this time, there was great interest in our metropolitan strategy work in and out of the government, and I consciously spent time present-ing in public and in government circles, gathering views. Though this could not be called real public participation, it became a formal consulta-tion program and the feedback was useful in modifying our plans.

Technical work on the approach approved by the HCC brought back fully developed forecasts and strategies in December, with detailed mod-elling work to culminate in a further 'cut' in April 1984 for approval by September that year in time for the impending environmental impact statement for Sydney's second airport.[30] This 'second cut' seemed insensi-tive to alternative options, and major corridor patronage forecasts went down because work had shown there would be more dispersion of trips among centres than we had assumed, even though we edged up the extent of likely urban consolidation.

I was concerned about the lack of commitment to fixed rail investment implied by the strategy because cars and buses would otherwise fill the roads and spread employment, but there was little political encouragement in this direction. For the northwest and southwest sectors, regional environmental plans were being prepared, and we modified assumptions for them, though Peter Kacirek, the chairman of the Macarthur Development Board and ex-chief planner of the State Planning Authority, was recalcitrant about DEP intruding into his domain.[31]

Work otherwise went smoothly. Agencies accepted a size-related rather than time-related approach on the basis that metropolitan growth management, particularly through the urban development program, could be adjusted for varying rates of population, household and employment growth. They were, however, concerned at the 'end state' feel of it, that it paid too little attention to social and technological change likely over the period. They were also sceptical about urban consolidation targets, being by then actively pursued, the prospects for decentralisation beyond the region implied by the numbers, and the appearance that the plan equated public transport with fixed rail provision yet made no new transit proposals.[32] I agreed with these concerns but shared the frustration of the strategy team that we could do little on the latter point.

Peter Self, an eminent British academic and policy adviser, who had been engaged with DURD, also reviewed our work in progress. He argued that the timeframe was too long, that social changes had not been given the attention that employment had, that conflicting objectives had not been reconciled, that the CBD and growth along the eastern seaboard had not been sufficiently considered, and that the strategy closed off alternative options too drastically and should be explored more.[33] Most but not all of these were taken into a revised work program going into 1985, including a number of further issues papers that played out alternative scenarios. However, deadlines and shortages of high-level professionals limited our taking up other comments.

By September 1985, work was well advanced and it was time to take the department's executive through the latest draft in detail. I circulated working drafts in December 1985 and April 1986. The land use and transport assumptions were settled so it was possible to contribute to the decision to locate the second Sydney airport at Badgerys Creek without a final plan being in place. The transport and aviation authorities were happy to have reliable forecasts to present their recommendation as a technical, not political decision. They were also happy to recommend, through the metropolitan strategy, the removal of superfluous road reservations and infrastructure proposals that had been in the Sydney region outline plan since 1968.

As a result of regular meetings between NSW and Victorian planning executives, which were very useful to both sides, Evan Walker, the Victorian planning minister, and David Yencken, his department head, invited me to spend some time transferring the NSW urban development program into Victorian practice, ultimately to become their metropolitan services coordination system. They were very impressed with it. My departmental leaders were happy to release me for a week or so, given the prestige in transferring the NSW know-how. I realised this might divert my work on Sydney.

I forwarded a presentation of advanced work in progress on the Sydney metropolitan strategy to the DEP executive to be considered while I was away for a week in Melbourne. I was not too concerned because Bob Meyer and John Roseth knew the work well and should have been able to handle it. However, it did not turn out well.

In my absence, my executive colleagues did not feel it was ready for exposure and were critical of some of its elements. Around that, some feelings had built up that the CPD in general and I, in particular, were not fully 'loyal' to the department, that we were serving the needs of government as a whole through our efforts on urban service and finance coordination, that unlike other divisions we were not driven by the EP&A Act, the department's raison d'être, and perhaps that we were over-friendly with those around the HCC who too often 'had it in' for the department. Whether these factors were true or not, on return to Sydney

I faced a departmental reorganisation in which I had a new division to run, planning division (south). I was very disappointed with the lack of support from my colleagues and at my own poor political judgment.

In truth, the executive group was not harmonious. Dick Smyth earlier recognised that and hired Tony Eddison, a prominent British corporate planning expert, with his partner, to lead us through quite deep psycho-social territory. As part of this they tested us to define our Myers-Briggs personality types, in an effort to understand why we were not a particularly coherent team (my type was ENTP: extroversion, intuition, thinking, perceiving), and find ways in which we might work better. This type of management intervention was popular during the 1980s. The agreements to work better together with honesty and transparency worked for a time, but the executive team stayed strained.

Back at the research division, into which the old CPD was now merged, the final draft of the metropolitan strategy was produced in November 1986. The draft was not very different from the one I had framed—smoother, certainly—and it was frustrating to have little say in it anymore. It went through more versions before it was published as *Sydney Into Its Third Century* by the new planning minister, Bob Carr, in 1988.[34]

The metropolitan strategy did not take the form of a regional environmental plan (REP) under the EP&A Act; like SROP, it was intended more as a management guideline than a statutory policy. Its projections, for example, were tied to regional population thresholds as we intended, rather than particular years. Population forecasts had been the bane of SROP's implementation, as growth inevitably defied the planners' and demographers' timelines. The aim was neither to promote the growth of Sydney, nor to discourage it, but to manage better its waves of growth and change, particularly the indirect effects of changing overseas migration and direct foreign investment. I was very interested in foreign investment into urban development, chairing an Australian Institute of Urban Studies (AIUS) commission into finance and investment.

I would lunch regularly with developer friends. I liked that they were doing real things, like building the city, though I refrained from talking about projects in which I had a stake. Long lunches were part of doing business then, notably on the iron lace clad veranda of the old New Hellas restaurant overlooking Hyde Park. Dining with developers was not common practice among the career planners in the department, for whom many were the enemy. I must admit, there were some unconscionable developments being pushed onto Sydney at the time, including a wily operator buying surplus rail land near the airport and putting up ugly thin buildings and billboard structures there.

For planning Sydney there was still a premium on predicting population and employment growth, and the department published good demographic forecasts at regular intervals. We proselytised this way of managing metropolitan growth and of accommodating high levels of international migration, defensible for economic and multicultural reasons, and for a while Minister Carr went along with it.[35] Given decent forecasting and land release and infrastructure programming, any rate of growth could be accommodated. My technocratic idealism was showing through, but everyone around me agreed.

I learnt from Bob Carr about how to prepare advice. He would ask for the 'clinching statistic', a single powerful fact that could lead a headline. He had a sense of humour, too. Once, at a function when Barry Unsworth (a later Labor premier) was droning on, my young daughter Maya started grizzling loudly. He turned around and said, 'I don't blame her'.

On his and our advice, Neville Wran went to a premiers' conference with a proposal for favourable commonwealth infrastructure funding to help accommodate growing migrant intakes to Sydney. But he was shot down by Queensland premier, Jo Bjelke-Petersen, who said something like 'international migrants might go to NSW but more people are moving to Queensland after that!' It was true: Queensland did have many net internal migrants from NSW. That stung Bob Carr, who later set out to limit Sydney's suburban growth to promote urban consolidation, earning him, fairly or not, a reputation as the originator of the year 2000 catchphrase 'Sydney's full'. Deliberate slowdowns in the urban development program after I left, and the residential land shortages that resulted, helped set back Sydney's metropolitan planning for more than a decade, with Melbourne taking over as the metropolis of largest absolute population growth and contribution to GDP.[36]

But the story is getting ahead of itself. For the metropolitan strategy in the 1980s, when it came to small area forecasts, such as at the local government area level, it was essential to feed in current and proposed population and employment distribution policies but not to believe in their immutability. Of course, for land release and infrastructure phasing careful timelines were essential. The decision to pitch the metropolitan strategy at the 4.5m regional population threshold was taken on the grounds that the 4m mark was already well within medium-term urban infrastructure commitments, and that the 5m mark was too far away.[37] The keynote was to create a robust framework for urban management into an unknowable future, rather than impose an exciting, if contestable, vision onto the region. The strategy was intended for periodic update and review, and even before the decade was out, the first update was published.[38]

The strategy was a modernised version of SROP matched to the new tools of the EP&A Act and growth management programs like the urban development and urban consolidation programs. It covered the conventional topics of population, land and housing, economic development and employment, manufacturing and services sectors, transport, regional open space, recreation and tourism, but had stronger inclusion of human services and public finance. Key spatial elements were the promotion of regional and sub-regional centres and selected business parks through growth in tertiary sector jobs, evidence-based designation of areas for expansion outside areas unsuited to urban development, and the protection of regional open space.

The strategy was not accompanied by full public infrastructure or transport strategies. However, less visible as direct outcomes of this work were a number of important decisions from agencies only too pleased to accept authorised forecasts of population and employment distribution and medium-term land development schedules. The decision to locate Sydney's second airport at Badgerys Creek (if not, unfortunately, to get on and implement it); the dramatic rescheduling of Sydney's freeway system and release of unnecessary road reservations; the alignment of the proposed very fast train and the rescheduling of water and sewerage major works all came out of the working groups on metropolitan strategy.[39] The state transport study group played a vital role in creating a shared information and analytical capacity for transport and land use decisions, something that Victoria, by comparison, lost through outsourcing its transport modelling capacity to universities that had to beg for funds and ultimately dropped the activity.[40] Then NSW followed suit this way and threw away its metropolitan database and modelling capacity too. The cities are the poorer for this type of 'hollowing out of the state'.

Improvement to public transport in Sydney was less a priority for metropolitan planning in part because it tended to be seen as an operational issue—for example, the regulation of expansion of suburban bus lines—other than advocacy of essential heavy rail links connecting corridors. Some of the other major new investments in transport infrastructure Sydney now enjoys were then not on the agenda, other than a new Sydney Harbour tunnel, studies for which drew me in. The state started outsourcing infrastructure development to public–private partnerships, favouring expressways, and shifted priorities for preparation for the 2000 Olympic Games. It lost track of coordinating urban infrastructure, and Sydney's growth has been served since by a succession of poorly linked and poorly scheduled infrastructure projects.

The shelf life of the 1988 *Sydney Into Its Third Century* was not long, as metropolitan plans go, replaced by *Cities for the 21st Century* in 1995. In urban development, by contrast, lead times are long. Though the premier's clamp on Sydney's expansion did hold back the region's growth, land shortages ultimately contributed to higher densities and infill development.[41] The succession of other plans that followed also contributed to Sydney losing its reputation for good metropolitan planning.

Boosting Sydney's centres

A clearer success of metropolitan strategy, in that development as planned was realised, came through the metropolitan centres policy, with the official designation of business centres in Sydney giving confidence to private development and setting priorities for accelerated, and even sometimes coordinated, infrastructure at selected centres.[42]

The plan designated Parramatta as a regional centre—to counterbalance central and north Sydney—and 19 sub-regional centres in hierarchical order. The aims of the policy were to:

+ Encourage a fairer distribution of office jobs in the Sydney region
+ Promote and accommodate job growth in the centres
+ Promote the use of public transport, keep centres the major focus for retail and community services
+ Improve the urban environment in the centres, and
+ Encourage higher-density housing in and around centres where appropriate.[43]

The policy needed a campaign of persuasion, especially for local areas missing out, but the act of designation itself spurred private sector interest and development, making the campaign enjoyable and, over time, successful.[44] In 1986, in an act of integration of strategic and statutory planning, DEP recommended, and the minister 'made', a Sydney REP for commercial centres, codifying policy for the central area and north Sydney, sub-regional centres, secondary centres, commercial premises, retail premises, bulky goods and business parks.[45]

Before that, in 1982, based in part on our division's work and led by Glen Searle, the government, once Treasury was persuaded there were savings to be gained, showed its resolve by deciding to relocate, by 1990, 7000 government office employees, largely from central Sydney, to Parramatta (4500, the first phase), Liverpool (1000), Campbelltown (1000) and Penrith (500), with a pilot project to Blacktown to consolidate nearby office employment.[46] All were key designated sub-regional centres.[47] In what must have been a rush of blood to the heads of ministers, these moves covered headquarter offices, including the Department of Education. I thought this part was too much, bound for a backlash, but was happy with the results overall.

These moves picked up from our Whitlam government experience of a decade before, and a failed previous state effort. The relocations were justified at the time by the prospect of $89m rental savings on central city leases and later again after the coalition Greiner government came to power in 1988 on further savings from a program of relocations out of the city centre but not to the west. While the choice of so many centres in the metropolitan strategy, with Fairfield added in 1989, has been criticised as politically motivated, particularly the choice of centres for state government office relocation, at least the centres chosen were generally consistent with employment growth forecasts in the metropolitan strategy, and vice-versa. That is cause for satisfaction.

There was government-wide concern with the administrative efficiency of dispersal to different centres, and in 1985 the DEP and Public Service Board reviewed the program and recommended recalibration to build up Parramatta more and scale back the other sub-regional centres.[48] Parramatta, designated as the 'second CBD' for the region, needed more support. By then private office development was suburbanising strongly.[49] The government was not sufficiently disciplined to resist more local proposals and by 1988, when the government changed, employment relocation destinations included Bankstown, Hurstville, Chatswood, Ashfield, Rosehill, Alexandria and Surry Hills. The Western Sydney Regional Organisation of Councils (WSROC) objected to this spread strongly because they were for the most part outside western Sydney and undercut the primacy of Parramatta.[50]

The growth of suburban offices was abetted by the deregulation of the financial system, and particularly the relaxation of Foreign Investment Review Board constraints on direct foreign investment in real estate, for which I chaired the AIUS investigation.[51] Parramatta and Chatswood, in particular, underwent spectacular booms, and other centres, given the nod by state policy, attracted tertiary employment through private office developments around railway stations. Further out, centres like Campbelltown and its Macarthur Development Corporation, originally supported through state and commonwealth growth centre programs and their successors, continued to fall short of the social and employment goals of the 1980s, especially with respect to the balance between sub-regional population growth and employment. They faced high sub-regional unemployment. Dispersed industrial zones, no longer likely to accommodate factories, were opened up to a miscellaneous category of developments, including high-tech start-ups and 'big box' retail, which no longer fitted the land use categories envisaged by the Sydney planning system. Where metropolitan planning was able to steer private development near to where it might have gone anyway (for example, to metropolitan sub-centres), it tended to meet its aims, but where major changes in policy or spatial structure were needed, and a redirection of major patterns of metropolitan growth attempted, they did not succeed. This is not a criticism for trying. The regional balance between jobs and work lies at the heart of what makes cities liveable.

This imbalance in Sydney has since worsened. Employment location cannot be planned with the certainty of housing land releases, and if anything, the physical development planning visions of Sydney in SROP and the County of Cumberland plan had better staying power, if less relevance to the central issues of government, than the more sophisticated managerial style of metropolitan strategy of the 1980s.

Efforts to address employment generation and economic development, including in the built-up areas, marked this generation of metropolitan planning over the previous one. The urban economics of the Hunter–Sydney–Illawarra regional complex were little understood despite their obvious movement to an integrated labour market and their inclusion in transport-land use modelling. It is good to see later versions of Sydney's metropolitan strategy, of which there have been several more, recognising these interrelationships.

Because of the relative lack of jobs in outer Sydney, I encouraged more work on employment planning and economic development, some of it sponsored by local councils or trade unions, and much of it led by Edward Blakely, my Berkeley friend now living in Sydney.[52] Sadly, much of this groundbreaking work attracted little interest; I recall Ed at a press conference on a hot day to announce the results of the Illawarra employment study, resplendent in a three-piece suit, but only a handful of uninterested journalists turned up.[53] From around then, though, local authorities, especially in outer urban areas, started to hire economic development planners in the hope of attracting investment and generating local employment; this was a field in which Ed was a pioneer.

Alongside the new local economic development planning was a

change in the style of regional mobilisation within Sydney, particularly in Sydney's west. A rise in regional consciousness, promoted by earlier commonwealth assistance to regional organisations of councils (in this case WSROC), and furthered by the location of several pivotal electorates and some key hospital and university decisions, built up a surge in regional entrepreneurship and political power that has not turned back. Whether or not this is 'dressing up the suburbs' or a deeper-rooted self-reliance, the repositioning of western Sydney's image has had a major effect on patterns of investment.[54] Much of its development was affected by how well urban expansion was organised.

Managing urban expansion

Sydney has been unusually prone to fluctuations in the residential land market. The incoming Labor government in 1978 set up a DURD-style public land developer, Landcom, mentioned earlier. Its aim was to bring downward price pressure through competition with the private sector, and thus make housing more affordable. It was able to acquire a large land bank from overextended private land developers. Many decision-makers held a belief that there was adequate land released, such as that rezoned under SROP, but in practice much of it was not coming onto the market through delays in detailed development control planning, disputes over road locations, fragmented land ownership and speculative withholding by private owners. Agencies disagreed on how much land was really available. The land price spiral was becoming a potential political crisis, affecting other regions too, if less acutely. The development coordination committee of cabinet hired Pat Troy urgently to review land availability and what should be done to bring it into urban development in a coordinated way. His report was as much about the coordination of planning and services as about raw land availability.[55]

On that basis, in 1980 the government pulled together information on stocks and flows of residential land at each stage of the pipeline, and formulated a rolling five-year program to try to ensure this would not happen again. The first urban development program (UDP) sought to produce 55,000 lots and keep two years' equivalent of supply available at any one time. I supported this as a means of helping keep new houses affordable, but I was under no illusion that zoned and serviced land automatically would come onto the market. The inter-agency urban development committee was formed, reporting to the housing committee of cabinet.

When I joined DEP in 1982 my division was responsible for coordinating the program and I was in the thick of it.[56] It was the largest of our responsibilities as it required good forecasting, integration with long-term and medium-term plans (as a means of implementing them), contact with myriad service providers, public and private, and disciplined resolution of urban policy issues over whether and when to release land. In other words, it was the key decision-making arena for the expansion of Sydney and its adjoining regions, and I felt well prepared to lead the work. We saw a number of ways the program could be developed further.

The original decision to establish the UDP required urban development schedules to include costs and timing for each public authority, by release area where appropriate, and reports on this came back to the UDP in 1981 and, in a fuller version, in 1982. The link with DURD's urban and regional budget experience was obvious to me, and this seemed a great opportunity not only to signal to government the cost implications of different release options and feed the best options back into sequencing decisions, but to highlight the complex financing issues holding back adequate service delivery and support the government's reform processes and its intergovernmental finance-raising campaigns.

The inadequacy of suburban services was a major social and political issue, with backlogs and gaps to be addressed. The issue went to the heart of social equity as many people with limited means could afford to live only in newer fringe suburbs. Early in 1983, DEP won the 'all clear' from Treasury to proceed with prior 1980 obligations to report on infrastructure financing, to feed into that year's Loan Council negotiations with the commonwealth. At the urging of Julie Walton in the minister's office the urban development financial program was extended to the Hunter, Central Coast and Illawarra regions, in a form simpler than Sydney.

The early stages of the urban development financial program needed work by agencies that had not previously held financial data by area in consistent ways. Different agencies used different planning methods, standards and sub-regional boundaries. Some were reluctant to account for full costs. In 1985 the parliamentary public accounts committee insisted that the UDC, and particularly Landcom, do just that.[57] Agencies whose services depended crucially on the timing and location of urban development were supporters of the program. They tended to be the capital-intensive network infrastructure providers: water, sewerage, drainage, roads and electricity. Telecommunications (semi-private) and gas services (in Sydney, private) were more content to follow urban development decisions and not to lead them.

Services delivered from particular locations, and not through networks (community services, health services, schools, technical and further education, welfare services), were less sensitive in terms of cost-effectiveness to alternative patterns of urban development, even if they incurred substantial capital costs overall. However, human services were most sensitive to the relationship between new urban development and areas of high need, past service backlogs, and social equity. Some services were so 'lumpy' that their catchment areas covered whole subregions rather than particular release areas; for example, airports, major hospitals, bridges and rail extensions. They were vital to urban development planning but not always relevant to choosing small-area priorities.

Treasury and its capital works unit understood the concepts and were generally cooperative—a welcome change from the commonwealth Treasury a decade before—but they were reluctant to release publicly small-area data, or total estimates of finance requirements, for fear of raising public expectations. The program certainly had ambiguities in this respect, being a combination of objective reporting and area advocacy. On the one hand, it put to ministers the forward capital costs of urban development, with estimates of what could be recouped from charges and what unrecouped costs would need to be financed. This helped the government in the budget round and in setting borrowing priorities, the latter including bids for federal assistance.

On the other hand, it was designed to press upon government the financial requirements for services to particular areas that may or may not be fully funded, hence Treasury's discomfort. Also, area budgets can cut across functional budgets and therefore ministerial preferences and prerogatives, so there was discomfort from here too. Nevertheless, the program developed on a confidential intra-governmental basis with some limited disclosures made. In 1985 Ken Booth, the treasurer, assented to full disclosure in the 1985/86 state budget papers and thereafter. I was glad to bring my DURD experience to bear.

More than now, most urban service providers were public entities, and the requirements for water, sewerage and drainage connections a much-used hook on which planners could hang their zoning plans and development consents. The provision of state-controlled services during this time became the focus of political conflict and the metropolitan strategy provided an arena for playing out policy responses. Two sets of issues dominated.

The first was to do with the pricing, supply and management of water services: water supply, sewerage, drainage, environmental protection and related open spaces. As the straitening intergovernmental financial climate conflicted with the generous land release provisions and high service standards of the past, the pressure on capital works and pricing policies was sharp. User pays mechanisms were strengthened to rationalise service use and raise revenue, and private providers such as major development companies were able to move their prospective release sites up the land development queue if they could financially supplement the headworks services planning work of the over-stretched utilities, or provide lesser items of infrastructure themselves.[58] I was happy with this nod to neo-liberalism.

The second, related set of issues played out more at the local level and in the NSW Land and Environment Court. The well-intended inclusion of Section 94 in the EP&A Act, designed to allow but limit local authority exaction of contributions for local services, opened up hundreds of disputes and threatened a number of major development decisions. My division took on a number of research projects about development costs and contributions, including review of the extensive experience overseas.[59]

Though DEP provided guidelines for local governments squeezing out development contributions, and upper limits particularly, in matters that would come to the minister, well-reasoned local service plans, and rulings by the courts as to what made up a reasonable nexus between a development and service needs arising, continued to cause conflict and confusion. The placing of limits did not endear Bob Carr, minister for planning and environment, to local government.[60] The urban development committee and the housing committee of cabinet were the key arenas both for guidelines about development contributions (the NSW Land Commission with a seat at the table arguing for the developers) and for the metropolitan plan, and the policies could be linked. Though they were at different ends of the suburban development pipeline, I was happy about this.

The Sydney metropolitan strategy made itself useful for providing more explicit development policy for the region on which servicing plans and development contributions could be based. But no amount of rational thinking and clear strategy could stop controversy about urban growth—including urban consolidation, levies on developers, using up rural land for urban development—which rage around most metropolitan regions in the democratic world. Even the best of technocratic planning cannot avoid—should not avoid—the contestation of interest groups and political parties.

In any case, I now had to bring my mind to practical regional planning, not urban development financing policy.

Regional planning, NSW-style

The latter part of my work at DEP, as head of planning division south, was a change of pace and style; it focused on more orderly negotiations with proponents of development and local governments rather than state agencies. Its territory covered the southern and far west of the state, including Sydney south of the harbour, though Sue Holliday, deputy director and my boss, tended to handle key City of Sydney issues. It entailed working with our regional managers, who reported to me, and handling recommendations about major local environmental plans (LEPs), regional environmental plans, approving developments of state significance, and being involved in big projects that might not—or at least at the stage I was involved—require a plan or approval. This work had to be very careful, and the managers' and my desks were piled with thick files secured by real red tape. More pleasantly, the work involved chairing multi-sector regional planning and development committees for most of my regions, meeting people across the state with many issues to push.

The Kosciusko (as it was spelt then) regional planning committee meetings were typically held on Fridays so that people could stay the weekend in the Australian Alps, though accepting invitations from Hoyts, the operator of ski-town Thredbo, was clearly a no-no. That didn't stop us joining them off-piste at our expense, at least until one of our group was seriously injured in a skiing accident. The national park was formally excluded from our ambit, but clearly plans and development consents had to be harmonised.

The Illawarra region was obviously larger and more complex for regional planning. Key tasks here were to prepare a regional plan for the region and run the urban development program.[61] Wollongong was led by Lord Mayor Frank Arkell, murdered in 1998 after being named in the Woods Royal Commission into a Wollongong paedophile ring. Alongside regional plan formation and major development consents there was a complex pattern of coal mine consents that allowed road haulage down the steep coastal escarpment only by ministerial consent. More than once a tramp carrier appeared unannounced out to sea, typically on a Friday afternoon, needing urgent contact and my recommendation to the minister to approve road haulage of coal at short notice, hardly an accidental opportunity for the hauliers.

The Murray–Darling river system is the lifeblood of inland NSW and the department proposed a regional plan regulating riparian development rights, seeking to keep developments off flood-liable and otherwise-sensitive lands along the river banks. Typically for the federal system we have, the plan was not paralleled on the Victorian side of the Murray, with NSW territory technically 'owning' the river space.[62] Steering this one past the irrigators and farmers, local development interests and environmentalists took navigation worthy of the rivers themselves, and many meetings in interesting riverine towns like Albury, but we did the work and the regional plan was 'made'.[63]

Very fast train proposals along the east coast of Australia have come and gone, but the plan by a joint venture of BHP, Elders IXL, Kumagai Gumi and TNT, formed in September 1986, was the first of the serious ones. Originally conceived by Paul Wilde of the CSIRO, it captured the public's imagination and came close to realisation. My task, on behalf of a four-government group (NSW, Victoria, ACT and commonwealth) was to combine, or at least coordinate, the planning approvals and environmental impact assessment processes so that the proponents faced one regulatory course of hurdles, not four. With painstaking work, endless meetings and tedious collation of regulations, we came a long way towards that aim, so that the concept report, completed in December 1988, could reflect a harmonised regulatory process.[64] I was very satisfied; I thought I had brought a breakthrough. Then Victoria broke the consensus on the inland route and opted for a coastal route for reasons of regional development, not transport cost-effectiveness, and the deal fell apart. My friend Mal Logan chaired the review that came up with their position. This was not the only reason the venture failed, another was the inability to get special federal concessions for accelerated depreciation write-offs, but it was a fatal one. I ended up disappointed.

There were of course many other issues to deal with in planning division south. It was on the whole a pleasant and worthwhile time—good regional managers to work with, a good boss in Sue Holliday, and a learning curve on the instruments of the EP&A Act, on which before, as a strategic planner, I had been somewhat dismissive. I had more respect for them now.

While working at DEP I kept an interest in international issues of urban development and took leave from time to time to travel. To that we now turn.

Bonding with China

The AIUS visit

For years I'd followed China's development, through the Whitlam government's normalisation of diplomatic relations and the battles of the

Californian Left around Maoism (the NCA was not Maoist but other pre-party formations were). Vivian's extended family was in mainland China (she was born in Taiwan but grew up in the USA), and her involvement with the US China People's Friendship Association added to my interest. Low-key sister relationships between NSW state and Guangdong province on the one hand, and the City of Sydney and Guangzhou, Guangdong's capital city, on the other, were started some years before I returned to Sydney. Thankfully, and unlike Victoria and Melbourne, these NSW relationships were 'nested', that is, Guangzhou city fitted into Guangdong Province.

Vivian and I thought it would be fun to organise a professional visit of China and asked around for interest in an urban planning/public health themed tour. We found 15 or so people, mostly friends, and mostly urbanists. But for Vivian and Jeremy Dawkins, both of whom had visited during the Cultural Revolution, the rest of us were new to China. It turned out to be the starting point for many relationships and agreements to follow.

Vivian's extended uncle, Hu Qili, was in the politburo of the Communist Party of China, and her aunt, Hu Qihung, was president of the Chinese Academy of Sciences, so it was sensible on the basis of our *guanxi*, our connections, to arrange for the Science and Technology Commission to host the visit.

These were early years in China's reforms. My Chinese phrasebook still told me how to make dinner toasts like 'Long Live the Glorious People's Cultural Revolution' in Mandarin. Hu Qili visited Australia with Hu Yaobang in April 1985, and Vivian and I joined him at a state banquet. We invited him home on another night, and he slipped out of a dinner to come over to Balmain. Little did we know that for his visit the armed holdup squad of the NSW police closed our street for the occasion, to the puzzlement of frustrated neighbours, planting security people all around. We were only informed on the night, and handed out beers to the police after Hu left. In 1987, he was elected to the five-person standing committee of the politburo. He was the 'number two' in the country, and stayed there until he was purged in 1989.

For the Australian side, we flew flags of convenience. I chaired the international committee of the Australian Institute of Urban Studies, so we affiliated the visit with AIUS.[65] While in Guangdong and Guangzhou we carried the good offices of the NSW government (see the coming pages) and put NSW people to the front: David Chesterman, who ran an architecture and planning firm and was adept with the urban politics of Sydney; Henry Wardlaw, who chaired Landcom, ran one of DURD's divisions, and was once the equivalent of chief planner for Singapore (and who looked so much like Santa Claus he drew a crowd and relented, on a Shanghai boat trip, to sing *Jingle Bells*); Jeremy Dawkins, a fellow student from my Sydney days mentioned earlier; John Toon, our lecturer from the University of Sydney who had let Jeremy and me loose on the planning institute journal; Di Talty, who would go on to head the Darling Harbour Development Authority; and others. In a like manner, while in Tianjin, sister city with Melbourne, Lyndsay Neilson came to the front as he and his wife, who accompanied us on the trip, were Melbourne-based. Blair Badcock came from Adelaide but we flew no Adelaide flag.

Ties in Guangdong

Our mission from NSW was to 'find the gardeners'. Guangdong had offered a Chinese garden for Darling Harbour, a waterside development then in its planning stage, as a gift to NSW. The NSW sister state committee was somewhat ambivalent about China's intention in the relationship, as in 'What do they want from us? Will they take our technology?' But the minister for public works, Laurie Brereton, asked us to have a look at gardens in Guangzhou and find the 'official' agency for developing them. We took a map of the Darling Harbour development plan with us, showing where the gardens were to be. While we were away the Darling Harbour Authority changed the plan, shunting the garden to a less auspicious site, virtually a forecourt to a hotel. But we didn't know that.

We learnt that the Guangdong style of garden is informal, always features water, and is guided by *feng shui*. After some delightful garden visits and garden banquets, with David Chesterman at the front, we left a copy of the map containing the old site with our new friends in Guangzhou. We reported back, and later the province and the state reached agreement to proceed. When Laurie Brereton went up to sign the agreement, they showed him the old map with our designated site. Rather than lose face, he returned to Sydney and told the Darling Harbour planners to put the garden back where it had been originally planned. We were the accidental saviours of the site of what is now one of Sydney's most beautiful attractions.

Naturally, we did what we could to help the gardens get built. The deal enabled the gardeners, who transferred to Sydney for the project and for the most part had never left their country before, to bring in ceramics, but they had to source other building materials, plants and rocks from NSW wherever possible. Their exploration in the west of the state found some wonderfully convoluted limestone boulders, and the plants, many now mature trees, make the gardens what they are today.

These visits gave me an idea: why not exchange planners too? My DEP colleagues, including the director Gabrielle Kibble, went along with the idea, but we had to figure out how to fund it as the state wasn't in the business of funding overseas development projects. The Guangdong side was willing to put up all local expenses, so the living expenses of any NSW participants would be little. When we circulated for interest in an as-yet-undefined planning project in Guangdong, we made it a condition that the secondees put aside money enough to pay the costs of their Chinese counterparts while in NSW. This seemed to work: Gillian Reffell and David Kanaley were chosen to go to Guangdong for six months and four planners from there to NSW for three months.

What would the four Guangdong planners do in NSW? We accommodated them in a house left vacant by Madeline McClean and Craig Knowles, her then husband and later NSW minister for planning, as she moved west to run WSROC. The Guangdong planners came to work in DEP and essentially became professional interns, joining meetings, shadowing executives and doing some analytical work, a more casual design for learning than today's international internships. They certainly enjoyed it. I kept in touch and visited some of them on later trips to Guangdong.

What would the two NSW planners do in Guangdong? Given its origins in the 1984 delegation, the host agency was again the Guangdong Science and Technology Commission, not the Construction Commission where urban development responsibilities normally lie. Their hope was that our intrepid two would transfer modern techniques of urban planning to Guangdong. The commission chose a small town of Sanshui, a county (now district) in Foshan prefecture, and asked Gillian and David to make a 'plan' using modern techniques. As any urban planner in NSW knows, that's not quite how it works; there is a prescriptive Act setting out a process, and making the elements of a local plan is largely informed judgement, not all driven by data or technique. It would be hard to transfer technology or even know-how.

Nevertheless, Gillian and David soldiered on, gathering information, coming to understand local conditions, and on the whole settling into life in small-town China. After some months, though, the tension grew and approached a crisis point: what can they possibly do that is useful? I went up, ostensibly to do a mid-project review, and spent time reassuring this able pair. Just draw up an outline plan, and don't hold back with any recommendation, I advised. At the least, it might give them some useful ideas. The project came to a satisfactory conclusion with a well-produced report, and the planners came home.[66] None of us thought much would happen, but that was okay.

Some years later, David revisited. He was amazed—almost everything he and Gillian had suggested or recommended had been implemented. The town centre had been relocated, a coal dump had been removed, and more. He said it was the most fulfilling moment of his career. This was certainly the first exchange of actual government workers between the state and the province, but we could not make it a continuing program. That is a pity. Perhaps more government-to-government staff exchange with China might have eased a little the tensions we now see building up.

Ties in Tianjin

If Guangdong is known for its entrepreneurship and free-wheeling business climate, Tianjin is known for its grit and determination. Vivian's uncle Hu Qili had been mayor of Tianjin between 1980 and 1982. Both were significant port and manufacturing cities facing enormous urban challenges. After the Tangshan earthquake in 1976, Gough and Margaret Whitlam's presence inspired Peter Nicholson's cartoon of them in bed: 'Did the earth move for you too, dear?'[67] It was no laughing matter when we visited; the city was still recovering, many of the sidewalks lined with emergency housing still occupied. Behind those shanties, in the old concession areas, lay an extraordinary heritage of buildings and streets resembling European and Russian cities. The foreign concessions had competed to build grand neighbourhoods.

This time we talked about an agreement between AIUS and the City of Tianjin, with further Melbourne linkages in mind. Here, Lyndsay Neilson was moved to the front. The talks seemed to be going nowhere, though the hospitality was generous and the site and agency visits welcoming and interesting. It seemed a pity, but after dinner on the last night we all went to bed. At 11 pm, Vivian and I were woken by a knock on the door and the whole Tianjin group, still in their suits, asked us to work through a draft agreement. We obliged, in dressing gowns. There was no typewriter, so we entered text into the telex machine, and in the morning at breakfast both parties signed a long scroll of telex tape.

The memorandum of understanding covered the waterfront, all the areas on which we might cooperate and exchange, including strategic planning, urban infrastructure and urban conservation. A number of commercial opportunities were identified. We also thought that Tianjin had much to teach other cities in areas such as fast-track construction, integrated economic and physical planning, waste water, recycling and bicycle planning. Its economy was opening up at speed.

We later promoted these urban sector opportunities, leading to further engagement in at least three directions. [68] First, I returned with Dean Forbes of Flinders University to do a more thorough planning and infrastructure appraisal, which we published and promoted. [69] Our Tianjin partners were happy to work further on it and other sources to build up the case for a successful multi-billion World Bank loan and grant package, then one of the bank's biggest ever in China. Dean continued joint work with Tianjin some years after I moved on. By good fortune, in 2004, I led a team of international experts for the World Bank and the China Development Bank to do a rapid review of infrastructure finance opportunities and priorities in Tianjin, and it was helpful to have a good background.[70]

How the city has changed! In 1984, and even during the 1990s, the scale of Tianjin's ambitions was unbelievable. Tianjin, Beijing and Dalian were the key cities of the Bohai Rim, a string of cities around the sea for which the Chinese authorities planned coordinated development. At first, planners were stuck on old British practices of satellite cities and green belts, and kept national restrictions on big city size and a 'one-child' family rule. In 1984, Tianjin proper housed 3.24m people, and as a big city faced a year 2000 limit of 3.8m, notwithstanding its favourable status as a city-province. Dean and I visited the important port of Tanggu, serving Beijing and much of the north of China, just east of Tianjin. On a muddy wasteland next to it, Tianjin planned an economic-technological development area (TEDA), announced the year of my first visit in 1984. Dean and I politely wrote that the regional expansion plans were 'perhaps overly ambitious'.[71]

They weren't. TEDA went on to be a stellar success, rated by the Ministry of Commerce as the best such zone in China 12 years in a row.[72] And around it, the Binhai New Area now houses close to 12m people. And around that, *Jing-Jin-Ji* (Beijing, Tianjin, Hebei), once a sketch in homemade briefing documents, is a megacity cluster of around 115m people joined up with fast trains and advanced logistics, 8 percent of China's population and 10 percent of its GDP.[73] Years after standing on those uncomely mudflats, I learnt what is humanly possible with the scale and pace of urban development in east Asia, something that university sceptics years later hadn't learned when they doubted an undeveloped marshy campus site in Vietnam, as discussed in a coming chapter.

The people we met in Tianjin in 1984, like Wang Zuokun, stayed friends over the years through multiple visits in both directions. One Tianjin friend, Qu Weiping, moved to Melbourne and even married an RMIT member of staff. Happy memories of Tianjin itself stayed with me. I visited whenever I had the opportunity. My favourite places were the *Goubuli Baozi* dumpling house ('a dog wouldn't eat here', now a national chain and its homely original site long gone) and the *Yangliuqing* new year poster workshop (still there), home of those famous lino prints of chubby red-cheeked babies pasted onto windows.

We were also taken with the extraordinary living history of the Western and Russian precincts (some of them it must be said, were inappropriately used, like a synagogue serving as a warehouse). In 1988, when I moved to RMIT, thinking what usefully might come to RMIT from the Wilmoth–Forbes list of opportunities made in 1984, I started up an urban conservation exchange with counterparts in Tianjin. The idea was that we would bring a team of urban conservationists to draw up a strategy for the western concession areas, and the Tianjin side would prepare the equivalent for the old Chinese quarters. Each side would learn from the other, Tianjin about western urban conservancy methods, and Melbourne about the conservation of Chinese heritage. About 15 people went from Australia on the project. The Tianjin leadership was understandably ambivalent about conserving reminders of a humiliating period of China's history, but recognised the quarters as assets in the city's quest to be seen as a cosmopolitan centre of finance and technology.

We raised funds for the project. Together with Evan Walker, no longer planning minister but my counterpart dean at the University of Melbourne, I steered the project.[74] Miles Lewis, a specialist at that university in the field, claimed Tianjin's pre-war modernist architecture was among the best anywhere. The implementation phase in Tianjin, out of our hands, met heavier weather, as the most senior officials of the construction ministry, flush with investment funds from the government and the World Bank, and being engineers, tended to favour road-widening over conservation. Moreover, when they did restore the neighbourhoods and districts, they moved the whole population out of each quarter so as to do the work wholesale, ending long-standing local social structures and not rehousing all of the prior occupants *in situ*. Nevertheless, today Tianjin is well-known for its heritage districts, including its 'ancient culture streets' which clearly reflect its history.

A third result of the 1984 visit was less direct. After 1988, when I was working at RMIT, I was responsible for international programs, and we built a strong relationship with the City of Melbourne's sister cities office. For Tianjin, we at RMIT combined with the two city governments to set up an office there, alongside other Melbourne-based ventures. That helped to recruit students, and for a time be a hub for our several partnerships in Tianjin, including with Tianjin and Nankai Universities (the former being equivalent in mission to RMIT, and the latter, more prestigious, hosting a centre for Australian studies), Rolls-Royce and the Civil Aviation Administration of China (CAAC) aviation management school. The university entered into a well-funded long-stay training program in Melbourne for promising leaders of the City of Tianjin which was repeated for a number of years. It helped for some of the time that Ivan Deveson, the Lord Mayor of Melbourne, had been chancellor of RMIT; he was an enthusiast for the partnership. Here, too, a Chinese garden was part of the deal, but it is a smaller place, an elegant sliver of stone, water, statuary and plants on Spring Street in Melbourne.

Urban policy on the ground

This time at DEP marked the end of my full-time career as an urban planner, and the beginning of my career in higher education, though both threads were interwoven ever after. I felt the six years in NSW were an evolution from the three years in federal government, and was able to continue work in similar directions. The Berkeley years of activism and radical theory were an interregnum; I came back to being a bureaucrat, albeit on the reform path. Work at the state level was obviously closer to urban development as it actually occurs, and less dominated by policy settings, but I'd kept continuity by working as a policy specialist for most of the time. I could see, more clearly than I saw in DURD, the power of good bureaucrats like Bob Meyer who hunkered down for years and shepherded through policy changes across changes of government, the sort of quiet heroes extolled by Hugh Stretton.

Still, I found that so much was wasted through internecine politics, within and between parties. Labor stayed in power until 2011 without distinction in planning. My greatest disappointment was to witness the beginning of the end of the framework we had built for good urban growth management, especially the growing currency of the idea that stopping suburban development would bring a more compact city with few social or economic consequences. After having helped to lead the charge against prescriptive statutory planning as a shaper of city form, I was unhappy to see the sophisticated combination of strategic planning, development monitoring, infrastructure coordination and financing largely neglected, and with it the means of ensuring a productive city region and more equity in the distribution of jobs and services within it.

The rise of the private sector in urban development—corporatisation, outsourcing and privatisation—has been a mixed blessing at best. Many of the services and infrastructure investments are now made by the private sector, so it is much more difficult to coordinate growth than when led by the government sector. Public–private partnerships (PPP) had, and still have, potential for efficient procurement of what cities need, but the state's use of this method has been lazy, inept, and sometimes corrupt. It is far easier to advance PPPs for toll roads where the private party carries much of the market risk than for heavy rail, hospitals, housing, community renewal and other sectors where the public has to carry more of that risk. This has distorted priorities between sectors and chopped up the orderly development of what should be city-wide networks and systems into single less-connected and out of phase projects. It isn't the tools we use for managing urban growth, it's the way they are used. From this angle, good metropolitan governance is more important than good strategic plans and programs, a view I reached after leaving NSW.

Not all was lost, of course. The centres policy held, and helped shape Sydney. A degree of coordination of growth in new areas remains. Local economic development planning is now a normal practice among councils and supported by the state. Much regional open space has been protected. Sydney's second airport landed in the right place. The housing industry has shifted towards a more diverse mix of dwelling types, though social housing has been cruelly left out of the state's direct investments, at least until now, and is still too little.

Vivian and I were enjoying Sydney, living in Balmain among friends, including American expats like Lori Mooren, and bringing up little Maya, born in 1987. We were both working hard. Vivian was becoming influential in public health policy in the state, building up a national and international reputation, and was open to moving again for work if opportunities opened up.

Reflecting on the directions I found at Berkeley, which I had fully assimilated by now, I felt I was able to address structural change in cities, particularly Sydney, but I was boxed in by administrative structures I had little power to change. I felt running the planning division for the state government was causing me to slip from strategic planning back towards statutory planning, and I didn't feel I was able to put my values fully into practice. Though I was still able to research issues, publish articles about my experience, travel and build up international contacts, it was time for a change. I felt my career should keep renewing, not digging into one track.

Over those six years I had become involved in Victorian planning and urban development coordination, negotiating joint developments like the very fast train, making regional plans that abutted Victoria, helping transfer know-how and exchanging experience, all while working at the NSW DEP. With a network of friends and colleagues in Melbourne, I joined an advisory committee for RMIT's faculty of environmental design and construction. Then staff of the faculty encouraged me to run for the deanship when it became vacant.

In November 1988, I moved to Melbourne to take the job.

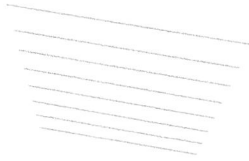

SEVEN

HELPING BUILD A UNIVERSITY

or the next 17 years I worked at the Royal Melbourne Institute of Technology (RMIT). It is difficult to go through the ups and downs of those years in detail, and the eight or more jobs I had within the institution. I was at first unfamiliar with university management, so it was an intense period of learning by doing. This was accelerated by taking a lead role in two large mergers, one unsuccessful, and the rewarding work of putting the framework for a modern university in place once RMIT gained university status. I was able to bring some urban planning experience to the mix, but my international experience and interests were more important as RMIT very quickly internationalised. The turbulence of the mergers, changes of leadership and a crisis of governance over an IT crash brought several changes to my job, all good for learning but stressful on my sometimes tenuous hold on the senior positions I held. Those formative years cover the three chapters ahead and discuss managing the university, its internationalisation, and leading a large new campus in Vietnam.

Stepping back, I see that these were experiences shared by many around Australia in the sector, such as bringing universities into a unified national system of mass higher education, merging complex institutions into big multi-campus universities, stoking their internationalisation through a period of rapid globalisation, realising that these multi-billion dollar enterprises were just as in need of good corporate governance as other business enterprises, and more widely keeping alive and enriching the distinctive historical mission of universities, these enduring parts of our civilisation.

A short-lived deanship

I started as dean of environmental design and construction at RMIT on 1 December 1988. To stretch Groucho Marx, why would I join a university that would accept me? It was a mark of RMIT's focus on engagement with the professions that they would take someone from outside an academic career track into the position. Anyway, RMIT wasn't a university then, and I knew little about how to run a faculty in any kind of institution.

Though not a university, RMIT offered PhDs and ran a large research program. The contribution of such proto-universities was under-recognised, blurring the binary divide in higher education well before the Dawkins Labor government creation of a unified national system. Traditionally called the 'working man's college' because it provided courses for those at work, RMIT was at the heart of Melbourne, figuratively and geographically.

With advanced education and technical and further education (TAFE) sectors, it was one of the largest tertiary education institutions in the country, a straggling mix of faculties and schools bent on being practical and industry-related, well-known for its engineering, design and technology programs in particular. It used to be an affiliate college of the Victorian Institute of Colleges, uncomfortable with that institute's intent to expand the number of colleges and thus reduce RMIT's domination. Then in 1983 it became self-accrediting.

In 1997, RMIT celebrated its centenary, producing a very readable book about its colourful history and a report from a centenary commission on the way ahead.[1] In that year the RMIT council resolved to keep the technical college and the advanced education sector under one principal and one council, though not to merge them, reversing an earlier presumption that they would eventually separate.[2]

My faculty was made up of advanced education departments of architecture, planning, interior design, landscape architecture, and building and construction economics. It was well-regarded, with areas of national leadership and some of the leading academics in their fields. The department of architecture was a lively spring of ideas, akin to the Architecture Association of London, from where its head, Leon van Schaik and others had come. Even before Leon, the department was at the forefront of architectural thought and practice through Graeme Gunn and others. The department of planning was also among the best in the country. Many of the disciplines of the faculty were represented in the schools of the TAFE division at RMIT, to and from which there were credit transfer paths (though not enough to make good on the potential; by and large they stayed different parts of the education system).

RMIT was built to show that separation: red brick buildings on the Carlton side for the technical college, echoing the British 'red brick' stigma of vocational education, and fortress-like grey buildings on the city side for the advanced education sector. With the even uglier buildings then of the University of Technology Sydney, these institutes of technology had been starved of capital funds and had to build in the cheapest possible ways. Nor was RMIT a coherent campus in the city. There were over 100 buildings and sites scattered around inner Melbourne under different forms of ownership and lease, and the headquarter campus was surrounded by security barriers and locked at night.

My welcome was warm, including from Mike Berry, head of the department of planning and erstwhile acting dean, and Leon van Schaik, who jointly with Mike had also run for the job. I organised a brunch in the park not long after my arrival in Melbourne, with a note that if it was raining at the designated time it would be in my apartment nearby. It was raining lightly, so that is what we did—start the party in the apartment. On Monday, a little irked, Leon asked, 'Where was the party?' as nothing was happening in the park. It was an embarrassing way to learn what counted in dreary Melbourne as 'rain'.

In the faculty, and across the university, there was an exceptional concentration of design expertise, all the way from graphic design through fashion to aircraft design. In the early months we put together a proposal for the national key centre for design, and after a period of drafting, making political representations and lobbying industry, we were successful. Work on the bid started before my arrival. Chris Ryan wrote the submission and then headed it up, an innovator with a passion for eco-design that, for any product, encompassed its whole life cycle sustainably. The environmental slant helped it win funding.[3] The field of design has stayed one of RMIT's greatest research and teaching strengths.

I felt able to continue my research and practice in planning outside of the university; indeed, unlike at DEP, this was an expected part of my job. National urban policy was coming back onto the public agenda, and I gave lots of talks on the topic. Andrew McCutcheon, Victorian minister for planning, a modest and genial man, the only person I knew who had been a minister in both senses of the word, and a friend from the DURD days when he was an activist at the Fitzroy Ecumenical Centre, asked me to prepare alternative big-picture scenarios for Victoria's urban development. He gave me a free hand (though the report was later bookended on publication with departmental prose) to sketch out settlement futures and publish them for discussion.[4] I also joined up with new colleagues, Des Eccles and Kevin O'Connor, to write a report critical of Melbourne's metropolitan planning.[5]

At the request of Tom Roper—then state minister for employment, post-secondary education and training, and who thus represented the owner of the state universities—whom I had admired since his days as an education activist with the National Union of Australian Students in the late 1960s, I reviewed the sensitive matter of whether Monash University should establish a campus at Dandenong or Berwick. The state's urban policy clearly pointed to Dandenong, intended to be Melbourne's 'second CBD', but the state's education policy, to locate university campuses in unserved sectors, just as clearly pointed to Berwick. I opted for the latter, giving primacy to the aims of the ministry commissioning the study.[6] This seemed to disappoint Tom, but delighted Mal Logan, by then Monash University's vice-chancellor. Both the poor performance of state governments in pump-priming Dandenong's tertiary industries, and

Monash University's exit from Berwick from 2017, tell us in hindsight that this was the wrong advice.

In summary, through these projects, and collaborating on others in the faculty (for the first six months), then across RMIT and internationally, my early years allowed something of an urban sector practice. This fell away after that short period as dean with the intensity of university management and turbulence of institutional amalgamations that followed.

Going to 'building one'

Not long after I settled in, Brian Smith, director of RMIT, left to accept a job as vice-chancellor of the University of Western Sydney, a creation of the Whitlam government. David Beanland, dean of engineering, was to act in the director's post and Brian asked me to act as associate director in charge of resource administration, running the institute's finances, human resources, campuses and other administrative matters. Little matter, in his mind, that I was new to tertiary education management. He thought as a former government executive I must know how to run that side of the place. I appreciated his confidence, but I wasn't well-prepared to run the resources of a large dual-sector tertiary institution.

Looking back, I regret leaving an enjoyable and academically rewarding deanship so soon. But ambition and a liking for learning to swim out of my depth won the day, and I accepted the job. Many in the faculty were unhappy they lost their new dean so soon to 'building one', for most of them a world away, after all the trouble of the search.

For five months, I tried to get on top of the work of the resources position and there were no disasters. On the building front, it helped that I had planning experience and good working relations with my old faculty, as together we led recommendations to RMIT council on a number of buildings, including a cheeky (read: incompatible) extension to the iconic Graham Andrews 'Glasshouse' student union building, now designed by Peter Corrigan, with exteriors to brighten up the dull grey façade of Swanston Street and each floor's interior decorated in the colours of a Melbourne-based Australian rules football team. Under Leon's tutelage a new set of architects who were awarded contracts for this and other buildings stayed involved for years to come, weaving in and out of faculty and contractor roles, giving RMIT a more adventurous environment and buffing its reputation for work-integrated learning on its own projects, while offending Melbourne's more established firms who missed out on being in the group.

The institute appointed Ruth Dunkin to the substantive associate director resources position from August 1989. From a state government background and Harvard master of public administration, Ruth was smart and energetic, up to speed with the latest organisational development thinking. She later ruefully commented she had no decent transition from me into her job, but truthfully, there was not much wisdom I could pass on. At her appointment I took the acting job as associate director for higher education (that is, academic affairs not including TAFE, which was the domain of Bob Bangay, another associate director). Thus came the unenviable job of supervising the deans and, through them, the seven faculties and the graduate school of management. It would be fair to say the deans were not excited by my acting appointment, but for my confirmation into the position later in December they were not opposed either.

Just before I joined RMIT, David Beanland, into whose old job I was promoted, led an 'integrated [i.e. dual-sector] task force on changes related to the creation of a university of technology', long an aspiration of RMIT. It was informed by the opportunity coming from commonwealth government changes to allow university status, and did not at that stage recognise any pressure to merge with other institutions. The RMIT task force found 'general, but not total support' for closer cooperation between the TAFE and higher education sectors, and 'significant, but qualified support' from external stakeholders for designation of RMIT as a university of technology.[7] But, as noted, it recommended against structural integration on the road to university status, keeping the sectors separate within the same organisation.

As a dual-sector institution RMIT was tied to two entirely different funding and reporting regimes, different career paths for staff, different priorities for research and different union representation. Though we promoted articulation between the sectors—'from apprenticeship to

PhD'—the pathways were patchy and not well laid out; indeed, across the system more students transferred from higher education to the vocational sector than vice-versa (for example, property graduates gaining real estate certificates). These pathways would have to improve.

I was enjoying the work very much, learning as I went. The leadership term was coherent and life around the campus, its restaurants, galleries and events, was fun not only for me but for Vivian and our children. Maya Lin, our first daughter, came down to Melbourne with Vivian when it was time to join me. I was a proud father, and spent a lot of time with her, trying to keep equal time with Vivian on household duties and rearing Maya. Vivian took on successful public health roles in the state government and then La Trobe University, so our timetables were very full. Vivian was particularly well-organised. We got better at it than in Sydney, when once I had to pick up Maya at the police station because Vivian and I each thought the other would pick her up from childcare. Then, in 1991, Sasha Wilmoth was born, and four years later Kina Lin-Wilmoth.

These were happy days, though without grandparents nearby and frequent travel for both of us, the children had to be self-reliant early. We fell in with a close and active group of friends in Elwood, including playmates for the children. But a complex institutional merger early in my period in Melbourne brought tension and things began to change. A full life with the children was being compromised by intensifying work for both parents.

Up the merger hill and down the hill again

The tertiary education sector in Australia was in upheaval at the end of the 1980s. The Hawke Labor government was determined to open higher education access more widely, gear it to economic development, and to get cost-effective growth by abolishing the stratified tertiary education system of universities, colleges of advanced education and institutes of technology. The national education minister, John ('Joe') Dawkins, brother to Jeremy, my university classmate from Sydney mentioned earlier, set about bringing together the university and college of advanced education sectors, expanding and redistributing access through funding increases and later an income-contingent national loan scheme, and pressing the merger of apparently sub-viable small higher education institutions.

The Dawkins agenda in tertiary education in Australia was revolutionary. The 1987 green paper led quickly to a white paper in which the program of reform was laid out:

- Abolition of the binary system (universities and colleges of advanced education, CAEs) and replacement by a unified national system
- Consolidation of institutions through amalgamation to reduce their number and form larger institutions
- Increased enrolments
- Priority to fields of study important to economic growth
- More selective priority-driven research funding
- Changes to university governance to be more like corporate governance
- More autonomy and power to vice-chancellors
- Greater staffing flexibility
- Promotion of institutional effectiveness and efficiency
- Greater reliance on student and trainee fees, and
- Encouragement for supplementary institutional revenue-raising.[8]

Upgrades to university status for CAEs and institutes of technology through consolidation were especially controversial, and institutions around the country variously started courtships or spurned potential suitors. Providing better higher education to regions through consolidation of institutions within them was a sensible aim, but university complacency about merging with nearby institutions was sometimes trumped by better offers from more distant suitors, such as Monash University merging with the College of Pharmacy under the University of Melbourne's nose.[9] In particular, the Australian government aimed to serve historically disadvantaged regions with more access to higher education, an aim I also supported. And indeed, I still support the Dawkins reforms in principle. They put a bomb under a confusing and segmented tertiary education sector and created the conditions, if in a messy way, for the wider access to higher education we see today.

At the time I joined RMIT, it had long been seeking university status. Earlier efforts had been rebuffed for reason of its inclusion of a TAFE college, the retention of which RMIT strongly asserted, and the reluctance of the state government regulator, the Victorian Post-Secondary Education Commission, to agree to RMIT's singular request over other aspirant institutions. The commission did however create a representative working party to prepare an issues paper canvassing the options.[10]

Now, with the Dawkins reforms running, and other states converting CAEs into universities, RMIT's vision of becoming a university of technology looked within reach. Other institutes in Victoria were making their merger moves to mass up to the scale needed. Big RMIT didn't need the numbers, but it did consider merging with Swinburne and Footscray institutes of technology. That did not progress once Swinburne withdrew as it intended to develop a campus in the eastern suburbs at Lilydale.

The Labor state minister for education, Joan Kirner, and Caroline Hogg, minister assisting her with responsibility for post-secondary education, both with electorates in western Melbourne, said they would consider it only after the future of higher education in Melbourne's western suburbs had been dealt with. They blocked RMIT's solo proposal for university status going to state cabinet. This was part of a pattern of trying to trim back RMIT's aspirations.

Evan Walker, president of RMIT council, was close to the government but unable to bring the proposal to fruition. (He was a colleague of mine when, as Victorian minister for planning, he and David Yencken asked me to help transfer NSW's urban development program know-how to Victoria). Swinburne Institute of Technology and Footscray Institute of Technology (FIT) started discussions and invited RMIT to join the talks.[11] In April 1988, RMIT council resolved not to support that federation proposal. However, Brian Smith, RMIT's director, was favourably inclined to pursue affiliation with the newly-formed Western Institute and on this other potential merger RMIT council agreed, against internal staff and academic board opposition.

This was overshadowed by an announcement by Joan Kirner and Caroline Hogg in November 1988 to form a new university for the western suburbs of Melbourne, in which the Western Institute would sit. A commonwealth–state joint working party on university education in the western suburbs of Melbourne, set up in December 1988, recommended merging RMIT, FIT and the Western Institute to create a university large enough to make a difference quicker than organic growth of the separate institutions would allow.[12] This was a big challenge to RMIT. Would it join the new university?

A number of concerns had to be weighed by the RMIT director and the council: potential dilution of research, the presumed better standing of RMIT's higher education courses, worries about slipped rankings on other measures, and doubts about whether RMIT's efforts to internationalise and capitalise on its metropolitan-wide centrality would be diverted. Premier Kirner's intention to fund each of the three institutions equally still rankles David Beanland at the time of publishing.

Against these concerns were the attainment of university status, greater scale, likely financial inducements from commonwealth and state governments, and opportunities to be more deeply involved in western Melbourne and to right some of the wrongs of area discrimination, an aim dear to my heart.

There was also some attraction beyond social justice. Werribee was a designated state technology precinct and a newly merged institution with research concentration might quickly build up an international cluster in food and technology R & D there. That, too, attracted me. Western Melbourne was, and still is, a big region with a workforce forced to travel eastwards because of lack of local jobs. A university-led resurgence of employment in knowledge-based industries could boost the regional economy.[13]

The case had heavy political support. Both commonwealth and state governments were Labor, and RMIT's governance was not yet fully independent, with state appointees on the council and detailed federal control of its education profile matched to funding.

Nevertheless, council's first answer was 'no', under the cool and courageous leadership of Yolanda Klempfner, president from 1987. It resolved instead to remain independent and seek itself to be the institution on which expanded higher education in the western suburbs should be based. But Evan Walker was inclined otherwise, towards joining the discussions about a merger. In April 1989, he persuaded the presidents of the three councils to form a working party. By July he brought the RMIT council around, announcing that RMIT, FIT and the Western Institute would indeed set up a working party to prepare heads of agreement for a new university. Internal RMIT resistance surged. Council based its agreement to participate in the working party on seven conditions, including use of RMIT's name, recognition it would be the core element of any new university, and retention of the TAFE sector.

David Beanland was acting as director. The heads of agreement for the merger, negotiated under Brian Smith's watch, came to RMIT council in October and David argued they were inadequate and grounds for rejection of the full merger, with six core issues unresolved: academic structure, council representation, headquarter location, the university's name, TAFE issues and resources.[14]

The pressure was on. The other two institutes resolved to support the merger. Minister Dawkins made federal funding to RMIT for capital renovation conditional on an institutional merger, and RMIT could forget university status if it stayed out. David Beanland's recollection is telling:

> The Federal Education minister requested me to attend a meeting with him (and approximately 30 of his departmental staff) and stated that $30 million would be taken away from RMIT if I did not agree immediately to join the two western Melbourne institutions. I categorically refused his proposal. Ruth Dunkin attended as a witness. The $30 million was taken away from our capital funding for building 8 (architecture on top of the library). Without us requesting, the Canberra staff [later] progressively restored the $30 million![15]

The media and coalition state opposition parties were weighing in too, the latter against the merger. RMIT was not in a strong financial position, especially on its capital account, with an old campus and enormous maintenance and replacement requirements and backlogs. I'd noticed the possibility when I was associate director for resources, responsible for finance and campus development, and it worried the staff in the division too. The underlying problems with RMIT's capital stock became even more apparent when Ruth Dunkin took over, from August 1989.

An atmosphere of crisis grew across the campus. Meetings and communications were diverting normal business. Could RMIT snub the two governments and go it alone? We toyed with radical solutions. One idea was to sell RMIT's main city campus and relocate to Melbourne Docklands, a planned precinct nearby. The answer was that we couldn't. Very few of its major assets were in RMIT's own name; most were in the name of the crown or the minister.

Minister Dawkins and RMIT ex-president Evan Walker, who was Victorian minister for higher education, were working together behind the scenes, and Walker addressed council on 25 September.[16] The heads of merger agreement from the working party came to council. On David Beanland's advice, on 23 October, council rejected them.

The academic board, of which I was a member, was divided on the question. I was now acting as associate director for higher education, and later appointed. The job covered undergraduate, postgraduate, higher degree and research, RMIT libraries, the computer centre and student services. It was a big portfolio, serving nearly 14,000 students through nearly 1000 academic staff. I was able to cope through delegation as most of the deans who reported to me were capable, or the staff around them.

On balance I was not in favour of the merger, nor were the deans. But the elected membership of the academic board included influential members of the National Tertiary Education Union (NTEU), aligned with the Labor Party and in favour of the merger, perhaps with the hope that university status would lighten workloads. The debate, conducted in the language of academic principle, was highly political. The academic board on 3 November 1989 rejected the draft university position and supported the merger. This hurt. I made a note for the future to see what we could do to get more membership of the board independent of the union. I stopped my union membership as it was a conflict of interest.

Western Melbourne local government councils weighed in too, and I spoke to a number of mayors, travelling around the western suburbs. The mayor of Werribee said the western suburbs were 'determined to have their own university'.[17] Meanwhile, Dawkins telephoned Beanland on 27 November 1989 with a threat to remove funding for an extension to building 8, the largest of RMIT's building projects, to remove student funding for 400 student places, to shift further student funding westward to the other two merging institutions, and to cap further growth funding overall for RMIT.[18] This was brutal. Those who knew, including me, were incensed.

That evening, the background pressure and lobbying came to a head. RMIT council agreed 'in principle' with the terms of the new university. It would be named Victoria University of Technology (VUT). The terms agreed that activities at the RMIT campus would still be known as under RMIT at the VUT, that its headquarters for at least five years would be in the Melbourne business district, that the three institute councils would continue to operate until the end of 1991, while ceding to the new university council the powers to set educational profile (the publicly funded composition of the student body), one-line funding and consolidated funding submissions to the commonwealth, one set of academic awards and the selection of a new CEO.

The government of Victoria proceeded to draft the legislation. I was acting director at the time and had a hand in this. I declared that 'we believe the bill is a satisfactory basis for its establishment and ongoing operation ... While RMIT has had difficulties with some of the early amalgamation proposals, the issues have been resolved to our satisfaction'.[19] The Act started simply by saying that RMIT is a university, without changing its name.

I persuaded myself I was not selling out RMIT because it was mostly about whether the bill fulfilled the conditions of council's consent. It was introduced to the Victorian parliament in March and the *Victoria University of Technology Act 1990* came into law on 1 July 1990.

The institutes would combine under one council, one vice-chancellor and one academic board, and be guided by an implementation steering committee to integrate fully by the beginning of 1992, with an option for any party to withdraw on reasonable grounds within a year. Creighton Burns, former editor of *The Age*, was appointed chancellor in August 1990, and Professor Jarlath Ronayne vice-chancellor in January 1991. Neither was an office holder of any of the merging institutes.

Some participants held high hopes, but tensions among the merging institutions continued in the new council, the implementation steering committee, the executive group and the academic board, and cascaded throughout the academic structure. Some staff stayed in outright opposition, fed by fears of mismatching missions and weakened RMIT influence over directions through a lack of majorities on the new university council and academic board. The dual sector nature of the merging organisations (both higher education and TAFE) presented the same questions considered earlier by RMIT, but with greater complexity. Should the two sectors be in separate structures? What should be the basis of merged faculties and departments?

I joined the other academic leads to work through the restructure. Paul Clark and June Gleeson, my academic deputy counterparts at FIT and the Western Institute respectively, were friendly and cooperative, but answered to their leaders on strategy and tactics, just like me. My boss, David Beanland, had strong views. The first big task was to plan an integrated structure for the higher education faculties, deciding on their composition, spilling senior positions and reappointing leaders and deputies on merit. This process cascaded down through academic departments to discipline leadership, a stressful process for all, directly involving many of the academic staff. At RMIT, it was a tough time persuading deans and heads of department of long standing, and in some cases distinction, to enter into a 'spill'. Most reappointment results went RMIT's way, other than for a new faculty of arts, the leadership of which went to a very able Rob Pascoe from FIT.

Though based on agreed criteria, the restructuring process was fractious, during and after appointments, and the campaign of resistance continued to grow, with anonymous newsletters, media leaks and manifestos of dissent. By and large this did not come from the main unions (the NTEU and the Association of Professional Staff), which, Labor-aligned, stayed in support of the merger. Instances of opportunities and decisions lost by majority vote mounted, but executives from all three institutions, including myself, tried to hold to the merger course we were on.

These collateral costs weighed on the work. I chaired Victoria's Knowledge Precinct, a kind of chamber of technology for Australia's largest R & D cluster, which included the University of Melbourne, RMIT and the many research institutes, especially biomedical, along the Parkville strip. The University of Melbourne and RMIT were well towards a shared major ICT building in the neighbourhood between them, putting together the best of each institution into a state-of-the-art shared space.

The two Davids who ran the institutions, Beanland and Pennington, got on well together, in part because their organisations had different missions. The commonwealth decided funding on the basis of competing bids, and for big capital projects like this, only the best would get up. The RMIT part of VUT failed to persuade the other parties in the new university on its priority. The joint centre and building project was bumped to second priority in VUT's bid, dismaying the University of Melbourne and failing to get funding at all.

This was just one example of the costs to RMIT of being in what seemed more and more a regional university, not an international or metropolitan one. While keeping its core values of access and practicality, RMIT had high aspirations. We had to face the fact that there were basic differences of values and strategy between RMIT and the other institutes. They seemed reconcilable in the early days but now affected almost every major decision. Bob Glass in his detailed account, on which much of this section relies, points out that difficulties began even before the new Act was proclaimed over the university headquarter building not being in the central business district as agreed, lack of Western Institute consultation over senior staff appointments and titles, and a professoriate proposal from that institute at variance with FIT and RMIT's agreed proposal.[20]

In my work, the integration of the faculties was well advanced, but earlier RMIT research and internationalisation strategies were being thinned. Staff in transition from RMIT were not confident about the direction VUT was taking. Differences in academic board over teaching and learning strategies were becoming clearer, and more decisions were voted on institutional lines against RMIT in the vital implementation steering committee.

The splits were sharper in the new council and among the three merging CEOs, and discussion about withdrawal came out in the open. Eventually, RMIT members of council considered their position. External members of council, led by Yolanda Klempfner, showed courage standing up to intimidation by governments and internal staff representatives. The governments knew it was not going well and continued to threaten negative funding consequences for a standalone RMIT.

The RMIT council (still in operation during the formation period) resolved on 26 April 1991 to give notice of withdrawal, effective from the end of the year, and not revokable by the other parties. *The Age*, VUT chancellor's erstwhile newspaper, in an editorial headed 'the high price of stubborn pride', called it 'a high price to pay for academic vanity, institutional pride and parochial self-interest'.[21]

I was relieved. In the higher education portfolio, though, the omelette was largely made, so I knew unscrambling it would be a complicated and painful process once again. After the RMIT decision, my academic merger counterparts stayed mainly constructive, probably relieved their 'big brother' (RMIT's persona was still masculine then) was leaving, and that life ahead would be simpler for them.

Financial disentanglement was a nightmare, including changes to the commonwealth-mandated teaching profile and the cost of the interim headquarters and top structure. Recovery from this dead end took great effort. David Beanland recalls wryly that some years later, as Evan Walker was resigning as minister responsible for post-secondary education, he was directed by Joan Kirner to admonish David for opposing the western region university development. He requested a meeting with David and told him he was to consider himself admonished, then took his close friend of more than 50 years out to lunch.

The remnants of the merger kept their new university status, even without reaching the scale intended for a university for western Melbourne. Over the years that followed, in its title as 'university of technology', the last two words got smaller and smaller in print until VUT eventually became Victoria University as it is today. I still have some unused VUT business cards.

More love the second time around

During this disengagement another possibility came up. The leaders of Phillip Institute of Technology (we didn't call it 'PIT') had been unhappy with the way they were treated by La Trobe University, their near-neighbour in Bundoora, northwest Melbourne. I had the impression that Phillip's concerns were as much about thwarted dignity as lost outcomes. Its director, Leo Foster, a genial and practical educational leader, invited David Beanland to lunch at a Vietnamese restaurant at Box Hill and opened discussions with him about merging, authorised by a February 1991 decision of his institute council.[22]

This merger proposal was explored thoroughly and carefully by RMIT senior staff. There were many issues to resolve, but David Beanland cannot recall there being any difficulties, as the shared objective was to expand RMIT as a university, incorporating the two previous organisations with shared educational philosophies. He recalls united organisation and decision-making, and no friction; even the state government was mildly supportive. He still sees it as one of the most successful university mergers in Australia at the time of writing.

In April, the same month RMIT council resolved to withdraw from VUT, I sounded out the deans on what they thought of merging again. My notes of the meeting show 'lukewarm', 'will dilute research', 'warm because niche courses', 'very negative'. More meetings followed, including one at the aptly named Bypass Motel. The deans warmed more to the prospect when they reviewed the benefits more closely. New fields of study beckoned, including nursing, education, complementary medicine, sports science, and area studies, as well as expansion of RMIT's presence in the northern suburbs and building scale to become Australia's largest tertiary education provider. Phillip also had a highly respected leadership role in the Bundoora technology precinct.

First, the name needed work. Both parties agreed the merged institution would bear RMIT's identity. The Royal Melbourne Institute of Technology was granted its royal charter in 1954. But in December 1991 the secretary of the Victorian Department of Premier and Cabinet advised, in the event that RMIT sought to be renamed as the 'Royal Melbourne University of Technology', that the use of the title 'Royal' in association with the title 'university' would not be permitted. Though there were other 'royal' educational institutions in the British Commonwealth, including the Royal College of Art in London that RMIT cited in its original application, there were, and still are, no 'royal' universities as such.[23] I understood that, if we sought to renew the royal charter on such a basis, consent from every other university in Australia would be needed. I did not think this would be assured. In any case, the secretary of the department advised that if RMIT kept its original name it could be treated for administrative purposes as a university under the relevant Act.[24] The problem was solved, at least for the time being. I was happy about this.

Second, what corporate shape should RMIT take? It had long been a company limited by guarantee, and we at RMIT sought to keep that form for reasons of independence and familiarity. I was acting as director at the time. The new Australian Catholic University had succeeded in this, smartly vesting their assets in a standalone trust and setting up an effective framework for university governance. Unfortunately for RMIT, this was not on. The government of Victoria was absolutely set on legislating to make RMIT their statutory authority.

The third issue was to define the objects of the bill. The drafting lawyers wanted a long list, but I was concerned that the more you added, the more unintended exclusions could slip in. We rationalised it somewhat, to the point where it was hard to think of what the university might conceivably want to do that was excluded. Though not elegant, at the end it was a shorter list.

The Act came into operation on 1 July 1992.[25] Ivan Deveson, ex-CEO of Nissan Australia and chairman of the Seven Network, a driven businessman, was nominated foundation chancellor, and David Beanland, the hero of disengagement from VUT, foundation vice-chancellor. The investiture on 9 September 1992 was a grand occasion, with an inauguration parade down Swanston Street to the Melbourne Town Hall, an air force flypast (the Royal Australian Air Force happened to be an important corporate client and partner of RMIT), then on to dinner where guests were each given a commemorative bottle of Australian port. Mine sits in the cupboard, unopened to this day.

The newly dubbed vice-chancellor set out themes for the coming years. One was a clear statement of the attributes of graduates, who would be 'sought after for their critical and creative approach, their well-developed sense of responsibility and the ethical underpinning of their professional practice'.[26] Other themes David Beanland continued from the earlier 'Vision for 2000' were the use of advanced teaching techniques, the internationalisation of programs and their growth onshore and offshore, leadership in applied research and development, and industry research funding. These were prospects saved, at least to an extent, from the failed VUT merger, and pursued with vigour by David.

Back at the campus there was much to do. This time, in the new merger implementation committee and elsewhere, the ground was solid. Once more, senior positions, including academic positions, were declared vacant. I had to apply for a new deputy vice-chancellor's job, and was successful. However, this time in the reappointment process, the old RMIT group did not keep every position. Nonetheless, the different departments cooperated well. Having established a professoriate, we were able to evaluate fitness for professorial titles during the merger reappointment process. Developing criteria and processes for appointment and promotion to reflect the values and aims of the university was a long but satisfying project.

A second opportunity with academic structure was to resolve the nature of discipline leadership on a more considered basis. We designated discipline leaders university-wide, with consultation roles across faculties where their disciplines were also taught or researched. This was difficult for those whose professional development had been directed towards Phillip's policy of interdisciplinarity (e.g. by which nursing sourced all their own management subjects), and for those who had not concentrated on one discipline alone. But the greater risk was that, over time, with university designation and a quality ranking regime ahead, those academics might not be able to keep up with their multiple disciplines in sufficient depth. Of course, this did not remove the benefits to those with established disciplinary depth from collaborating with, or themselves being experts in other areas. Cross-disciplinary work was still recognised and valued in the professorial and academic promotion and appointment criteria.

A third related issue of academic design was how to handle those without a record of research, or otherwise settled in teaching-only positions. The solution lay in the academic staff promotion and professorial criteria, which allowed weighted consideration across three fields: teaching and learning, research and development, and community and professional engagement. There's nothing like promotion to motivate academics' choice of work priorities. Within limits, applicants could choose variable weights if they aligned with the university's mission. In other words, teaching-only positions and awards of title were possible with outstanding achievement. Alongside it, though, we funded a research capacity building program to encourage all willing academic staff to widen their research competence. After we worked through these and other issues, the academic part of the merger settled down.

The academic board was a fourth focus of restructure. Merger was readily achieved, with the retention of an elected chair. Previously, the position had gone to academic staff members affiliated with NTEU. I remembered painfully the academic board's opposition to university management views over the VUT merger and was determined to lead the academic board and management into better alignment. Over the summer of 1992–93 I quietly lobbied members-elect of the forthcoming academic board to support management's nominee, who was Bob Gray, ex-deputy director of Phillip Institute. I invited Ivan Deveson, the chancellor, to come to the first meeting of the year to speak about directions ahead, a kind of pep talk. Ivan was good at pep talks. I achieved the aim: our candidate was duly elected and after that the chairs were always elected from the management team. This may appear like—and it was— another incursion of managerialism into the university's academic affairs, but the chairs that followed were fair in representing and leading the new university collegiate.

The merger brought new responsibilities for community engagement, on which Phillip had a good record, and opportunities for campus development.

Campus development

Though the Coburg area had promise as an educational cluster, with a high school and the John Batman TAFE campus, RMIT decided to wind the campus down and dispose of the site as it was likely to stay under 5000 student equivalents for some time, not a viable scale for RMIT's ambitious student servicing plans. A strategic facilities plan encompassed this in July 1993.[27]

The business and management disciplines at Coburg were able to relocate to 12 floors on Bourke Street, in the heart of the city, courtesy of a large if self-interested gift from the Hong Kong-based Chan family, the owners of the Tivoli building, who kept the lower retail floors, with renewed profitability, to serve the thousands of students who used the building. That building housed the business faculty, renamed the business portfolio, until its move in 2012 to the superb new Swanston academic building, on prime land held for a number of decades. At one stage, the property services group allowed an impoverished man to live in a little attic apartment on an otherwise unused building there. Unfortunately, he died and his body was not discovered for days. Acting as vice-chancellor at the time, I had to comfort the distraught member of staff who found his remains.

The RMIT leadership liked the idea of locating departments in the working districts of their students' fields to promote industry connections and workplace culture—aerospace at Fisherman's Bend was such a case—though it made access difficult to more centralised services such as the library, and for intermingling with other faculties. During the Phillip merger we tried to minimise cross-campus travel for students and staff by avoiding replication of departments on different campuses. Smaller buildings distant from the main campuses had no special advantage and we sought over time to relocate their activities back to the main campuses, as lease expiries and resources permitted. In tightening financial circumstances for RMIT the leases and upkeep were costly burdens.

The Bundoora campus expanded onto a large campus across the road acquired from the discontinued Melbourne Metropolitan Board of Works (MMBW) northern headquarters site. There is an interesting story behind this. The MMBW was a long-standing independent utilities authority with wide urban planning powers by virtue of its control of network infrastructure and planning controls. It was led by Alan Croxford, a legendary strong-man whom I knew well through AIUS, and near whom, sadly, I was when he died suddenly.

The MMBW got itself into serious conflict with the Labor government of Victoria through its independent planning directions and in particular its pursuit of freeway development and high-rise public housing, long after these policies were on the nose with much of the public. John Mant, a friend from Tom Uren's office, and then Gough Whitlam's office, was commissioned to plan the unbundling of the MMBW and the return of its responsibilities to more direct control by the respective ministers. I helped him with the metropolitan services coordination system transplant from NSW which I had guided. The idea was that inter-agency coordination within government could, with a system in place, be just as effective as intra-agency coordination, countering the argument to keep one mega-authority alive.

This issue went to the heart of whether modern strategic planning, of which I was a devotee, was better than having old-fashioned independent infrastructure authorities operating under more prescriptive plans. The failure of modern planning and coordination of urban development since then across the NSW government, in particular, and their difficulties in Victoria too, now call for a mixed verdict at best. Anyway, as a consequence of MMBW's shrinkage, RMIT benefited from divestment of their Bundoora site. Later, it was also the beneficiary of a city-to-Bundoora tram extension to the campus under Brian Howe's Better Cities Program.

The effort to consolidate and grow the city campus took longer, as leases were expiring slowly and capital expansion was controlled by the commonwealth through competitive bidding. However, there was much we could do without new buildings. Simply opening up the gates of the main city campus in a gesture to the precinct about the university— including the State Library where many students studied—helped the city become the extended campus and the university strengthen its CBD engagement. Melbourne became UNESCO's second 'city of literature'.

In effect, a learning city was coming into being, an urban setting with rich learning resources, and in RMIT's case an easy flow of students and non-students off and on campus.[28] Being at the intersection of education and urban planning, I took an active interest in this emerging field, with international networks of learning cities and government funding all coming on. The book returns to that theme in the coming chapters.[29]

The wider process of integrating the city campus with its surrounding precincts is one of the great stories of RMIT. As the city is filled with international students, and as the City of Melbourne and the new stable of preferred architects and urban designers cooperated in joint precinct planning and building delightful small urban spaces, the 'buzz' that had long been latent in RMIT's activities became manifest. Before too long new buildings returned to RMIT's city campus, off-beat, bright, engaging. This was extended in the 'urban spaces framework' drawn up by Peter Elliot, one of the chosen few, to guide future campus development strategies in the city, Swanston Street and Carlton precincts.[30]

With a less-regulated capital project approval regime from Canberra and growing revenues from asset disposals and full fee-paying international students, the funding of city campus development improved. After long efforts, in November 1997 RMIT acquired the adjacent magistrates' courts on the corner of Russell and La Trobe Streets, a heritage building that had for a long time been unsuitable for court purposes on grounds of efficiency and security.[31] It has a rich history, including murders on site, Eureka Stockade prisoners acquitted of high treason, the trial and acquittal of gangster 'Squizzy' Taylor, and the trial and hanging next door of bushranger Ned Kelly. As late as 1986, a lethal bomb was exploded outside the court. It was good to talk to my cousin Wendy Wilmoth, then a magistrate of that court, about some of the issues. The university executives, including me, moved into the building once it was refurbished, with concessions for film crew access from time to time. On filming days their entourages created an atmosphere of excitement about the building. I had a wonderful room in it for many years until nabbed on reasonable grounds by Margaret Gardner, an incoming vice-chancellor.

Some development opportunities came by chance. The long vacant Carlton & United Breweries site across Swanston Street from RMIT in Carlton—against whose world headquarter building development RMIT objected in 1986—had since 1994 been owned by the Republic of Nauru, reserved for high-rise development as 'Pacific Central' in partnership with RMIT. Incidentally, the university provided the country's teacher training, and its minister for education had been good enough to join RMIT's business partner panel during a commonwealth quality audit I supervised. The Pacific Central development concept was to provide student housing for up to 1500 beds, a focus for international activities within RMIT, a place for prospective consulates and other appropriate tenants, and accommodation for a concentration of IT and media activities, including a supercomputer cluster, as part of the Knowledge Precinct.[32]

When Nauru's entire sovereign wealth was put at peril through an arrangement with a suspect financial adviser in Melbourne, they had to sell the site at short notice. Acting quickly, Sam Smorgon, the chancellor, approved the purchase over a weekend in 1998. Unable itself to develop the site once acquired, RMIT held it for a number of years—too many years, it drew public opprobrium—and then modified its possible uses to include a design hub.

A KPMG strategic review of university properties was considered by council in December 2003 and it adopted an integrated infrastructure plan enabling the property to go to market shortly thereafter, offering to bidders a choice of different deals, including public–private partnerships and 'design and construct'.[33] The review also recommended a rationalisation of the property portfolio through sales and other developments, and work towards relocation of the business portfolio onto what is now its magnificent building on Swanston Street. By then I was responsible again for campus development, and oversaw the closing stages of the CUB site bidding competition, which Grocon eventually won. Its actual development occurred after I left, a happy conclusion to a long saga.

Academic leadership by the non-academic

From 1989–94, years of some upheaval, I stayed responsible for higher education, which included research and the higher education part of international education for most of the time. David Beanland encouraged me to act often as director or, after the position was created, vice-chancellor. I accumulated nearly a year at that, sometimes during critical periods. This work was under a series of employment contracts, with some good results, but I never felt fully secure in the job, and in renewals I was seldom given an enthusiastic endorsement of my performance. I was working ridiculous hours and under stress.

Some breaks were helpful—summer programs in university leadership at Harvard and Melbourne Universities, time to publish and travel professionally—but the job of helping build a university was pressing. I was determined not to let this ruin time with the children, and I went to some lengths to avoid this with Maya, Sasha and Kina. They went to RMIT's children's centre in West Melbourne, a warm and interesting place for them to learn, but they also played in my office and came to so many university meetings and receptions that workmates and council members got to know them all too well.

An old issue resurfaced in this time. As recounted earlier, the terms 'royal' and 'university' could not be reflected in RMIT's official name. I believed we should stay RMIT, just as MIT (the Massachusetts Institute of Technology) does not have 'university' in its name. Market research did however show that prospective international students wanted to know clearly that RMIT was a university, and later the move came to brand (but not formally rename) the institution as 'RMIT University'. I opposed the idea but lost the argument. Perhaps this was not a big issue, but it came back to irk me from time to time. I led the debating team for the Australian Club, one of Melbourne's oldest clubs. In one debate, the opposing team from the Savage Club, all senior counsel in their day jobs, had the audience laughing out loud as they mocked my day job for being at the 'Royal Melbourne Institute of Technology University'.

I also opposed, unsuccessfully, the consolidation of RMIT's Melbourne graduations into one big stadium, where we, the university leadership, sat on a rotating stage in front of tens of thousands of distant graduands and supporters. Sometimes my unwelcome contributions came by mistake. When the chancellor in council asked 'David' what he thought of the proposed new logo for RMIT (still there today), I thought he was looking at me and said, 'It looks like a big red spitball'. Of course, he was really asking David Beanland. There were too many Davids in leadership at RMIT at the time—at least six on my count—but there is no accepted collective noun. A den of Davids, perhaps?

I allowed myself to question academe and higher education, as much as I had questioned urban planning. What makes a university? I read Cardinal Newman, but his universal liberal pedagogy didn't seem much about RMIT, separation from the church hardly having been an issue. Nor did most of the US critiques of university education at the time. Free discussion, universal, autonomous, yes, but neither the dictates of the Dawkins reform (effectiveness and efficiency, growth to meet the economy's needs) nor RMIT's long-standing ethos (technical and professional orientation, a strong TAFE sector, work readiness, applied knowledge) quite fitted that broad, liberal tradition.[34]

Powers to accredit its own programs within the government approved profile, and to set its own directions, were gains well won, but there was much more work to do. RMIT as a university wished to become even better known for its practical learning and teaching, industry engagement and applied research. There are very few dual-sector universities in Australia and not many more around the world. Challenges were to strengthen teaching and learning, including through a distinguished professoriate, develop a limited number of key research strengths, build a major international presence, and bring order to the strong but scattered pattern of engagement with the different communities that often took RMIT for granted.

Many able educators did not feel equipped for expansion of research, especially in the 1990s when RMIT rewarded research winners to position itself in the Dawkins-era competitive research funding environment. The Australian Research Council (ARC) and its funding system was new. Metrics were important and political. How big should a concentration be before a group could be designated a 'centre'? How to measure research outcomes and impacts across the fine arts, architecture and business, as well as engineering and the sciences? Decisions on these questions were tough, but there were some exceptional groups already with standing. At the same time, we channelled significant resources for seed funding to new researchers and to university entry into chosen strategic fields. RMIT, and other universities in the Australian Technology Network (ATN), a group of similar universities, tended to centralise and direct research priorities more than traditional universities, which were decentralised and more curiosity-driven. And what about those who were less interested in research, or who were well back from ARC-like standards?

One driver of change was the design of a professoriate and an academic staff promotion scheme discussed earlier. I was helped with research and academic strategy by being on the ARC Research Infrastructure and Australian Vice-Chancellors Committee academic DVC (deputy vice-chancellor) committees. Another key factor for RMIT and my thinking was adoption of the Boyer model of scholarship (of discovery, integration, application and teaching and learning), allowing recognition of a wide range of self-reflective educational practices in this practice-oriented university.[35] These settings, along with an active academic development program, set much of the institution's culture, as academic staff had clear criteria for advancement. In the inaugural professorial round, I too had to face my peers' assessment against the criteria.

Procedures for new courses or major changes were cumbersome, not meeting the aim of RMIT becoming nimble, and they needed work. Like most universities in Australia, RMIT had a system of dual governance with the academic board reporting to council parallel to management. There was healthy dissenting advice to council from time to time, and on the whole, it had become an effective arena.

The course advisory committees were a force in RMIT's transformation. Every course had to have one, and demonstrate that external members from industry and the relevant communities had influence over the creation and directions of them. Along with near-universal requirements for student industry experience in courses, this furthered RMIT's 'real world' mission. Course advisory committees had the right, when necessary, to make representations to council. Though this hardly ever happened, it kept pressure on departmental academics to pay attention to advice.

I have to admit such advice was not always wise. Industry representatives, sometimes corporate recruiters rather than senior executives, tended to look for immediate work-readiness rather than attributes with longer-term usefulness, and sometimes wanted to crowd the curricula with prescribed hours on professional topics. Occasionally, industry chairs with particular bees in their bonnets were appointed. But making course advisory committees effective added a lot to RMIT's engagement with industry and students' learning experience.

'Paid outside work' policy was another less-recognised force in RMIT's transformation. By its nature, the university attracted academics and researchers from industry who were encouraged to stay involved. One means was through paid consulting, outside teaching, sale of creative works and provision of other services. Too much, and core work was diverted; too little, and they would get out of touch. After some trial and error—and testy discussions with unions about who owned the intellectual property from courses (apart from earlier contracts of employment, the university did)—a regime came into place in 1992 that encouraged such engagement with supervisor approval, but levied university overheads when the topics of outside work were inside position descriptions.

These are but a few of the many things, less visible and less organised into 'projects', that together make up a working university going through rapid growth, constant government policy changes, an uneasy mix of autonomy and accountability, and the upheavals of the two major mergers and more TAFE mergers not covered in this memoir.[36] There had to be a means of assuring quality. RMIT was very diverse, sprawling across many disciplines and industries, different sites and ways of working, and with different standards of quality.

Quality assurance can be interesting

Quality assurance really mattered. Being technical and tuned into industry trends, RMIT was more sympathetic to quality assurance in general, and total quality management (TQM) in particular, then sweeping corporate practice but shunned by traditional universities. To improve the standard of the education programs and promote TQM across the university, in 1991 the vice-chancellor set up a quality development office. It was to 'guide all operational areas in questioning their efficiencies and exploring ways of involving staff in quality management'.[37] David Beanland was impatient, for good reason, with those who thought of quality as just a standard, as in 'high quality'. He promoted the view that quality assurance was a process of continuous improvement, not a measure of outcome. I strongly supported this.

The Australian government created the independent Committee for Quality Assurance in Higher Education (CQAHE) in 1993 to review universities, and provided a further $70m for each of three years to be allocated on a competitive basis on the standards of their own internal quality management and the excellence of their outcomes.[38] The first review asked the following questions: What quality assurance policies and practices does the institution have in place or is developing? How effective are these? How does the institution judge the quality of its outcomes? In what areas and in what ways are the outcomes excellent? What are the institution's priorities for improvement?

Like the other universities, RMIT opted in. Reputation and money were at stake. I went 'off-line' from my normal job to lead a full-time project team with the quality development unit, to bring RMIT's submission portfolio into shape and to go through the necessary self-assessment and preparation for audit. This was helped by going to the 1993 conference of the international network for quality assurance agencies in higher education in Montreal, a gathering of higher education quality agencies and interested universities. Despite David Beanland's push for TQM and some ISO (International Standards Organisation) certifications, the university was not in great shape. It still had a collection of different policies and processes, and the faculties, schools and groups were doing their work in their own way, each adapted to their different environment, and still coping with the aftermath of the VUT, Phillip and TAFE mergers.

While we took urgent steps to improve quality management practices in time to show the CQAHE audit team they were in place, we also took advantage of the diversity of stories and strengths of post-merger quality management, writing up a large number of documented case studies for each CQAHE category, all in a standard format. Time was short, and the intense work with non-negotiable deadlines pushed some of the team into stress leave. I felt bad about this. While normally a genial manager, I could push work targets too hard. Those affected were able to join us later in celebration of our success.

It was a voyage of discovery, finding lesser-known groups, pockets of high achievement and some very innovative practices, especially in areas like community and professional service where patterns of engagement had not before been documented systematically.

The three-volume result was like an encyclopaedia of RMIT, and it was well-presented, if too long.[39] Beyond the documentation and the last-minute implantation of quality assurance in all units, we established parallel processes of training in quality management and preparation for the visit of the review panel, including trial audits. It was a pleasure to use the TAFE plumbing school's boardroom for CQAHE's visit, a statement that *this* is RMIT too.

When the agency reported its results in 1994, RMIT found itself in the third group, along with Flinders, Griffith and La Trobe University and the University of Tasmania, a group above the other ATN universities.[40] Considering RMIT's position, I thought this was a good result. At a celebration of the result David Beanland said it was 'probably the most corporately focused activity that we have ever undertaken here at RMIT'.[41] The team felt very proud. But we did better. The next year, with a focus on teaching and learning, RMIT was in a large group 2, but three other Australian Technology Network universities (universities like RMIT) were in group 1.[42] Then, in 1995, the review put RMIT in group 1 for both research management and for community service, and in group 2 for both research outcomes and research improvement.

These reviews contributed to the transformation of universities across the country to become more effective mass providers under the Dawkins regime. To critics, the reviews were exercises in rampant managerialism. To David Beanland and me, they improved RMIT. Denis McMullen, then head of student services and a participant in the RMIT process, put it as follows:

> The effect of the Quality Audits has been to force the Universities to accept that they have been subject to a massive, fundamental and irreversible change, a change which they have been loath to recognise for many years, but which has had a profound effect on the Universities, moving them from elite institutions to agencies of mass education.[43]

Efforts on quality management continued. In 1996 Technisearch, the university's main commercial subsidiary, was certified at ISO 9002 (general management quality without product development). The international division, under my control, was certified in 1997. The whole of the university's academic activities were certified at ISO 9001 (i.e. covering product development) in 1998 and then upgraded to the new version in 2003. This was most unusual for a university, as they usually opt to certify their non-academic services first, if any at all. Now all of RMIT's main subsidiaries were certified. A widespread view of certification in the ISO 9000 series is that it gives only minor improvements externally—showing the badge—but significant benefits internally.[44] This was my experience with RMIT's efforts.

The quality reviews and ISO certification gave us some insights into the local quality framework for the international programs, but they did not cover transnational (i.e. cross-border) delivery. For that reason I organised a quality review of the offshore programs through the international management of higher education group of the OECD, featuring Hans de Wit from the University of Amsterdam, Jane Knight from Ryerson University in Toronto (an RMIT-like university) and David Woodhouse, who would go on to be director of CQAHE's successor, the Australian Universities Quality Agency. They were, and still are, thought leaders in the field, and I have since stayed a colleague and friend with Jane. The review found some faults and gave us some directions for improvement, but, on the whole, it complimented us on what we were doing. That is revisited in the next chapter on international engagement.

Three more jobs

An academic services interregnum

I also learned much about RMIT's academic services during the quality reviews. After the merger with Phillip Institute in 1992, Leo Foster, its previous director, ran these for RMIT, including international programs. Leo retired in mid-1994, Ruth Dunkin took over higher education, and the academic services portfolio was offered to me, with international programs coming back. The disparate groups by and large ran themselves, but I had to give strategic direction and handle major changes and 'hot button' issues. The cultures of each group varied widely, as did the characters who ran them.

The student services group brought some fun to my work life. I got to know the student leaders, including those of the RMIT association of international students, and mixed with the staff, many of whom were activists in their own ways. Though I had contacts and friends among students before, I liked the new contacts taking part in World Week and in anti-racism campaigns and big open days. One year, the University of Melbourne broke a tacit agreement to have our open days on separate weekends, so we hired a light plane with a big banner to circle over that university advertising RMIT's open day down the road. A bit juvenile, perhaps, but that taught them!

Student housing was also part of the group's remit. RMIT could not offer the residential colleges of the 'sandstone' universities, so we experimented with contracts to student housing developers and providers to assure decent housing was available for students and helped build a student quarter, at least around the city campus, and a shared student village at Maribyrnong.

The computer centres were very different, highly technical. Its director, Graeme Knox, was too. We reviewed and restructured the group. With the booming growth of the internet, teaching and learning were changing fundamentally, and RMIT was racing to keep up and extend what we called 'distributed learning' across all courses, and meet skyrocketing demand for computer labs and online access. The lead research groups were greedy for processing power too, and RMIT bought a Cray supercomputer in 1994 and created massive data storage capacity. Here, too, though, we had our activists. Some RMIT people were in the mix of setting internet standards through the World Wide Web Consortium (W3C), a bit like the wild west, and we hosted a stream of digital entrepreneurs coming through. I remember one MIT professor pulling a few baby robots out of his pocket and letting them run around the table. I was delighted that Graeme's group also donated decommissioned VAX computers to a university in Vietnam. In a way, it helped pave the way for an RMIT campus there.

The communications services group provided electronic and print services for the educational revolution under way, putting information onto media of all kinds, setting up videoconferencing suites and producing multi-media products for government and industry clients as well as RMIT. It was hard to put into practice David Beanland's vision of ubiquitous and simple stop-start video modules for blended learning, as many faculty were not willing to go online or on record with anything but polished presentations. RMIT helped create, technically broadcast and financially underwrite Melbourne's only free-to-air broadcast community access TV station, Channel 31, but this same misplaced perfectionism about production standards among lecturers prevented the channel from becoming primarily an educational broadcaster. At least all the little clubs and societies of Melbourne with their own community programs benefited.

A fan of libraries, I enjoyed helping push ahead the ambitious plans of the RMIT libraries. Don Schauder led a partnership with the State Library of Victoria to develop a state-wide VicNet, a local library-based public access internet system. They also spun off a subsidiary business INFORMIT, whose turnover grew 65 percent across my year and became the country's biggest digital data publisher, hoovering up databases of interest and putting them on searchable CD-ROMs. The Mormon church was a major donor and client. To them, and to my bemused understanding, making the entire births, deaths and marriage records of Victoria searchable on disc gave their immortal souls, once taken to the holy mountain in Utah, a better chance of getting to heaven.

A new international portfolio and major projects

After less than a year, I changed job again. From 1989, as direct supervisor of the deans, except for the academic services period, I had been in a position to oversee international programs or at least mediate between faculties and the dean of international programs on strategy and issues that arose. This changed from June 1996 when David Beanland, with council support, upgraded the leadership of international policy and programs. A new university executive structure recognised four portfolios, with each dean reporting primarily to Ruth Dunkin as deputy vice-chancellor (DVC) for teaching and learning, but also three ways to the other DVCs for research, resources, and my new position. This way I came to lead the university's international work full-time, the subject of the next chapter. Academic departments became dual-sector, integrating TAFE and higher education for the first time, a move I supported.

Over nearly the next three years this new structure of university management came under strain. Each of the DVCs was ambitious and driving for success in our respective areas. Faculties and schools (their TAFE equivalent) were under pressure to perform against targets in four directions, including for my division. Budget cuts and staff cutbacks were a feature of the late 1990s.

Two of the deputy vice-chancellors departed, leaving Ruth Dunkin and me. Ruth's responsibilities, teaching and learning, were clearly the dominant part of the faculties' business, and she had deepened her understanding of the field through a PhD in the area and innovative practice at RMIT. Though I felt more established and more able to lead than in my earlier years at the university, clearly Ruth was in a stronger position to run for the vice-chancellorship when David Beanland retired, should she apply. I happily carried on with international programs.

To hold operations together, David persuaded council to promote Ruth to sole DVC from the beginning of 1998, responsible for all the activities of the faculties, and simplifying the number of reports to him to three: Ruth, me and John Jackson as DVC resources. It looked like preparation for Ruth to succeed as VC. I was okay with that part of it; I thought Ruth was very able.

But in the reorganisation the position of dean of international programs was to be abolished too, and a new PVC (pro vice-chancellor) international position to be created would play a lighter role in providing policy direction and leaving the faculties to do more international coordination, and the domestic student service groups to provide for international students alongside domestic students. Its focus would be the internationalisation of all students' experience. While that was a fine goal in itself, I was concerned for the future of the international programs, and the dedicated services international students used to access. But I was powerless to stop it, as David had already briefed council and gained their support.

The PVC international job was advertised on 14 October 1998. Clearly it was not meant for me. The vice-chancellor wrote to me on 4 November saying the obvious: my job would cease to exist. The media speculated about 'staff upheavals' at RMIT.[45] The vice-chancellor replied to press comments about me that I was 'continuing' as DVC international, though he knew that I had a transition only until early 1999 before the job was to disappear. Tony Adams resigned as dean of international programs in disgust, went to Macquarie University, and took some good staff with him.

Now I was upset. This was arguably the best group of its kind in the country. In effect, I had been 'constructively dismissed'. Should I resign too?

What could I do? Given the centrality of work on a Vietnam campus which had been building up, and that I had sometimes gone off-line as a DVC to run key assignments like the university quality reviews, David offered me a position as PVC major projects, which still felt, despite assurances to the contrary, like a demotion, if not quite entry to the 'departure lounge'. I was reluctantly willing to do it, and proposed 'executive director' instead as a title to lessen the sting of titular demotion. I took up the job in June 1999, and it carried across the leadership transition from David Beanland to Ruth Dunkin in October 2000. Actually, on the whole, it turned out to be rewarding. And it was still mainly international, as the chapter on the Vietnam campus shows.

So, I was in charge of big projects. When I thought more about it, I'd been doing that at RMIT quite a lot. As well as the campus in Vietnam, I found the other projects interesting and useful too.

Asylum seekers, sustainability and fundraising

One project came out of a headline-grabbing rift in the university about whether or not to provide higher education services to detained asylum seekers. Mary Kalantzis, dean of the faculty of education, language and community services and others in her faculty, wanted to do so. Many others didn't want to associate in any way with a repressive detention regime set up by an Australian government that stoked 'border security' fears of people escaping persecution to Australia on boats. Ruth Dunkin, vice-chancellor, wanted to address it frontally and fully. I led a group to recommend 'action that RMIT can reasonably take in support of asylum seekers in Australia and elsewhere, in detention and in the community'. We were helped by a reference group made up of key members of the wider community, including Julian Burnside and Paris Aristotle, who were at the forefront of advocacy.

It culminated in an overflowing public forum and a report I wrote on possible actions. My bias was towards international actions—a strategic university partnership with the UN High Commission for Refugees to provide worldwide training support—but in the end the committee was more practical. Ruth bravely took up the recommendations and, among other actions in support, RMIT defied federal policy by enrolling asylum seekers as international students with scholarships.[46]

> The boldest recommendation is for a commitment to provide temporary protection and bridging visa holders with access to higher education programs. Temporary protection visa holders are currently able to undertake state government-funded TAFE courses, but they cannot access to federally funded higher education. RMIT's decision to open such programs is a direct challenge to the federal government's policies.[47]

Another cross-university project I led sought to embed sustainability into RMIT's policies and practices through a 'sustainability and triple bottom line' committee. The task was complex as it touched on almost everything that RMIT did: its curricula, its research, its campuses and utilities, its administration, its international activities, its culture and more. And although the work had near-universal support in principle, it was in danger of falling down in practice because it really did need serious changes across much of the university. My approach was influenced by Tricia Caswell, a long-time Queensland AFS returnee friend who was executive director of the global sustainability institute, GS@RMIT, one of only four such university institutes. Woe betide anyone who stood against Tricia when she was on a campaign! Within RMIT, it sought to 'make RMIT a walking, talking model of Global Sustainability', and beyond RMIT to work with founding partners to extend research, teaching and activism.[48] When Tricia left the job in July 2004 her able deputy, Carolyn Bayliss, took over.

In other words, this was not a new start. RMIT had adopted an environmental policy in 1994 and a group of managers and activists like those around my table had been working on it for a decade, helped by a set of indicators from 2001 from the global sustainability institute and a 'greening RMIT' program going since 1998. Katelyn Samson, writing when I took over, judges this preceding decade a failure, pointing to the continued loss of jobs dedicated to the task (including her own), commitments that were non-binding ('green-wash'), fragmentation of effort, underfunding of initiatives (admittedly over a period of financial stringency) and management uninterest. To her, the underlying causes were:

> (1) the establishment of extensive sustainability rhetoric that has not been applied in practice; (2) the implementation of isolated but effective pilot projects that were terminated; and (3) non-compliance with sustainability commitments and the deterioration of critical human and financial resources dedicated to the implementation of sustainability initiatives.[49]

My task was to work with GS@RMIT and the many other centres of activity to make serious progress towards reporting on greater sustainability on all dimensions, of which we counted four, adding governance to the 'triple bottom line' of social, environment and economic dimensions to be 'TBL+1'. The Talloires declaration of the association of university leaders for a sustainable future, which RMIT had signed, gave the committee I chaired a good starting point.[50] Our aims were to advance RMIT's performance on all four dimensions which would be reflected in reporting from the university and its subsidiaries. This was locked into my 2004 individual performance plan, as I was wont to say to those involved: 'Professor David Wilmoth highlighted that RMIT's compliance with its public sustainability commitments has intrinsic relevance to his job as PVC Governance'.[51] I was driven to get results, saying to the committee, 'to paraphrase Marx, we can measure our university performance in various ways, the point is to change it'.

I expected the hard part would be to 'green' the campuses, transport, utilities, energy use and waste practices, but found the property services group continuing supporters, already signatories with the commonwealth government under the greenhouse challenge program to reduce emissions and the greenstar sustainable office program. However, the vice-chancellor's executive had not accepted an RMIT operational sustainability plan, and the property services group, with their own funding constraints and the campuses' old and poorly adaptable buildings, still had to make up ground. Monitoring community and professional engagement also improved; the strategies and progress were much more explicit than shown in the CQAHE rounds of the 1990s.

Getting the strategic plan categories lined up, and widening financial reporting, were tougher, the pace of change on inclusion of sustainability into curricula was slow, and though some research groups were driven by the goals, others took their own time. My advocacy in the executive group had some effect, and after I left RMIT in 2005 the work became more mainstream, with several pro vice-chancellors on the supervising group. A look at RMIT's recent annual reports shows a greatly strengthened level of commitment, with progress towards different goals, including its own carbon neutrality by 2030, the first university debt financing facility of its kind, for $100m, that rewards it for meeting performance sustainability targets, and a 62 percent reduction for 2020 in emissions under the 2007 baseline.[52]

A third 'major project' of mine was leading the university's development or fundraising strategy and servicing the RMIT Foundation. The work of the foundation was straightforward: promoting, receiving and disbursing income from gifts and bequests. Not all gifts to RMIT went to them, including the Atlantic Philanthropies gifts for RMIT Vietnam discussed shortly, in that case for reasons of efficiency in sending funds on for development and operations in Vietnam. Nevertheless, the foundation board and its staff did a good job, at least by Australian standards, in helping the parent university and giving satisfaction to donors and ultimate recipients alike. Clearly, more was needed, and with advice I formed a new approach to fundraising and university development. Perhaps this task was included in the portfolio because I had been successful, albeit at first serendipitously, in raising so much money for RMIT Vietnam.

It seemed to me that 'friend-raising' was as important for the long run for RMIT as fundraising, and that the strategy should simultaneously cascade down and bubble up, through all the different arms of the university. In other words, big gifts promoted to attract smaller gifts, and at the same time many small contributions, including online, to build up scale. University development was defined as the planned raising of benefit for RMIT. Benefit could take the form of funds but could include gifts in kind, bequests, collections, equipment and, importantly, the time and goodwill of influential supporters and of many thousands of people who supported RMIT voluntarily. We identified priority areas for prospects and priority areas of RMIT activity and need. There was interest and support across RMIT, including in council, from where major offers had been facilitated in the past. But against the noise of recovery strategies (from a crisis recounted below) and other issues, it was hard to get traction. The changes went through and we hired fundraising consultants, but the effort did not build up as I had hoped.

The Vietnam campus development project, covered in the next chapter, was taking up more and more of my time. I had been overseas a lot of the time, and now I was spending most of it in Vietnam. In practice I was working there almost on a week-in and week-out basis. Vivian was travelling a lot too, building up an international practice, especially with the World Health Organization. This was not easy on the children, Maya then 15, Sasha 10 and Kina 6. They were too often left to their own devices. This certainly instilled independence, but was it a subtle kind of child neglect? Vivian and I took them into our offices and overseas with us whenever we could, and this narrative includes some of those stories in coming chapters. The children, now grown up, don't think they were so abused, but they certainly remember stories of absence and near misses with organising pick-ups and drop-offs.

While I was preoccupied by these projects at RMIT, storm clouds were building up around us, and to them we now turn.

University crisis and rebuilding governance

Crisis and restructure

The crisis from 2002 was largely of RMIT's own making. It suffered arguably Australia's most disastrous IT crash then to date, and took a long time to recover.[53] I took little part in its causes—though no executive at the time can be exempt—but a somewhat larger part in recovery from it.

Counting its higher education and TAFE sectors, RMIT was the largest university in Australia, with over 57,000 students in many programs, onshore, offshore and online. Its size, growth and complexity were straining the old student record system, first installed in 1982, for which in two of my previous jobs I had been responsible. That old system felt the weight of ever-changing reporting and compliance requirements for the different education systems, and provisions for a greater load from online learning.

In 1999 the university started an academic management system (AMS) implementation project, and in July 2000, two months before Ruth Dunkin was appointed as vice-chancellor, David Beanland signed a contract with PeopleSoft, market leader in the field, to implement the AMS. The project's aims were to integrate student management into one consolidated system, and to streamline student management processes, including enrolments. It therefore needed close interfaces with finance, general ledger and human resources data served by another complex enterprise system, SAP, installed only the year before.[54] As my own projects went to council's finance and major initiatives committee, I was there to see the progress of this project too, and I recall Paul Kennedy, once an NTEU (academic union) powerbroker and now the project director for AMS implementation, saying it would be backed up.

The project went live in October 2001. Problems piled up from the start. On 16 January 2002, as the annual enrolment load was building up, Ruth Dunkin got a message at home that there were problems and she drove straight in on a hunch they were serious. The system had buckled under the massive load of transactions.[55] The preparatory 'business simplification project', an effort at business process reengineering, a management approach in vogue at the time but really needed to make the merged systems work, had not been enough to simplify the number of transactions down to a manageable computing load, and early work with PeopleSoft implementation was fraught with arguments over contract and scope.[56]

Massive data files were lost and would have to be replaced, to the extent they were available at all, from legacy systems and paper records. The immediate consequences were dire: lost debtor and creditor records, including from fee-paying students, inability to issue student debt statements, delays in advising enrolment details, and more. These were documented in excruciating detail by the Victorian auditor-general who reviewed RMIT on behalf of its owners, the government of Victoria.[57]

The financial consequences mounted: costs for replacement and remediation, lost revenue, diverted management resources. At the turnover of vice-chancellor, the university's finances were precariously leveraged, a risky position to be in even before the crisis.[58] The auditor-general's office issued a qualified opinion on RMIT's accounts in December 2002, citing 'clearly unsustainable' negative financial trends. Lynne Kosky, minister for education and training (importantly, also minister for finance), was losing faith in RMIT's capacity to solve the crisis, and in February 2003 gave what amounted to an ultimatum to RMIT to fix it in six months. She asked the Victorian auditor-general to review the financial position and budgetary outlook again.[59] The auditor-general found that the root of the problem was not technical, but poor project governance. RMIT 'did not establish the required governance arrangements, including senior management involvement, or support, to ensure the implementation project was effectively managed', 'staff in key project positions … lacked relevant project management and/or implementation experience', and it was 'difficult to identify clear and concise documentation on the governance process during the early implementation of the AMS'.[60]

It should be noted that other universities were having similar problems with PeopleSoft.

It was extremely hard on the staff involved. They had to recover business-critical data and operate the university while repairing and rebuilding an AMS with a defensive and litigious PeopleSoft, and critical and sometimes hostile media. It was certainly big news. Tragically, in April 2002, the AMS project director at the time of the crash, Paul Kennedy, died while taking a break from work. This was very hard on the leadership team, as we had seen a lot of Paul both in his union and project leadership roles. Sadly, some time after John Jackson left in 2005, he also died. John had been dean of business in my team and then a peer in the executive group, responsible for oversight of the AMS project. Both John and Paul had been friends with many of us.

In the meantime, in the wake of the crash, Ruth Dunkin and many others involved worked mightily to stem the losses, but university finances continued to deteriorate and information was insufficient to enable the auditor-general to form a full opinion. Ruth cut back non-academic operating costs, including staff numbers, and prepared to trim the capital program further by deferring maintenance and selling key assets such as the CUB redevelopment site, described in previous pages, and the Janefield technology park at Bundoora. This yielded savings of $29m. These campus opportunities were lost to RMIT, but the financial sustainability of RMIT was at stake.

There was a chance of a small operating surplus of $3–5m, but for 2002 the result was an operating loss from ordinary activities of $17.7m that took account of $34m spent on the academic management system, much of that unexpected when the budget was set. It was little comfort that, alongside the large operating loss declared for 2002 for RMIT proper, the consolidated accounts for the university group showed a surplus before tax. This was because the operating results for RMIT Vietnam Holdings, $18.5m, reflected early payments of gifts for RMIT Vietnam and learning resource centres in Vietnam, projects described in the coming pages.[61]

Despite these results, as 2002 turned into 2003 there was some optimism in the air and positive indications coming onto the books. Continuing cuts in operating expenses and programs, asset sales and project deferrals had their effect, and progress towards financial recovery was helped along by commonwealth government supplementation of $7.5m.

But again, these signs of recovery did not continue long. Within RMIT morale had deteriorated markedly and it would take a long time to build up. The auditor-general stated that 'the AMS project's culture was viewed as being one of blame rather than one which aimed to resolve problems.'[62] The media on the whole stayed critical of RMIT, in part from the less than transparent way they claimed the university had disclosed the problems. *The Age* reported that:

> Senior managers at RMIT University botched virtually every aspect of the implementation of a $47 million software system that collapsed last year, an auditor-general's report has found. The system will have to be scrapped.'[63]

In fact, it was not scrapped, nor should it have been. *The Australian* and *Crikey.com* were worse, attacking the vice-chancellor personally.[64]

During late 2001 and into 2002 there was disagreement within council over how deeply to cut spending, and some members wanted to take it out on management. In the midst of the conflict the council forced an executive reorganisation through Ruth Dunkin, the vice-chancellor, over her opposition.[65] I wrongly thought this was Ruth's making. Different members of council wanted different executives sacked, and some members opposed her appointment of several women into the new positions. There were many meetings to try to sort out such matters. One council 'retreat' at Bundoora was meant to be informal. In casual dress, but coming early, I saw council members gathering in business clothes, so I jumped back in the car and went to the nearest shopping centre to buy a cheap suit and tie and get back for the starting time. Tension between the chancellor and the vice-chancellor, including over the latter's replacement of the finance director, Ian Raines, was building up.

It bounced along and came to a head late January 2003 in the middle of dealing with the worst of the technical and financial crisis. Knowing he did not have the support of the majority of council for a harder-line approach to cost-cutting and reform, and after three reported meetings with a 'select group' of councillors, Don Mercer surprised most people by resigning as chancellor, effective from 1 February.[66] Ruth saw this as mainly over two of her appointments into executive positions, one in particular. Within two weeks, another five members of council left, including the deputy chancellor and chair of the audit and risk committee. Council was reconstituted, of course, but the media mostly stayed sceptical.

After urgent discussions in government, rumoured to be like 'receivership' talks, by 7 March Professor Dennis Gibson was appointed as chancellor. He was a recently retired vice-chancellor of Queensland University of Technology (QUT), smart, affable, and very experienced with universities. Sometime before, I had served on his appointment panel for his DVC, and we had contact as members of the Australian Technology Network.

Having won through the conflict with some of the old council, Ruth gained the respect of the new members, pointing to some financial recovery off the 2002 results. She kept the support of some staff by continuing to quarantine cuts to as many of the academic programs as possible. But as the AMS reinstallation costs rose (now forecast by the end of the year to be $47m, three times the original budget) she was still under harsh public scrutiny and in state politics opposition Liberal Party attack. Minister Lynne Kosky made another demand to turn the finances around in six months or 'face the consequences'.[67]

The aforementioned restructure of management occurred just before the change of chancellor, and was pushed by council. It was designed to make good on the adopted strategy of 'dissolving the boundaries' and took effect in July 2003 after a long period of consultation. Ruth worked to fit it with her approach to university leadership and modern educational practice. In a sense, the usual pyramid was to be inverted, with students, enterprise and communities of engagement at the top, served by front line academics, researchers, teachers and trainers, who were backed up by specialist portfolios for product development (such as new course design and development), infrastructure and governance.

To break the symbolism of 'building one' as the centre of power, Ruth moved the vice-chancellor's office across the road into modest rented offices.[68] Combined with new approaches to teaching and learning, new business processes and the aftermath of the IT crash, she sought to bring new principles of organisation design to the university, to 'dissolve boundaries', turn the focus to better engagement with students and other clients, and be more innovative.[69] The executive structure was greatly flattened. A matrix of seven discipline-based academic portfolios and four horizontally integrating portfolios came with changes to practices and culture. All this change at once was not easy, and the restructure pushed by council came at the worst time.[70] In the reorganisation, I had a new job once again.

Poacher turns gamekeeper

While I was director of major projects the planned campus in Vietnam came to take up almost all of my time. Constant travel to Vietnam was becoming a grind for me, though we were well represented there by Tricia Roessler, my deputy director described in the next chapter. I was not angling to move there as Vivian and I were not confident of schooling and health care for the three children. All the family had visited Vietnam with me and took part in the decision not to try to go. As a non-resident CEO of RMIT Vietnam (and RMIT Vietnam Holdings), I thought it time for transition to a full-time resident CEO. By late 2002, the transfers of RMIT Vietnam functions to Michael Mann, previously Australian ambassador to Vietnam, and its Melbourne coordination functions to the PVC International, were complete. What next?

Crisis recovery brought an unlikely opportunity. In the reorganisation, Ruth offered me a new division and position as pro vice-chancellor (group governance) to help clear up the organisational mess. John Jackson, previously dean of business and DVC resources who had been doing the group governance job, as well as overseeing AMS installation in its earlier days, had resigned in July 2003.

I acted in that job for the transition, and then took it on as PVC group governance. Its primary functions were improvement of the governance framework of the university and its group of companies. I was to take leadership of internal audits, compliance and risk management, subsidiary companies (including servicing the RMIT foundation), the council secretariat, legal services, and property services and campus development. Some of this I knew from work on risk management, subsidiary companies and property, but much of the rest was new to me.

This time I was not the entrepreneur, the company start-up leader, the protector and defender of risk-takers. I was to reform the corporate governance system of the RMIT group and where necessary clean out the stables. I felt less Augean and more like a poacher turned gamekeeper. I was concerned it might be a little too dry and administrative.

It wasn't. I liked the work. It helped to have clear auditor-general recommendations behind me—woe betide anyone who resists them!—and my work must surely be useful under the straitened circumstances. Council approved a program of work to respond to the auditor-general's findings, and more. We started the first compliance management system. Council received the improved risk management system well, including disaster response, management and recovery. Helped by Monash University, which had handled a deranged shooter on campus, we ran a major incident simulation on the city campus. This event reminded me of an earlier incident that caused me, as acting vice-chancellor, to close the city campus as a result of the Coote Island chemical plant disaster not too far away. The human resources director had then recommended closing the campus, contrary to the recommendation of the authorised person in the disaster manual, the director of property services. It was hard to tell who was right—and I was off-campus at the time—but I felt I had to err on the side of caution.

Much of the governance group was in offices across Swanston Street near the main campus, and staff remembered 1997 when students, protesting RMIT taking up the commonwealth-created opportunity to charge fees, occupied and damaged the finance group offices for 19 days. My office in 'building one' suffered more than one occupation over those years too, but unlike elsewhere on campus, the occupiers were reasonably respectful. The more frequent intrusions into our office area came from occasional deranged people coming off the street, or drug-users looking for a place to inject.

The costs of an open campus.

Internal audits should have been on the front line of the reform work, as the group had undertaken an earlier review on university governance and there was a newly revised and urgent program of audit reviews before us, as well as continuing normal oversight of fraud and other risks. But there were issues of appropriate conduct within the group and, within a few months, after a KPMG report (who audits the auditors?) I saw to it that all three full-time auditors had gone, not necessarily in disgrace.

A Victorian review in 2002 of the governance of university controlled entities recommended better oversight of commercial activities and a more businesslike handling of risk management.[71] The subsidiary companies of RMIT, 11 of which were fully owned, some unincorporated entities and many with only part-equity participation by RMIT, needed straightening out.[72] Fully owned companies need good reasons to exist, otherwise why not just use the executive arms of the parent university? They had no role in lightening the university's balance sheet, or debt profile, as Australian regulations had long since removed any 'corporate veil' of liability: councillors, as directors of the parent university, had responsibility for the performance and compliance of the subsidiaries just as if they were an inner part of the university.

The rationale for keeping most of them boiled down to the need for undivided focus on business performance in a specific area, some advantages in terms of employment and industrial relations, and in some cases, preparation for spin-off. In all cases we made sure there were majorities of independent directors on the boards. The board lines of reporting had to be direct to council, not through an extra university line of management. All this was consistent with good 'corporate parenting' practice.[73] Dennis Gibson understood this, though Don Mercer, the chancellor before him, perhaps more used to ANZ practice of batched meetings of multiple subsidiaries through executive lines of management, appeared to me not to.

The council secretariat needed tightening, but not radical reform.

Reporting systems into council needed work and better oversight. To mention just one example: the auditor-general found that the council failed formally to approve the annual budget at the depth of the AMS crisis. This was an embarrassing lapse, but RMIT's response noted that the university continued to act without interruption on the basis of the draft budget at the time. It was just a matter of key people forgetting to formalise a provisional arrangement.

All my RMIT jobs, with the possible exception of the deanship, required close interaction with RMIT councillors, internal and external. Though sometimes frustrating because of contested views and the need for reasonable executive solidarity, this was one of the most interesting and often pleasant parts of the work, and I am friendly with some members to this day. For example, Terry Francis, who was then chair of the council finance and major initiatives committee and experienced with public–private partnerships, later joined me to lead risk assessment in a university project in Botswana.

Meanwhile, through executive restructure, continuing tensions nagged at RMIT's recovery. The AMS was still being rebuilt, just a 'vanilla' version, stripped of most modifications, with elements borrowed from a similar system at the University of South Australia. Step by step, unevenly, RMIT's finances, information systems and governance were improving. Year 2003 brought a net operating surplus of $36.6m. But during 2004, expenses and losses still kept coming to book, and conditions looked difficult again. The net operating result for RMIT was headed for a loss.

The continuing internal changes kept a level of disquiet simmering, and a covert campaign, reminiscent of the VUT anti-merger movement, whispered that the vice-chancellor, despite her PhD qualifications, came from an administrative, not an academic background (actually, like me), and that her professorial title was not earned but came with the appointment. The facts that she was the first female vice-chancellor in Victoria and that some of these criticisms had a misogynous cast have to be faced. In Ruth's words, 'I find it difficult to believe the public debate would have been couched in quite the same way if I had been male'.[74] Despite some staff appreciating her efforts, and in particular for protecting teaching and learning and research from cuts as far as she thought possible, others continued to blame her for the AMS crisis and its handling, even though she had inherited its project design, and system of project oversight, as well as over-leveraged university finances.

In the words of Victor Del Rio, whose doctoral thesis was on major corporate crises in Australia, as financial recovery hopes faded at RMIT, media attacks on her 'reignited', some of them questioning the quality of her PhD thesis and reproducing a so-called 'staff motion of no confidence' in her that alleged 'ineffective, non-consultative and divisive leadership'.[75] Ruth rightly saw much of this as 'rumour and innuendo … [that was] not going to go away'.[76]

Her transparency-driven honest warnings of financial challenges ahead perhaps unintentionally stoked these fires. The mix of sceptical public support and divided staff opinion kept her leadership in the news. *The Age*, previously critical, ran stories of how she had 'pulled RMIT back from the brink' and acted with composure.[77] But concerns were building up again in council, too.

Exits

Ruth resigned on 28 August 2004. Chris Whitaker, previously CEO of Melbourne Ports and PVC business at RMIT, took over as interim vice-chancellor. With finances deteriorating, Chris promised deeper cuts again.

> [H]e said the university would cut up to 180 jobs this year and slash costs at a 'magnitude and intensity that has never been seen'. He predicted the austerity measures would help achieve a $40 million surplus by 2007.[78]

Indeed, the year did not end well, with RMIT carrying an operating deficit of $24.4m for 2004.

The search for a replacement was quick, as university appointments go. Margaret Gardner, a Queenslander like Dennis Gibson, and wife of Glyn Davis, vice-chancellor of the University of Melbourne, started as vice-chancellor of RMIT in April 2005. This fed speculation about how much say the council really had in the choice, and whether the Victorian government acted independently of council to bring in an outsider vice-chancellor, as they had earlier brought in a new chancellor. Was it a kind of involuntary receivership installed by the university's owners? While acknowledging the serious financial conditions, Margaret set her first task as clarifying the vision and direction of the university ahead. The theme of her inaugural address was a clever riff off Dickens' *A Tale of Two Cities*: 'It was the best of times, it was the worst of times, it was the age of wisdom, it was the age of foolishness ...'[79]

I expected to get on well with her, as she had an academic research interest in urban social movements, an interest of mine too. Rather than take Ruth's office across La Trobe Street, she took a liking to my room, a magnificent old Victorian judges' common room, and I was happy she took it as her own. It was time for the vice-chancellor to move back onto the campus. She supported our work on group governance through my remaining year, but I couldn't help feeling she saw me as a remaining part of the 'old guard' and wouldn't mind too much if I went. Her main task was to steady the ship and steer it onto a reliable, sustainable course ahead, which she did well. Although she supported RMIT Vietnam—as had Ruth earlier, a creature of neither of their making—her period over RMIT's international activities was marked by a lower appetite for risk and innovation.

Her promotion of care and caution did help governance. With the reforms mostly working it seemed to me that a PVC portfolio for governance was not needed any more. I put a plan to her in which I would wind up and transfer responsibilities to other portfolios, and be free to retire. There was no push from her for me to go, but she accepted it. Despite liking this recent job, I felt I had stayed too long at RMIT, 17 years in all, at least eight different jobs, and I was tired. I would have left earlier, but I wanted to help recovery and not be seen leaving a sinking ship.

Vivian had long thought, somewhat ruefully, that I was 'married to RMIT'. During my time as the international deputy, I was overseas a lot. Though Vivian and I had a wonderful group of friends, we were both under work pressure and, despite trying, I had not found a balance between work and home life.

I missed the urban sector work of years ago, and wondered how easily I could get current again. Peter Drucker said a pathway for the second half of your life is to develop a parallel career.[80] Before leaving RMIT I tested the water for consultancy work by doing a short urban sector review of Vietnam for the World Bank, and leading, at the last minute, a World Bank/China Development Bank rapid review team in Tianjin. From these forays I thought it might not be too hard to get back into the sector.

On 2 September 2005, I retired from RMIT and its companies. At the retirement lunch, shared slightly awkwardly with someone whose departure wasn't entirely voluntary, I was given no gold watch but an edgy ceramic piece made by Fang Po-Ching that looked like a tissue dispenser.[81] Whoever chose it must have known I liked RMIT's fine art departments' odder student works, which I used to rotate through my office. But a tissue dispenser? Going into the carpark after the lunch, I slipped and it fell, breaking into dozens of fragments.

That felt apt.

How did we go?

It is not easy to sum up 17 years and eight jobs at RMIT, especially as there are two more chapters on the period to come. The changing back-drop to RMIT may have resembled that of other institutions, but the scenes on its stage between 1988 and 2005 were dramatic and distinctive. RMIT grew from 29,000 students in 1987, with 200 overseas students, to 57,000 in 2005, of which 18,000 were international students. It greatly expanded its teaching and learning programs, both in TAFE and higher education, and moved from face-to-face and distance learning modes to a variety of electronically distributed ways of learning. It kept its strong focus on teaching and learning as it built its research capacity, not always easily, but with continuing innovation. It never abandoned its focus on industry relevance and job-readiness for students, through continuation of a strong culture in those directions, and through specific policies such as work-integrated learning and course advisory committees. In the latter part of the period some of the promise of articulated learning pathways both ways between TAFE and higher education were realised, especially after the difficult decision to create dual-sector schools.

Its research capacity and performance built up strongly (but quite unevenly) over those years, as RMIT embraced selectivity in internal support, a consequence of results-based commonwealth funding policies and success with public and private funding for particular centres. Fields of excellence in research aligned broadly with the best-regarded of the courses.

By the very nature of its commitment to the professions and industry, the fairly free flow of staff and students in and out of workplaces and community settings, and the location of its campuses, RMIT's community engagement, in all its dimensions, has always been strong. However, during this long period it became much more organised and recognised, including in criteria for staff appointment and progression, a powerful incentive for setting academic priorities anywhere.

These three transformations, and the international changes discussed next, did not flow along smooth curves. They came fast and slow, bumped by constant changes to the educational profile as the university and the institute before it manoeuvred to respond to changes in public funding rules and policies, including merger opportunities. The changes to public funding and policies were seldom favourable, so retrenchments and reorganisations were more frequent than would have been desirable. However, some of these reorganisations were driven by internal conditions such as changes of vice-chancellor, pressure from council or ideas to modernise management. More rarely, but dramatically, mergers and institutional crises dislodged RMIT, issues building up glacially and then fracturing suddenly.

As RMIT grew and became more complex, its management had to become more sophisticated and more corporate in style. Running TAFE and higher education sectors together was a particularly difficult task, as by then, taking all sectors into account, RMIT was Australia's largest tertiary education institution. I was struck by the scale of our work when

I attended the Harvard higher education summer school in 1994. Most of the other participants were leaders of colleges and universities tiny by comparison. Putting in place the systems for research management, the professoriate, quality assurance and generally the framework for better academic governance was satisfying and successful. I was grateful that RMIT accepted me into leadership with my non-academic background. In 2005 it was bigger, smarter and much more international than in 1988.

After the first year, I regretted leaving my short-lived deanship because it had a balance of scholarly activities and management that I would have preferred to my half-won hold on more senior university leadership. However, if I had stayed I might not have liked working in this shatter zone between constant university manoeuvring around changing government funding rules and the implementation of cutback after cutback. I know my friend Leonie Sandercock, who was for a time head of school in that faculty, hated handling those cutbacks instead of doing her core academic job.

In a way, the first merger and the systems crisis were damaging events from which RMIT had to rebuild and recover. While hard to characterise these as creative destruction, they certainly did focus the university's leadership on its core values and how the future of the university should look. That was the same for me. My jobs and ways of working had to change after each of them, going towards making decisions that were more sustainable for the longer-term future in the areas of corporate governance and robust academic policies.

We made some good headway on modernising curricula and distributing learning electronically, including for international delivery. However, we never really came close to completing that huge task. Though I put work into it, my vision was complementary to those of David Beanland and Ruth Dunkin, not distinctively my own. Opening up the city campus into a lively urban precinct and developing the other campuses was satisfying work. There too, though I was responsible for campus development in two of those eight jobs and enjoyed the planning and the deal-making, I had a minor hand on leading its direction. My role was more to do with enabling others to do the work.

Leadership should be mainly about having a vision or sharing one, finding good people, joining them in strategy making and then leaving them to get on with the job, with course corrections as needed. That I did, though once or twice I was a party to bad appointments, including a poor choice of dean.

While sometimes I showed courage and more often determination, I did not take big steps ahead of conventional wisdom and draw people with me. I showed real courage only when I believed principles were at stake or injustices might be done. My forte was more in collaboration and management. I enjoyed problem-solving and finding solutions 'out of the box' through lateral thinking. We hosted Edward de Bono, the guru of lateral thinking, a number of times. At least I had wide communication roles, in the early years often representing our leadership in the media because I had some experience in public affairs.

The feedback I sometimes received was that my directions were not clear. Curiosity led me to consider too many options, too many 'if this, then that' instructions. That was confusing for my teams. Although the peer feedback I received included statements like 'visionary leader with strengths in intellectual capability and creativity … a caring individual and a model of integrity', they also included comments like '… he does, however, need to get to the answer in terms of the processes used to ensure people are brought along'.

Curiosity and willingness to find unconventional solutions coupled with enjoyment of entrepreneurship, through starting ventures, guiding our various commercial subsidiaries and spending good time outside the university. I was prepared to take risks myself, and support staff who did so too, particularly with international programs. This sometimes brought failures which, on the whole, we learned from. Only later did I learn professional risk management and come to enjoy using the tools of corporate governance, the gamekeeper role described earlier.

Just as my technocratic belief in strategic urban planning in earlier years did not hold up in practice—witness the NSW government's abrogation of the framework we built up for Sydney in the 1980s—and caused me to focus more on better urban governance, so my belief in the power of university strategic planning was found wanting and my attention shifted to the need to implement the basic principles of good corporate governance.

My self-management was not top class. I let my reserves of energy and stamina become an excuse to defer sorting out priorities, to do too much myself to meet deadlines, taking home trays of work and interfering with family life. I cut back on that when, acting as vice-chancellor, I found I'd taken home a commonwealth government cheque for tens of millions of dollars in my briefcase.

Perhaps I did well as a deputy? Most of those years I worked with David Beanland, who was decisive and assertive, occasionally to a fault. On big tasks like starting up RMIT Vietnam, we worked very well together and have remained friends. On all the jobs I had plenty of scope to make decisions, of course; RMIT was big and my portfolios were wide. Working with Ruth Dunkin was good and practical, and sometimes fun, but during some of her time as vice-chancellor the environment of trust around the senior group was challenged. Working with Margaret Gardner was correct and professional, but as mentioned above, we didn't become as close as I had hoped.

Was it that I was better at management than leadership? I think it was more about my leadership style. I built support, and people followed my directions when they were clear, through common understanding of aims and strategies. Most had respect for my decency and aligned with the aims. But I wasn't the conventional 'out in front' leader. At the time, Henry Mintzberg, the management theorist, was vital reading among the executive group, and important to Ruth's thinking in particular.[82] He said that the role of strong leaders was overrated, that leaders without management got out of touch, and managers without leadership were rudderless. Leaders can be 'incomplete', in the sense that Ancona *et al* mean:

> It's time to end the myth of the complete leader: the flawless person at the top who's got it all figured out. In fact, the sooner leaders stop trying to be all things to all people, the better off their organizations will be. In today's world, the executive's job is no longer to command and control but to cultivate and coordinate

the actions of others at all levels of the organization. Only when leaders come to see themselves as incomplete—as having both strengths and weaknesses—will they be able to make up for their missing skills by relying on others.[83]

I made many friendships among fellow staff, councillors and students, some of which have endured beyond the RMIT years. Perhaps I may have been something of a Pollyanna: in daily work I seldom disliked anyone, or made enemies. Opponents on some issues became supporters on others. At times I felt like one of those 'wise fools' in Russian novels, conscious of occasionally being manipulated, bypassed or talked about behind my back, but going along with the collective effort that got my friends at RMIT through the good times and bad in the big job of making a university.

These reflections cover all my times at RMIT. The next two chapters explore some highlights in more detail: the growth of an international presence and the development of RMIT University Vietnam.

EIGHT

INTERNATIONALISING THE 'WORKING MAN'S COLLEGE'

This chapter goes back through my time at RMIT to trace the surge of internationalisation that occurred over the period, looking at the 'what and why' and especially the 'how', including the Penang campus and other offshore ventures. From my AFS experience I had easy empathy with international students and did all I could to make RMIT international in all its dimensions, including cross-cultural engagement. There was an obvious connection between this work and urban development, as international students made up a big proportion of the population of the City of Melbourne. I learned a lot about how to identify international opportunities, shape them up into ventures, and deliver them across borders. This became the core business of my work after RMIT.

RMIT had a history of international engagement going back to the 1950s Colombo Plan, through which promising students from the larger southeast Asian region studied on scholarships in Australia.[1] A flow of private international students also came from Papua New Guinea. The Jackson report of 1984 paved the way for expansion of intakes to meet the demand for education in developing countries so that Australia could 'develop its education institutions into a major export sector'.[2] A countervailing report from a government committee chaired by John

Goldring argued against the commodification of full fee-paying international student programs and in favour of tying them to multicultural tolerance, but it was overshadowed by the Jackson report.[3] In 1986, the government allowed publicly funded higher education institutions to market their programs overseas and charge full fees, and in 1988 it ceased subsidies to international students.[4]

In 1987, the year before my arrival, there were 200 overseas students at RMIT. By 1992, international student enrolments had grown to 2310 onshore and 865 offshore.[5] In 2020, there were over 36,000 international students overall.[6] This was explosive growth, but the onshore international student program was just one of several.

Turning entrepreneurship into systems and strategies

The faculty of business had the largest number of onshore international students and the most active offshore programs, led by deans John Milton-Smith and then, on an acting basis from 1990, Tony Adams. I remember John characterising RMIT as a Chinese emporium—a disorganised big jumble with some wonderful products tucked away on the shelves. International programs were a bit like that. They were growing in variety and numbers through the decentralised entrepreneurship of the faculties and departments. Systematic growth was held back by a lack of strategy and working policies, procedures and standards, with only 'semi-formal' arrangements in place. Perhaps the movers at the time might have said they were in reality enabled by those absences. This was not only the case for international strategy, but for the whole movement to reform corporate processes for strategic planning and targeted budgeting.

By 1991, the international programs started a new phase, with greater strategic development. The university corporate plan acknowledged internal pressures for coordination of the international student program, international strategy, scholarships and offshore project approvals. That year we created a new university office of international programs (UOIP) in a direct report to me, with Tony Adams the dean after his stint acting as dean of the faculty of business. This was the first non-faculty deanship and its title only weakly supported by the faculty deans, who feared the wider spread of their titles. Tony was an excellent appointment as he knew well the pioneering faculty's programs and had a vision and a passion for what might be achieved, a flair for international deal-making, and a capacity to build loyalty among his staff.

He led the drafting of an international strategy which clearly categorised the programs and set directions for each of them: an international onshore student program, education abroad, offshore programs and projects, offshore campuses, international research and the internationalisation of the curriculum.[7] Each had clear university-wide leadership identified and, step by step, clearer administrative policies and processes.

A more detailed structure grew under the international programs. The UOIP steadily created and brought together documentation of procedures.[8] Rules-based behaviour followed, and captured after the event, the informal practices of the travelling academic trailblazers. However, they were not comfortable when compliance (read 'red tape') caught up with them from time-to-time, nor always was Tony Adams, who was inclined to forgive a creative but non-compliant event and encourage more experimentation. But as the procedures echoed their practices, they were useful for faculties other than business to build up their own scale and emulate business faculty practices. This aligned with a push from external councillors and growing interest from the state auditor-general to install more business-like approaches to university management.

We kept a live register of significant international contacts, negotiations and agreements, picking up lesser known agreements in place (some which I didn't know about) and requiring approval before any further agreements could be entered into in the future, even friendly but vague memoranda of understanding (MOUs) typically signed by deans or department heads on overseas trips. This was intended, in part, to avoid parallel agreements with different partners in the same city by different parts of RMIT, and it had the advantage of seeing the whole pattern of international engagement. It allowed us to brief comprehensively and accurately RMIT visitors to those countries, or visitors from them when they came to Australia. RMIT had the largest number of international exchange and cooperation agreements among Australian universities. I didn't think this was a good indicator, and acted to rationalise them by discontinuing inactive agreements. We also renewed an uncomfortable number of out of contract agreements which had continuing business.

The 1992 strategic plan aimed to develop staff familiarity with countries in the region, enable RMIT to be responsive to the needs of those countries, provide opportunity for RMIT students to study abroad, support Australian companies in the region, and form a network of alumni offshore. This was a good start. By 1994, the international strategy had matured to be ready for council adoption, reported as the first of its kind in the country.[9] It linked to one-year operational plans with performance targets across the university, priorities among countries, and detailed individual country and area strategies.[10]

Depending on the level of maturity of engagement in a country, we established a number of country 'desks' in Melbourne, with time allowances made in individual work plans for some chosen desk leaders cum country 'champions'. They were well-informed about the area, knew most of what was happening across the university in their country, and were encouraged to network with other country enthusiasts and experts, often through committees with other scholars engaged in the area. Importantly, they had no 'veto' power over others' work, though from time to time they did raise compliance issues needing escalation to resolve them.

We also set up a number of in-country 'posts' in high-priority countries, alongside the network of recruitment agents abroad managed by Technisearch, RMIT's main commercial subsidiary. Typically alumni or ex-staff of RMIT, the in-country appointees were part-time appointments, with 'light touch' coordination responsibilities across all RMIT's in-country program activities.

The UOIP serviced a number of university committees to operate the programs, such as on international student scholarships and on offshore project approvals. Staff of the office were bright, convivial and many of them unconventional. I enjoyed their company a lot, but on some issues I could not escape the 'building one' tag, of being a member of the executive group. Parallel bidding between faculties and Technisearch sometimes occurred, so we required Technisearch to give the faculties 'first right of refusal' on any opportunities before Technisearch could hire independent contractors, who were typically more used to delivering international projects on time than fully academic teams.

We channelled around two percent of gross onshore international student program revenues into a vice-chancellor's discretionary fund to seed major international projects. This funded a joint building on the Vietnam National University (VNU) campus in Hanoi and feasibility work on the Penang campus and the Vietnam campus. A more logical pattern of international engagement was coming into place.

Making strategy from practice

The overall goal of the international strategy was to:

> internationalise the curriculum and educational experience of RMIT students through development of a culture which values the globalisation of education with all its implications and effective action in ... the international student program, education abroad, offshore programs and projects, and internationalisation of the curriculum.[11]

Classification of programs gave shape to the strategy. In a way, they reflected the classic trade-investment ladder and the classification used in the WTO General Agreement on Trade in Services (GATS) negotiations then under way.[12] The onshore program was trading our programs through students travelling to learn, joint international research was similar, the offshore programs were a means of taking the programs to the students in their own countries through trading partnerships, as were international development projects exporting the university's expertise. The development of joint ventures and then wholly owned campuses were further steps involving direct investment. Across these were growing student and scholar exchanges, and organised study abroad arrangements in and out of Australia. And through them all was a commitment, not clearly defined at first but always asserted, of 'internationalising the curriculum'. These programs each warrant a closer look.

Onshore programs

The onshore international student program was the first and largest of the programs. It was not at all well organised, and so we decided to outsource much of it to Technisearch. For that, Tony Adams and Technisearch CEO Bernard Cronin locked themselves away and hammered out an arrangement, that with my support, was accepted by the other deans and endorsed by council. Under annual performance contracts Technisearch took over responsibility for marketing, student recruitment, fee collection, fee distribution, visa and other statutory functions, negotiating course targets with each dean and the TAFE division, and reporting on progress towards the targets. Clearly, RMIT proper kept responsibility for all course delivery, academic services, counselling and other services once students enrolled. This included extensive service support dedicated to international students through the UOIP and representation through an active RMIT association of international students, which brought out outstanding leaders, with some of whom I still stay in touch.

These arrangements laid the basis for very fast growth, 59 percent year on year to 1991. The international student program accounted for over 13 percent of the university's income and we aimed at 20 percent in our 1994 strategy. It cross-subsidised other international and domestic activities both directly, through overheads charged on higher fees for international students, and indirectly, as the costs of educating each extra international student were borne at just a marginal rate, at a time when domestic students were tending to spend less time on campus.

By 1999, the year I left the job as deputy vice-chancellor international, the onshore program enrolled 6855 students, still growing at 11 percent that year and by my estimate in the university's annual report the largest of its kind in the world.[13] Combined with offshore programs and including TAFE numbers, at 12,125 RMIT enrolled Australia's largest number of international students, representing 16 percent of total student load at RMIT. It had been ranked first for total international onshore numbers in Australia since 1995. This took Technisearch, to which we outsourced fee collection, to be the largest university subsidiary in the country, according to income, and RMIT and Technisearch together were ranked 254 among all exporters from Australia.[14] Even so, as Carmelle Le Vin and Tony Adams point out, the organisational culture at RMIT was at that time self-effacing, with little inclination to make extravagant claims.[15]

But this growth did change the character of the university. Though the domestic student body and RMIT staff also came from many cultures and countries, the presence of international students from over 100 countries greatly enriched diversity. This growth came at a cost. Services dedicated to international students were well-organised, but the demands on them, academics and other service providers, strained the university's capacity. We established training programs in intercultural learning through staff exchanges (for example, student services personnel to and from China), offered a graduate diploma in intercultural learning from the University of British Colombia to staff, and did what else we could to build that capacity. Academic quality assurance stayed a challenge even though the new foundation studies and professional communications programs prepared international students for university study through English language learning and modern study methods. The marketing arm, for much of the time Technisearch, pressed faculties and schools to take more international students. Some external members of council pressed, unsuccessfully, to dilute English language standards of entry, and a subterranean business of selling assignments had to be quashed at one stage.

The university had almost no dedicated housing, a disadvantage for international and non-Melbourne Australian students alike, and an impediment to international marketing. We made affiliation arrangements with student housing developers and providers where we could, as mentioned in the previous chapter, ranging from a large suburban 'student village' in Maribyrnong to a small 'shop top' over Toto's Pizza around the corner from the city campus. Assuring quality of provision and the compliance of university-associated housing providers was not easy, as housing developers saw it as an easy way to make money. Unlike some other universities, RMIT resisted the urge to take on market risk, by not guaranteeing occupancy or revenue to housing providers.

Community reception of international students was generally good, with the City of Melbourne especially supportive through events and programs. Their numbers were building up. By 2010, 48 percent of the resident population in the City of Melbourne were students.[16] The university adopted a strategy for 'RMIT in the city' that committed RMIT:

> to contribute to the economic, social and sustainable development of the City and the planning and design of the built environment, contribute to the artistic and cultural life of the City, develop opportunities for intercultural exchange adding value to the experience of RMIT students and the community, further develop a strategic approach to meeting the education and training needs of the City and contribute to school education, add value to industry and business, contribute to the provision of health and community services, assist community groups in the City and ensure quality management of RMIT's community service in the City.[17]

The RMIT Association of International Students became very active, cooperating in identifying issues and running programs. In many ways, well documented by Paula Durance, the international students led some of RMIT's international policies and much of the university's transformation of the city, not just engagement with it.[18] The association's leaders worked well with the centre for international students, where they had a drop-in centre, UOIP more widely, and university management. Some of them went on to make careers in international education and youth leadership. A number of country international student associations formed as well, with the Indonesian students association running a large and profitable annual music and culture festival. From 1994, RMIT, prompted by international students, ran an annual World Week celebrating the diversity and enrichment brought by international students and other students and staff of international origin and diverse cultures. It started on-campus but spread across the CBD.[19] I very much enjoyed taking part in it.

Not all was sunshine. During the 1990s, in a period of economic downturn when overtly racist political movements built up, exemplified by Pauline Hansen's One Nation Party, many international students were harassed and some assaulted. This was bad news abroad. Media in east Asia covered the events closely and loudly. With international students we organised anti-racism campaigns of some power and sophistication, rallies and a media presence, including mine.

While we lauded the contribution of international students to life in the city, there was another dark side, as Ruth Fincher and Kate Shaw pointed out at the time.[20] Access to affordable housing, exploitation on jobs, and lack of friendship with Australian peer students were all too common. These have become bigger issues now as the dependence of universities on international students for fees, and collapse of the market with the global pandemic, have left universities exposed. There is now an opportunity to provide for international students in a way that is less financially exploitive and more culturally inclusive.

The community in the southern Grampians, a rich sheep-raising region in western Victoria, was worried about their economic future during the slump. 'The future is international', they concluded. 'How can we be more connected? RMIT has so many international students. Why don't we ask them to visit?' In 1993, there followed an unusual flow of homestay students working on school intercultural education, Landcare, art exhibition and other projects, organised at RMIT through the UOIP and championed by Yaso Karthigasu (now Nadarajah), a brilliant, energetic member of staff, and Kaye Scholfield, the local coordinator who knew everyone. The program, named RMIT international community exchange, or RICE, was housed in a Hamilton learning centre and became 'the university's largest regional project, involving all academic portfolios, a large community network, 32 schools, tertiary and other adult education providers, 150 host families and most local businesses'.[21] Looking back, Yaso describes RICE's vision as also to

... bring together a local-global network of researchers, scholars and engaged community activists, working together to better understand and affect the nature of community and its social transformation through exchanges of information and ideas and comparative research programs.[22]

The state governor, Sir James Gobbo, saw the region bucking a trend of rising rural xenophobia, and chose to support it. This is what vice-regal representatives in Australia, often too tame to take a mildly political stand, should do more often. It was a pleasure to travel down with him and attend a concert at the culmination of a round of student stays.

Two female Korean art students worked in the well-regarded Hamilton Art Gallery, challenging by day the locals with confronting contemporary art. At night, they were confronted themselves. They stayed in a quiet farmhouse with one of the hosting families, a new experience for these city-dwellers, and were terrified by the thought of wild animals in the empty darkness. That's cultural exchange!

Much more was to come. Helen and Geoff Handbury, local residents and part of the Murdoch family of News Limited fame, pledged $2m to extend the RICE program. This enabled RMIT to develop a mini-campus and offer nursing and other courses directly to the community. But in that scaling up, with its inevitable bureaucratisation, something of the spontaneous magic went out of the program. This is but one vignette in the transformative role played by international students onshore at RMIT.

Offshore programs

Offshore programs were just as exciting. The number and scale of these transnational programs, through which RMIT provided the whole or part of its courses with local partners for students whose families were often not able to afford to send to Australia, grew very quickly.

When I joined RMIT some were already delivered offshore, notably through Jim Hurley of administrative studies with the Singapore Institute of Management, and Barry Cooper of accountancy with Taylors College in Malaysia and with the Singapore Institute of Management. In 1989 the business faculty already taught 500 students offshore. These were pioneering programs, the first 'twinning' programs in southeast Asia, and these two champions real entrepreneurs.

RMIT had a number of exchange and cooperation agreements then, took part in development assistance projects, mostly in east Asia, and aimed further to 'internationalise' its activities. Le Vin and Adams describe the conditions for offshore programs in the late 1980s as including a national higher education policy at last conducive to growth of international engagement, RMIT valuing entrepreneurship throughout the institute, a practice of departments 'owning' courses rather than the faculties, and decanal encouragement in business and administrative studies, later the graduate school of management.[23]

Offshore programs had high costs of travel and management, and were not as profitable as the onshore programs in Australia. By July 1993, there were 2000 enrolments in Malaysia and Singapore, where fly-in-fly-out arrangements for teaching staff were feasible. They reached more students, gave the flying academics good international experience and built their cross-cultural competencies, not to mention their CVs.

The 1994 international strategy aimed to maintain RMIT's leadership in the field, reduce dependence on Malaysia and Singapore, and develop RMIT mini-campuses.[24] By 1996, countries and regions further away, including Vietnam, Hong Kong, Japan, China and Nauru, had joined the list, often under franchised agreements that included quality assurance, professional development and teacher training provided by RMIT. Risks and responsibilities were equally shared with 50/50 fee splitting, or else governed by a services agreement where RMIT's partner bore all the market risk. Sometimes there were different programs and different partners in the same countries or cities, and in Malaysia we experimented with bringing the local partners around the same table in an RMIT advisory committee.

I was involved in negotiating many of these programs and being at signing ceremonies and graduations—a major annual roadshow—so I became friendly with many of our partner principals, an interesting group of successful businesspeople. Some were wealthy and entertained us lavishly, others were bent on tough negotiations and more frugal with their hospitality. All were friends of RMIT. We roped in Australian politicians when we could. For example, when I was travelling in China with Brian Howe, deputy PM, he witnessed our signing ceremonies in Shanghai. The annual offshore graduation rounds were complex roadshows involving more than 20 people from RMIT, usually including the chancellor and members of council. Nothing could be allowed to go wrong. This was a big task for my office but they became good at it.

There were other hazards. In Wuhan, while staying at the small RMIT campus, I accepted an invitation for a group to join senior executives of the Baoshan steel company, thinking the leader may be interested to invest in offshore programs through our emerging campus there and help RMIT deepen its links with this huge company. At the banquet I found out his son was an RMIT student and he asked what it would take from him, his father, for his son to get higher grades. This was an alarm bell. Best to be friendly but not seek favours when his son was a student. We agreed to go to karaoke for a while after dinner, but fell into a honey trap. Female RMIT staff took their leave, and I should have taken their cue. Young women started coming into our karaoke room and some RMIT staff disappeared from the room, escorted. It was time to round everyone up, wherever they were, give our thanks all the same, and get out fast. The next day, we seemed to have escaped incident. Years later, however, I was told we missed one of our staff that night. This was not a big incident, but indicative of the thin line to be trod in the university's offshore relationships. Bribery and corruption offshore were prominent discussions in the executive group, leading to a hard-line decision to oppose them in any form.

The different regulations in each country were important to know. Keeping in touch with the Ministry of Education in China, for example, was vital. Vivian's aunt, Hu Qihung, had been president of the Chinese Academy of Sciences, but after her alleged role in the Tiananmen incident that *guanxi* wasn't there with the ministry anymore. Arrangements for twinning programs and campuses changed frequently and were not clear.

RMIT had a good relationship with Fudan University in Shanghai in management and technology research and training, built up by Peter

Burgess, director of RMIT's enterprise executive management centre and one of those classic offshore entrepreneurs. I enjoyed several stays in Fudan's hospitable guest house. With the pledged support of $1m from a banking family in Hong Kong, we planned a joint centre on the main Fudan campus. This was not a big amount of money for Fudan, which as one of China's top universities was then being showered with corporate and government largesse from around the world as China's economy opened up. The relationship needed careful cultivation. And there was a hitch, too. The donor family wished to name the building after their patriarch, but the Chinese government, through the Ministry of Education, did not allow foreign naming rights for fear of endorsing, inadvertently or otherwise, in Deng Xiao Ping's phrase, any 'flies' that might come through China's open door. A lower-key form of recognition was negotiated and the centre went on to do good work for a number of years.

By 1999, when I left the international affairs job, the portfolio of offshore agreements to provide courses jointly grew to 46 offshore programs, enrolling 5270 students. Keeping good relations with partners, in a huge east Asian region where partner contacts, not contracts, were the key, took a growing commitment from the RMIT executive team and me, in particular, away from home a lot. It was not good form for deputies to turn up in place of principals. Good sincere relations with offshore partners were what we learnt from our pioneers.

If moving courses to people instead of people to courses was one step up the trade-investment ladder, developing offshore campuses was the next step up. Some twinning programs, like the chiropractic site in Tokyo, with big RMIT signs, looked to people like the Australian ambassador as campuses already, but strictly speaking international branch campuses need bigger investments.

But before we turn to that let us take stock. We made 'internationalising the curriculum' the first goal of strategy, but what this meant was not always clear and was not front of mind in marketing or negotiating agreements.

Internationalising the curriculum

The 1994 international strategy stated the goal simply: 'the interna-tionalisation of the curriculum and international experience of RMIT students'.[25] All courses would include a global perspective, international language streams would be introduced, and the movement of staff and students to and from other countries would be encouraged, including through more funding. In faculty performance plans I set targets for every course to build in at least of one of these dimensions: a global perspective in its curriculum, languages other than English, or organ-ised international movements of staff and students, including through offshore delivery. We expanded the teaching of languages other than English, previously not a strong suit for RMIT, even though 44 percent of all students spoke English as a second language, and built up a leading accredited interpreter course. A quarter of academic staff were expected to have an active international practice, and this was backed up in their professional development programs.[26]

The RMIT office of educational quality assurance and research devel-opment led a taskforce of 84 members of staff and trained a further 200 in international aspects of their specific disciplines. In different ways we aggressively built up cross-cultural competencies among students and staff. Though the overall goal was simple enough, there were many ways to pursue it, and with the fast growth of international programs, needs and demand kept rising. Of course, the international programs themselves also contributed to the internationalisation of the curriculum, especially inbound and outbound education abroad programs and the exchange and cooperation agreements that underlaid them.

By 1996, when RMIT was helped by a commonwealth staff develop-ment grant to review internationalisation of the university, policies and practices had become richer and more diverse. The reports recommended that academic leadership take a strong lead in endorsing internation-alisation and explicitly state RMIT's anti-racist position (the theme of a student–staff campaign at the time), that faculty teaching and learn-ing strategies explicitly include internationalisation, and that university capacity to do this be built up through expansion of cross-cultural and diversity training and through more exposure of staff and students to the different cultures already within RMIT.[27] I supported these and other recommendations and sought to define and measure internationalisation better. I was also attracted to the framework of the University of Technology Sydney where students of most degrees could tack on an international or languages stream to make them double degrees. I brought globalisation of the curriculum up into first place in the international division's 1997 performance plan, along with promotion of a strong international culture and cross-cultural understanding within RMIT, set targets and allocated resources. The transformation was continuing.

After the closure of my international division in the 'upheaval' in 1999, ironically the year that the university won Victorian and national export awards for education, the vice-chancellor, Ruth Dunkin, sought to shift the focus more onto global awareness for all.[28] She hired Fazal Rizvi, an internationally recognised scholar in globalisation, as pro vice-chancellor international. He thought previous approaches were not touching on the fundamental changes needed, stating that

> ... for RMIT to become a truly global university, growth in student numbers is not sufficient. A new paradigm for conceptualising internationalisation appears necessary, that takes into account the rapidly changing context in which education now takes place.
>
> A global university must now be characterised by its engagement with the processes of globalisation, its international networks and its internationalised curriculum.[29]

He sought to strengthen engagement with the forces of globalisation, to build a stronger global outlook across the university. This effort to change the culture of RMIT further as a self-proclaimed global university was associated with the 'mainstreaming' of services to international students: all students and staff would be part of the same project. We were all global now. Though the years since have seen RMIT international programs ebb and flow, and RMIT's international and global ethos, built up in the 1990s and 2000s, may not have met Fazal's high bar, much of that has endured.

International development projects

Participation in international development projects with aid agencies, such as the Australian International Development Assistance Bureau (AIDAB, later to become AusAID, the Australian Agency for International Development) and the World Bank, predated the build-up of other international programs, typically the missions of individual experts or projects won by Technisearch or the faculties. Their contributions were positive and the work built up international understanding and experience among staff and those students who took part. However, because of the vagaries of measuring time spent and accounting for expenses, I could not tell whether overall the financial contribution of this program was positive or negative.

At the time we outsourced onshore international student recruiting to Technisearch, we also clarified project bidding and delivery responsibilities, empowering the subsidiary to bid for big projects—always with faculty and school rights of first refusal. Technisearch had some outstanding international project managers, notably Daryl Hill, who had been managing director of the Overseas Projects Corporation of Victoria, a state government agency. Having started international projects in China before working at RMIT, I joined in on some of RMIT's international development projects, including one in the Philippines.

When from 1998 Technisearch was wound up and the international student program returned fully to RMIT proper, international projects became the core business of a new subsidiary company, RMIT International Pty Ltd. The number and scale of that company's projects grew very fast. Their value grew from $1.8m in 1997 to over $6.7m in 1999, by then having accumulated earnings of over $90m in this very competitive market. Besides the intangible benefits mentioned above, this work was profitable, even when staff time and university overheads were fully accounted for. The university has continued to be a strong presence in the market, adding to the skills and capacity of its staff and those students involved.

Education abroad and exchange

I was keen about study abroad, as my AFS year changed my life. Tony Adams and his team were up to the task, but we all realised RMIT's programs had a long way to go. The 1994 strategies were to develop more cooperative agreements to enable students to spend part of their courses overseas (10 percent of students were to do so by year 2000, off a low base of only 113 movements in 1994), to accredit courses jointly with other providers, to create international degrees (one per faculty by 2000), and to expect up to 25 percent of staff to have international professional activities by 2000.

Study abroad could be through bilateral exchanges, study tours, studies abroad, conferences, internships and clinical placements. We started hosting many groups of exchange and study abroad students from around the world. Those from Singapore consistently performed very well, as did their onshore students, and those from the US were a headache, being for the most part out to have a good time while in Australia. I chaired the offshore initiatives review committee that oversaw the programs. Debra Perry of the education abroad centre managed cooperative agreements, student and staff exchange programs and the study abroad program. She was loyal to Tony and a loss to us when she followed him to Macquarie University after his deanship was discontinued.

Importantly, the programs and targets applied to the TAFE sector as well as higher education. By joining the US-based Community Colleges for International Development (CCID), the university started tapping into huge opportunities there, initially with the University of Hawai'i system that, like RMIT, was dual-sector. I worked on this in Honolulu to strengthen the relationship and we looked forward to recognition of credit and articulation among compatible courses and programs and a two-way flow of joint advanced diploma/associate degree students in business. However, those relationships need a lot of work, and the full potential was never realised after RMIT strategy changed and Tony and I left our jobs.

RMIT was clearly a leader in offshore higher education, through which RMIT courses were offered abroad. But I enjoyed working on 'reverse-twinning', too, whereby international programs were offered at RMIT. Chinese traditional medicine (TCM) was the most interesting of this class. We came to an agreement with the Nanjing College of Traditional Chinese Medicine to translate their highly regarded course into English, and translate its pharmacopeia into scientifically validated medicines. No bears' paws. Accrediting the course within RMIT and with industry associations was no small feat, only made easier by key people who had battled and gained Australian Medical Association support for an earlier chiropractic course, and the leadership of Charlie Xue when he arrived. Chinese traditional medicine was eligible for Medicare public funding support, and Vivian, my wife, who was accomplished in public health and fluent in Mandarin, came to chair the Victorian medical registration board for TCM.

By 1997, there were 185 working cooperation and exchange agreements around the world, tidied up from earlier in the decade, and by 2001 600 study abroad movements, though still two-thirds of them were inbound to Australia, not outbound. The next steps up the ladder were to dedicated campuses.

Offshore campuses

From the early 1990s, experience with twinning programs was making some of us keen to ensure that the university had more control over provision of courses offshore. In some countries the standards of prospective partners were not high, or the higher education sector not well enough developed, to justify joint venture partners. David Beanland and I aspired to develop international branch campuses.

In December 1991, David commissioned an internal report from Tom Yardley on the possibility of RMIT establishing a campus in Asia. It argued that if RMIT wished to provide a distinctive education, only its own offshore campuses could be consistent with standards in Melbourne. It recommended that RMIT seriously plan to establish a network of campuses throughout Asia. Malaysia, Singapore, Indonesia and Thailand were the recommended priorities, in that order of preference.[30]

The 1994 international strategy took a staged approach, to 'develop mini-campuses' like the one in Wuhan. From a joint Australian govern-ment program with the China Ministry of Metallurgical Industry to train managers for the iron and steel industry, in 1994 RMIT took over responsibility for a small residential campus that was adapted to house ten Australian international trade TAFE students. With 26 Chinese students accommodated by the Wuhan Iron and Steel University (later to become the Wuhan University of Science and Technology), this associate diploma was designed to help China build capacity before joining the World Trade Organization.[31] With knowledge of China in business and some facility with Mandarin Chinese, the Australian graduates were highly sought after by Australian firms in China, and likewise the Chinese students by multinational and Chinese firms. The program expanded to the Shanghai Institute—now University—of Foreign Trade, and became a full degree program, enrolling over 2000 students. A network of similar mini-campuses was envisaged by the international strategy.

David Beanland and I were thinking beyond mini-campuses to larger campuses. Publicity about RMIT's offshore success brought a stream of proposals for international campuses in a range of countries, from governments, companies and counterpart universities. Dato' Tan Chin Nam, a Malaysian property tycoon, noted for the refurbishment of the Queen Victoria Building in Sydney and ownership of the winner of the 2008 Melbourne Cup, even asked David Beanland and me, in the course of discussing finance for offshore campuses, whether perhaps the whole of RMIT might be available for sale.

Most offshore proposals we received were grand but impractical. In our promotion of international campus strategy, I would talk about perhaps one large campus each decade, and when Leo Foster took responsibility for international programs for a time from mid-1994 he too shared this realistic ambition.

At that time China was our first priority for campus development, and we had good relations with the national government. Despite our access to other arms of government, dealing with the Ministry of Education in Beijing about a possible campus was difficult, and the road ahead paved with restrictive regulations.

This is where Guangxi Zhuang Autonomous Region came in. The equivalent of a province but with more independence, the regional government seemed to have wide latitude in allowing a foreign campus to develop, relative to that of a normal province. Its leaders, especially the party secretary and mayor of Beihai, the coastal city mooted for the campus, were most enthusiastic about it on their visit to RMIT.[32]

Close to the border with Vietnam and across a strait from Hainan, China's go-go subtropical island province, the city seemed to have good long-term potential. The regional and city governments were confident of more than sufficient capital funding; there seemed good prospects for this to be covered. Leo cultivated the relationship through mutual visits. An RMIT team drew up a possible strategy for him to present, including an enticing graphic vision of an RMIT campus drawn up by Leon van Schaik.

The Ministry of Education in Beijing was less enthralled; they saw the region as a wild frontier and wondered why a foreign university was interested there at all. They preferred new campus entrants to 'go west', away from the better served east coast. The 1994 country action plan drawn up by Tony Adams' office noted, for the Beihai project, that 'Chinese regulations on the introduction of foreign degrees may hinder this possibility as well as difficulties in coming to a final agreement with potential partners'.[33] He was right. The talks wore on and eventually came to nothing.

At the same time, two country action plans identified the development of campuses in Penang and Vietnam, both covered elsewhere in this account. Meanwhile, RMIT was growing investment in international programs, including executive capacity.

Mobilising for international growth

From the beginning of 1996 when David Beanland upgraded the leadership of international policy and programs, my job was as DVC international. The new structure was supported by new commercial subsidiaries in each portfolio, which continued the businesses of Technisearch, now split up. This was done mainly to build integrated businesses in each of the four new domains of RMIT's reorganised structure, and because Technisearch had over-concentrated on the lucrative international student business. Technisearch's leadership had also strayed too far from council control over unrelated matters, such as its own efforts to find accommodation outside the university's campus strategy. Technisearch had good quality assurance, though, having gained early ISO 9001 certification and been given favourable comments from multiple audits from the Victorian auditor-general.[34]

There was continuing disquiet about the core university delegating so much of its business away from faculties and schools, whose leaders, characteristically, thought they could do a better job with international student recruiting than Technisearch. The view of my colleagues was that to make all of RMIT international there should be less organisational separation of international activities, and concerns about the separation of international student marketing from domestic student marketing brought about the 'mainstreaming' of international student recruitment back into one unit in the university proper.

A new company, RMIT International Pty Ltd, was formed to keep a focus on commercial activities in the international realm, particularly the international project services described above. I chose to be CEO of that company rather than chair the board, so as to be more hands-on in harmonising its business with the university proper. We developed policies and procedures for avoiding overlap. I also became a director of RMIT Training Ltd, which ran the market-leading RMIT English Worldwide, and sought to commercialise further training and executive education internationally.

Some of the executive group put on pressure to 'mainstream' more than student marketing and recruitment, to include services to international students, and thus to abolish the centre for international student services in UOIP. I thought this was crazy. International students have special needs and their higher fees were capable of funding those services. Tony Adams and I made a strong case for keeping special services for international students separate from those for domestic students, such as drop-in centres, arrival and settlement assistance and concurrent language support. The centre continued for the time being.

During this period RMIT international programs prospered further. Tony Adams saw 1996, the year of the restructure and a deepening of commitment to internationalisation, as the beginning of a new phase.[35] The international programs grew richer and deeper through the internationalisation of curricula on all their dimensions, albeit late in the development of the programs. Through my office and UOIP we applied for awards, and won Governor of Victoria export awards in 1998 and 1999, and the inaugural Australian export award for education (awarded to me by singer Kylie Minogue) in 1999. We paid a lot of attention to the entry submissions we made, and where allowed, prompted friends of the university to vote for us.[36] These awards built up morale further and helped attract external support. Tony Adams was recognised as a national leader in the field and the feedback of international students onshore was good. The Penang campus was an exception to this success.

Learning from failure: a campus in Penang

RMIT's interest in a campus in Malaysia was investigated in 1992 by Ruth Dunkin, then deputy director for resources, who visited Malaysia and recommended a more strategic approach be taken to offshore programs in Asia, a Malaysia strategy along the lines discussed below, and an in-Asia resident academic director to focus on quality control in the region.[37] She recommended a deeper primary partnership with a local education partner, such as Dato' M. S. Tan, of Taylors College, rather than keeping on adding multiple partners. Her aim was to see a Malaysian campus become a jumping-off point for wider regional engagement, working in parallel with any corporate partnerships (such as with M. S. Tan), and with governments and other universities on development assistance.[38]

The aims in the international strategy at the time were to offer students a network of choices, including on our own campuses, and to deepen relationships with students, business, governments and civil society in the region. RMIT's linkages in Malaysia were strong—twinning programs with the Malaysian Institute of Management, Metropolitan College, Limkokwing Institute of Creative Technology, the Malaysian Stock

Exchange and other partners in chiropractic and life sciences.

Consistent with that strategy, we formed a Malaysia 'desk' in Melbourne, a representative 'post' in Kuala Lumpur run by an alumnus and ex-staff member, Lai Ah Chek, a logistics expert, and a Malaysia advisory committee made up of the principals of these and other partners to discuss RMIT's further development and harmonisation of programs in Malaysia. Those around the table mostly knew each other, and were pleased to take part. One meeting was chaired by Sam Smorgon, RMIT's billionaire chancellor, who was committed to the university's expansion in Asia, and our guests were most impressed.

Malaysia stayed a priority country for campus development, and we favoured Dato' Tan as the seed partner. We prepared a licence application for RMIT International University Malaysia under a relatively permissive new Malaysian law.[39]

Penang was also a prospect for a campus, a distinctive state of Malaysia with long history as an international entrepôt, a mix of Malay, Chinese and Indian cultures, great tourism, a good university, some good schools, and a cluster of multinational electronics and other companies. It had a strategic plan to build 'a fully-developed, post-industrial society'.[40] Koh Tsu Koon, the chief minister, a family friend through Vivian's months researching in Malaysia and our children's visit, made a proposal for a new shared campus on Penang island sponsored by the Penang Development Corporation. It was to involve the University of Sydney (for whom Murray Wells, director of that university's graduate school of management and public policy, was the leader) and RMIT. But the University of Sydney, when pushed, seemed to want a 'big brother/little brother' relationship in which RMIT would concentrate on VET programs while they would be dominant in higher education. So we said, 'No thanks'.[41]

The University of Sydney went ahead with the venture, but with little experience in managing an offshore campus, even for a small start that was not much more than a twinning program, and even with an excellent local 'hand', Michael Leigh. After some years trying, including efforts to bring in TAFE NSW, the venture passed into the management of INTI, a Malaysian private education company.[42] I give the university credit for trying, but offshore campuses do not come naturally to the elite Australian 'sandstone' universities (Monash University excepted), who tend to see their home campuses as the mecca for all their students.

Meanwhile, an alternative possibility arrived in the form of John Fong, a Penang businessman, who visited RMIT in Melbourne late in 1993. He and David Beanland hit it off and talked about a campus at length. David proposed a feasibility study. In the limited due diligence time available we noted he ran a conglomerate built around the Adorna jewellery company, 'a family affair [founded] in gold, diamond and precious stones'.[43] Typically for family run conglomerates in the region, the group's business affairs were opaque, in this case linked to the Kelantan royal family, and RMIT had little capacity to uncover the details of this.[44] Fong had no direct experience with education, other than meeting some of the training needs for his construction companies, hotels and resorts, for which he argued he had plenty of 'internal' demand for graduates to justify a campus with RMIT.

Penang seemed a good location, with successful hospitality and technology companies and a pleasant island reputation. But John Fong wanted to develop a campus at Jawi, on the mainland part of Penang, well away from urban areas, even if near planned technology estates. As the Victorian auditor-general later noted, visiting architects for RMIT in September 1994 found the quality of Adorna construction on their sites was 'poor to average' by Australian standards. Brian Stoddart recalls 'looking out the window one day [on campus] to see a guy hanging from a drainpipe on the second floor across in the next building, an arm around the drainpipe with a paint can hanging from it, the other hand painting!' The auditor-general also noted that RMIT research on the prospective campus found a weak market in the short term, with high capital expenses likely for technical courses. Nevertheless, John Fong gave strong undertakings to underwrite capital and market risks. David pressed us to move to an agreement.

Before too long detailed agreements were drawn up by Hunt and Hunt, a good legal firm, led by Bill O'Shea, who had facilitated Caulfield Grammar School's Nanjing campus, where Sasha and Kina, my children, spent time as part of the school's program. The children and Vivian also enjoyed visiting Penang with me. Who wouldn't enjoy holidaying there!

The joint venture was named Adorna Institute of Technology Sdn. Bhd. (AIT)—note, not using RMIT's name—in which the Adorna group would hold a majority stake. However, RMIT's name was prominent in marketing. The university would hold 20 percent of the equity in recognition of its intellectual property, not as crystallisation of royalties, which, with normal service payments to RMIT, were covered by a separate service level agreement. In other words, RMIT licensed its courses to AIT.

It would be the first Australian true international branch campus anywhere (by contrast with the more prevalent form of twinning program). Our experience in the region told us that these types of agreement might take six months of hard fought negotiations. We were pleasantly surprised when John Fong accepted our first ambit claim without question, covering generous payments for course development, course delivery, and growth of equity in the joint venture (JV). The Adorna group was at the time making significant profits from property development and would have education venture tax deductibility for this business, not to mention property value uplift around the campus and good favour with the government of Penang.[45] We should have thought more about signing these dream contracts, especially into a minority position on a joint venture. But the vice-chancellor remained keen to go ahead, and in February 1995, we entered into agreements on the joint venture, services provision from RMIT and a lease for a greenfield site.

We created an Australian subsidiary company, RMIT Malaysia Ltd, and a Malaysian subsidiary company, RMIT Malaysia Sdn. Bhd., for both of which I was CEO, as vehicles to hold our 20 percent interest in the JV, alongside three other parties: Adorna Education Sdn. Bhd. (60 percent), Fatimah binti Adbullah (10 percent) and Yayasan Bumiputra Pulau Pinang Berhad (10 percent). David and I served on the board as two of ten directors. It was chaired by the late Tunku Dato' Dr Ismail Jewa, nephew of the founding prime minister of Malaysia, Tunku Abdul Rahman, and a member of the Kedah royal family. This fulfilled in part Malaysian requirements for *bumiputra* (literally 'sons of the earth', ethnic Malay) composition, which also explained the other minority participants in the joint venture. The Tunku (prince) was genial and well-connected to the Malaysian elite, but he stayed aloof above all the goings-on. At the beginning his role seemed mainly symbolic.

The academic plan was to offer foundation studies and advanced diplomas in engineering, IT, hospitality and tourism, all leading to bachelor degrees. Australia and Malaysia signed an MOU on cooperation in education soon after in 1996, and we had good diplomatic support throughout the history of the venture. That same year Malaysia also enacted the law allowing foreign institutions to deliver cross-border education in Malaysia, including higher education programs.[46] We had drafted a licence application with Dato' M. S. Tan under these provisions, but on reflection did not submit it as the Penang campus was moving ahead. Later, like other Malaysian twinning partners, he came to say he did not understand why RMIT bypassed its traditional partners for a new and untried favourite.

In Penang we thought it better to proceed with a campus under a vocational education licence. It seemed quicker and easier to register, and was suitable for the form of the VET higher education awards that we intended (i.e. advanced diplomas leading to bachelor degrees). These dual-sector programs were experimental for RMIT, and if successful we would extend them across other, Melbourne-based programs. A higher education campus registration could come later. Even the VET licence took much longer than planned, frustrating our operational planning. By 1997, RMIT was named by the Malaysian government as one of four universities under consideration for foreign campus status in the higher education sector, but notwithstanding RMIT's earlier proposal, we decided to bide our time until the VET institution was ready to convert to a higher education provider under the name of RMIT.[47]

The campus-to-be was on a disused palm-oil plantation in Jawi. It comprised a multi-purpose hall, administration and teaching buildings, library, lecture theatres, a canteen and union building, residential accommodation and sporting facilities. The site was populated, as such plantations are, with king cobras among the oil palms. This would become an unwelcome exotic feature for the Australian families who transferred to live in the 14 specially built bungalows among the palm trees. Brian Stoddart, campus director for RMIT, recalls that one student was bitten chasing a stray football into the grass, and he asked that something be done about it. So a sign went up: 'Do not go on the grass'. The cobras and introduced barn owls did not eat all the rats, though Brian recalls the contractors reporting that they had cleared 'all 673' or so rats.

At least it was near the military complex at Butterworth for making links with industry employers, and a number of technology and industrial estates were built or being planned nearby on the mainland. The free trade zone at Bayan Lepas on the island side of the bridge also turned out to be a key location for work experience links, set up through Brian's connections with industry leaders and prompted by the shortage of skilled people.[48]

Once built, the campus was pleasant enough, though too remote for student and resident staff convenience and with some deficiencies in buildings, fixtures and equipment. It was financed directly by our partner, we were told, as part of the group's equity in the joint venture.

We appointed Brian as academic director, professor and pro vice-chancellor. A senior academic with long experience offshore, particularly in India, he reported through me to RMIT. He and his wife Sandra settled well into Penang life. At first, Dr Rasiah Ratnalingam, a Rhodes Scholar and eminent academician, was appointed by Adorna as CEO, in charge of human resources and other administrative matters. He was a good appointee who worked well with Brian. But as finances later became strained, Adorna replaced him with Dr Terri Hew, a much tougher prospect for cooperation, though able in her own right. Worse, the chair of the board (the Tunku), after a do-nothing start, began to meddle in operational matters. The majority partner corporate group treated the college more as their proprietary subsidiary than as the business of a joint venture. Add to this the common problem of international branch campus directors feeling remote from the home office of RMIT in Australia, and university and Malaysian decision-making processes not timely enough for Brian to keep the start-up on track. This included delays in getting work permits for foreign staff, thus generating many weekend renewal trips out of the country, because the campus operating certificate was held up. Ostensibly this was because of a problem with a drain in one corner of the site, but Brian thinks it may well have been because 'the appropriate person had not been paid'. There are few harder jobs in a university than being a start-up international branch campus director. Nevertheless, there was goodwill among the parties at the beginning and a number of enjoyable events to relieve the hard work.

After the delays with a licence and other approvals, and a police cavalcade with sirens chasing off illegal workers on the site, the campus finally opened in January 1996. The brochures touted it as 'the perfect place to study'. The plan was to grow to 2050 students by 2002. By 1998, 302 were enrolled. Local students expected a choice of completing in Penang or transferring for later years in Melbourne. Of around 600 students enrolling between 1996 and 1999, around 350 did transfer to Melbourne. The first group of Australian students arrived in 1997, many of them motivated by an international experience en route to their degrees, and by fees lower than in Australia. The degrees gave them a pathway to a bachelor degree through two-year advanced diplomas, leading to engineering degrees after two more years in electronics-computing, civil or manufacturing-mechanical engineering, a building and construction degree of the same length, and business and tourism degrees after one more year.

The students overall were an intrepid group who put up with the teething problems on the new campus. The Australians and Malaysians seemed to mix well together. With a decent local academic recruitment pool, Brian Stoddart's decision to recruit young academic staff with modern ideas about teaching, RMIT preparatory training and academic quality assurance, teaching standards were actually very good, with high student retention rates. Local staff were active in customising curricula, but struggled sometimes to reach 'parity of esteem' with their remote Melbourne counterparts, as distinct from the cooperative RMIT staff transferred to Penang. Though we made a point of ensuring there were lines of communication to faculties and indirectly to the academic board, some of the local academics thought the university's approach was marked by a touch of 'superiority'.

The plan required timely development of facilities. The second year of the original courses (or third year if the foundation year is included), and the start of further courses, required more buildings to be completed, with kitchens for hospitality and more advanced labs for engineering. The Adorna group built more than adequate space to begin with, but equipment was in short supply and repairs were often not undertaken. For example, when the PABX was destroyed by lightning the college had to suffice with six separate hard-wired telephones.[49]

By the time the further investment was needed, in mid-1997, the majority partner ran into financial difficulties, despite a contractual obligation under the joint venture to keep sufficient funds available for future development. These problems became more acute as the 'Asian financial crisis' of 1998–99 worsened. The Adorna group had overextended itself, diversifying too quickly by moving into sports stadia construction and even the commencement of a one-plane airline, Adorna Airways, trading as Asia-Africa Airways.

The start of building for campus extensions was put back later and later, and after blowing a fog of vague intentions, John Fong announced that they were unable to commence the next stage of development at all. Without these facilities, the students would not be able to continue, nor could the college responsibly enrol more. Relations among RMIT staff and the chair (the Tunku) and CEO (Terri Hew) deteriorated over these and other issues. Against good practice, the chair took a direct hand in management decisions, and in the final terms delivery of the courses started to suffer.

Understandably, this became intolerable for Brian Stoddart, who unfairly took blame from Adorna. He returned to Australia. Mick Mileshkin, from RMIT aerospace engineering, tried with mixed success, given the conditions, to rebuild relations. Already in arrears, the joint venture company was in no position to fulfil its obligations or make good on payments from penalty clauses to RMIT. We negotiated some terms for late payment, but without facilities in place and with poor information, RMIT was faced with a hard choice. It could take legal action to require Adorna compliance with their obligations, but advice to RMIT was that the Malaysian courts were unlikely to be neutral in such a matter.

Denied access to the details of the capital financing, and as a Malaysian company director at risk (not to mention an RMIT executive with his neck on the line), I went to see the manager of the bank in Penang that held Adorna's accounts. He told me that the construction loan was secured on the JV itself, and that repayments were well in arrears. This was a surprise. The campus assets were meant to be vested in the joint venture as equity. Brian remembers that even the chancellor, business-man Sam Smorgon, had earlier assured him the campus was not funded by debt. The board papers had not been clear on this, and our questions unanswered. John Fong started making himself unavailable to Brian and me, to put it mildly.

I found out through the media that Adorna's construction company was finishing a new aquatic venue in time to host the world youth diving championships because there were media reports that the diving boards had not met the International Swimming Federation (FINA) standards (their cement was too fresh safely to hold the bolts securing the diving boards). Nevertheless, the opening ceremony was going ahead, with Koh Tsu Koon, the chief minister, cutting the ribbon.

I went along and took a front row seat. As the official delegation entered into the crowded stadium to music and applause, I jumped the fence and walked up to the front of the official party. I said hello to the surprised chief minister, turned around and button-holed (these days we might say 'shirt-fronted') John Fong in front of the crowd. I insisted we talk right away about the unpaid bills. Embarrassed, he took me into the dope testing room beside the pool and we argued. He was bitter about the high levels of payment he had to make to RMIT under the agreements and he resented paying any more—as if a contract wasn't a contract. We thrashed out a further repayment schedule, but I got nowhere on the construction schedule. The first payment was duly made on time, but in the form of over 50 individual collected cheques from parents under a so-called 'RMIT levy'. After that no more money came.[50]

Closure loomed. By then we had contingency plans, but there were no good options. The company may have been trading while insolvent, but we could not get sufficient information to tell. In late 1998, RMIT gave formal notice of terminating the service agreement, to take effect from February 1999, and this would also automatically terminate the JV agreement. Some students were completing their RMIT program or taking a foundation studies course which was widely transferable to other providers, so they were little affected. But another 123 students were stranded by the wind-down. We put into action plans to teach them out one way or the other. Students would be given credit to transfer to equivalent providers in Malaysia or come to RMIT in Melbourne on concessional terms.

The college was wound up by the end of 1999.

This was painful and expensive for the students and for RMIT, as to that date the trial dual-sector hospitality-tourism sequence was operating only in Penang and its further years would now have to be custom-provided in Melbourne. The engineering faculty loyally provided a special six-week series of laboratory classes in Melbourne at no charge to students who could get to Melbourne, in part to make up for laboratory work unable to be completed in Penang due to the lack of facilities.[51]

In accord with the implementation plan, staff were given notice of termination or transfer, including the Australian staff, who were mostly repatriated. We met with the Australian high commissioner well in advance and had a communication and media plan, so although there was some negative publicity and obvious student and staff hardships, it could have been much worse.

In the months and years that followed, ex-Penang students stayed in touch, including through annual reunions organised by Mal Rowe, a loyal RMIT Penang returnee and passionate engineering teacher. Brian Stoddart took a senior position at La Trobe University where he became vice-chancellor, and then went on to work with the World Bank, ADB and other agencies in situ in a number of countries. The Adorna group tried to find a use for the campus, but over time nature reclaimed the land and looters stripped the copper wire and even the window frames. Mal Rowe visited the ruin in 2002 to find it badly damaged by rain.[52] Now the site has been refurbished and is used by ILKM-MARA (Institut Latihan Kecemerlangan–Majlis Amanah Rakyat, a government agency to support *bumiputra* education and training): not a bad outcome, but with oil palms still on one side and suburban development on the other.

Working at RMIT in the aftermath of the Penang affair was not easy as most there thought it an unmitigated disaster. It was investigated by the Victorian auditor-general, on whose draft report I drafted a rather defensive reply:

> RMIT did not directly invest any monies in AIT. The continued unfunded provision of academic services to students was the result of RMIT's commitment to ensuring that all students at AIT were able to complete their studies. More than half of the AIT students articulated to RMIT's Melbourne campuses and the academic performance of these students and their subsequent employment profile proved highly satisfactory. The onshore international student fees paid by this cohort of students more than offset the AU$2.3 million notionally owed to RMIT.[53]

RMIT had to book that $2.3m in unpaid service fees, even though it benefited from other fees from the flow-on of students from Penang. When it became obvious that the university would never be paid, RMIT council agreed to write off the debt. I thought it worthwhile to formalise the lessons to council.

My assessment of the project covered difficulties, successes and lessons to be learnt.[54] The difficulties that arose included delays in campus construction, causing curriculum rescheduling and deferral of the tourism and hospitality program; long delays in college license approvals and in the appointment of effective college management; a continuing lack of separation of the affairs of the joint venture college from the affairs of the Adorna group, particularly on finances; lack of experience of the partners in private education (for example with respect to work permit requirements for foreign teachers); growing tension and operational conflicts between college administration and RMIT academic management, including over non-compliance by the partners with the basic agreements; and delayed payment and non-payment of invoices from RMIT, growing into a financial crisis by 1997.

Melbourne campuses benefited and the academic performance of these students, some ranking in the top group of engineering students, and their subsequent employment profiles were very good. As I stated to the auditor-general, the onshore international students fees paid by this cohort of students more than offset the $2.3m owed to RMIT.

Achievements were few but worth mentioning. They included the establishment of a residential technology campus, acknowledgement of RMIT for the initiative and for its attempts to contribute more widely to Penang and Malaysia, some very effective teaching at the course level through Malaysian staff and dedicated RMIT staff, and successful student graduates and transfers to RMIT Melbourne, including cross-cultural exchanges between Australian and Malaysian students.

The lessons were most important. The inexperience of the Penang partners and inability to get due diligence information on a privately-owned family company caused RMIT in future to be more vigilant in the choice of offshore partners. The market research done by both prospective partners was not enough to pin down the demand for courses at a relatively remote site at Jawi, with little nearby urban or industrial development. RMIT undertook to do more thorough market research in future, and more readily intervene in offshore problems before they become serious. The university's leadership became wary of any offshore ventures that were intrinsic to property deals, a feature of Monash's more successful Malaysia campus too.

The joint operation of an offshore college with intertwined operational responsibilities made management difficult.[55] As a result, RMIT thereafter sought management control of operations in such ventures, including sole ownership where possible. The exceptionally good conditions gained by RMIT on paper out of the original negotiations (in both corporate and service agreements) left a residue of resentment which by rhetorical design or genuine bad feeling compounded resentment at RMIT's attractive conditions. As a result, after that, RMIT was determined to ensure that prospective partners fully understood the commitments they were making.

The remote location was a mistake that could not be compensated by reasonable initial standards of the campus or by marketing. After this, RMIT preferred proximity to, or location in, established areas, such as with the Vietnam campus and the centre at Fudan University in Shanghai.

Finally, ironclad paper agreements did not protect RMIT from partner non-compliance and reputation losses in Penang. The majority partner tended to treat the college as a fully owned subsidiary rather than as a cooperative joint venture. Classic east–west differences of emphasis between RMIT's alleged legalistic focus on meeting written obligations and the partner's propensity to rely on unwritten understandings were also factors. Particularly stinging to me was the misleading passage of loan liabilities onto the joint venture company and thus onto RMIT and its directors, the council. As a result, in the aftermath of the regional economic crisis of the late 1990s, RMIT brought tighter controls over contracts with, and payments from, its 30 offshore award partners in the region. For any ventures that put a financial risk on RMIT, arrangements were made to cover any financial losses, and to be tough on financial delegations to the leaders of future transnational ventures. This last lesson came back later to bite me in the Vietnam campus project.

The painful experience of this big project did not dampen David Beanland's and my keenness to establish an international branch campus, as we will see in the following chapter. The Penang work stretched my experience, a combination of education and planning.

An agent of internationalisation

My international work at RMIT was the most satisfying of all the fields of work there, and on the whole we were very successful. The university was ripe for this development, and I felt well prepared by my experience.

The explosive growth of the onshore program was enabled by early allocation of clear responsibilities between Technisearch and the faculties, and a well-structured international strategic plan. Credit for both must go to the leadership of Tony Adams and the enthusiastic sponsorship of vice-chancellor David Beanland.

It is true that this growth preceded systematic thinking about the internationalisation of the university's programs and the complex and different needs of international onshore students. However, for the latter, a set of matching services were soon put in place. The needs for the university to respond to rising racism in some Australian communities and to protect and promote the multicultural character of domestic students and staff brought synergy to managing the international onshore student program. The plan clearly differentiated the international programs, gave form to more detailed plans by program and country, and put in place monitoring and quality assurance that steered the growth well.

This was true for offshore programs as well, where I helped put systems around the successful practices of a number of entrepreneurs who had made up the rules as they went along. RMIT moved quickly to create a presence in many countries, which was recognised nationally and internationally by emulation and awards. I particularly enjoyed the travel and deal-making with offshore partners, some of whom remain friendly with me after the RMIT years.

Lifting the low international mobility of Australian students was a continuing challenge that surprised me, given Australians' high general propensity to travel, but at least it grew, and education abroad (inbound and outbound) became well mixed with growing exchange programs. This field was later to expand more when successive commonwealth governments finally saw the advantage to the country of putting real money into it. I kept a warm regard for this work, remembering how my AFS year abroad had changed my life for the better.

As the university climbed up the 'trade-to-investment' ladder, the offshore partnerships moved to campus development opportunities. These were recognised in successive international plans and supported by David Beanland and then Ruth Dunkin as vice-chancellors, but they needed good strategic choice about which projects to pursue and good arguments for the support of an often sceptical university council.

But about RMIT's international programs as a whole, I was very disappointed in 1998 when David and Ruth yielded to the arguments of some deans and others to dismantle a successful framework for international programs. I was not able to turn the tide of events. Then, buffeted by the financial and governance crisis of 2002, the university became less innovative in its international programs.

Tacitus' adage that victory has many fathers, but failure is an orphan, rings true for RMIT's international branch campus adventures. This chapter covers the biggest failure, a campus in Malaysia, in which I had a key role, and therefore carry a key responsibility. As I look back, it was no failing of management, appointment or technical preparedness. The groundwork was done reasonably well in those respects.

It was a failure of courage, including mine. First, I shared qualms about the choice of Penang partner, but did not work hard enough to budge David Beanland's enthusiasm. The due diligence was not rigorous enough. Second, as an economic geographer I knew about the risks of locating the campus away from the centre of Penang and remotely on the mainland, but I went along with the project when the property development partner was adamant about building there on his land.

The next chapter covers the biggest success, RMIT International University Vietnam, for which there are many fathers. Courage aplenty was needed for that too, but we learned the lessons of Penang. I helped persuade RMIT to take better strategic decisions, and luck rewarded our preparedness.

NINE

VIETNAM'S FIRST
INTERNATIONAL UNIVERSITY

The origins of RMIT Vietnam have been much celebrated, and documented in part by my co-founders and friends Nguyen Xuan Thu and David Beanland.[1] But other people also sowed its seeds over the years before its creation. RMIT's early international strategy sought an offshore campus, and by 1996 the Penang campus was in operation. Though RMIT hosted many international students and staff originating from Vietnam, its early engagement with that country did not plan for a branch campus.

Merger with the Phillip Institute accelerated engagement through Dr Thu and the enthusiasm of Leo Foster, its director. Under the coordination of the office of international programs where dean Tony Adams took a particular interest too, the new RMIT expanded a scholarship program for students from Vietnam to study at RMIT and set up a joint master of systems engineering program with Vietnam National University Hanoi (VNU Hanoi), the country's most prestigious university. RMIT ran English language learning programs in Ho Chi Minh City, Hanoi and Vung Tau.

In 1994, Dr Thu, who had been senior lecturer in Vietnamese studies at Phillip Institute, then RMIT, left to return to Vietnam and acted as a consultant to set up a representative office, consistent with our international strategy of having a 'post' in high-engagement countries. That wasn't easy. As one-time director of documentation and research in the Ministry of Education for the anti-communist Republic of Vietnam in the south, Dr Thu was followed continuously by police. He was eventually, and justifiably, cleared by the minister for interior, which ran the police, of any association with outside agitators.

Things accelerated from these beginnings. They included donations of VAX computers (with some upkeep support) and container loads of books to universities; work with Ford Vietnam to provide training and executive development services for their truck assembly start-up; provision of English language programs for the oil, gas and airline industries; and continuing the master of systems engineering program with the Center for Systems Development at VNU Hanoi. A joint VNU Hanoi–RMIT conference on 'higher education in the 21st century' in May 1996, led on our side by Tony Adams' office, was momentous for a number of reasons. It was one of Vietnam's first truly international conferences after the start of the *Doi Moi* reform movement. Seeing this, the government asked RMIT to run conferences in Vietnam for university rectors to undertake their roles better.[2]

The link with Vietnam's leading university really blossomed, to the point where we agreed to fund a building on their main campus to house the centre and deliver the program, funded by $160,000 from the international project fund we'd set up out of a levy on international student income in Melbourne. Its rector, Professor Nguyen Van Dao, was an influential national figure and friendly to RMIT. Vietnam National University Hanoi was outside the Ministry of Education and Training (MOET) and there was always some friction between them. The centre was opened in April 1997. Some of its costs were meant to be defrayed by RMIT visitors staying in the centre itself, which had accommodation, thus saving hotel bills, but this did not happen much. To this I plead guilty too, having negotiated a good deal for any RMIT visitor at the historic Metropole Hotel. Though the building later reverted fully to VNU Hanoi control and had no RMIT affiliation in its name, these— the conference and the building—were both signals to the government that RMIT was serious and there to stay. It became a talking point for a possible RMIT campus.

Deep cover

As Dr Thu records (he was an adjunct professor at the time), conversations about a full campus started with his voluntary advice to the Ministry of Education and Training (MOET) from April 1994. Prior to a visit to Vietnam, David Beanland, vice-chancellor, asked for MOET's views on establishing an international university in Vietnam. Then Dr Thu drafted MOET's reply, as he was wont to do. He really had extraordinary access. It was sent in April 1996, turning the question back to RMIT to set out its views on establishing an international university in Vietnam. While in Hanoi at the abovementioned conference, David met with the MOET minister Tran Hong Quan, who asked what an international university would look like. Those of us around him at the time joined to draft overnight a short punchy reply, which he sent on. David met the minister again, who said he liked it, and asked for a more detailed proposal, which I later crafted with David and submitted in July, still just six pages.

It proposed that the university be fully foreign owned, have academic authority within Vietnam law but independent curricula, be able to raise its own capital, be provided with land free of charge, require infrastructure available at least to the site, and be entitled to cover its costs from fees and grants. It sought to have 20 percent of the student body from outside Vietnam (including from RMIT Australia), teach in English, and provide professional development to local and international staff.

That was quite a big ask. The new institution would start with dual higher education and vocational education programs in business management, accounting, communication engineering, computer science, manufacturing engineering and construction technology, and be followed by others we listed in the proposal. From early investigation we proposed a 70 ha VNU HCMC site at Thu Duc, 20 km to the north of the city centre, that had been set aside for international higher education.[3]

Dr Thu records that the minister sent the proposal to the office of the prime minister, Vo Van Kiet, whose representative replied that the government lacked a regulatory framework to approve any such project, and instructed MOET to get started on a statute for the establishment and operation of foreign universities in Vietnam.[4] (Vo Van Kiet later became prime minister and was very supportive of the venture.) Quietly working both sides, Dr Thu helped draft some regulations and sought my input every step of the way. The first drafts were for non-profit ventures, reflecting RMIT's constitution and intention not to repatriate any profits. But Vietnam's adherence to Marxist–Leninism, distrust of foreign non-government organisations (including US NGOs pursuing the remains of service people missing in action), and fears (surprisingly based on some real evidence) that fifth column anti-communist agitators were getting overseas support and grouping in the hills, brought us around to the clearer path of helping frame regulations to cover for-profit ventures.

Back at the Office of the Prime Minister by January 1997, the draft was delayed by a change of prime minister and a widening of the scope of the proposed regulation to cover health and scientific research.[5] Once the decree—in effect, enabling legislation—was promulgated, Dr Thu, who stayed on as RMIT's representative in Vietnam, resubmitted to the Office of the Prime Minister an expanded version of the original RMIT proposal. That was in December 1997.

Getting to 'go'

Breakthrough came not long after, on 23 January 1998. Deputy prime minister Lai Van Cu agreed in principle for RMIT to establish a campus and invited RMIT to develop a full proposal to be based on foreign investment law, assessed by MOET, and re-presented to the prime minister. It was the first licence 'in principle' of its kind (a step now well-established in Vietnamese law by two further decrees), and we had first-mover advantage for establishing a branch campus.[6]

Back at RMIT, and indeed in the Australian government, whose diplomats and ministers had been informed and supportive all along (if without a hint of any money), the realisation sank in. We were starting to be committed to what David Beanland called RMIT's biggest ever project.

Leadership of that was to be my job. The opportunity came at the time of one of RMIT's reorganisations and I went onto it full-time, though still as executive director of major projects. David was determined we put the necessary resources into the task, and encouraged me to see it as a career-making move. Having lost my favourite job as DVC international, and then the brilliant Tony Adams, dean of international programs, over that reorganisation, I was not sure how grand the prospect really was. I set about forming a full-time team in a new major projects unit and commissioned RMIT International, through its then CEO, Madeleine Reeve, to do more thorough pre-feasibility work at arm's length, so as to back up a full submission.

After some work, Madeline and I returned to the vice-chancellor to say preliminary indications were that it did not stack up financially. The fee-paying market for in-country international higher education in Vietnam was unproven, there was still regulatory uncertainty, and the costs of developing a large greenfield campus would be very high. Undeterred, and characteristically, David sent us back to revise our assumptions, which with more work was indeed able to show reasonable financial feasibility, if at higher fees, faster rates of development and lower construction costs than assumed before. The study was completed in draft by July 1998 and 'finalised' in September, recommending RMIT proceed to the next stage, but press the government of Vietnam to provide land free, enter into suitable equity partner arrangements for investment, including possibly through Australian or multilateral aid programs, and explore acquiring initial premises by lease.[7]

The site originally envisaged was no longer available, and the alternative 12 ha site offered at Thu Duc, a designated higher education zone in the same area, would be too small. That site was one of the options identified by a team led by Ron Davison, head of systems engineering at RMIT, who did some contributing pre-feasibility work, including site investigations, with Dr Thu. His team's work, when completed, painted a positive picture, but its most useful contribution was a review of some site options which David and I, with others, went up to inspect. One site at Thuan An in Binh Duong Province had plenty of land (some pockmarked by B52 bomb craters from the American war, now circular duck ponds), but it was too far out.

The best land seemed to be back in HCMC in District 7, near a giant Taiwan-invested Saigon South urban redevelopment project. It was close in, 5 km from downtown, but its access relied on completion of promised bridge projects, and the consistency of the land was 'like yoghurt', in the words of one of our consultants. Its riverside location raised the possibility of ferry access, or so I thought. And at least there was a clear government and planning framework for the area through the Management Authority for Saigon South Development (MASD), supposedly, but not really in practice, a 'one stop shop' for investment and development. This location was recommended by Ron Davison's study.

David was happy, and on that basis, we sought RMIT council approval to proceed to the next step. Members of the major initiatives and projects committee of council, charged with project oversight, showed some nervousness. The failure of the Penang campus was clearly on their minds. David masterfully managed the issues, stressing the uniqueness of such an invitation from the government of any country, keeping council informed, and promising to come back to them every step of the way.

By October we had their approval to go ahead with an application for investment licence. I helped by ensuring every submission showed the timing and cost of the nearest exit point, and providing honest and thorough documentation. This was the pattern of council persuasion for the steps to come—approval just for the next step, never a big leap into the dark, always a way out if needs be. Their continuing concerns included the size of the market for fee-paying students, financial viability, Vietnam's country risk, health risks (on which we had to commission an independent study), the sheer scale of the venture and our capacity to manage it, and later, site conditions and flooding.

Over time, most members of council visited first-hand, but the visits didn't all allay their concerns. It was hard for most Australian eyes, unfamiliar with Vietnam's breakneck speed of development, to see undeveloped marshland becoming a mature campus in only a few years. Later, after the long-term site was fixed and the Pham Ngoc Thach campus in the city opened, I still liked to take visitors to the new campus site by launch from downtown, to show how close it was to the city and to promote water access. But one time some boys dropped two big bricks from a bridge onto visiting council members cruising underneath, cutting through the canvas cover, grazing and only narrowly saving the head of Bob Frater, a key member of council, and Christine Chow, a member of my team, from serious injury or worse. Persuading council was not easy, though once the venture was established, Dennis Gibson, chancellor and chair of the board, gave it strong support and played a key role in the governance and oversight of its operations.

A lot of work was ahead, on many fronts. A more rigorous feasibility study was needed; a detailed foreign investment licence application had to be drafted in both languages; we had to set up a governance structure effective for both educational oversight and financing; and, far from least, we had to find the money. RMIT was in no position to find around US$30m to develop it. We were able to fund just the technical work from the same project fund that had supported International Cooperation House in Hanoi, but even this, we estimated, might need around $1m. We hoped this amount could be capitalised as equity into the venture. (At the end of the day, project development costs were about twice that.)

The feasibility work needed a lot of detailed planning, with specialist inputs from staff and consultants on courses, labour regulations, campus design, building, infrastructure, site conditions, market research, legal conditions, legal agreements, and more. It also needed a communications program, not only with the university community, but with leaders in both countries and the public at large, though we had little definitive to say at that stage. The full feasibility study was finished in August 1999, just as the parallel work to prepare a licence application was finished.[8] Our assumptions were conservative. When later the Victorian auditor-general reviewed offshore campuses of all the Victorian universities, he found that only RMIT Vietnam did not have 'overly optimistic' student enrolment estimates.[9]

When negotiations started with possible investors, we engaged the Commonwealth Bank of Australia, the university's main bankers, as we expected them to have some stake or other ahead. Debra Knight led their team, a bright and ebullient analyst, and as it turned out, wife to one of Vivian's US friends. She stayed supporting the negotiations until the deal was closed. Detailed business plans came into shape, with constantly changing details. I enjoyed running this part of it as I was learning project finance on the job, and years later, after RMIT, this kind of work became my consultant company's bread-and-butter.

Unrestricted access to land was critical. In Vietnam, land is owned by the state and leased to occupants with land use rights. We had to commit to a site and prepare a lease before having a full legal presence in the country beyond a representative office. Working with MASD and Ho Chi Minh City People's Committee, we gained land use plan approval from the city in March 1999 for a site in District 7, Saigon South. We really preferred a better site, 62 ha on the eastern side of the river, but it was already committed to another developer. It was worth asking for a change anyway, and to our delight Le Thanh Hai, chair of the people's committee, the city government, reserved it for us through a process taking little over two weeks. In the face of grumbles about the slow pace of government decision-making in Vietnam, I am still struck by the contrast between this efficiency and the 11 months it took the Victorian government to approve the project. Le Thanh Hai later became party secretary, and stayed a staunch ally of RMIT Vietnam and friendly to me.

The second requirement of the licence application process was to commit to levels of investment, both 'invested capital' (like subscribed capital, not needing to be provided up front, but contributed later over the 50-year period of the license) and the 'legal capital' needed at the outset. By the time of submission, these were the major hurdles to be overcome. When eventually approved, our nomination of US$51.5m invested capital turned out to be Vietnam's largest foreign investment for that year, for *any* sector of the economy. We were in the deep end now. The more the preparatory work progressed, the higher the stakes for RMIT rose.

The governance and management structures weren't easy to design either. We wanted a start to operations as early as possible after licencing, at interim premises while the new campus was being built. Unlike Singapore, Kuala Lumpur and even Hong Kong, where programs could be served by fly-in-fly-out lecturers (alongside local staff), RMIT Vietnam would need a complement of resident local and international staff and a good local management structure, as autonomous as possible under the circumstances.

The whole basis of the proposal to RMIT was that the business would stand on its own legs, requiring an incorporated structure in Vietnam and a service level agreement with the university proper, similar to other structures we'd set up for RMIT International and RMIT Malaysia. This concentrated RMIT's interests, rather than risk the different parts of RMIT having their hands directly on operations. Monash University's governance problems with their South African campus seemed at the time to have this problem.

Academic independence was critically important. We insisted on the university's right to set its own curricula, along with its own student numbers and fees. After all, the courses were to be accredited offshore in Australia. With the support of the Ministry of Planning and Investment, the Ministry of Education and Training (MOET) went along with this, but remained uncomfortable about their lack of control, apart from a small mandatory course they set on citizenship, Vietnam-style. To allay a concern of MOET that the RMIT courses might not be provided in Vietnam at the same standards as in Australia, we negotiated an agreement for annual MOET–RMIT exchange visits to monitor and assure academic quality alternating in each country. These visits helped our regulators see how a large modern university assured its academic quality, still a challenged area of policy in Vietnam.

Dr Thu coordinated much of the investment licence application. Requirements for demonstrating economic and technical feasibility for a foreign investment licence in Vietnam were different from Western practice, and it took some months for the data to be generated for, or adapted to, their regulatory template. A set of document boxes holding the application was delivered to the Ministry of Planning and Investment (MPI) on 9 August 1999. They circulated it among agencies of government and came back with more questions. This supplementary document was submitted in November.

On 20 April 2000, a full investment licence was approved for RMIT International University Vietnam. This was of course a cause for celebration. In August 2000, RMIT council gave the venture full approval to proceed. I became general director, that is, CEO, of the new university and Don Mercer, the chancellor of RMIT, became chair of the entity.

As conditions of financing later became clear, it seemed necessary to have an offshore vehicle to hold RMIT Vietnam. Singapore was a good possibility, as were the British Virgin Islands, but they would need non-RMIT nominee directors, and the 'look' of a third-country holding company would not have appealed to our sceptics, whose concerns— and in some cases in RMIT active opposition—lived on after the licence was granted. So, we interposed RMIT Vietnam Holdings Pty Ltd, an Australian company, to hold RMIT's stake in RMIT Vietnam, and it made sense that I become CEO of that too. Later, Dennis Gibson as chancellor chaired the board, and being an informed supporter, played a key role in the governance of the start-up and the oversight of its operations.

Starting up and operating

During the period of preparing the investment licence application we looked for places to start without building a new campus. We knew that having a working presence on the ground would show commitment to prospective investors, and let us test the market and education conditions in Vietnam. We looked at sites right downtown, but they weren't suitable. Motorcycle and scooter parking would be too expensive for students. We looked in the Tan Thuan export processing zone next to the development area of the eventual campus, but though it was a good space it was too expensive. We looked at buildings along the river near one of the expatriate areas, but they weren't fit for purpose.

At the time when RMIT's campus intentions came to be known we were approached with a number of proposals. One of them, in 1996, was to form a joint venture with the International Grammar School, an Australian-originated international school then using the NSW secondary school curriculum. The idea was to occupy the school's old campus on Pham Ngoc Thach Street in District 3 to develop an English language learning centre once the school moved out to its new campus in District 2. We didn't pursue it because it would have undercut our entry into the higher education market and diverted our energies. But the deputy director, Simon Dawe, was on the job market with some relevant experience, if not in higher education. We hired him in October 2000 to lead the first start-up tasks for an interim campus, along with Trish Chapman as manager of pre-campus programs, an RMIT stalwart deeply immersed in Vietnam who stayed through those tough early years, and two others. Simon was well connected to the owners and operators of Dragon Capital, a successful equity fund, so we thought this might be useful in the future too.

He said he knew of a possible site, and one night after dinner he took David Beanland and me to a dark property on that same street. We jumped up on the front fence to see over. It was a disused Shell company executive compound with a grand but dilapidated French villa (later known as 'the castle' by students), an overgrown tennis court, long grass and a mouldy swimming pool, green with slime visible even in the dark. It was perfect! It was owned by the Foreign Affairs Bureau of the city, and after some haggling we signed on to a five-year lease, renewable up to 20 years, and at a fixed rent. District 3 already had a number of prestigious schools and universities nearby, and was a relatively well-off district on the edge of the city centre and on the way to the airport. The team started preparations for renovating the main building, and staffing and equipping it for the first courses to be offered.

From RMIT Melbourne Patricia Roessler was appointed as deputy CEO and moved up. She was a talented Harvard-trained manager in the institutional planning section, self-reliant and not afraid of taking decisions. Simon Dawe left, and Tricia initiated work to renovate the buildings and grounds as well as recruit and gear up for the courses. As my deputy she ran much of the whole start-up on the ground. My experience told me not to stand in the way of a campus director far away from Melbourne. This worked for me. I was spending a lot of time in Vietnam but not intending, after family discussion, to seek to relocate there.

Tricia and I worked closely together by necessity. It was very hard for her doing all the things to get started from scratch. Hiring and firing were difficult issues, sometimes landing in the courts where judges were not impartial. They were tasked with finding solutions, and unfortunately open to improper influence, though never offered from RMIT. More generally, the external working environment was corrupt. More than once, local officials made unannounced compliance visits and sought to levy informal fines.

On such practices RMIT Vietnam took a hard line—one breach and we would be known to be open to influence. It was difficult, for example, to keep up ICT integrity when the whole economy seemed to run on bootlegged software. Even Microsoft, with whom we were seeking to be an education partner, offered us unauthorised versions of their own software when out of stock of the real thing. But to the puzzlement of some commentators, we held the line and paid only for authorised software and equipment.

The team of people who formed in Ho Chi Minh City were a pleasure to work with: Tricia's staff, including Trish Chapman, Dr Thu on his many appearances, the advocacy of Michael Mann as ambassador and Lisa Filipetto as consul-general, and the background support of Nguyen Thanh Hoang, the Australian-Vietnamese owner of the Norfolk Hotel group, in whose apartments and hotel the RMIT people stayed, and whose inside advice we valued.

But start-up funds were tight. Memories of Penang were fresh in the minds of council members and my delegations as CEO were limited to $10,000, though even in those early days, gifted money was building up in the Australian holding company. One time the venture was running low on cash just before payday, so Tricia and I went down to the ANZ Bank in Ho Chi Minh City and I put the payroll gap on my corporate credit card.

This was ridiculous. We needed decent delegations. On return to

Melbourne in May 2002 I called an extraordinary meeting of the board of RMIT Vietnam. It was do or die for me. I made an ultimatum: I would have to resign as CEO if the matter could not be resolved effectively. I knew this might see me leave RMIT too. This infuriated the chairman and chancellor, Don Mercer. I circulated the papers for the meeting to his home fax well after midnight, its loud and long chattering keeping him awake. But I was in a state too. Lori Mooren, then a visiting friend from Sydney, remembers me storming home for dinner angry earlier that night.

After a tense meeting the board gave me the delegations I needed, but at a cost. Ruth Dunkin, the new vice-chancellor, established a large and obtrusive implementation oversight committee made up of many managers of the university to keep watch. Added work though it was, it turned out useful, allowing my team to inform sceptics and supporters alike of what was happening, and enabling Ruth to have detailed oversight, which grew into strong support.

Once refurbished, the campus looked beautiful. More importantly, it worked well for the students. The first courses were a continuation of the master of systems engineering and English language learning, preparatory studies, and bachelors of science in computer science, software engineering, and information and multimedia. In its first year, 2001, 369 students enrolled, broadly on track with our conservative forecasts.[10] Pham Ngoc Thach Street was a buzz of activity, with modern open learning spaces, good connectivity outside the Vietnam firewall, trimmed lawns, a pool that was a venue for teaching children to swim (many people in Vietnam who can't swim die in floods), and active student associations. Tricia deservedly was later recognised in the Order of Australia awards in part for her contribution. After an interregnum leased out as a school, the Pham Ngoc Thach Street campus operated inside RMIT until recently as an English language learning and conferencing venue.

Looking for money

During licence preparation we worked to seek funding and arrange financing, listing and talking to many prospects. The idea was to minimise RMIT's capital exposure by attracting up to 80 percent equity and to gear it up as much as prudently possible with debt. The business plan was a basis for talking to interested parties: banks in Australia and Vietnam, equity funds, superannuation and pension funds, foundations, aid agencies, individuals and companies that might be interested, for commercial or corporate social responsibility reasons, to invest in a new university. This was very time-consuming and involved meetings, meals, pitches and travel. My list of prospects to work on was over 60 and growing.

For equity we were making progress towards a stake from an industry superannuation fund, and a convoluted financing vehicle with one of Australia's major banks which really amounted to quasi-equity, having a 'put' option enabling them to convert their equity to debt at their will. There was no prospect of the Australian or Victorian government taking equity.

By contrast with equity, there was no limit to institutions' interest in providing debt; of course, at a price. But interest rates in Vietnam were very high, and all the commercial lenders seemed to want RMIT's full guarantee under the loan, a risk the university council would be unwilling to take, given its ownership by the state and in turn the state's loan limits under the commonwealth–state loan agreement.

As an urban planner I had long been interested in urban infrastructure financing, having practised infrastructure coordination for optimising NSW finance, and publishing a little in the field myself.[11] At a talk in Melbourne on public–private partnership financing by Wolfgang Bertelsmeier, director for Vietnam of the International Finance Corporation (IFC), I twigged that perhaps the World Bank, in which group the IFC sat, might be a possible source. He was not an expert on education financing, but said a new education group had formed at its Washington DC headquarters and they might possibly take an interest.

Yes, I found out, they would be interested to hear what we were doing, but their mandate was for the private sector, not public institutions like RMIT. With favourable World Bank equity from country member funding, the IFC makes a surplus on lending to businesses that would make a positive development contribution in developing and emerging economies. It also provides equity, security packages, and advice. The IFC people I contacted said they would be happy to hear us out, and as RMIT Vietnam was technically a for-profit entity it would be eligible. So, it wasn't too long (August 1999) before David and I were standing before their lead education group in Washington DC pitching our plans.

It was a splash of cold water. They didn't seem much interested at all. The project size was small for them, they weren't interested in equity for a deal like this, RMIT's 'skin in the game' was too small ('think more than 50 percent'), and our debt gearing ratio was too high. They did however think Vietnam was ready for a venture like ours, offered technical assistance money for preparation, and encouraged us to keep talking to Wolfgang. Sadder but wiser, we went away to think about it.

They were probably right. Our team tweaked the business plan yet once more. In our chase for equity we continued to present ourselves to others as preferred minority shareholders; no way would RMIT council agree otherwise. Why not put a little pressure on the IFC by bringing in another international financial institution, like the Asian Development Bank (ADB)? A similar process followed, with me pitching the project in Manila.[12] They were definitely interested, though they didn't have a private sector financing arm like the IFC. Importantly, they'd look at a project financing deal secured by the project itself, not requiring a full guarantee. With a better idea of what might work, we reverted to both agencies and by the end of 1999 found ourselves negotiating two mandates for due diligence.

The Washington DC meeting taught us a lesson, but nothing like the workout that was to follow. Negotiating a terms sheet was the most difficult because everything of importance was in it. This work was integrated with legal preparations, with Freehills law firm joining our team and chewing up much of the project's development budget on a set of documents that were in the end even bigger than the licence application. I counted over 20 agreements, the most important of which were the loan agreements, the guarantees and pledges, and the educational and administrative services agreement between RMIT and RMIT Vietnam. With the IFC and ADB loans in the offing, we restructured the licence to interpose the holding company between RMIT and RMIT Vietnam (as described earlier) and to reduce our invested capital to US$33.6m and our 'legal capital', the equivalent of equity, to US$16.5m.

The IFC team was led by Seung-Hee Nah, a brilliant business-woman with good humour but an iron will, and ADB was led by Cheolsu Kim, a level-headed economist familiar with big capital sources in east Asia. Isabella Stoehr, a smooth French national from the Multilateral Investment Guarantee Agency of the World Bank in Japan, joined us too, possibly seeing an opportunity to sell RMIT Vietnam a security package. The project benefited enormously from entering into the mandates. At the start, in Singapore, I indicated our willingness to modify some financial assumptions and forecasts. Seung-Hee laughed—the IFC expected us to throw out the lot. The financial model was rebuilt on the screen as we talked, aided by Carole Merman, a French IFC modelling wizard. The weeks and months ground on for our team of RMIT people, CBA and Freehills, talking in different locations and time zones, communicating and getting advice from the board of RMIT Vietnam and the rest of the university.

There were some sticking points. We needed a project financing model that minimised, if not eliminated, recourse to RMIT, which ultimately was on the Victorian government's balance sheet. We were asking for US$15m between them. As a result, the IFC and ADB tried to tie up securities in multiple and intrusive ways, and charge us a premium over the spread that we knew the commercial banks could offer. Combined with an eye-watering list of obligations that the international agencies required on environmental, resettlement and other areas, it was looking like RMIT could never be fully in compliance with the loan conditions. I was concerned about presenting an unacceptable terms sheet back home. The IFC also required us to commission more work, but at least paid for it with technical assistance money: the feasibility of a proprietary student loan scheme, and a resettlement action plan to estimate payments and processes for the involuntary relocation of people living on the intended campus site, many of whom were long-term informal settlers (read: squatters).

One particular issue became a real problem. Experience, including the painful one in Penang, told us that payments under the service agreement between RMIT Vietnam and RMIT must have top priority. The IFC and ADB wanted to subordinate to the interest repayments those payments for essential services that RMIT would have to provide. At the time my colleagues at RMIT were nervous about what our team might come back with, and I knew what they would think, so we dug in. They were most certainly not disguised royalty payments, as our would-be financiers suspected; they would not even be sufficient to cover the costs of course development and conversion necessary for delivery in Vietnam.

The IFC and ADB wouldn't move. Now that we saw the costs of money and the security package we had to commit to, commercial financing was starting to look more attractive. We walked out of the meeting with sincere intent, not as a tactic.

We'd had enough. Debra Knight and I went down to Orchard Road (in Singapore) so that we could talk more, and she could buy some shoes. An hour later Seung-Hee called and conceded. So, we left the shoe store and went back to the negotiating table, the biggest hurdle overcome.

Back at RMIT, the vice-chancellor and even members of council were delighted that we had reached a deal, glad such reputable funders as the World Bank and ADB had endorsed the plans, implicitly covering much of our country risk. Vietnam at the time depended on development assistance from those two agencies, so any problems that might arrive had a chance of being fixed at the political level.

One more big step was needed—due diligence. It was another painstaking collection of information, and a round of visits to Melbourne and Vietnam in July 2000. The ADB required us to prepare yet another market research report to address their concern that a presence in Vietnam would face an entirely new and unproven market in a country with officially documented low incomes and an unmeasurable 'grey' cash economy. Cheolsu's (the ADB lead) conversion came through the river of motorcycles that fill, and give a raffish charm to, Ho Chi Minh City's streets. Outside a Honda motorcycle shop he said, 'Stop the car' and went in for 10 minutes. He came out, and with some drama, said, 'You have your project'. How could people in a low income country afford so many

Honda Dreams? They put down $1000 cash and paid the rest off over a year. For university education in Vietnam, a dream bigger than even a Honda, they would surely be able to find the cash.

The due diligence team also worked over RMIT thoroughly. Ron Perkinson, a Kiwi, rugby coach and IFC's most senior education specialist, disappeared into the faculties in Melbourne to quiz ordinary academic staff about their educational philosophies and their views on RMIT Vietnam. He was pleasantly surprised. The educational thinking was good and the project by then had wide support among academics. However, our visitors knew RMIT was not willing to provide equity in full, and was still in discussions with prospective investors. Would we get across the line? This hung uncomfortably in the air on the last night of their visit as we hosted farewell drinks in RMIT's Story Hall.

At the very same time, on another part of the campus, another event shaped the future of RMIT Vietnam. To understand this, it is necessary to step back some months.

A friend calls

After we'd started up RMIT Vietnam there was a lot of publicity and my office had many calls asking what was happening, with offers to provide consultant services or otherwise become involved. David Garner was manager of my office and took a lot of them. I'd asked him to get details of each call and batch them up so we could answer them the best way. He had a call from a Ron Clarke, whom he didn't know of (being younger than me), and took a message, saying he'd pass it on. 'Ron Clarke', I said, '*The* Ron Clarke? The famous runner?' Sure enough, that was him. He knew David Beanland and wanted to connect RMIT with a friend of his who might be able to help RMIT Vietnam. Would David and I come up to Brisbane to meet him? We thought it worthwhile, so up we went in January 1999.

Charles Feeney was a US American, a shy man. He had read about RMIT Vietnam in a magazine in a coffee shop in Danang, and that day offered to donate US$80,000 for scholarships for the systems engineering program with VNU Hanoi. It was hard to find more information about him: through a non-disclosure agreement he insisted we not disclose his name or the identity of his foundation, Atlantic Philanthropies, which was incorporated in Bermuda. There was no malfeasance to cover; on the contrary, he wished to stay behind the limelight, despite the fact that in 1997 the *New York Times* had already 'outed' him as a reclusive billionaire donor.

He invited David and me to visit his activities in Vietnam. I joined him in Danang where we spent an evening on the river with Helga, his wife. I got to know Juliette too, his daughter, who had a French foundation for urban heritage conservation that might take an interest in restoring the city hall in Ho Chi Minh City. Chuck often visited the East Meets West Foundation in Danang where he joined with them on development projects.

That foundation's CEO, Mark Conroy, another US American and a veteran of the American war, was most influential. He and his Vietnamese wife would visit impoverished villages in central Vietnam on Mark's motorbike, talk to local people and their leaders, and pledge what was needed to help them out of poverty without needing to get back to Atlantic. Chuck trusted him and honoured the pledges every time. We looked around local hospitals which Atlantic was funding, but Chuck also expressed particular concern about the awful standards of student housing in Danang, in which he thought the future leaders of Vietnam had to live.

We learned that he had been co-founder of DFS Duty-Free/Galleria, a multinational company that pioneered the modern concept of duty-free shopping, sold his stake at the top of the market in 1996, and wanted to spend up to US$8bn on improving other people's lives before he died, 'giving while living'.[13] He was particularly focused on education, public health and hospitals in Vietnam, which were not in good shape.

Other meetings followed, including lunch in Ho Chi Minh City at Lemongrass Restaurant (after a slightly proprietorial look at the Galleria duty-free store nearby), with his confidant, Walter Bortz, an eminent Stanford professor and geriatrician. I talked up our plans for the next

272

stage of RMIT Vietnam, thinking of student housing or perhaps the library as possibilities for gifts.

Time went by and Chuck topped up his support for the scholarships he'd earlier pledged. As David Beanland records, he asked for an impromptu visit to RMIT while in Melbourne.

Now we return to 9 August 2000, that final evening of IFC and ADB due diligence in Melbourne. At David's request I walked over from that to join Chuck and David in David's office. Chuck said he'd like to help RMIT Vietnam more and had his copy of our business plan I'd left with him in Vietnam. He pointed to one of the financial pages. 'Oh, that's our lunch at Lemongrass', I joked, thinking he had taken my hints about student housing or library support. It indicated US$300,000. 'No', he said, 'I mean the line above'. That was the equity requirement, US$15m. 'I'd like to fund that'.

The meeting being unscheduled, David had to go elsewhere, and I had to get back to the drinks with the IFC and ADB. Would he like to join us and meet the co-funders? 'No thank you.' Chuck walked off alone into the drizzly Melbourne night. Over the years that followed, more generous gifts followed from him for scholarships, a building on the Pham Ngoc Thach Street campus, student accommodation, a gymnasium, standard-setting for libraries in Vietnam, a set of learning resource centres in four domestic universities developed by RMIT, discussed below, and more. All up, US$22m came for RMIT Vietnam alone, and over US$50.7m to RMIT for all projects.[14] A frugal and modest man, he was and still is a hero of RMIT Vietnam.

To our embarrassment, he had had to return to Melbourne to persuade the Victorian government, RMIT's owner, to allow RMIT to accept the gift. The RMIT council members' suspicions were hard to assuage. A commitment to secrecy about his identity? Constituted in Bermuda? What does he want in return? But the state government was more sceptical still. The gift, as we know from the section before, was leveraged with loans from the IFC and the ADB, and despite RMIT's financial exposure being quite small in the hard-won deal, the Treasury treated the project as if we, RMIT—and thus they, the government—had to guarantee it fully. The same Treasury that was a world leader on innovative public–private partnerships seemed to have no clue about what project financing was. The situation was not helped by the minister of education, Lynne Kosky, also being minister for finance. So, into the full cabinet meeting Chuck went, to plead to let RMIT accept his gift. Chris Oechsli, Chuck's right-hand man before and after Atlantic Philanthropies was set up, and later CEO of the foundation, said he hadn't seen Chuck put on a tie, as he did that day, for many years.

After a delay—324 days, actually—the state government gave its approval, in August 2002, to draw down the funds, but on the condition that RMIT make hedging arrangements against the US dollar, and that we take out country and political risk insurance for Vietnam. On advice, we did not take out a hedge facility. It would be very expensive; we had a natural hedge by keeping offshore US dollar gifts to pay for further development, and we were setting US dollar denominated fees which would go to purchases of library books, equipment and so on. And the funding partnerships with the World Bank and ADB were themselves good country risk insurance.

We held the donated money in the holding company (RMIT Vietnam Holdings Pty Ltd), not RMIT Vietnam itself, to be transferred as needed. The way was now clear to develop the Saigon South campus, to start up in Hanoi, and, we hoped, to set about transforming the lives of many young graduates to contribute to Vietnam's development.

Developing the campuses

The original leased 63 ha site in Saigon South was mainly marshland, occupied by people with low income and used mostly for farming and fishing. There were 50 households living on the extended site and 84 off-site using it, along with 785 graves, which are ubiquitous around the city and reflect a cultural practice of burial near family homes, not just the legacy of the American war. The occupants, users and graves would have to be involuntarily relocated. This was an established practice for land development in Vietnamese cities, covered by detailed regulations and standards, and overlain with more rigorous IFC and ADB requirements.

The author, Koh Tsu Koon and David Beanland at Penang campus graduation ceremony, 1998

Dinner in Osaka, 1994
From left: Renata Howe, Brian Howe, Deputy PM, Jenny Macklin, then Director of Australian Urban Policy Review, the author

The author in a flight simulator, China Civil Aviation Flight College, now Civil Aviation Flight University of China, Guanghan, China, ca. 1995

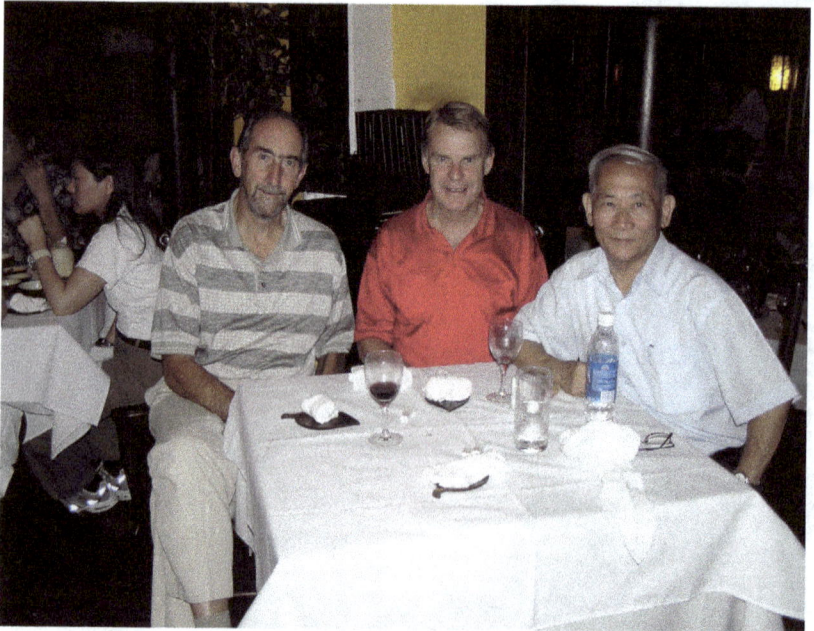

RMIT Vietnam founding team
From left: David Beanland, the author, Nguyen Xuan Thu

Christine Chow, a member of the RMIT Major Projects Unit, using an umbrella where boys from a bridge over Saigon River dropped bricks on a launch carrying visitors to the RMIT campus site, just grazing and narrowly sparing Bob Frater, a council member, 2003

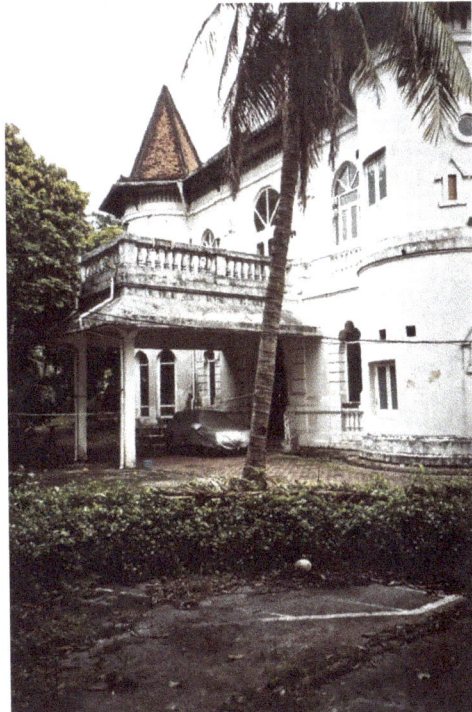

Pham Ngoc Thach Street main building, in its original state, 2000

The family at a wedding
From left: the author, Sasha, Kina, Vivian, Maya

Signing ceremony, Asian Development Bank and RMIT, Pham Ngoc Thach
Street RMIT campus, Ho Chi Minh City, 21 February 2002
From left: Mr Myoung-ho Hin, Vice-President ADB, the author
(courtesy RMIT Vietnam)

Conditions at RMIT Vietnam's Saigon South campus site, 2001

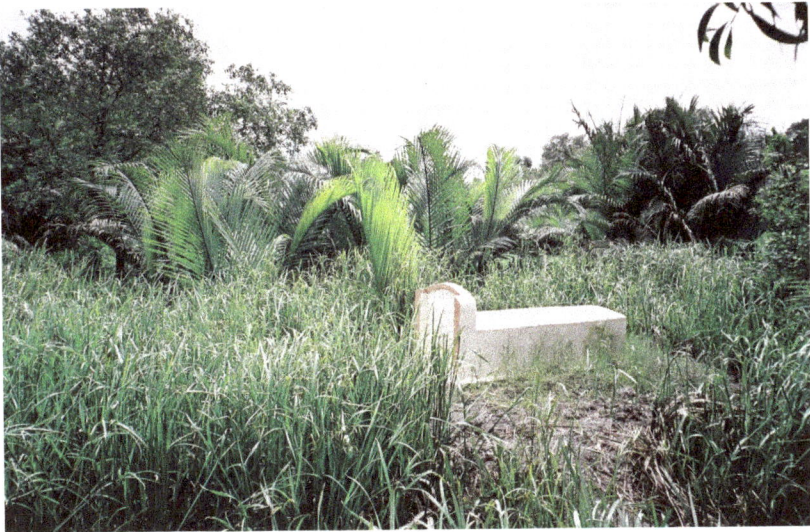

One of 758 graves to be relocated,
RMIT Vietnam's Saigon South campus site, 2001

David Beanland and Victorian Minister for Education (and Minister for Finance) Lynne Kosky at the opening of RMIT Vietnam's Saigon South campus, 2004

RMIT Vietnam long-timers at Saigon South campus launch, Ho Chi Minh City, 31 May 2004
From left: the author, Dr Nguyen Xuan Thu, Professor Nguyen Van Dao, ex-president of VNU Hanoi and adviser to RMIT Vietnam, Ms Thanh Bui, personal assistant to RMIT Vietnam's president Michael Mann, and Professor David Beanland

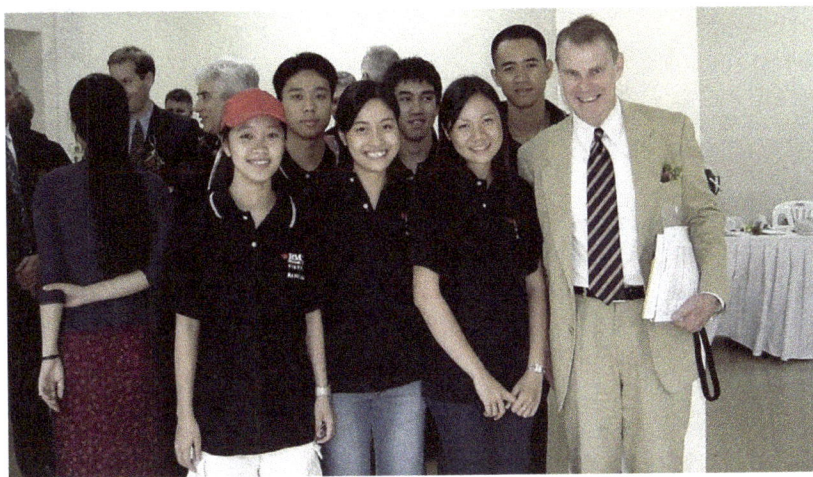

The author with students, RMIT Vietnam, Ho Chi Minh City, 2002

*Chuck Feeney inspecting the state of student housing,
University of Danang, 2002*

Asia Injury Prevention Foundation corporate-sponsored crash helmets distributed to school children, Hanoi, 2002. Recipients must agree to take part in publicity if they escape injury or death by wearing their helmets.

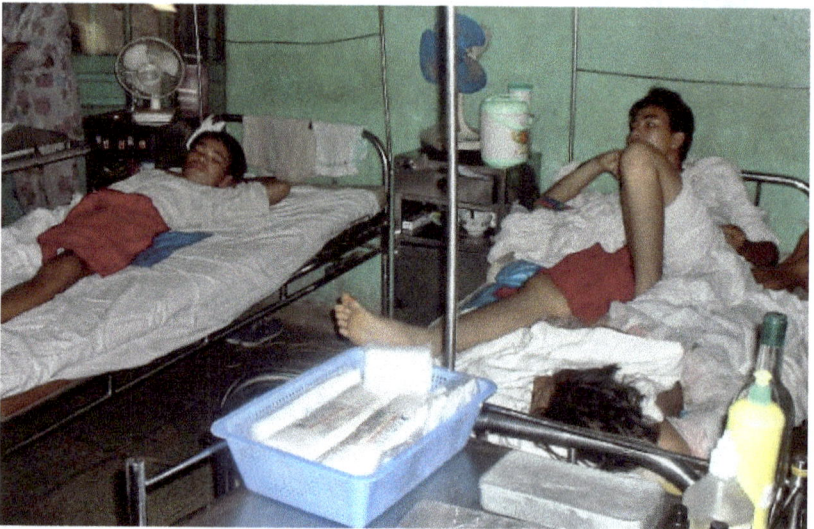

Orthopaedic ward at Viet Duc Hospital, Hanoi, with two to a bed, part of directors' inception program for Asia Injury Prevention Foundation, 5 October 2001 (courtesy VietnamPlus)

*Botswana International University of Science and Technology
designated campus site, Palapye, 2007*

*IFC public–private partnership team prior to Botswana government cabinet
briefing on International University of Science and Technology,
Gaborone, June 2008*

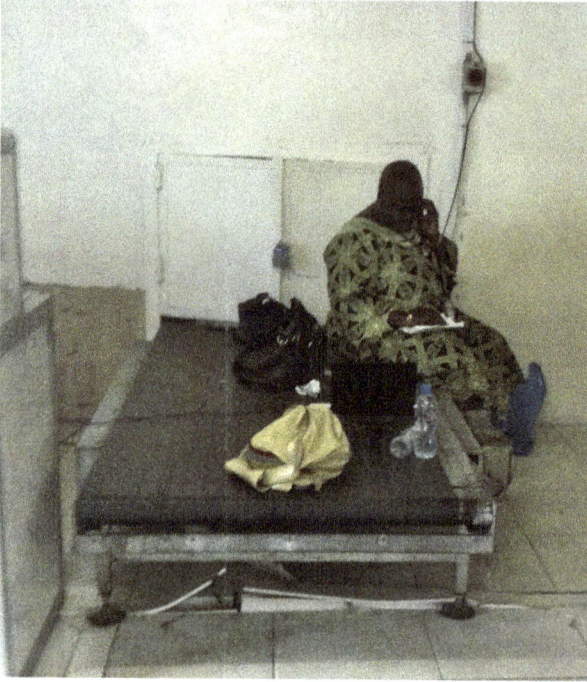

The ticket counter at Monrovia International Airport, June 2012

International Leadership Institute graduation, Dar es Salaam, Ethiopia, July 2016 (courtesy Badeg Bekele)

University of Central Asia, Naryn campus,
Kyrgyz Republic, 2019 (courtesy UCA)

SABIS® village school, Soran, Kurdistan, 2014

Tribal nomadic people near prospective campus site, Khedbrahma, India, 2010

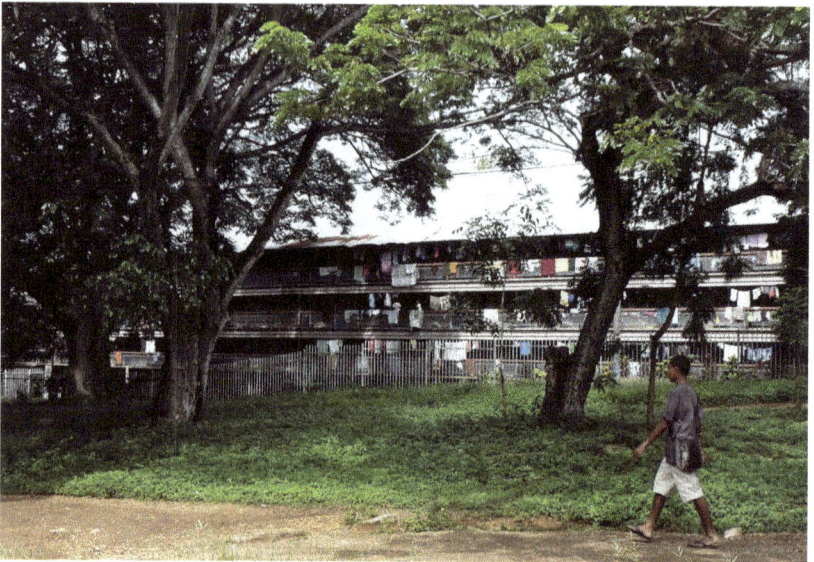

Student housing, University of PNG, Port Moresby, 2012

In the Gulf on Monash University work, January 2008
From left: Ismail Al-Bishri, University of Sharjah, Stephanie Fahey, the author
Photo courtesy of Nizar Farjou, Monash University

Departing for board meeting of Blue Mountains International Hotel
Management School, Rushcutters Bay, November 2012
From left: Rachel Argaman, Brian King, Ingrid Moses, Guy Bentley,
Arie van der Spek

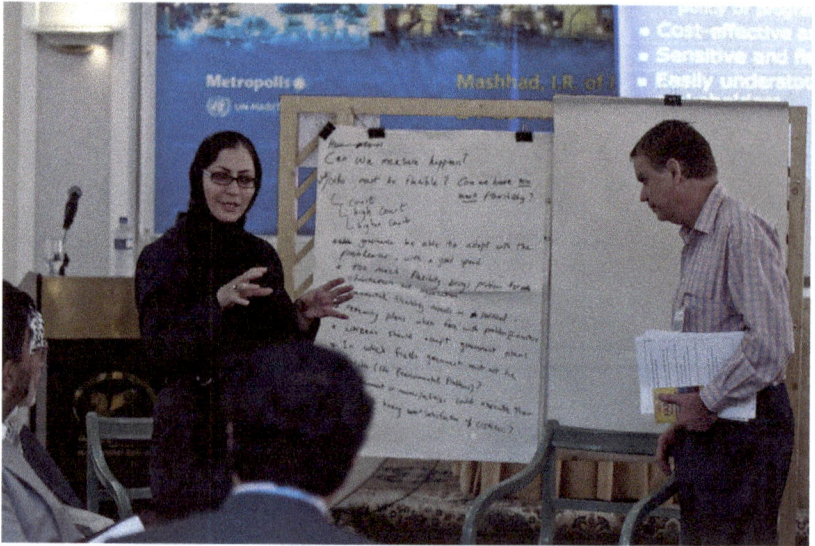

'Can we measure happiness': Workshop on urban governance performance indicators, Mashhad, Iran, 2012

A friendly reception from children of a landowner's semi-formal settlement near Tabubil, PNG, 2008

AFS Australia board dinner at home, 2019
From left, clockwise: the author, Eduardo Assed, John Shuey, Frances Baxter,
Izumi Taniguchi, Kylie Farmer, Marcela Lapertosa, Sarah Nielsen, Martin Piron,
Justin Grogan, Lori Mooren, and Robert and Kai Zarr

'Come home now': AFS staff working to repatriate pandemic-stranded students,
18 March 2020
From left: the author, Frances Baxter, Sally Farquharson, Léa Bouillet,
Claudia Rojas, Hannah Allum, Elisabeth Hansen, Alexis Ong

Family at home in Melbourne, 2010
From left: Sasha Wilmoth, Vivian Lin, Kina Lin-Wilmoth, Maya Lin, the author

Family in Brisbane, 2018
From left: Kina Lin-Wilmoth, Sasha Wilmoth, the author, Maya Lin

The details went down to how many banana trees the occupants and visitors grew and how many ducks they had (the latter, of course, open to temporary additions overnight for counting).[15]

Another complication with the land was that it needed to be cleared of unexploded ordnance. Experienced Vietnamese military were engaged to undertake this task and some 30 pieces of ordnance were found. They were mainly unexploded mortars. The site required extensive landfilling. Hundreds of trucks completed this task. At that very time a worker was killed in an industrial park in Vung Tau. Even when our site had been cleared, it was apparent that unexploded ordnance had been brought in with the landfill. Consequently, all the landfill was then checked with three more pieces of live ordnance found.[16] Kenn Crompton, the campus development manager, recalls of me that 'the management team had complete faith and confidence in your leadership as we followed in your footsteps when we walked onto the site for the first time after the ordnance was cleared'.

It was also necessary to move graves found on the site. We attempted to find the families of those buried to get permission to move the bodies and move them to a new burial site. We funded the new graves and accompanying religious ceremonies, and paid further compensation where necessary. For those whose families could not be found we arranged the appropriate relocation through the local government.

I walked over the site many times. I talked, through interpreters, with some of the occupants. They showed no hostility whatever. Little wonder, I suppose. Settlements of this type tended to be generous, particularly from foreign-invested developers (the typical displaced farmer could retire to a new house and set up a little retirement coffee shop), and that year we were the biggest foreign investor in the country. That was the problem. The bargaining position of the local ward was strong, and despite the resettlement action plan estimating US$2.7m for resettlement and compensation (including moving allowance, job retraining and more), the asking price kept rising. At one point Le Thanh Hai mentioned to Michael Mann a US$25m total cost of compensation. Discussed in the previous chapter, Michael was my successor from March 2002, previously the Australian ambassador to Vietnam. He recommended shrinking the site to a 12 ha roadside strip that had already relocated settlers, paying retrospectively only for those people's relocation. I could live with that as a first stage, but thought it small for the long term.

But what to do with the rest of the site? In effect, thanks to Le Thanh Hai, who had secured the whole site for us, we had a free option. The land could remain undeveloped, and over the next 50 years, RMIT would grow across the unused site and for each step pay resettlement compensation. Sure, that might cost, but resettlement would have to be paid only as needed.

Michael and most of the RMIT Vietnam board later took the view that there was a real risk that the government might 'call up' payments in advance for compensation, and so RMIT gave up land use rights to the rest of the site, which these days is developed out by other new private universities. It is ironic that, with RMIT Vietnam's success 20 years out, the smaller site taken up has now nearly reached capacity, and before too long the university will have to find more land, a scarce resource in Ho Chi Minh City.

The RMIT leadership, including Ruth Dunkin when she became vice-chancellor, insisted that the design of the new campus remain in the hands of the successful stable of RMIT's Melbourne-based campus architects, discussed earlier, though none of them had direct experience in Vietnam. I didn't oppose this either, provided that the lead project management company had that experience. And it did. Norman Day was chosen as lead architect, coincidentally the boss of the practice where my daughter Maya had her school work experience placement.

In the early planning there was a choice to be made between an international modern feel and using locally comfortable Vietnam themes. We were warned off using anything like the dreadful yellow colour of government institutions in Vietnam, and from making any reference to Vietnam's national symbols, such as the red star, so disillusioned with government were our prospective middle-class student families. That was good advice.

The talks with prospective project managers (which we wanted to be international companies) and construction firms were interesting. Chuck's suggested company, Delta Constructions from Danang, took me over the recently built US consulate complex, including its deep underground fortified rooms, such was the memory of the US' ignominious retreat from Saigon in 1973. The city authorities had memories too, letting the grass on the outside nature strip of the complex—their responsibility, not the Americans'—grow unkempt in an otherwise well-trimmed precinct.

Ground was broken in 2003, the year that the other campus enrolled 619 students. Though there were some issues of cultural translation in its development, on completion the new campus looked and felt like an RMIT place, cool and contemporary. The opening of the campus on 31 May 2004 was a grand occasion. Behind the dignitaries, David Beanland, Dr Thu and I gathered with some of our colleagues from day one, and felt proud.

It is a common saying among foreign investors in Vietnam that you need a presence in the north and a presence in the south. There were still hints that, so many years after the American war, the two sides are still not fully united. Northern-based ministers still brought their security attachments when visiting. Anyway, that's where the two biggest cities were, so a Hanoi campus made sense. RMIT had always stated its intention to have a campus there, but it ultimately needed a fresh licence approval.

Originally, we thought that the strong relationship with VNU Hanoi might be the basis for a joint campus, and at least continuing joint programs. I visited with interest VNU Hanoi's new intended headquarter campus, really, a new high-tech city, at Hoa Lac, west of Hanoi. The university stayed keen to cultivate RMIT Vietnam further. The rector, Professor Nguyen Van Dao, an eminent analytic mechanics researcher and a kind man, presented David Beanland with a large wooden bust in David's image, disconcertingly looking like Vladimir Lenin. Professor Dao stayed a friend of RMIT. Once he retired, he chaired RMIT Vietnam's Advisory Board, and then joined RMIT Vietnam on staff for public affairs and other roles. Sadly, he was run over while exercising in Hanoi in 2006.

Notwithstanding this VNU Hanoi interest, it seemed better to establish RMIT in Hanoi in its own right, not least because there was a possibility of more Atlantic Philanthropies money for a greenfields campus. In the meantime, we leased and refurbished an apartment complex next to the United Nations International School in the diplomatic district. Michael Mann's inside knowledge of foreign affairs properties was pivotal here. We even looked through the long-vacant Bulgarian embassy in the district, a striking brutalist concrete structure broken by courtyard gardens, but the disputed legalities of prior Soviet ownership sent us running.

This first campus in Hanoi was fitted out and operated successfully. I taught a short course there on urban growth management. But the spaces were too limiting. It has since moved. Today's modern high-rise RMIT campus (opened by Australian prime minister Julia Gillard in November 2010) is better, and not far away from its original location in Ba Dinh District.

Learning Resource Centres
Birth of the idea

Developing RMIT campuses was one set of tasks, but we also developed four learning resource centres around the country. Chuck Feeney and Chris Oechsli had the idea. Chris asked that I set aside some weekend time in the new IT building on the Pham Ngoc Thach Street campus that Atlantic had funded, to talk about Vietnam's universities.

We started broadly. We talked about the unreachable demand for places (one of the reasons RMIT Vietnam was set up) and Vietnam universities' poor resources. They were a weak link in the country's development strategy. Vietnam was trying to create a more advanced information society through communications and information technology, a nascent software development industry, and an effort to train professional staff in information literacy and modern management. But lack of access to information resources in the universities was a bottleneck to university development and any transformation of teaching and learning away from rote learning.

The idea was to fund a network of information resource centres—basically, electronic libraries—in the metropolitan and regional universities, using RMIT Vietnam as a turnkey provider for the buildings, collections and training. Chuck saw it a positive 'bomb' under the rigid and unchanging university managements and 'passive, lecture-style model of education'.[17] Students and young faculty would right away take advantage of the electronic learning and research resources, then the mid-level faculty would follow, and only later, when change was already irreversible, the rectors and senior managers.

After more talk with librarians, we decided to call them learning resource centres (LRCs), to reflect their wide role. Their aims were to improve student and staff access to information; upgrade information resources and library management systems; create open working platforms for independent learning and research; support regional engagement including extension of community linkages to address the 'digital divide'; provide training and capacity building for the LRCs, their users and stakeholders; enhance collaboration; and show that each project could deliver a low-energy, low-cost, sustainable centre.[18]

If we waited for curriculum reform to create a demand for distributed learning resources, we'd wait for ever. It was decidedly a supply-led project idea, not what conventional development theory supports: build it and they will change. Why did Chuck and Chris choose RMIT for project delivery? One reason was to avoid the corruption and cronyism that could accompany direct payments to universities in Vietnam. Another reason in Chuck's mind was that this would give RMIT Vietnam, relatively new to doing business in Vietnam, quick experience with delivering major projects, and it would give the universities and the local companies engaged in the project exposure to RMIT's international standards of project management and probity. These new regional learning centres would be consistent with one of RMIT's reasons for establishing a campus in Vietnam—to trial innovative education processes and systems.

The turnkey projects would require planning, design, acquisition, procurement, commissioning and review, and also training, professional development, modern-style staff recruiting and scholarship schemes. We were talking in the range of US$30m. Eventually US$28.7m was spent through RMIT on them.[19]

Front-running candidates were the top regional universities in Danang, Hue, Can Tho and Thai Nguyen, with Vietnam National Universities in Hanoi and Ho Chi Minh City potentials too. Atlantic committed funds to RMIT Vietnam to get them started and asked us to talk to the universities and come back with detailed project and funding proposals.

One basis for Chuck's commitment became clearer. The central region of Vietnam, though tragically not alone in Vietnam, was ravaged by the American war, and Chuck's early success in duty-free retail had served the US troop presence. I felt that this might be motivated, at least in part, by a private desire to make some reparation. He had a deep commitment with Ireland, famously funding the US centre for Sinn Fein's peace negotiations. I agreed to mentor John Joyce, James Joyce's grandson and aspiring planner, and spent some time with him. I was coming to admire Chuck enormously.

The commitment of RMIT to equity and inclusion, and its mission to provide learning pathways to all, continued to motivate me as they aligned with my values. But the work in Vietnam motivated me this way even more. RMIT Vietnam itself would appeal to more wealthy Vietnamese, even though there were generous scholarships. But here, we were really helping impoverished universities, and there was an element of war reparation in both Chuck's and my thinking.

We started with Danang and Hue, where Atlantic were also funding hospital development, medical equipment and training. Then we went on to Thai Nguyen University, in the northern mountainous area, and Can Tho University in the Mekong Delta region. The national universities in the two big cities were dropped off as Chris eventually thought they were funded from other sources better than the regional universities.

Danang LRC

The University of Danang was a multi-campus university (like many, the result of unfinished institutional mergers from the 1990s) with colleges in technology, foreign languages, education, economics and a vocational school. It hosted a library under construction:

... while in Da Nang on the first visit, Feeney and Oechsli paid a call on the city's university, where the two men saw an unfinished library building for which the university had run out of money, according to Oechsli. "The idea of completing that building," Oechsli recalls, "became the first major grant that Atlantic made in Viet Nam." ... "It had an impractical design," Oechsli remembers. "Contemporary Vietnamese design at the time had a light well down the center of the building, which Chuck thought was a waste of space. He worked with the university leadership to completely redesign the building."[20]

This redesigned and technology-enriched 'information resource centre' downtown was assisted by the University of Queensland, whose librarian, Janine Schmidt, was first rate. RMIT Training, a specialist subsidiary company of RMIT of which I was a director, did a post-occupancy review of it, including of the locally developed Lac Viet library management system as installed. Michael Robinson, librarian and LRC project manager for RMIT Vietnam, began the program in Danang and stayed involved all the way. As for the building, the promise of a more efficient and modern LRC on the city campus was realised. The University of Queensland also developed, with Atlantic funding, an English language institute in Danang which would help build LRC capacity. Now, in 2021, RMIT Vietnam has an English language centre in Danang too.

For some time there had been a pressing need to provide the fast-growing college of technology, inside the University of Danang 9 km from central Danang, with adequate information and learning resources, as well as the nearby college of education. The college campus had a student body of about 10,000, of a total of 16,000 at the whole university. Given the university's stop-start experience with the first information resources centre downtown, the rector was reluctant. He was not sure he wanted to throw out his plans for a project whose delivery the university wouldn't control. Michael Mann, then the Australian Ambassador, warned me that leaders in central Vietnam were renowned for their hard-headedness. This was just a generalisation, but the discussions at times were difficult. For one, the rector refused to have any product made in China on his campus. He eventually came around on the LRC. Who would not accept US$13.3m for two gifted modern libraries?[21]

The US$3.8m project for this second LRC was awarded to RMIT to develop a four-floor 5400m² centre. It was to be networked with the other campuses, share resources, and link to national networks. For the turnkey project we appointed GHD Pty Ltd as project managers and collaborated closely with Vietnamese government and others. The East Meets West Center was the Atlantic-designated builder. At times delivery of this LRC was tough going, and for RMIT something of a diversion from the Saigon South start-up. Nevertheless, it was a pleasure to go back in 2006 for its opening.

Hue LRC

Discussion with Hue University about their LRC also had its moments. The university's main library was housed in an old French bank on Le Loi Street, Hue's strand along the lovely Perfume River. The university's library holdings were pitiful by our standards—sparse, old, damp and seemingly little used. Chuck insisted the bank building, which had flood-and-bandit-resistant walls over a metre thick, was unfit for purpose and had to come down if the university wanted the project. As with the University of Danang, what reasonable rector could say no?

The project steering committee was made up of the host university, the donor, the provincial people's committee, East Meets West and RMIT Vietnam. The project team was led by RMIT Vietnam with expertise from Melbourne, made up of a project manager, library/resource centre specialist, architect/designer, information technology specialist, and others. A reference group of international and Vietnamese experts was available to call on as necessary.

For building design, I hired David Chesterman, a campus planner and long-time colleague from Sydney, with a fine record of greening and redeveloping the University of NSW, among other campuses. User-based design and documentation were kicked off through a big workshop. It was a delightful few days in which we at last connected well with the university people. And who could miss the extraordinary world heritage-listed complex of Hue monuments, including the citadel, down the street and across the river from the LRC?

It was hard to demolish the old bank, and sad to see it go. David Chesterman was happy to prepare an outline design for a 7000m², 900 place electronic library building with a sophisticated take on ecological sustainability, one of his trademarks. For example, air circulation bottom-to-top would remove the need for air-conditioning in most areas, and natural lighting would draw little energy. By the time East Meets West's people had turned the design into drawings, some of its sophistication was lost, but practical changes were made. The air circulation system originally was to include a labyrinth, a maze through which the fresh air would come in. We learned that in Vietnam this would attract vermin, so that was ruled out. I called a chapter I wrote in a book on this project 'Rats in the labyrinth'.[22] Designing and building this LRC, buying the books and computers, and training the people to be involved became a learning exercise for everyone. Chuck took a close interest and joined steering committee meetings.

The building went ahead to construction, fit out, furnishing and equipping. Hard copy holdings and e-resources were bought, along with the same aforementioned library management system. Based upon needs assessments and university strategies, a big training and staff development program went in parallel with physical construction. We insisted on modern, open, competitive, staff recruiting—something of a novelty for the university. The LRC was finally made operational and handed over. It became a site for developing information programs in specialist areas, including public health and medicine, for which Atlantic was funding other projects in Hue.

That new LRC was part of a comprehensive campus development plan, more truly a learning hub than Danang's. The plan aimed to consolidate separate campuses into one, letting the LRC serve as the hub of the new cluster, engage with its spread-out communities, provide modern learning infrastructure and generate research results. The project cost was US$6.4m. The building was completed by 2005, but Atlantic funding carried through until 2012.[23] At first the rector refused access to students—staff only—but this was rectified.[24] It has been successful in its aims since it opened.

Thai Nguyen LRC

To me, Thai Nguyen was the most enjoyable of the LRC projects: a relatively remote university in a green region with great cultural diversity. The rector of Thai Nguyen University was more receptive at the start than those of the first two universities, grateful for what must have been unexpected support in the face of the big regional challenges he faced. The university serves the development needs for the northern mountainous area, an economically less-developed group of 16 provinces between Hanoi and China, home to a great variety of ethnic minorities. It was one of three regional universities recognised for national minorities, with a mission to contribute to their sustainable development. At the time it enrolled 30,000 students in medical, education, industrial engineering, agriculture, fisheries and vocational colleges, and now hosts over 88,000 across its network.

A university campus development plan consolidated separate campuses into one, letting the greenfields LRC to serve as hub for the newly developed university. In the workshops the university leaders were keen to modernise their learning and research methods. The feasibility study looked at distributed learning and information resources in this regional context, to help the university engage with its mountain communities, sometimes very remote and often very poor. Its aspirations to extend modern learning infrastructure to the region were held back by lack of such basic things as surfaced roads and electrification.

The negotiations and site visits were not without hazards of their own. The hospitality and keenness of our hosts were impressive indeed. So long and liquor-laden were the lunches that even for the team's day visits from Hanoi the university booked us hotel rooms to sleep them off. We were unsure of the origins of the 'wild meat' we were eating, and drew the line on eating turtles. But they were effective in partnering to build the

LRC, with its library, student-led learning spaces, computer centre and meeting rooms, not fully completed until 2009. All up, it cost US$7.3m.[25]

Can Tho LRC

The last of the LRCs was developed with Can Tho University, in the city of the same name, the centre of Vietnam's Mekong Delta region in the south. Founded in 1976, the university was an amalgamation of colleges built around agriculture, forestry and fisheries, with three campuses in the city, 15,500 students on campus and 14,500 enrolled in extension programs through satellite training centres in the region. The curriculum covered the sciences, veterinary medicine, engineering, information technology and electronics, education, economics and business administration, medicine, dentistry, pharmacy and law. Satellite programs in the region offered undergraduate courses and vocational training in teaching and business administration. The university was growing fast and had attracted funding for new campus development from the government and the World Bank.

Its library services were better-organised than the other LRC universities—having already adopted international Dewey Decimal standards for cataloguing, for example—and it integrated them with its network of distance learning centres. However, the spaces, information resource holdings and infrastructure were insufficient for that time, let alone the growth planned ahead.

I thought the university was among the best-managed of all the universities in Vietnam, not stuck with half-finished institutional amalgamations like others, and led by a business-like rector. It was not given sufficient autonomy to be effective by the national government then, and still inexplicably lags in having these powers in full. The proposed new LRC was part of an ambitious campus development plan, more truly a learning hub than the other LRCs. Taking account of the other LRC projects, the plan was led more from RMIT in Ho Chi Minh City than Melbourne, with Michael Robinson managing and Michael Mann in ultimate charge, and did more to set up a learning network across the region than the other LRCs. The university was further down the path of transforming its teaching and learning too. The hub in Can Tho was big, 7200m² of floorspace, eventually costing US$9.1m. After inception and planning of the project I had little more to do with it. It was not finally completed until 2008, after I'd left RMIT.[26] But with my more recent work to establish a museum of the Mekong Delta in cooperation with the university, it is the LRC that I see most now; an elegant, well-located, busy building.

National standards and a network of LRCs

As I child, I spent days on end in the Toowoomba library and developed a love for libraries' potential for imaginary adventures and free-range learning. At RMIT for a while I was responsible for the university's libraries, helping form a partnership with the magnificent State Library of Victoria across the street. But I knew little of the invisible systems that underpin modern libraries.

Such footings were badly needed for the new LRCs in the universities of Vietnam, especially consistent national standards for electronic management and educational resources. The Ministry of Education and Training was also grappling with these issues as they developed the sector with help from a World Bank higher education loan program. Under the LRC program we brought key policymakers and stakeholders in Vietnam together on different occasions, alongside international experts willing to contribute. The aim was to identify technical library management system issues needing national or collaborative resolution, and to promote policies helpful to the development of interactive libraries and learning resource centres throughout Vietnam, especially in the university sector.

Efficient and effective library software systems, reliable internet connectivity, low-cost access to national and global information resources, and dedication of information resources to the learning and research clients of the country were all critical to reaching international standards in library management across Vietnam. Issues as basic as a consistent and shared classification system, common standards for cataloguing materials, choice of multi-lingual search engines and collaborative e-subscriptions and collection development all had to be addressed.

We held a national discussion on what were the likely nodes and what should be the network with key national institutions. Atlantic saw this and supported the effort financially. The future state of the internet in Vietnam (technically and price-wise), university connectivity and firewall restrictions were all issues to be addressed, and part determinants of what ICT standards and infrastructure should go into any LRC. In an ideal world, updated decisions about national systems and standards should precede local procurement, but that was not possible. A national framework of standards, such as catalogue and classification systems, search engines, acquisitions, publishing, lending and sharing, LRC administration, communication/internet, had to be put in place quickly to meet the timetable of the regional LRCs.

The universities were not taking advantage of economies of scale in buying, managing and distributing information resources in Vietnam. The costs of licenses for hard copy and electronic materials, and their on-going maintenance, were high. Integrated library management systems were very expensive too. There was merit in consortial buying, through associations of libraries and institutions or via the government. Vietnam had good standing as a fast-developing country and it seemed possible to negotiate concessional prices alone or with the support of multilateral agencies in the field like UNESCO and the World Bank. With the concluded US trade agreement and possible accession to the WTO, Vietnam was in a position to drive good bargains, in exchange, say, for a stronger compliance regime for protection of intellectual property rights.

Common issues for the LRCs came up early. The University of Danang wanted to use Lac Viet, a locally produced library management system, but all the international experts advised buying a better one off the shelf and sharing it. But what if the local suite could be used for all the LRCs, and others, and become an IT product for Vietnam? The universities had different cataloguing systems and no inter-library loan system. They bought electronic and hard copy books and serials separately, leaving themselves open to exploitation by the big publishing companies and missing the opportunities that other developing countries had taken to negotiate discounts for consortial buying. Less-developed internet protocols made it difficult for the libraries to cooperate, the internet firewall was an obvious barrier, and Vietnamese-language search engine standards were not well developed. There wasn't even a common standard for machine recognition of diacritics—those little phonetic marks that adorn Vietnamese writing.

These weren't just problems for the LRC universities; consistent national standards more generally were also needed.[27] Atlantic rose to the occasion by funding resolution of these bottlenecks. Into the RMIT program came the relevant national agencies, the US Library of Congress, the Dewey Decimal System company, Simmons College Boston (a strong international library school), the University of Queensland and RMIT libraries, and the World Bank, whose firewall-exempt Vietnam Development Information Centre we used for Hanoi meetings.[28]

The results were remarkable, mainly due to the sense of urgency of the Vietnam participants, and over US$30m of Atlantic funds at the end of the obstacle course. In a little over six months, the key agencies agreed on a set of technical information resource standards, including for most of the issues mentioned above, for the country as a whole. Even the local library management system software proved its worth for wider use. Some might see library development as humdrum, but this work was truly exciting and important.

The LRCs now

After I left being CEO of RMIT Vietnam, the aim of collaborating with their host universities abated somewhat because RMIT leaders wanted to focus more fully on the start-up in Ho Chi Minh City and feared, unreasonably in my view, that those universities might be stronger competitors to RMIT. That didn't stop professional completion of the turnkey projects. It was good to return to see them opened and operating. Atlantic Philanthropies were proud of the accomplishments and reviewed the outcomes generally favourably.

Each LRC has gone its different way. Every one is used actively, perhaps not always for their high connectivity, but as good libraries and meeting, teaching and research spaces. They are pleasant learning places.[29]

For me the experience was important. I enjoyed leading a serious contribution to Vietnam's development. Its methodology was unconventional, very much a 'supply led' approach, but as discussed in previous pages, Chuck Feeney's instinct to do it was right, as students and younger faculty were much more receptive to good IT platforms for learning and research than the quite traditional university leaders. It was also a good way to work closely with Atlantic Philanthropies, including their board, and that led to other contributions.

Extending the relationship with Vietnam

Safer roads

Association with Atlantic led me into road safety. Any visitor to Vietnam in the 1990s and 2000s would be shocked to see—let alone try to cross—the streams of motorcycles and scooters flowing along the streets, some of them with unwieldly cargoes or four or five family members on board. There may be a certain grace in the way people ride at close quarters, but almost nobody wore crash helmets. Too often I would see crowds formed around crashed bikes and injured people; less often ambulances as there were very few available. To me this was just an unpleasant feature of Vietnam's exciting cities, nothing I could do much about.

This changed in an unexpected way. Chris Oechsli, by now a friend, asked me if I would be interested in being on a road safety board. While as an urban planner I could see some relevance, I was curious why Chris would think of me. He made it clear: Atlantic were gifting a million dollars to enable a new NGO, Asia Injury Prevention Foundation (AIPF), to build a crash helmet factory. The donor wished to nominate me to the board to keep an eye on their investment, though Chris understood as a director my duties would be to the company and not to Atlantic. Once I looked closer, I was happy to join the board of this Arizona-incorporated company.

The idea was that AIPF would establish a commercial subsidiary in Vietnam—Protec—to manufacture, market and sell lightweight 'tropical' motorcycle helmets designed to international standards but to let the air flow through them, and thus not be among the hated 'rice-cookers' that riders were required to wear, at least on highways, but hardly ever did. Profits would be returned to its foundation parent to fund road safety campaigns, including campaigns for better compliance and enforcement, what would be a virtuous cycle as more people bought the helmets.

Other members of the board were helmet safety researchers, corporate chiefs, lawyers and business people from Vietnam, the USA and Singapore. Greig Craft was CEO of the AIPF, an American businessman long-resident in Asia with an exceptional network and persuasive ability for fundraising. With a father in the armed services, young Greig lived in many countries, including a stint at Brighton Grammar School in Australia. He was certainly not afraid to ask any prospect for money. We were inducted in part through visits to the orthopaedic and neurological wards of a Hanoi hospital, a truly shocking illustration of the problem. Vietnam's public hospitals have improved since, but then we saw scores of seriously injured patients, many two to a bed, sharing very basic facilities, some intertwined with traction slings. And it seemed the majority of the cases were road trauma. Those we saw were the lucky ones who had made it the hospital.

How could we make a difference? The helmet factory punched out, and mechanically crash-tested, helmets designed for typical Vietnamese heads: the return of scientific phrenology! They didn't sell well at first because the national government and most cities, Danang perhaps excepted, were not enforcing helmet regulations. Instead, Greig and his team persuaded big corporate sponsors like BP to buy hundreds of thousands of child helmets with their logo on them and have AIPF distribute them to schools. A condition was that the family whose child received a helmet would, if involved in a collision—we don't call them 'accidents'—consent to whatever publicity can be drawn from the incident. Children's safety became the main goal of AIPF, aka 'Helmets for Kids', partly on the belief that many adults found it too difficult to change their dangerous practices.

Michael Mann, president of RMIT Vietnam, was persuaded to sign up to the use of AIPF's Protec helmets for all staff using two-wheeled vehicles at their campuses and promote them to the students.

A public campaign backed the distribution of helmets, with one television campaign roping in prominent intellectuals with the catch-phrase 'protect your intelligence'. (Would an Australian campaign so venerate our intellectuals? It says something about Vietnam's admiration of scholarship.) Behind the scenes the team lobbied governments hard to persuade them to get serious about road deaths, in Greig's words, 'a jumbo-jet full of people killed every month'. Year by year, compliance and enforcement got better. These days, the rivers of two-wheeled vehicles still flow, but along them bob thousands of shiny crash helmets.

The foundation has become very successful, expanding internationally. Road injuries are still the biggest cause of death of 15- 29-year-olds around the world, a global public health epidemic. Greig spoke of the need for a 'global vaccination campaign' to reduce, and one day eradicate, this epidemic, appealing to mega-donors like Bill and Melinda Gates with the analogy. Of course, the circumstances vary greatly by country.

In south Asia, truck, bus and heavy vehicle injuries are more prominent causes of death than helmetless riding, with poor road behaviour, low compliance and enforcement, and fake driver licencing major issues. So Greig, Tu Anh, his deputy, Lori Mooren (a road safety expert and friend from Sydney days) and I went around governments, business leaders and donors in Nepal, Bangladesh and Sri Lanka to test proposals to expand into these areas. We made some headway, but not enough, possibly due to economic downturn at the time. Today, AIPF has offices and operations in Cambodia, China, Thailand and Vietnam; programs in India, Myanmar, and the Philippines; and activities in many other countries.[30] The Global Helmet Vaccine Initiative has come into being. I am no longer on the board of directors of AIPF but still on its board of advisers.

Upgrading a children's hospital

Another engagement with Atlantic occurred after leaving RMIT. During the RMIT Vietnam work, I came to know fellow donees from the Royal Children's Hospital (RCH) Melbourne, especially Garry Warne, a pediatric endocrinologist and director of RCH International, its international arm. The renowned hospital had activities around the world. It seemed to me that in its efforts to be more systematic, the hospital was going through a process similar to that which I had led at RMIT, namely trying to bring its diversity of international projects and programs into a common framework, in some cases rounding up the horses after they had bolted in the interests of a more effective approach. Before too long, Garry and hospital management asked me to chair their international board, RCHI, pronounced, of course, as 'Archie'.

More than this, among their Atlantic funded projects in Vietnam, they had an issue. The foundation was supporting the redevelopment of Hanoi's main children's hospital, the National Hospital of Pediatrics, offering matched funding to encourage other donors. Physically, it was a Rubix cube of vacation and development of buildings on a crowded site, moving one group at a time to new premises while vacating the space left for redevelopment, like living in a house while it is renovated. This big uplift in physical capacity, advanced equipment and the varying spaces a modern hospital would need, also needed a great leap forward in human capacity: in medicine, nursing, allied professions and management.

Atlantic were willing to fund that, but had not been satisfied with the plan put to them by RCHI. Garry asked me to draft an alternative training and development plan. He had seen some of the proposals I'd written for Atlantic that were successfully funded. The problem was, of course, that I did not belong to the medical or health services sector. We overcame this by forming a little team of pediatric doctors and leading nurses, both in Melbourne and Hanoi, to map out what a modern children's hospital would need. Atlantic's Vietnam chief, Le Nhan Phuong, himself a medical doctor, was key to this and the other Atlantic projects in the medical and public health fields.

The task was made more difficult by chronic overcrowding, the tertiary hospital providing primary care to children with sniffles, to exaggerate a little, and whose parents often travelled from far away to the most prestigious children's hospital in the country. Also, the hospital's capable and ambitious leaders wanted to develop high-tech capacities such as pediatric heart surgery, when the greatest value for money appeared to come from more prosaic tasks like raising the level of hygiene and infection control.

After much work, the hospital leadership accepted the plan with modifications, and Atlantic Philanthropies agreed too. It was costly, involving overseas medical training and advanced equipment, part of an overall campus redevelopment costing around US$62.5m. The government of Vietnam stepped in to meet some of the matched capital funding challenge from the donor, and took from RCHI their brilliant preceptorship approach to nursing training for roll-out nationally. In this approach, each new course combined normal delivery with train-the-trainer and replication by Vietnamese nurse trainers, while the senior RCHI nurse inceptors went back to prepare the next course in the series, to be implemented and replicated the same way.

It was a pleasure to make a small contribution to the medical and health services sector. Though I was involved with the formation of the French–Vietnam hospital in Ho Chi Minh City because they and RMIT were both working with the IFC at the time, and I dabbled with being a project broker for very favourable investment opportunities for private hospitals in Gujarat, I sensibly did not try to deepen engagement with the sector.

However, I was then, and still am, struck by a contrast between hospital and university development. If a government or company would like to develop a hospital, there are consortia that will handle the whole pipeline, from vision to operation—an enormously complex task. For the universities sector, this is not so. Almost all sponsors of new universities, from inception through planning, financing, hiring, development, accreditation to operation, use a string of different advisers, consultants and project managers. I have often felt that, having had the privilege of experience in every step of the way, I could build a consortium around the world that could offer to do this. There would be an enormous market. This opportunity still beckons.

Getting out of RMIT Vietnam

After financing RMIT Vietnam, building the RMIT Saigon South campus became the main task. I spent a lot of effort in campus planning but it was clear, to a commuter from Melbourne, that RMIT needed a full-time CEO living in Vietnam. David Beanland and I started searching. There was plenty of interest and a strong field. David and I had become friendly with Michael Mann, the Australian Ambassador, as had Ruth Dunkin, the new vice-chancellor. We asked key people for leads, including Michael. After a few conversations, Michael said he was interested himself. A journalist before joining the Australian Department of Foreign Affairs, Michael had senior business experience, at one stage running Australian TV for the Packer media group under a privatisation deal with the Australian government, as well as the ABC and Seven Network. He would be a stable hand on the leadership, with a calm way and excellent network. Ruth and I talked through his complicated appointment on the phone as I was walking around the amazing cloisters of Angkor Wat, an odd experience.

The transition to Michael through July 2002 was smooth enough for me, if not Tricia Roessler in Vietnam. I kept involved by staying on the two Vietnam boards, but letting go of control is always hard to do and Michael and I had different views on issues like the LRCs and the size of the Saigon South campus site. In 2006, we gave tandem presentations to an IFC conference on views 'before and after' the start-up of big education investment projects, and the message was that there are always big differences between inception and implementation.[31] As the reader will see in the coming pages, we stayed friends and colleagues and both later contributed to another new university, Torrens University Australia.

The story of RMIT Vietnam's build-up is a good one. It kept broadly to its business plan, though concentrating more on the cost-effective business and IT programs and deferring engineering. It did a good job of providing the courses and the services that go with them, and the Saigon South campus looked better and better as it matured and added buildings and services like student housing and a big gymnasium. It started to win national prizes and publicity (including by enrolling film stars), establishing an elite position and defraying the high fees with scholarships. RMIT Vietnam was definitely not the 'working man's college' of RMIT Melbourne's reputation. This was clear when I later advised RMIT on testing the market for RMIT Vietnam to enter vocational education and training, a risk given Vietnamese families' and young people's shunning of the blue-collar image of vocational courses, even those leading to high-level skills. The poor fit between extreme skill shortages and the provision of training and vocational education still plagues Vietnam.

By contrast, RMIT Vietnam's engagement with industry set a new benchmark for the country. Companies welcomed the work-integrated learning that students shared through internships and real-world projects, tracking the most promising students to hire them in a very competitive professional job market. For domestic companies this had not been normal accepted practice. The job ready students did very well in their early careers, contrasting with high unemployment among less practically trained graduates from many public universities. A minor downside to this success was found by Anh Pham in her doctoral research: some RMIT Vietnam graduates disappointed employers by carrying unrealistic expectations of rapid advancement to management, demonstrating a feeling of entitlement.[32]

The first-mover advantage continued to help RMIT Vietnam as regulations and regulatory practice made it difficult for other foreign-invested higher education providers to enter Vietnam, though a number of new international branch campuses and institutions have started up. With some ups and downs on student numbers, pricing and leadership, RMIT grew to become the largest university international branch campus in the world, with over 5000 enrolments in 2012 and 6000 enrolments in 2020.[33]

On my visits to Ho Chi Minh City, I try every time to go to the Saigon South campus, and am always welcomed kindly. With the normal turnover of staff, many do not know much about the early years, and I always enjoy talking about them. That was one motivation to write this chapter. David Beanland, Dr Thu and I were recognised on the tenth anniversary of RMIT Vietnam and we are looking forward to reliving the twentieth, as pandemic conditions permit.

LEARNING CITIES

Education and urban development are twined around each other in modern cities like DNA, each a part of the other and responsible for much of what comes as a consequence. When I left RMIT I realised that this had been a theme of much of my career, so I named the company I set up Learning Cities International. After 17 years in higher education, I returned to the urban sector to mix it with education. The company works with other associates who have country knowledge and language, or skills I don't have such as architecture or quantity surveying. The work I most enjoy is where cities and universities intersect. Some of the examples to come cover work while at RMIT, others after I set up the company.

When the two domains come together they can take many forms: knowledge precincts and science cities, education hubs, city developers wanting to host universities, or communities setting up learning centres. Cities, as jurisdictions, also learn from one another, often deliberately through networks of communication or exchange. A good single term to cover experience at this interface would be 'learning cities'. It has several meanings here: cities that learn, cities in which people learn, and my learning about cities.

UNESCO defines learning cities, in part, as cities that effectively mobilise their resources in every sector to promote inclusive learning from basic to higher education, including lifelong learning.[1] There is a learning cities movement, a global network of learning cities, and more than one international program seeking to promote learning cities.

The examples that follow view the interface between cities and education from different angles. Even those that are primarily about education or intercultural learning have a location in the environments that nurture them, all with variations on the theme, and all that I enjoy exploring.

A knowledge precinct for Melbourne

Ed Blakely, my Berkeley friend now living in Australia, advised the Victorian government in the 1990s on setting up technology precincts. The government set up boards for them to engage stakeholders and ensure that all measures possible were taken to make them a success.

From 1991, David Beanland, the vice-chancellor of RMIT, asked me to chair the board for Melbourne's Knowledge Precinct, the area encompassing RMIT, the University of Melbourne and the biomedical and other research institutes and companies through to the 'Parkville strip'. The board represented Australia's then biggest concentration of research and development workers. The aim was to act as a kind of 'chamber of technology', promote the area and its companies and institutions, bring the education and research providers together, and act to clear up any constraints or bottlenecks to development or cooperation. With RMIT entering into the VUT merger, it seemed wise to me to enlist the University of Melbourne more strongly, and after some meetings of the board I asked Barry Sheehan, my counterpart there, to co-chair it with me. In truth, member enthusiasm for joint action among members was never high, as we all saw there were few regulatory constraints to be overcome, and by and large the participants were happy with their own institutions' promotion and the state's generic marketing of the area.

The small secretariat did some work to design a consortial seed finance and venture capital fund, which generated interest but implied, unrealistically, there would be shared decisions and finance to set it up. Basically, in a competitive environment lacking in deep cooperation, it was a diversion of effort. There were no particular planning constraints to members' success in the precinct, though there was more we could have done on a wider stage with place-making, student housing affordability, creativity and inclusion.[2] But these were busy times, and Barry and I, with the approval of the state government, decided to wind up the board, keeping the knowledge precinct brand for entities in the area to use. That brand is still in use, and the many companies and institutions in the area continue to cooperate informally for this key part of the city.

A city lost in translation

Sometimes whole cities take on the knowledge development theme. Like all urbanists in Australia, I took great interest in a proposal in 1997 from the Japanese Ministry of International Trade and Industry (MITI) to develop jointly in Australia an advanced city around tourism, leisure, education, science and technology. I was familiar with this thinking as grand high-tech cities were popular in Japan and I had visited Tsukuba and Kansai science cities there.

For the Australian new city, MITI's concept paper claimed it would 'become a forum for international exchange in the region and a model for new industries and new lifestyles looking ahead to the twenty-first century'.[3] Its name, 'multifunction polis', translated awkwardly (not just because it combined Latin and Greek roots). Extensive and expensive feasibility studies were done in 1988 and 1999. In MITI the concept came from an idea to find a future for the aging population of Japan in a high-tech city with a leisurely lifestyle in Australia. This was not widely understood in Australia, to say the least.

The cabinet of the Australian government was perplexed, but the government commissioned joint feasibility studies anyway, and took the next steps.

> Cabinet documents from 1989 show the minister asked his colleagues to approve a further $1m from within his existing budget to keep the feasibility study rolling. There were consultants to feed, not to mention working committees and thinktanks and pilot concepts and steering committees.

But government departments were lukewarm at best. It was a time when increasing Japanese investment, particularly on the Gold Coast, was causing a low-level racial rumble so familiar in Australian politics.[4]

Originally it was not-so-subtly intended for the Gold Coast, but the joint feasibility study identified 'spatial attributes', or location criteria, that opened the project up to other states and territories. New South Wales, Queensland, Victoria (on which I did some work for the MFP education working group) and South Australia all made proposals. Even a consortium for north Queensland formed.[5] The Queensland government, conscious of a right-wing anti-Japanese backlash, failed to indicate it would consolidate the land necessary on the Gold Coast, and the commonwealth chose MFP–Adelaide as the headquarters site instead.

The idea and its origin, the feasibility studies (which continued on and became more specific after Adelaide was chosen), and the location decision itself, for a partially degraded site, themselves generated great controversy. It was a challenge for Australia to translate Japanese intentions—obviously coming with major investment prospects—into what would work for a technopole in Australia, and in particular to handle its unexpected location in Adelaide. Japanese interest waned with that choice, fears and confusion about Japanese and Australian government intentions grew, and the debate widened into the nature of Australia's urban future. It was party political too, with the coalition opposition strongly opposed and promising to can the project if it came to power.

In December 1987, Senator Button, minister for industry and commerce and responsible for the MFP, briefed cabinet that 'some criticism could be expected from certain community groups; the feasibility study will canvass community and business attitudes, and will provide information to the community'.[6] This was mentioned again in the May 1989 progress report, but it was opposed by Treasury, and not only on its cost:

The proposal for a public awareness campaign seems premature, given the vagueness of the MFP concept and the fact that the

Government does not intend to make a decision on its participation in any MFP until after it has considered the completed feasibility study.[7]

The question of community consultation was thus kicked down the road.[8] It was not until May 1990, after the completion of the joint feasibility study, that Senator Button released a media statement saying the MFP would not proceed unless there was broad community support. He obtained cabinet endorsement to that in August 1990, with terms of reference for a consultation program.[9]

To gauge community views about whether the project should continue, and if so, under what conditions, so that provision could be made in the 1991–92 budget, the minister formed a community consultation panel of three.[10] They were Bob Lansdown as chair (my previous DURD boss, by then retired from the public service), Deidre Jordan, a Catholic nun and chancellor of Flinders University with a vast amount of experience, and myself. It was a convivial group, and our work together, as distinct from facing sometimes hostile audiences, was most enjoyable.

During the consultations of May 1991 the MFP–Adelaide management board report identified information and communication technologies, environmental management and education as the MFP's key areas for commercial development, but also health, space, tourism, media, entertainment and transport.[11] The education industry proposal was a good deal more modest than the 'world university' proposal of the joint feasibility study in the original concept, as were most other elements of the Adelaide plans.[12]

The development was found to be feasible on the criteria set. It would be 'a mosaic' of villages in the Gillman/Dry Creek area, linked to Technology Park Port Adelaide and The Levels campus of the University of South Australia, and connected with a high bandwidth 'information utility', set in a green and aqueous environment, ultimately housing around 100,000 people. In some versions it was 200,000.[13] The commercial clusters would be highly international. But by then Japanese investment interest had virtually disappeared, with media stories running that Japan had been left out of MFP plans entirely.[14]

My panel had contributing reports already available, such as David Yencken's excellent social issues study, and the reports of the original investigations, but to us these were just part of a flood of submissions, books, reports, articles, media programs, public meetings and rallies around the country. Much of the written material was forgettable, but the debates never were, and we met some extraordinary people with big and well-argued ideas.[15]

Our engagement process came late in the life of the project. It should have been part of the MFP process right from the joint Australia–Japan announcement, and the Treasury cabinet advice against it at the time should have been ignored.[16] As Yoshio Sugimoto noted early in the process:

> The Multifunction Polis project has been a moving target. More precisely, it has been a moving amorphous phantom whose exact shape still remains unclear. The MFP organizers have been extremely secretive about their design and apt to refrain from presenting their ideas in detail publicly.[17]

From this inauspicious start, we published a progress report in December 1990, but still before the MFP–Adelaide feasibility study was complete.[18] That study produced its own report in May 1991, giving us little time to consult on the new information before we had to report finally in August. And in the middle of this, while considering our interim results, the commonwealth and state governments announced the project would go ahead, at least to the next major stage. The government pledged $12.3m for this step. Commentators were cynical that our work was window-dressing after the fact. They included Australian Democrats spokesman John Coulter, who disrupted Senator Button's press conference. The panel work was a 'farce', he said.[19] That wasn't true. We had been empowered to make a recommendation to discontinue the project and did indeed consider that, as we listened to national and local sentiment. We had a free hand, but it was a difficult task. At the meetings and events around much of the country we felt the heat and debated the issues backward and forward without a pre-conceived view.

Some of the strongest criticism was couched in broad terms—infatuation with high technology, insufficient emphasis on sustainability, over-emphasis on commercial development at the expense of social justice. I could see that. But even some of the critics saw the prospect of the MFP being a better kind of international engagement with the western Pacific region than in the past, 'despite its confusion, bungling and utopian hype', as Gavan McCormack put it.[20] Other national issues were concerns that technology would not transfer, that relaxation of immigration controls would enable a Japanese enclave to form, and that ownership of key assets would pass to foreigners, a particular concern of the then-xenophobic Returned and Services League of Australia.[21]

Earlier concerns that a national urban policy should determine the location and nature of the MFP rather than a bilateral deal—an issue dear to my heart—were, by the time of our consultations, turned towards broad support that Adelaide's MFP might enhance the 'clever country'. The site environment brought its own issues, as might be expected for a degraded peri-urban site near water, including strong criticism of its ecological unsuitability. Local and regional criticism of the lack hitherto of any significant participation or project transparency was strong, along with concerns about the formation of an elite enclave, whether Japanese or not. The likely governance framework, not yet fully spelt out, drew great suspicion about special deals bypassing normal planning protections.

From that process, presented to us in the terms of reference, we drew detailed proposals for future consultation design and participation mechanisms. On any scale of community empowerment, like Arnstein's 'ladder of participation', the engagement was low-level, with consultation largely after the fact. It was not really participation or empowerment, though it was much better than any involvement to date.[22]

We concluded there was general national support for the MFP, and on balance acceptability at the local level, recognising some strong local opposition. We did not commission an opinion poll, noted by some of the critics. As Parker implies, our judgment of acceptability was still contestable.[23] A motion to reject MFP–Adelaide was proposed at one of the Adelaide public meetings and was seconded, but not recognised by the chair, Bob Lansdown, so a vote was not taken on that occasion.

We recommended that the MFP continue ahead but on a number of specific conditions, including verification of costs, retention of resources for existing residential areas, an attack on environmental health issues and social disparities, pursuit of social and not only commercial objectives, consideration of leasehold ownership, change of the MFP name, and formal inclusion of independently-run public participation.[24]

The recommendations were accepted by the minister. MFP–Adelaide continued to the implementation phase as announced, and its name gradually went out of use. It attracted much less investment than originally intended, especially as Japan entered into its long deflationary slump through the 1990s. What remains is the well-planned and environmentally innovative suburb of Mawson Lakes (at The Levels), developed by MFP-related companies Delfin and Lend Lease, and an expanded and successful Technology Park Adelaide.

The report certainly contributed to the fate of the MFP. After our panel findings, in 1993 the government asked the Bureau of Industry Economics to evaluate the form and level of commonwealth budgetary support for the MFP. Its April 1994 report found that the project was not value for money in terms of budget expenditure, but could in theory be warranted on the grounds of regional development, meeting international obligations in the interests of investment reputation, or developing knowledge-based industries nationwide. It concluded that only the third argument might have direct economic welfare benefits, and that even this case was unproven. If none of the reasons was compelling, the bureau argued, 'wind back of Commonwealth support would seem indicated'.[25]

The commonwealth went ahead and phased out its participation in the MFP, and in 1996 ended funding. The South Australian government kept it going longer, but announced transfer of the MFP development corporation to a city centre development role, and it too lost funding in 1998, a decade after the idea was first proposed.

The MFP is little remembered or lamented. In a way that is a pity. The original idea came from overseas, and the ideas and debates about a visionary new city for Australia even among supporters showed something like a lack of confidence, a weak national urban policy and an unwillingness to embrace big ideas and aggressively develop them.

But it did create a national debate about what kind of society, economy, environment, technology and cities Australia would like to have, and it popularised ideas about a world university and smart cities, the latter now part, if not the essence, of the conservative coalition's national urban policy.[26] The consultation panel was a part of that, and I was proud to be involved.

Japanese urban dreaming

An internationalist mayor of Ogaki, Gifu Prefecture, Japan, sought to put his city on the map for new ideas for the information city, hosting a number of futuristic gatherings in 1988 and 1989 to play out the ideas, and feeding us tubs of caviar at receptions.[27] The city is famous as the starting point for Zen poet Bashō's *The Narrow Road to the Deep North*. The little stream at the very start of his journey that still flows through the city is these days commemorated with concrete municipal engineering. But Ogaki's 1980s were Japan's glory days too. The conferences and the activities around them were memorable for both their ideas and their people. Visionary planners, designers and developers came from Japan at the height of their boom, when proponents of new science cities like Tsukuba and of corporate mega-developments started with the wildest ideas possible to attract interest, and used inflated language to match: floating cities, underground cities, mile-high cities, cities of learning, 'softopias', 'technopias'. Then they would scale them back to get development consent, the very opposite of practice in Australia where developers try to slip through consent as quietly as possible and factor up scale through variations in the planning and development approvals later. The MFP, dating back to 1987, was discussed at almost every meeting in the Ogaki series.

Their main theme was the information city, and thus learning cities were a key part. The Japanese thought leader was Professor Yoshinobu Kumata from Tokyo Institute of Technology, a charismatic entrepreneur with an ebullience not unlike that of the television host of *Iron Chef*. Through our friendship RMIT formed an exchange and cooperation agreement with that university. From other countries came similar vision-aries and sceptics, including friends from MIT and Berkeley. Over several events and many side trips and site visits, we discussed and critiqued con-cepts and plans, with Ogaki and other pro-development cities taking part.

I returned on my own to Ogaki more than once to explore a campus project with Ogaki Women's College, but it didn't progress because they wanted to manage the curriculum. Here too, the side trips were unusual. One was to spend an un-touristic morning in Inuyama, Gifu, with the Imperial cormorant *ukai* fisherman, a gentleman with overseas post-graduate education, wearing a straw skirt, living in a thatched hut, and salaried to keep the ancient art alive. Another was a visit to the little old village of Tsumago, near Nagoya. I liked it so much I returned to it again, and in a teahouse met Masao Yagi, a conservation architect working with locals who wanted to conserve the whole village, a first for Japan. We struck up a friendship, with Professor Yagi spending a sabbatical at RMIT in Melbourne with his family. Later, in 2012, he and his wife joined my friends on a pilgrimage around Shikoku, the famous Buddhist trail, and in 2016 on another long walk with his family along the Kiso valley, back to Tsumago to have a reunion with those visionary villagers—those surviving, anyway.

As for Ogaki, its big plans were not realised. Not long after the Ogaki meetings, Japan slid into its long stagnation. Australia licked its MFP wounds, and mega urban development projects were not considered in Australia for years.

The city and its universities

I was keen for 'town and gown' work after leaving RMIT, that is, work on the links between universities and their urban environments. I'd worked closely with the City of Melbourne on their sister cities programs, especially with Osaka and Tianjin, which I visited several times for that purpose. In Tianjin, we at RMIT and the city set up a joint office and negotiated a long-lasting executive training program in Melbourne for Tianjin city officials.

Because the wellbeing of both RMIT and the City of Melbourne depended on the size and vibrancy of the city student body, we meshed our community engagement programs closely. So, when I left RMIT in 2005, Melbourne's city management asked me to design a study of the contributions that the main Melbourne universities made metropolis-wide. The end result was published in 2007, along with a paper I wrote with Geoff Lawler, the city's director of sustainability and innovation, on town and gown relationships in the City of Melbourne.[28]

This interest stayed with me as it was a perfect connection between urban affairs and education. The central role that universities play in the economy and society of cities is greatly underestimated: not only through teaching and research, but as generators of employment and economic development, demand and supply links in the structure of local economies, hubs for social, political and cultural affairs, and providers of housing and services. Too many studies of this topic focus on impact, and not enough the other way, on what makes good city 'hosting' of universities. I found myself giving talks and writing on the topic, including a chapter on the Botswana education hub for a book edited by Jane Knight.[29]

A new university and education hub in Botswana

The RMIT Vietnam project had been an early success for the new education group at the International Finance Corporation (IFC) and its leaders brought me in after RMIT to work on their side of the table in other public–private partnerships (PPPs). Botswana was one of those. Tanya Scobie Oliviera, a New Zealander in the IFC group whom I'd met at various IFC activities, specialised in PPPs and had deep experience in southern Africa and a spirited commitment to economic and social development.

She asked if I would be interested in bidding for technical lead of a PPP they were planning in Botswana to finance the country's second university, the Botswana International University of Science and Technology. The IFC saw it as a long shot but worth trying. I certainly was interested, but it was too big for my little company, outside the maximum company share of annual turnover set by World Bank guidelines for any one project. I turned to Darrel Conybeare, from the Sydney Clarke Gazzard days recounted in chapter two, to see if he could join us on the basis that they, Conybeare Morrison International, a much larger

306

company with good international university campus planning experience, took the project lead in bidding and agreed to my still being project director. This was fine with them.

Like some Gulf states, Botswana provided free university education, and if the field of interest was not available in Botswana, the government paid all overseas education costs. This was having a negative impact on the national budget and its foreign exchange position. Also, the country's leaders wanted to develop knowledge industries at home, but faced serious shortages of skilled managers and professionals even for its present industries. Though Botswana was expanding tertiary education places at 10 percent a year, its leaders wanted to do more. A new, second, university would be a big part of that expansion.

The rationale for the Botswana International University of Science and Technology (BIUST: sounds like 'beast' in that wonderful deep Batswana growl) echoed other emerging economies. It was to build national education capacity, overcome skill shortages, reduce the costs of sending students overseas to study, and promote social inclusion and equity.

Palapye, a provincial town—which happened (by coincidence, of course …) to be in the president's electorate—was chosen as the location for the main part of the university, to foster decentralisation and regional development. Formally, the university was established in 2005 and a large site of 2500 ha was dedicated to that purpose.

To finance its development, Botswana entered into a mandate with the IFC in 2007 to create a PPP. That was our job, mine as lead transaction adviser. We had to do a feasibility study and help find the private sector partner to deliver the university; specifically, to help the government determine the best project delivery option, develop a master plan for the campus and a plan for academic and educational services, and find a private sector provider for its infrastructure.

The government did not seek private participation to make up capital shortages alone, but to bring innovation in finance, project management, design, construction and service provision. For jurisdictions where capital is short, education infrastructure PPPs can be powerful means of attracting investment, provided that market risk is mainly carried by the public sector party and that the country's sovereign risk is manageable.

We formed a team of engineers (Dermot Knight, based in South Africa, still an associate of LCI), quantity surveyors, and finance people including Debra Knight, from RMIT Vietnam days, and Terry Francis, a big player in Melbourne PPPs and a colleague from RMIT council days. Terry covered risk assessment. Tanya Scobie and, later, Catherine Commander, were also constant participants from IFC headquarters. The IFC attracts some of the smartest people in the regions they operate, and Emmanuel Nyrinkindi, based in Johannesburg, and their consultant economist, Francis Ogutu, based in Kenya, were no exceptions.

It was a big project and the work was demanding. Dick Nugent, the lead from Conybeare Morrison, was a travel companion for many of the visits from Australia and a constant workmate; we struck it off well. We still tell stories of a champagne breakfast (the bottles brought in duty-free) at the Gaborone Hotel as we watched Barack Obama cross the victory line in the US presidential election, the country of Dick's upbringing. He developed a good master plan for the huge Botswana campus, which, with modifications, the university today reflects.

As the whole proposal shaped up, its full project costs grew beyond US$1.5bn, reflecting the high standards on which the government insisted, so we had a number of discussions with the ministers and the full cabinet. Importantly, to cover market risk, the government would have to sign on to 35 years of student funding on lines of policy similar to those in place then, a big commitment to education policy ahead. The cabinet seemed up to the task.

But despite strong private sector interest at our investor conference, the deal didn't come off. After the government accepted the PPP proposal, the inaugural vice-chancellor, Professor Kweku Bentil, thought it possible to finance university infrastructure through shaving off parts of what he thought an excessively large campus and co-developing them. The cabinet also became more concerned at project costs as economic conditions became less favourable.

I still think the PPP could have been saved. The IFC didn't seem dedicated enough to closing the much delayed deal, and I know from seeing the vice-chancellor later, in Melbourne when he was visiting students from Botswana, that he could have been brought around to a variation in the deal to bring in more self-financing from university land sales and property development. But as merely a consultant, even the lead consultant, it wasn't my job, as I had learnt, and the World Bank decision-making network was far too complex for me to penetrate. This was frustrating. However, the university is in operation now at Palapye, built along our campus development lines, if at a smaller scale and slower pace of growth.[30]

On one of my visits, I was critical of the approach the government was taking to positioning Botswana as an international education hub. The country's leadership was unrealistically ignoring the need to develop its own capacity in education first, instead contemplating a billion-dollar finance facility to leverage foreign investment into the sector, following what was proposed, but on better grounds, for the Botswana diamond hub. My criticism turned into an unexpected invitation to advise the government on what it might better do, so not long afterwards I was back, this time working with Joyce Maphorisa, LCI's local partner in Gaborone, and I brought in Tony Adams (my old friend and colleague from RMIT) on just that.

The idea was to develop Botswana as a regional centre of excellence for education, promote economic development through education, training and research in key strategic areas, align skill development with social and economic needs, promote quality and access, internationalise local education provision and promote Botswana as a preferred education destination internationally. To do this, some parts were straightforward: write a strategic plan, establish a unit of government, and set up the framework for a marketing campaign.

Two other requirements were more difficult. The first came from the fact that the Botswana education sector was not in a strong position to attract many international students. With a secondary system going only to 'O-levels', the country was losing some of its own secondary students to study in neighbouring countries like Namibia and South Africa where school curricula went to 'A-levels'. And though its one university did attract some international students, this fell well short of a basis for establishing an international student industry. Reform to the education system was a prerequisite. This was not a comfortable conclusion to sell to the government, but try we did, and found that they got on the road to reform in a number of key areas.

The second challenge was that the government wanted a business plan. This is normally easy enough to prepare—one of the staples of my consultancy business—but to keep all the 'hub' plans aligned across the industries for which Botswana wanted hubs, such as diamonds, transport, tourism, the business plan had to show reliable rates of return. For a program that was not mainly investment-driven, nor easy to define in operational terms—in our advice there would be no physical development hub—we had to quantify guesses about costs and benefits to the country as a whole. This we did, but the results and recommendations were not comfortably received either. At least the government did go ahead, sensibly combining the operations of the Botswana education hub with the unit servicing its government-funded students abroad.

My Botswanan colleagues and I published a chapter in a book on education hubs and put a positive spin on the country's experience.[31] I didn't mind that as the education hub had to be promoted, but as Jane Knight later noted, the hub has not lived up to its hype.[32] I went on to learn that advancement of education in poorer countries can be even more difficult.

Skills for young people in Liberia

If Botswana was an exemplary economy in Africa, Liberia was one of its most challenged, a post-civil war country still then riven with regional and ethnic divisions, corruption, and a large number of unemployed international refugees. Much of this immense burden of unemployment was on young people, some of them ex-fighters. The fragile peace was kept with the help of 12,000 United Nations (UN) troops stationed just outside the capital, Monrovia (who have since been successfully demobilised). In President Ellen Johnson Sirleaf, the first elected female head of state in Africa, the country had an inspiring leader who was seriously focused on youth skills and employment.

In 2012 the IFC asked me to facilitate a national meeting of government and private sectors to find ways to promote private and other non-governmental vocational education and training that would be fit for the challenge, and write post-conference recommendations. I jumped at the chance.

The conference was a great success, in part because the relevant ministers stayed its course, and because they were in the middle of drafting legislation to enable just what the conference was about. I recommended a number of reforms and investments, including a national training fund and a national qualifications framework.[33] In Africa, Liberia was not alone in needing to develop a national framework for vocational education.

Monrovia was an interesting city with green vegetation, dilapidated modern buildings, sprawling suburbs and slums. I was well looked after at a seaside hotel at Mamba Point, the diplomatic area. I didn't see any mamba snakes, thankfully, if they still existed there at all, but I was warned about walking alone at night for other reasons.

Getting to Monrovia had been easy enough. Getting out was another matter. I was confirmed on a midnight flight and took a beaten-up taxi along the 56-kilometre road to the airport while the driver talked about how much he'd like to study in Australia. There seemed to be too little traffic, and when we approached the airport there were no lights and the gate was locked. My seat had been confirmed on a non-existent flight. Thankfully, my driver didn't leave me there. We took the long road back again, and I hoped the hotel might still have a room, which it did. Rebooking at 2 am was off as the airline telephones were not answering. My agent in Australia said go to the ticket office at the airport in the morning, so I slept on it and returned early to try my luck in person, packed to go. The 'office' was a woman in traditional dress sitting on an unused luggage carousel with a mobile phone and a credit card machine. But she was efficient enough in getting me out via Accra.

Any review of the technical and vocational education and training sector in Liberia today will show that significant progress has been made there, led in the public sector by a bureau of TVET, many more private providers, and some companies opening their training doors to communities. The 2012 project may have helped that along.

Leadership education in Ethiopia

A higher education task in Addis Ababa did not work so well. Through a finance sector friend in Uganda, Father Badeg Bekele, an Ethiopian-American, asked me to come and review the International Leadership Institute, a private graduate program provider whose leaders aspired to university status. Could I map out a strategy for growth and quality improvement and model the institute's finances well enough to support project financing, and help with the search for CEO? Sure. The institute was generally well regarded, housed in an imposing high-rise building, and counted many of the country's leaders among its graduates.

It was a long trip from Sydney, and I was exhausted on arrival. Badeg asked me to join a graduation ceremony as soon as we got into the city and I reluctantly consented. Sorry, no time for a shower or shave, just put on a tie. When I went up to the dais in front of the large well-dressed crowd, I looked through the program. There was my name, giving a graduation address! I didn't mind busy programs while travelling, but this was a stretch. Though I'd given several such addresses before, I'm sure I said nothing memorable for the graduands. Then, on another day, he asked me to front up for a searching quality review by their academic partner, the University of Greenwich, as a part of his team.

Badeg took me around the charitable enterprises he had founded, including a clinic for low income people. He seemed a good man in this regard: after all, he was an ordained man of the Church. I also had some time to explore Addis and its expressions of the culture and society of Ethiopia, its poorly maintained museums housing extraordinary artefacts of the country's religions (mostly Orthodox Christian), Italian colonisation (disastrous), and its chiefly and folk cultures.

I finished the work back in Australia and was satisfied with its quality, as were the leaders of the institute, so I sent in my invoice to Badeg. No reply. I sent it again. I tried telephoning him. No reply. I called others in the institute leadership. 'Yes, we'll see to it.' No further response. To this day, I haven't been paid. If only I'd checked to see who was Australian Ambassador then. I'm sure Lisa Filipetto, an enthusiastic supporter of the RMIT campus while she was consul-general in Ho Chi Minh City, could have helped. But that's wishful thinking now, as I look back at the only time running LCI that I have not been paid.

A global schoolhouse

From time to time my work engaged with schools, mostly setting them up or seeking investment in them, particularly in big urban developments. Through contact with the IFC and the World Bank proper, I was impressed with the potential for private schooling to meet the huge supply gaps in poorer countries left by inadequate public coverage. At biennial IFC private sector education meetings I met Carl Bistany of SABIS®. He was the head of a 130-year-old private company, his family being the 'BIS' in the company's name. They owned a large chain of schools around the world, ranging from elite boarding schools in Germany and the UK, through charter schools in the US (private providers contracted to deliver public education where it is difficult for government to do it), to village schools for low income families in poorer countries.

I worked with SABIS on school investigations in Australia, New Zealand, Singapore, Malaysia and Vietnam. I was at first sceptical of their educational model—highly centralised, relying on daily metrics on progress visible to students, teachers and parents. But it was cost-effective, enabled low fees, and had clever student-to-student arrangements for support. Udo Schulz-Mahlendorf, SABIS' global business development leader, took me around some of their operations to show how they worked. In Kurdistan, Iraq, we saw a typical range of their schools, from a good international school in Erbil to a small village school in Soran, near the Turkish and Iranian borders. The village housed Kurds forcibly displaced by Saddam Hussein's regime, some suffering from the effects of chemical weapons, and government support for the school, which surprisingly taught in English, was a kind of reparation. All the schools were serviced from a complex in Beirut (for 70,000 students in 20 countries), with curriculum developers and teaching facilitators for every settled continent. I was impressed with their education model.

A tribal university in Gujarat

I did like working with the IFC—they were highly professional, their people smart and international, and they paid quite decently. So when Tanya Scobie asked me whether I would like to bid for another PPP transaction in Gujarat, I was delighted to put in. Like BIUST, this was a long shot too. The local client was the Tribal Development Department, whose leaders wanted to develop a township—a 'special education area'—to provide university education and vocational training to tribal minorities and scheduled (i.e. low) castes. The development would be on tribal land, yet to be chosen. Like land eligible for native title in Australia, tribal lands in Gujarat were those with no significance for any other use, ruling out much more suitable and better-located sites.

The task was to give shape to the vision, estimate effective demand, devise student financing schemes, develop an educational and physical plan, cost it, figure out how to build local capacity to manage a big PPP, identify the procurement options, model the feasibility of public and private sector options, and search out possible investing and operating partners. Quite a job. The department was not experienced in big PPPs, though the state, under chief minister Narendra Modi, probably had the best know-how and experience in India on the topic.

As with the Botswana PPP, to do the work I formed a team of education advisers, campus planners, architects and financial analysts. Financial modelling was helped by the IFC, who, as always, knew well how to do it. The local champion for the project was Dr Kiran Shah, the retired vice-chancellor of Hemchandracharya North Gujarat University, a gracious and experienced man with a great deal of knowledge of how higher education around the big state of Gujarat worked. I spent many days with him and his wife, looking round and talking about how to fulfil the project, and innumerable site visits with the project team.

My son Kina joined us on one visit. He became fascinated with a poor informal settlement next to the hotel and its obvious social order and busy local economy, and we enjoyed an eye-popping day out with the Shahs at Akshardham temple in Gandhinagar, like a religious theme park.

Away from the big city, the main problem for the team was site selection. The township had to be on tribal land, almost by definition remote. However, the financial viability of the university depended on access to the market for non-tribal students, who typically lived further away in big cities. Some of the potential sites were near Godhra, site of an anti-Muslim massacre arising from a train fire from which Mr Modi has been unable to shake an association.

My status as a mere consultant dogged me again in Gujarat. Communications with the department were strictly channelled through the IFC, whose leader was a finance specialist who used to work with Standard and Poor's, the rating agency, very 'big city' and with a background seemingly distant from those of the senior departmental officials who were awkward about their inexperience with PPPs. I could see that communications were difficult, but being out of some of the key conversations with IFC's client, I couldn't help steer them back to safety. I was also puzzled why the very good PPP advisory agency of the state was not involved, but my team diligently worked through the steps anyway.

The preferred site was at Bakrol, near Vadodara, and the plans we devised were good. But somehow 'the file didn't move back to the department's desk', and it took forever for authorisations to be given by the central part of state government. I don't think the quality of our work put them off. As with Botswana, the state sought the whole PPP deal—a university, housing, vocational college, health centre, hospital, district shopping centre and more—but they were daunted by the financial obligations for many years that the PPP would put on them. The project lagged and lagged, and like the dry sands of the sites we looked at, drifted away.

Trying to cash up a university in Papua New Guinea

Links between universities and urban development can take interesting forms, as they did in Port Moresby, where the national university owned developable land around the city's new central business district. Seeing my work on education PPPs and a number of briefings I made about them in Papua New Guinea (PNG), the country director of IFC, Carolyn Blacklock, asked me to join the University of PNG and devise a way to realise the locked-up value of a large holding of undeveloped campus assets, turning them into jointly-developed affordable housing, new facilities and cash from sales for the benefit of the fund-starved university. In this Carolyn was imaginative and courageous. The university was keen, but the government was not. Ministers saw the university lands as a potential cash cow for the government, and worse, possibly a chance for personal benefit, and were not comfortable with the university profiting from these assets, the disposal or development of which would need ministerial approval anyway.

The university owned or had control of nearly 500 ha of land in Port Moresby alone and 20 other centres or open campuses around the country. Some had discontinued student housing and university building construction on them, a legacy of the university living hand-to-mouth off intermittent funding from a succession of fickle governments.

The university could benefit from development of the land in different ways. It could get the value of using new buildings, returns from leasing out new housing to staff and students even at subsidised rates, derelict or substandard properties would be freed up, some of the land value increment of privately developed land would revert back at the end of the project period, and know-how for the university's estate managers would come from working with up-to-date private developers.

There were several ways to do this, and we canvassed them with university staff as I went round looking at the sites. In the first place, the university could 'do it itself', develop housing and other facilities on its land and manage the developments. This would be slow, put pressure on the university's limited capacity and most likely not result in much innovation.

Second, it could enter into separate limited joint major developments for selected sites ripe for development. This would bring a better yield and could produce affordable housing, but it would be management-intensive and carry other risks.

A third option, an 'umbrella' development with one chosen partner, could work through available sites under a PPP of one sort or another,

316

perhaps a build-own-transfer where the private party develops and manages under a long lease, then transfers the properties back to the university at the end of the period. It would be a complex single transaction but would be relatively easily handled after that, and would bring the greatest returns. The paucity of development companies in PNG big enough and sophisticated enough to be contenders added some risk.

A fourth option, of selling land ripe for development with or without conditions, would bring early and high returns, but not have been politically possible.

We recommended the third 'umbrella' agreement, and discussed how to shape the transaction, for which the IFC would be well suited to arrange project financing. We had some good indications of interest to proceed, but the university took a long time and entered into a controversial process of changing vice-chancellor. After that, its interest waned. I was getting all too used to PPP transactions that went nowhere.

This project was mostly in PNG's capital city. Sometimes, though, opportunities for universities to contribute to their surrounding communities are a long way away from cities. There are few university locations as remote as the mountains of central Asia.

A university in remote central Asia

Knowing my work, a colleague in the Asian Development Bank (ADB) asked me in 2011 to bid to review the viability of the University of Central Asia (UCA) as a basis for ADB to consider a package of loans and grants up to around US$500m. This was a wonderful opportunity, but I knew very little about central Asia and nothing about the university. On top of that, I speak no Russian, the lingua franca of the region, and was to be responsible for arranging my own translation and interpretation.

For me, the deep end had seldom been deeper.

The university is virtually unique in that its constitution takes the form of a treaty among three countries and the Aga Khan. He is the hereditary Imam of the Ismaeli people, Shia Muslims under his spiritual care and tutelage. They are ethnically diverse, tolerant, and value education highly. Many of them live in remote parts of central Asia. First working through the Aga Khan Foundation, the Aga Khan committed to the development of an international-standard university with new campuses in three countries and a number of interim facilities while the new campuses were being built.

The ADB had an interest in building higher education capacity in those countries—the Kyrgyz Republic, Kazakhstan and Tajikistan—and through that, contributing to economic development and security in their remote regions. Because of the potential scale of funds, UCA gave my work high priority and appointed a full-time expert, Latif Jina, to work with me to help settle in and get the information needed.

Getting to start was an adventure in itself. The transit in Guangzhou was nine hours late, and I had the macabre experience of seeing a brawl at the terminal between angry passengers and resolutely uncommunicative airline staff. To add to the fun, the airline lost my baggage for nine days, causing me to search around the scattered shops and bazaars of Bishkek, capital of the Kyrgyz Republic, for clothes and essentials. The huge Dordoy Bazaar, where I met some of my needs, is one of the great markets of Asia, springing up after the collapse of the Soviet Union with vendors selling out of 7000 old containers across a sprawling area, and a place of refuge for organised crime.

Bishkek itself was an odd mix. I'd learnt a little about it through a trainee at a course I ran on urban growth management in Mashhad, Iran. He chose his assignment on how to deal with Bishkek's contested urban land ownership after its bloodless 'Tulip Revolution' in 2005. Now I was there. It still felt post-Soviet, not yet transformed, with heroic monuments and sad squares with morning drunks on benches. But I found the government quite competent, and the mix of ethnicities interesting. It is a pity the country's governance has gone back into crisis.

The university had high standards and even higher aspirations. Under Bohdan Krawchenko, its Ukrainian-Canadian vice-chancellor, sophisticated and multilingual, it was already teaching through interim campuses, and aimed to reach 'ivy league' standards. My task was to understand their operations and determine whether they were, or could become, financially sustainable.

The best part was visiting the new campuses. From Bishkek, Naryn was a four-hour drive, past yurts with television antennae and 4WDs, high into the snowy mountains. The campus was in early stages of construction, but the first stage is now complete.

Doing the work here was straightforward because Bishkek was the university headquarter city, and Bohdan saw to it that I had Russian language interpreters with me. Kazakhstan would be more difficult as many of my meetings would not be organised for me and I would have to hire my own interpretation and translation.

I'd earlier asked my daughter Maya, 24 at the time and a student at the University of Melbourne, to help me on the project, and she was able to join me for part of Kazakhstan and all of Tajikistan. She was interested in human rights and international development, and I thought it might help her education. It was also a great chance to be on the road together.

We found Astana (now Nur-Sultan), Kazakhstan's planned new capital, like Disneyland on municipal steroids, with grandiose buildings, including our hotel, on overbuilt boulevards. With few taxis, we just hailed any car and negotiated a price. The new campus site of Tekeli was not so remote from its capital as Naryn, near a strategic junction of massive road investments and the Chinese border, now part of China's Belt and Road Initiative. The Chinese head of the ADB office took particular interest in my appraisal of the regional development opportunities around the campus.

We then went to Dushanbe, capital city of Tajikistan. The university had interim campuses pending completion of its third campus in Khorog, high on the Pamir Plateau, by far the remotest of the three campuses. Maya and I were excited at the prospect of going to the roof of the world, but we never got there. The 12-hour drive would be highly dangerous, with trucks and vans frequently going off the hairpin bends. The university used helicopters instead, but day after day dust storms closed the flights. We would have to do the work in Dushanbe.

The city itself is perched in mountainous country, with green valleys upstream housing weekenders for the wealthy, and numerous carpeted public picnic spots for everyone else. With a colleague we planned a day off visiting one of the valleys, but Maya took ill and decided to stay in while I went along. On returning from a delightful day, I found her very ill and called in a doctor. It was amoebic dysentery; she'd have to go into the infectious diseases hospital.

That hospital, on the edge of town, was a forbidding Soviet-style fortress, secured by barbed wire and rolling steel barriers that were locked at night. After Maya was admitted, I had to go back out and get medicines, toiletries and bedding. The Hyatt Hotel manager kindly agreed to let me take some bedding and toiletries back to the hospital. Maya was very sick and would have to stay in there for 10 days at least, a rigid rule. This greatly worried me and of course confounded our mission. I checked with the people at the Aga Khan Foundation in Dushanbe who were in charge of our logistics. The news was not promising. This sort of confinement had happened to their staff before, and in one case the patient did not come out alive. The bare facilities at the hospital fed my concerns about their standard of care. Now I was alarmed.

The airlines needed a certificate of fitness to travel, and Maya was most definitely not fit to travel. But I had to get her out of there. 'No way', said the hospital administration. I talked to Maya's physician, an overworked woman perhaps in her forties who seemed quite competent. What would it take to get her out? 'Money?' I quietly suggested. Absolutely not, she said, making me ashamed to have tried to bribe her. 'She'll need to get better first', she said. After some days of rest and medication, Maya did improve a little, and she was less infectious, but the 10-day rule still hung over us. I pleaded with her doctor, stressing how important it was to get Maya home, making no criticism of her hospital. She finally agreed to certify—against the evidence, and again taking no money—that Maya was well enough to travel. So, after a slightly tense meeting of the doctor and me signing off with the hospital superintendent, Maya was free to go. Into a hotel room, never leaving it, and then, finally, we both left for the airport and went home. I felt grateful to the doctor, who put her position at peril, the more so when our doctor in Melbourne said that the medication and treatment Maya had received were quite proper.

My understanding of the university and financial modelling showed that the university was an outstanding educational venture, but miles away from financial sustainability, buoyed up almost entirely by his highness' limitless financial commitment. This is called 'moral hazard' in the trade. Any reasonable request from the vice-chancellor would be met, and so there are few incentives for financial discipline. The ADB aid package did not proceed, but the university today has three high-quality new campuses and is going from success to success.[34]

I saw a similar reliance on faith-based largesse in developing a strategy and business plan for a new Buddhist college for the well-known Nan Tien temple in Wollongong. Enjoying re-engagement with Buddhism, including staying overnight and joining meditation and chanting ceremonies, I prepared that documentation for the college's registration. Its head abbot was a warm and engaging female former Australian mining company executive. But here, too, it was difficult to work out financial viability because the temple was enthusiastically supported by its well-endowed mother temple in Taiwan, where from time to time large groups of pilgrim donors would descend on Nan Tien and bolster its finances. The college was registered, the course accredited and the venture is going well.

Switching to Monash

Other work was also more inside education institutions than at their 'learning city' interface. After leaving RMIT in 2005, I was head-hunted by KPMG for a place on the board of Monash College Group, Australia's biggest and best-regarded university pathway program (foundation studies, diploma programs, English language learning, homestays, internships and more, with offshore mini-campuses). I took it up with enthusiasm, not least because it was chaired by Stephanie Fahey, a highly Asia-literate friend from my University of Sydney days. This took me into the fray of another big university, where the issues were different from RMIT but the wars among fiefdoms familiar. The college had constantly to prove the students transferring into the university proper were as good as or better than those entering the university directly, and to keep the faculties happy with their diplomas outsourced to us for first-year provision. A part-time directorship seemed manageable.

At least until the CEO left. Could I step in part-time? That, too, seemed manageable; it would be for a short time until we could make a continuing appointment. Wrong. The job took 18 months, during which time, far from keeping the ship steady, I had to lead a major restructuring and acquisition of new businesses. We came out the other side of the changes well, but it took way more of my time than planned. Our eventual appointee, Jo Mithen, still runs the college, which is doing well.

Being inside the university led to other tasks. Monash's urban planning course was ripe for review, given the university's desire to train professionals for Melbourne's fast-growing southeastern suburbs, so I did that review. Monash was also expanding its franchised programs in the Gulf States, especially its medicine courses, and I reviewed and rewrote some of their agreements. Stephanie and I went to the UAE to visit partner universities and explore the possibility of a Monash campus, and I went to Sri Lanka to negotiate a Monash pathway college there. I was drawn into reviews of the university's other offshore campuses. I felt I'd made a decent contribution to Monash. At root, all these engagements were about promoting learning cities.

A hotel school and new university

Town and gown linkages in hospitality are always interesting because of the field's commitment to work-integrated learning. The Blue Mountains International Hotel Management School, and Torrens University Australia which merged with it, are no exceptions.

Around 2000, when I was looking for investors for RMIT Vietnam, I called Joseph Duffy and Douglas Becker in the US. Joe was ex-president of the University of Massachusetts and adviser to Doug, the founder of Sylvan Learning Systems. Sylvan was acquiring universities around the world. Sorry, they said, they did not like to have minority stakes in universities into which they committed funds; for any investment they wanted a controlling interest. But we parted on good terms. In 2004 the company sold its other businesses to concentrate on building up a network of 50 private higher education institutions by 2010, and become Laureate International Universities. I helped them on this, advising on a number of companies and travelling to Indonesia incognito to check out prospective acquisitions there for them.

My Laureate colleagues had their eyes on Australia, a key market for international private higher education. Their original strategy was to acquire one or more institutions as a basis for expansion, preferring to build up in new markets a cluster of higher education providers. Their first target was the Blue Mountains International Hotel Management School at Leura, west of Sydney, a prestigious institution set up in 1981 by Fritz Grubler, a Swiss hotelier, and others. Laureate people asked me to do the academic due diligence: what was the school's accreditation status, was its China campus shipshape, were there any 'skeletons in the closet'. My review tied up management for many days, but the Laureate people liked the report and in 2008 went ahead to buy the hotel school.

As a result of the review, they asked me to chair the academic council of their new acquisition. At first Laureate preferred a controlling business board over academic governance, but Australian regulations prevented a fully foreign-domiciled board running a higher education provider. So, the modified academic governing board took on most of the delegations of company directors except ultimate financial responsibility. We were 'shadow directors'. The board's members were eminent and experienced, and of course being in hospitality, our meetings as a board and with hotel industry partners set a benchmark for culinary excellence, in one instance on a member's yacht on Sydney harbour.

Meanwhile, Laureate's strategy for entry changed tack. There was an opportunity to start up a greenfields university registered in South Australia, rather than expand out from the hotel school I chaired. The Rann Labor government enacted it in 2013, among its last days of office, with the attractive promise of Bill Clinton coming to open it. He was honorary chancellor of the whole group of Laureate universities. Torrens University Australia was the first private full university to set up in Australia since Bond University in 1989. Michael Mann, ex-ambassador to Vietnam and my successor as CEO of RMIT Vietnam, led the start-up work and was appointed chancellor after a stint by Dennis Gibson, ex-chancellor of RMIT. How small is the circle of key players in the business!

Torrens was clearly now the main Laureate entry gate into Australia, and it set about acquiring companies such as THINK Education as well.

The hotel school was thriving. It was ranked number one in Asia-Pacific for an international career, in the top three in the world for innovation and best for professional success. It measured well against other elite hotel schools like Glion in Switzerland and Hong Kong Polytechnic University, both of which I visited. It also enjoyed good financial returns, helping by transfers Laureate Australia to finance the expensive business of starting a university. I enjoyed meeting with its students, in neat hotel uniforms and dedicated to service. It was a residential school and ran teaching hotels. Blue Mountains expanded to campuses in downtown Sydney, Malaysia, and Canberra—the latter only for a number of years, at the lovely historic Kurrajong Hotel. Over time it made sense to merge Blue Mountains into Torrens University Australia and THINK.

So, by 2015, that happened. The hotel school board was wary at first about Torrens keeping the brand and ethos going, but the merger process was smooth enough, reaccrediting the courses and enhancing academic quality. Naturally, the board disbanded, and I accepted a position as deputy chair, and then chair, of Torrens' and THINK's expanded academic board. Being a new university, we were able to apply best practice in academic governance, and month by month a lively collegiate across the university emerged. It was good to be able to design new courses and put new policies and practices in place without the difficult task of changing old ones, even as we went along a rapid growth path. Of course, COVID-19 added to the challenges, requiring reaccreditation for online delivery and the redesign of student and scholar support services.

My adventures in cross-cultural learning, and learning cities more generally, are not over. The same can be said for my interest in governance, another thread through all of this book, whether the governance of cities or the corporate governance of education institutions. To this final theme we now turn.

ELEVEN

GOVERNING CITIES

The reader will recognise the theme of governance running through the ups and downs of my career, the successes of contributing to good governance, and the destruction that poor governance can bring to the best of plans. As examples, recall my disappointment at DURD's demise, the years of researching how policy is made in the USA, the institutional politics of work in the NSW government, and the job at RMIT leading corporate governance. But it wasn't until I taught governance and decision-making at the University of NSW between 2014 and 2019 that I came to understand it better, and see more fully what good governance could be.

Governance is the formal and informal framework within which decisions are made, both broadly in relations between state and society, and in corporate governance within organisations. Though governance as a field of inquiry and practice dates from well before the modern nation state (think of Machiavelli), the 'new governance' came to prominence during the Thatcher and Reagan era of the 1980s, the use of neo-classical economics to provide public goods with market mechanisms and shrink 'Leviathan', the swollen post-war states of so many advanced economies.[1] This included outsourcing, privatisation and corporatisation within agencies, the destruction of traditional bureaucracies. Many of the urban services that I sought to coordinate in the interests of equity became harder to manage for the public good when they were in private hands, though I did try, becoming more expert in public–private partnerships.

The governance of cities goes to the heart of how they are constituted, and how key planning decisions are made, so it is little wonder that, as a consultant, I might be disappointed in the results of some of this work, and happy with its occasional successes. The stories of practice in urban governance that I share below come from different perspectives. They include government-to-government attempts in Japan and China to open up the urban sector to Australian interests, a review of municipal governance in the Philippines, capacity building for strategic planning in Melbourne, forays into Iran's unique urban governance, an attempt to map out the future governance of a mining town in Papua New Guinea, and devising a scheme of governance for a new town in Vietnam.

Helping the government

On the whole, the governance of Australian cities is good by world standards. I found that the export of this know-how can be a more powerful means of extending Australia's influence in the sector, and of expanding urban sector exports, than normal trade and investment promotion.

One memorable instance was a trip with Brian Howe in 1994. He was then deputy prime minister and minister for housing and regional development. He and Jenny Macklin (Brian's protégé, leading a national urban policy review, later to become a successful federal Labor minister and parliamentarian), asked if I could join them and introduce them to interesting urban sector people in Japan and China, beyond what the embassies might recommend, with the idea of finding ways to boost Australia's business engagement in the sector. They knew of my network in these countries. Renata Howe, Brian's wife, Andrew Podger (secretary of housing and regional development) and Brian Martin, CEO of Delfin, a big innovative urban development company, joined us.

In Japan we had exceptional access to the leaders of government and business, including meals and meetings with some of the leaders of the *Keidanren*, the equivalent of the Australian Business Council. At an Australian embassy dinner, the Ambassador, Ashton Calvert, assigned me to buddy with (that is, sit next to and look after) Shunichi Suzuki, the legendary governor of metropolitan Tokyo. At a lunch seminar of luminaries at the Tokyo Imperial Hotel, I didn't understand why my delightfully offbeat invitee, Professor Tatsuhiko Kawashima from Gakushuin University, was put at the head of the table. It turned out that he was father of the Crown princess' husband and always got the top seat. We visited some mega-developments, including Rokko Island, a big island development on reclaimed land, and the Kansai airport, about to open. Japan was in full flight then, its wings spread across the property world.

China was even more interesting. The same deal applied; I rounded up urban experts off the beaten track for seminars. The urban authorities were developing new cities and infrastructure at a breathtaking pace, and welcomed our ideas. But here the politics were important too, meetings with the leaders such as deputy premier and reformer Zhu Rongji. Lots of official photographs were taken at these events, but I didn't get copies. I happened to see myself on television meeting his nemesis, premier Li Peng, so at least got a photograph of that. At the Diaoyutai state guesthouse, my floor was guarded by a heavily armed official. I imagined in years past meetings of conflicted national delegations, each staying in different buildings in the compound.

I also felt awe when I visited Hu Qili and his wife Hao Keming, but they and Li were on opposite sides of history around the Tiananmen incident. Qili was second in line to party leadership, and with Keming were revered by young people, having risen to prominence through the Youth League. Each time I visited them I brought something unusual, like an out-of-season watermelon. An urbane English-speaking reformist, he was courted by the Hawke government, and Vivian and I would sometimes be a backchannel of communication between Hawke and Hu. At one meal with me in Zhongnanhai, party headquarters (of Chinese beef, 'better than the Japanese wagyu', he boasted), the couple seemed tense. Unusually, Qili was wearing a Mao jacket. This was just before the 'Tiananmen incident'. After the disastrous rift in the standing committee of the politburo over students' rights to protest, when Qili and Keming were under house arrest, I was still able to visit them, sometimes walking in a park, with his secretary five paces behind.

Later, rehabilitated to the position of minister for electronics industry, where he led the way for China's extraordinary development in this area, he opened the door to David Beanland and me to have RMIT form a privileged relationship with the ministries' universities. The opportunity was followed up by a delegation from the faculty of engineering in April 1996.[2] It came to some useful action but my colleagues at RMIT did not fully embrace the scale of the opportunity.

I learnt the lesson of doing top-down business for RMIT better by cultivating leaders of the CAAC, before cascading down to a successful aviation management degree in Tianjin and a flight training program with the Civil Aviation Flying College of China at Point Cook near Melbourne and in Guanghang, Sichuan province, an 'aviation coup' according to the *Australia-China Review*.[3] That college was oversupplied with flight simulators gifted from eager flight companies. They used them profitably to bring paying aviation students from western institutions around the world just to do the simulator parts of their courses.

Let us move back to 1994. For Brian Howe's delegation, Shanghai was grand in a manner different from Beijing. The highlight was a visit to the massive Pudong development, then under construction. This was no ordinary visit. To the wail of sirens our motorcade raced along streets closed for the occasion, as we stretched our necks to see the towers and cranes.

That visit had its lighter moments too. Back in my favourite city of Tianjin we dined at the Astor Hotel, famous as the place of many treaty signings and the haunt of Pu Yi, last ruler of the Qing Dynasty. It had been awfully refurbished in a Chinese version of high western opulence, and our meal was served by waiters dressed as distant copies of Versailles pages. Brian preferred western breakfasts over Chinese, and in Yantai, Shandong province, for the opening of an Australian-developed hospital, he asked for more jam on toast at breakfast. At the grand banquet that evening we were told there was a special dish. Out came a queue of waiters (this time dressed normally). When they lifted the cloches covering the plates, lo and behold! Jam on toast!

After returning from the visits, we ran a number of meetings and other events for industry leaders to promote urban sector exports and investment opportunities in the two countries. Austrade and Brian's Department of Housing and Community Development made it a priority.[4] It seemed to me the key was exporting whole Australian systems, along the lines of the clever knocked-down housing imported into Japan by Greg Clark, Nick Clark's brother, who knew the smart way to get through Japan's prohibitive tariffs, or of Sydney's coordinated adaptive traffic system (SCATS) being sold to multiple cities in China. Behind the export of such systems, developers, planners, architects and others who knew them could follow. It was some years before Australian urban sector companies 'cracked' the China market, and even today they have not met their potential in Japan. This 'systems' approach seems to have been successful in public–private partnerships, where Australia's clear and transparent guidelines and project details have been copied the world over (even to reproduce a typographical error, which I found in South Africa), to the benefit of exporters and investors. Australian companies do well in the urban development sector.

While at a less grand scale, I enjoyed some other, more personal, international efforts to improve urban governance.

Capacity building in the Philippines

At RMIT in 1999 and 2000, I worked through RMIT International to join in a two-person review of the performance of an AusAID urban sector project in the Philippines. The Philippines regional municipal development project aimed at the institutional strengthening and professional development of the personnel of seven city governments through capability building and community consultation processes. The project was well past its midpoint and there were problems with the way its separate parts fitted together. The Australian project consultants technically provided each of the deliverables of the project, if late (expressed in the mind-numbing logical framework, or 'LogFrame' system) to cover land information, engineering and solid waste services, planning and development, administration and project management. But integrated improvements to the cities' whole municipal capacities were weak; they would benefit from a city-focused approach to project implementation rather than a component-based approach.

Our workshops and site visits were in Manila, Cebu, Tagbilaran, Bacolod, and General Santos, the latter a Mindanao city then and now under challenge from Islamist insurgency, but hosting a wonderful tuna fishing (and tuna eating!) industry. Visits to some of the cities were cancelled for security reasons. But it was good to see some less-visited parts of the country. In Manila, I had a meal with my old university friend Alice Buckley and her husband John, who was Australian ambassador, and played a very sweaty game of golf with them down fairways protected by half-hidden guards with machine-guns. Alice and John later joined me for some long-distance walking in France and Japan; stories for another day.

The project got back on track, and though aid for better urban governance is contested by some countries—it often embeds anti-corruption work and the promotion of human rights—it is a worthy area of assistance and has been central to my work.

Helping plan for Victoria

Closer to home in Melbourne, right after leaving RMIT, Lyndsay Neilson, director of the Department of Sustainability and Environment, asked me if I could help with building up the department's strategic planning capacity, with whatever time I could give. The offer was attractive because Lyndsay was a progressive leader and the government was gearing up for a review and performance audit of its path-breaking *Melbourne 2030* strategic plan, and it had a relatively new strategy team. The plan was better built than its Sydney equivalent.

The first task was to help build up the capacity of his new strategy division. Its managers were mainly young, all were smart, but some lacked experience in senior state policy environments. The aim was to help build a team among them, advise on professional development, coach them so as to operate effectively across the bureaucracy and with the department's stakeholders such as the property industry. This was a delight. Virtually all of them have gone on to successful senior careers, including Julian Hill, at the time of writing the up-and-coming federal Labor member for Bruce.

Inevitably, working with the urban strategy team drew me into advising on metropolitan planning, land release policy and services coordination. The task there focused on 'strategic navigation' and metropolitan plan implementation, especially performance evaluation for the forthcoming audit of *Melbourne 2030*.[5] It was an active time for Melbourne's strategic planning because the team that followed those who produced *Melbourne 2030* had the task of aligning its policies and programs to the whole of government in its implementation.[6] Even aligning the operating divisions of his department to the strategy was a challenge (not unlike my previous role in NSW), but we had Lyndsay's full support.

Part of the metropolitan performance evaluation was to develop a set of indicators as a dashboard. This was not straightforward, as the authors of the plan had perversely fuzzed the measurability of its targets in the belief that it had to be seen as a totality and not sliced up into little targets by others. At the time, Victoria, a member of the World Association of the Major Metropolises, was leading a multi-city commission on metropolitan performance indicators, so through Mary Lewin, their key person for international liaison, I worked as lead technical consultant on a global Metropolis report on urban indicators.[7]

This took me to Iran (see coming pages), India and Canada. In Vancouver I led a preparatory conference for the World Urban Forum with Meg Holden on urban performance indicators. She is a professor active with community engagement and international urban affairs. The meeting was hosted by the innovative citizen-based *RVu* (sounding in Canadian drawl like 'our view'), at the regional Vancouver urban observatory, and I presented its findings to the main conference. But so vast was the conference, with over 10,000 attendees, that I am sure it got lost in the crowd.[8] Such a large gathering of the great and the good in global affairs, such daunting issues of global urbanisation, and such energy for solutions were intense for me. I found a pleasant retreat at the Vancouver Club, a corresponding club to my Australian Club in Melbourne, whose quiet garden and restaurant were by good luck right at the conference site, a place where I was able to entertain friends from different countries.

The Victorian government stint was altogether exciting work, if with some bureaucratic tangling. It certainly deepened my understanding of metropolitan governance in Melbourne.

Helping a holy city in Iran

As mentioned, my work on metropolitan performance indicators went international. Though urban issues were not explicitly included in the UN Millennium Development Goals (MDGs), unlike the current UN Sustainable Development Goals, big cities were grappling with how to 'localise' the MDGs when they were only sub-national in the structure of government. The word 'glocalisation' became popular for local actions that pursued global goals.

Mashhad, a holy city in northeast Iran, was a member of Metropolis, and with the support of a modernising mayor they established a municipal training centre within Metropolis, led by the charismatic Hamid Isfahanizadeh. In June 2007 I led the part of a three-day workshop on metropolitan performance indicators that focused on city governance. It was attended by mayors and others from around the region, though mainly from within Iran. That topic was especially sensitive. Under Iran's system of dual governance, a council of elders always vetted urban decisions and municipal election candidates. Currents of reform were alternately running hot and cold in Iran, but whatever the trend, women faced long-standing barriers to candidature for local office and then election.

We trainers had to use culturally appropriate methods to reach consensus, in my case to come up with a set of indicators of good city governance. I took this to mean letting the workshop find its own methods. My non-Iranian colleagues in the project team thought this was not so wise. The workshop—consisting of a combination of modern professionals, visiting Arab mayors (one whose several wives looked on), Iranian mullahs and feisty burqa-clad activist women—appeared to spin out of control. It was marked by passionate speeches, scuffling over control of the microphone, and a wandering agenda. But at the end we did agree on a set of indicators. Among the preferred indicators 'proportion of female candidates running for office' was first choice.

Mashhad hosts the tomb of Imam Reza, Shia's founder, the holiest shrine in the sect. As a result, the city is a major pilgrim and tourist centre. Everyone must visit the shrine, a magnificent quarter of the city. For me it was an unforgettable experience. We visited at the time of the equivalent of the Haj, with tens of thousands of men and women separately streaming towards the holy centre. From our group of 20 or so, one of our hosts quietly took John Goldsmith, a Canadian photographer and husband of Meg Holden (of course no photos there!) and me aside, and led us into the crowd. Were infidels forbidden? He gave us no clear answer.

The crowd thickened as we walked along tiny marble corridors, worn into sunken channels by millions of unshod feet over the centuries. There was no choice but to go with the flow, coffins held above, and frenzied, sweating pilgrims below. The corridors became rooms, gilded, magnificently adorned in ancient patterns, and sparkling with mosaic mirrors. As we approached and then touched the tomb itself, my apprehensions rose. John and I were obvious westerners and obvious infidels. But nobody paid attention—all were absorbed in their own intense prayers.

I returned to Mashhad with my son Kina Lin-Wilmoth, who was royally looked after by our hosts, the Metropolis centre, and with whom, of course, I visited the shrine again. Without telling me, naughty Kina snuck in a camera and took photographs surreptitiously. However, not all of Kina's trip was fun. He had a long stopover in Doha on his way to join me. I booked him into one of those desert tours while waiting, so he could kill some time. The airline assured me a 15-year-old would be fine. He wasn't. They detained him as an unaccompanied minor for 12 hours in an airline lounge with a stern guard. At least later he could talk about the adventure.

Over the years, my three children have accumulated too many travel mishaps with me, and mishaps of their own: Kina stuck here in Qatar and another time denied entry on arrival to meet me in Indonesia; Maya falling forward with me into the traffic of Manila as a baby, sick in Tajikistan, as described earlier, and another time needing medevac from Cuba, courtesy of me. Sasha, it seems, has remained free of the curse.

I ran similar training programs in Mashhad later on urban growth management and on innovative urban project financing. The people who attended were always interesting, and often impressive. In the urban growth management course, the Hezbollah-affiliated mayor of Baalbek, the site of world heritage Roman ruins, took as his case study the means of protecting precious historic precincts during the armed conflict then under way. The example was all the more moving because I treasure photographs of those same sites in Baalbek taken by my father during another conflict, World War II. Urban growth management is of vital importance to Mashhad because its growth has been dramatic and much of it unplanned, as hundreds of thousands of refugees migrated there during the Iran–Iraq wars. The Afghanistan border is close by, with some new instability, despite being tantalisingly close to some of China's Belt and Road transport corridors.

In Mashhad, during its surges of population growth, emergency housing could not wait for plans, normal urban infrastructure or regulated development. So much of it is informal. To the untrained eye the suburbs look like the result of standard urban development; certainly not slums. Now they are trying to retrofit services such as water supply and sewerage into them. To accommodate the overflow, the national government was developing new towns well outside Mashhad, one of which looked forlorn to this visitor, and too far away from jobs. Analysis since has shown it has indeed failed to decant population from greater Mashhad, allow access to jobs, or provide satisfactory living conditions.[9]

Sadly, my work in Iran now prevents me getting a visa to the US, where I lived for over six years and have many friends. From Iran work, I keep in touch with colleagues, some of whom pop up at other Metropolis meetings, along with Meg Holden and Ali Nemati, a friendly and scholarly mullah with whom I've kept a dialogue on Islamic urban economics (he likes the monetarists who eschew debt and loves Friedrich Hayek, of all people). Iran is underrated in the west as a sophisticated, cosmopolitan centre of Persian and Shia Islamic cultures, and coming to understand its dual governance was a learning experience for me.

A college town in the sky

Sometimes urban governance problems occur in smaller settings, in this case Tabubil, a town in Papua New Guinea (PNG). After the destructive discharge of tailings from the copper, gold and silver mine at Ok Tedi, above the town, in 1999 its owner, BHP, withdrew and vested its shares in a foundation: the PNG Sustainable Development Programme (PNGSDP). It was incorporated in Singapore at arm's length from the PNG government, and charged to contribute to PNG's sustainable development and, in particular, that of the Western Province where the mine was located.

In 2008 when I was involved the mine was still operating, but it had a limited life and was contemplating closure. The board of PNGSDP was chaired by Ross Garnaut, whom I knew from his days as Australian ambassador to China, and included Tricia Caswell, a friend since our days as AFS returnees in Brisbane, who recommended me for this project. They originally asked if I would review the mine's training centre and help them develop it to build community vocational skills before and after any mine closure. The proposed college was to be known as the Star Mountains Institute of Technology. I hadn't worked in PNG at that stage, and so grabbed the opportunity.

Though some residents worked in the mine, the skills base in and around the town was very poor. Traditional know-how had been degraded in part through easy access to expensively subsidised food and groceries in the mine canteens and shops, some of it junk food. Even the ways to grow taro, a traditional crop, were being forgotten. The health status of the population, numbering around 13,000, was poor, made worse by an influx of 5000–10,000 settlers, often squatting to take part in the informal cash economy generated around the mine.

The mine faced possible closure. I was diverted from work on the college onto the mine closure planning project to help map post-mining futures for the town. That is, if it was to have a future at all—abandonment of the town was an option. Other scenarios for the town economy included local services and logistics, regularised artisanal mining, building up a productive border with West Irian nearby (including shared training capacity), basing more mining and gas companies there, building up hotels, resorts and tourism, creating a university-level mining school, attracting university and vocational school branch campuses, developing a defence base, and starting a flying school for PNG's hair-raising aviation conditions, which Tabubil had aplenty.

This was a wide canvas. All the options had as their primary goal the generation of sustainable economic development for local job creation. The small team working on them initially included a mine closure specialist and an economist, but they were later to become a 70-person study of the options run by Cardno, a big consulting firm.

Build-up to a tourism and education hub was at the ambitious end of the spectrum. The nearby Star Mountains offer magnificent scenery, trekking and birdwatching, the 50 km long cliffs of the Hindenburg Wall were surely of World Heritage standard. Elite tour companies like Abercrombie & Kent were flying in groups to see rare birds of paradise. Mary Ann Law, my sister, once went there for that. The Fly River, notwithstanding deep damage from the mine tailings, drew in fishing excursions to its healthy tributaries.

Apart from tourism and hospitality, the town itself could become an international education hub, a campus town for tropical campuses of teaching and research institutions, and a place for remote seminars and meetings, a kind of tropical mountain Davos. While that might sound way out of reach, there were places somewhat like that, such as the Rocky Mountains Institute and the National Institute for Research in the Amazon, Manaus, Brazil. And Tabubil was probably the best-managed town in PNG.

Our work was complicated by pre-feasibility work under way on continuation of mining, to take out lodes more difficult to reach by using underground, not open cut mining. The task therefore might end up only a risk management exercise, but we were happy there could still be a mining future. The mine was providing 18 percent of PNG's GDP.[10]

What sort of governance is needed for transition from a privately owned mining settlement to a sustainable municipal town after mining? Answering that question was another task I took on. Ok Tedi Mining

Limited could perhaps continue to operate the town on behalf of provincial and national governments. This would be an expensive and slow road to self-management. It could revert to normal administration and standards under PNG law, but that could lead to catastrophic decline to the low standards of other towns in the Western Province such as Daru, notorious then for endemic diseases and disorganisation.

It could be constituted as a special purpose authority or its services incorporated into a new company, capitalised on its infrastructure assets. Those latter were the recommended directions. The more difficult task was to map the logical and pragmatic path through the stages ahead, tricky decisions under conditions of great uncertainty. The mining company and PNGSDP, joint sponsors of the larger planning study, put a brave face on the future and promoted the optimistic 'education hub' vision.[11]

Meanwhile, for the vocational college, we searched and found Trevor Davidson as CEO, who stayed from 2009 until 2013. He and his wife were experienced at living internationally and relished the new adventure. The institute got started in an existing building while a new one was being designed and built, along with staff housing and student accommodation. It went on to operate the international school in Tabubil and make plans for the future, including a school of conservation, heritage and environmental management, courses on behalf of Divine Word University in medical education linked to the Tabubil hospital, which could become a teaching hospital, and a campus in nearby Kiunga.[12] Brad Shaw, Trevor's TVET deputy, tells the early history well in his PhD thesis.[13]

The ventures—the college, the town's economic future and its governance—did not end well. The PNG government and Western Province were frustrated for many years at not getting their hands on the trust money and full ownership of the mine. The government moved to institute control over PNGSDP by taking control of the board, something barred by the foundation's constitution. They argued that BHP's rights to approve membership of the board (put into the original deal to prevent corrupt takeover of the foundation) amounted to continuing BHP control. The argument went on.

In November 2012, the government banned Ross Garnaut from entering the country, effectively preventing him from chairing the foundation and the mining company. It passed a law on 18 September the following year revoking BHP's immunity from prosecution for the disaster, part of the original exit deal, and cancelling PNGSDP's ownership of shares in the mine, issuing shares to enable the state to own it 100 percent.

The futures project, and all that might have come from it, ceased. Governance of the town would have to muddle through for the foreseeable future. The Star Mountains Institute of Technology passed to the mining company, its non-mining-related programs ceased and it was renamed the Star Mountains Training Institute. At least it continued to offer that training to some unaffiliated members of the community. But the loss of funding and momentum for the Star Mountains Institute of Technology and the Tabubil futures project was a loss to PNG's modernisation. I did my best.

Governing a new town in Vietnam

The reader will be aware of the prominence of Vietnam in my career. Keeping in touch with the country after RMIT Vietnam, I consulted on a string of projects and gave training courses on urban governance and university governance. Links with one client in particular lasted a number of years; indeed, but for the pandemic it could still be going. Originally invited onto a jury for selection of master planners for a private new town development, I introduced Conybeare Morrison International, friends and partners from my Sydney and Botswana days, to the developers. The town was branded Waterpoint, near Ho Chi Minh City, and the job of preparing the master plan went to Conybeare Morrison through the design competition.

The Vietnamese company then hired me and my associates to work out the feasibility of developing a university or branch campus in the town, an international school as well, and then to attract investors and operators to make them both happen. For this I worked again with Dick Nugent. Despite a number of investor negotiations and visits, interest stayed low at first because the evidence of fast development on this outer-suburban site was not compelling. It seemed well away from the city centre, despite a successful new urban development alongside Waterpoint to house those relocated from the site, a necessity for just about any mega-development in Vietnam.

But from 2016 on, construction accelerated, and market and investor interest rose too. Vietnam has shown consistent GDP growth over many years, and its cashed-up middle class, the target market for the new town, is growing fast. Overseas Vietnamese (*Viet Kieu*) can own property back in the country, as well as expats resident in Vietnam under certain conditions.

Launching into its first major precinct, those in the development company, Nam Long Investment Corporation, came to realise they had a very complex project management and town governance job on their hands. The nearest equivalent, the massive Phu My Hung project in District 7 of Ho Chi Minh City, has taken decades and is still developing. In a highly regulated, centrally planned economy, how can a private developer plan and develop, at high standards, all the infrastructure and services needed? What is the developer allowed to do and what will the government, mostly here the provincial government of Long An, demand they themselves keep doing? How can the different parties accomplish this division of responsibilities? How much independent power can the new town managers have as properties are sold and leased and communities built up for a town of 20,000 people? What say should owners, lessees and the community at large have over town management, and how can that continue sustainably and indeed democratically? What are the dos and don'ts from international practice?

With these questions and more, the job of writing a quasi-legal comprehensive town governance strategy came to Anh Pham, my dual-citizen associate, and myself. The idea was to establish a framework for every function, every scale, and every stage in the planning-development-sales-management pipeline, so as to enable the development company, the town management company, the government, the eventual owners and the other stakeholders to participate, creating a set of practices and a body of more detailed policies and guidelines to be drawn up within that framework. The chairman of the development company accepted the framework, and Waterpoint development is now well under way.

The work, incidentally, gave me a great potential case study for the master's-level course I was teaching at the University of NSW on urban decision-making and governance.

Coming together

It seemed as if the strands of my career were coming together, not only across the rich interface between urban development and education, but through the governance of towns, cities and education institutions. More than 15 years with Learning Cities International have been adventurous, and they continue. They are worth some reflection.

All those years at RMIT in Australia and overseas gave me a good network of friends and contacts, and perhaps a reputation for knowledge and project delivery. From 2005, for the first ten years or so, I could pick and choose work. Though some invitations involved competitive bidding, I did try making uninvited open bids to see what that was like. But I disliked being a small part of a someone else's big project, working to deadlines out of my control and pre-defined report outlines into which my work had to slot.

When the tables were turned, with LCI playing a lead role in large projects, such as in Botswana and Gujarat, it was different: I could form a team with trusted colleagues. Even if I had formally to relinquish contractual leadership, my friends at bigger companies like Conybeare Morrison were happy to keep me as project director.

But even when leading projects, or being lead transaction adviser, I never quite overcame the loss of power I experienced after my previous executive positions. Perhaps some of that was from my style of leadership, being consultative to a fault, sometimes unwilling to push myself to the front out of respect for the responsibilities of clients trying to land the project. The different board roles, especially chairing the boards, compensated for the lack of power over some project outcomes. However, board meetings slice up the diary, so that it is sometimes hard to find weeks clear for travel. It was demanding to spend hours in the middle of the night participating in international meetings online, a syndrome shared with so many now in international business.

The reader cannot help noting that some of the projects described above were 'failures', did not lead to further stages, or were canned a few years after the start of implementation. This is inevitable with such work. And always there are shades of success. The Botswana International University of Science and Technology used our work, including on campus planning and building design, even though the full PPP was not implemented. It is hard to measure the efficacy of advice; often it is not a matter of accepting or not accepting recommendations, but of ideas, proposals and suggestions being taken up less directly, or people influenced by one's work continuing as agents of implementation.

Having worked on capacity building right from 2005 when I reviewed the means of building urban planning capacity in Vietnam for the World Bank (a project not described above), I have been acutely aware that of all modes of development assistance, capacity building has been the least successful. Short foreign consultant engagements, flying in and flying out—as distinct from change management grounded patiently in local institutions, culture and knowledge acquired—are one reason for this to be so. I have to look at myself and say this is what too often I have been doing.[14] At least I can be pleased that I have worked with a number of the same clients over many projects and many years, coming to ground my work more fully in their companies or agencies and their ways of working.

When I formed the company I made up a business plan and kept to the criteria of taking work that had a chance of making a difference for the better, tasks where I knew I could perform but would go onto a learning curve, and places and people that sounded interesting. Though I kept good records of time and costs, typically I would spend much more time than budgeted. If I were on salary working for someone else, I doubt that I would have made them much money. I'd treat paid work and unpaid work, for-profit clients and not-for-profit clients with the same rigor (though with lower fees for the latter).

The best part of all this work came from, and still comes from, the people on the job. Many invitations came from friends of long standing (perhaps a touch of cronyism?) and almost invariably new clients on long jobs became friends. Even on short jobs my clients and I usually ended on good terms, with more invitations following. Being able to choose my associates for larger projects—people who knew the conditions in new settings for me (and their languages) and people with skills and qualifications I didn't have (such as architecture, engineering and advanced business modelling)—allowed me to build up a network of friends to whom I could turn for advice or subcontracted contributions. I can't say I did well in every cross-cultural setting, but I found that honest curiosity and being respectful do go a long way.

The typical cycles of feast-or-famine applied to my consultant work, especially after 2015. When I became overloaded, I delegated work and project management to others, once or twice making mistakes—for example, in my choice of sub-contractor for drafting a China education policy for the Victorian government—and had to step in more than I had planned to make matters right. Even consultancy projects need good governance.

It is a truism that every decision taken, or indeed not taken, is tied to an institutional or political framework around which it happens. That was at the heart of my doctoral thesis on urban policymaking and the state. But urban governance can be more systematically understood if we are conscious of the power of actors around us, and recognise more explicitly the arenas in which decisions are made. I came late to the understanding that good governance underpins all attempts at strategic planning and modern management.

Despite the persistence of most governance frameworks, change is not smooth and can be disruptive. Since university I have been drawn to Schumpeter's idea of 'creative destruction', reflecting Marx, the revolutionary drive in capitalism for technology to destroy old modes of production and replace them with the new.[15] It is of course an older idea, reminding me of Kali's devotees in Kathmandu, the destroyer of evil who embraces the destruction intrinsic to creation. For me, the failed projects and dashed hopes of reform recounted above tend to come back to give me direction and energy.

TWELVE

CREATIVE DESTRUCTION

The destruction of the pandemic from 2020, and the economic crisis that came with it, bring the seeds of change, a combination of interruptions, accelerations of earlier trends, and end points to an era. They also give me here a chance to reflect on what has been important in professional life over the past 40 years. Globalisation has been transformed. Intercultural understanding faces its populist enemies. Neo-liberal ideology and practice are on the wane. What should now be the norms of professional life, and what parts do changing values and personal support play in one's personal development?

Globalism interruptus

My career has coincided with one of history's great periods of globalisation, perhaps the greatest period if cross-border trade, investment and movement of people are counted. From the time of the 2008 recession global connectedness became more volatile, but it kept going until the trade wars and pandemic of 2020, and will take a different shape again.[1]

Lower demand, recourse to digital communication, disruption to global supply chains and more money printed on top of the liquidity sloshing around the world: these trends and more hasten the end of the long post-war wave of growth and speed the start of a new long-term wave—'Industry 4.0'—driven by ICT. The evidence changes the views on communications I formed through my master's research. Transformation of the ways we work will surely now disperse the business concentrations of big cities—towards the 'non-place urban realm'—and at the same time promote smaller clusters of activity accessible to workers spending more time at home and in communities building local climate resilience.

Recovering from the pandemic and confronting the climate emergency have to bring a stronger role for the state, including in Australia, and more power to civil society with a new-found sense of community. However, it is likely that right-wing populism and xenophobic nationalism will continue to grow too, and the post-war international order continues to fray, disrupting international connections.

A formative early year away set my course on work promoting international mobility and intercultural exchange, with luck in later years leading to RMIT's internationalisation at the very time borders opened up for students and universities embraced a more global outlook. In my career and my personal life, I have been a beneficiary of this great opening up. Now, as with trade and investment, so international direct student mobility is suffering a massive decline, ending that long run of growth with accelerated digital engagement.

In a reshaped world, this mobility will recover in a different form, and some previous trends, such as greater south-south movement, and a move away from Anglophone country destinations, will accentuate. The same will be the case across education more generally. It will grow and develop, but for a different, digital, world.

Student exchange: embers, not ashes

Cross-cultural understanding is key to any success across borders and within our own communities. This has been most evident in AFS work. The reader will be familiar from chapter one with my 1964–65 year away. Going on AFS to America in 1964 was my initiative, not that of my parents. To me, the USA was the future, and especially California, to where I wished afterwards to return. The year-long separation from my own family and friends taught me some self-reliance, but immersion in another culture, which I didn't expect to find so different, taught me more. An interest in different people and international affairs stayed with me and set my compass.

With my career, changes of city, and raising a family, I drifted away from AFS returnee affairs, just taking part in occasional dinners and reunions, and in Melbourne teaming up with returnees like Reg Smith. Separately, though, I was working a lot with international student programs at the higher education level, including student exchange, so I kept an interest in the internationalisation of schools and their exchange programs.

Reg became chair of the board of AFS Australia, and we talked about how the AFS programs might be developed. We agreed we might not 'start from here', running study-travel and exchange programs. By the turn of the century there were many private providers for that, not as good as AFS, but cheaper, and burrowed into the schools sometimes through attractive 'chaperone' trips for school staff on the shorter programs. Maya Lin, my daughter, went on one to France; it wasn't a great experience for her. Many families and schools now organise their own international travel for young people. Reg asked me if I would stand to be a director.

He and I clearly shared an aim to diversify AFS' programs. He explained that the organisation was in danger of losing its way. With my experience in international education I could help steer the board towards more diverse programs, some of which involved intercultural learning without travel at all. There were business opportunities in these directions too. This appealed to me and in 2008 I was elected to the board.

After Vivian and I separated in 2010, then divorced, I moved to Sydney to be with Lori Mooren, who was a research fellow at the University of NSW in road safety, and whom I had known since the early 1980s. Returning to the AFS board for a further term in 2015, and taking on the chair in 2019, I found the same underlying problems. A capable new team was finding success with the non-traditional programs around intercultural learning, but still slipping on its core business of student exchange.

During this time, being semi-retired, I had more time to do volunteer work, meeting and transferring students at the airport or bringing them home for short stays, which Lori and I loved. From many countries and backgrounds, these young people brought short but sincere international friendship into our home. Some were just in transit, some 'between families' (not every family placement works out first time), and some were on their way out of AFS entirely, with undeclared health preconditions emerging or other issues preventing happy family placement. But all students were a pleasure to host.

Since we had face-to-face board meetings in Sydney, Lori and I hosted dinners every time, hilarious gatherings where Ruth Pearce, an ex-ambassador good at chairing, would emcee the story-telling. This fun did nothing to keep the financial crisis at bay, and after a long and fraught negotiation for financial support from AFS International and other AFS partners, we made structural changes, including bringing three international representatives onto the board of the ailing body.

As the virus spread and borders closed, AFS programs closed down too; first, country by country, then the whole network. At least all our students to and from Australia were safe and healthy, but the business dried up. Some countries, even those with 'the curve' of cases high and growing, talked optimistically about reopening the programs later in 2020, but in Australia we knew that would not happen. We terminated or stood down all but three of the staff, wonderful workers for the cause, and that hurt. AFS International judged AFS Australia to be non-viable, and, given our indebtedness, red-carded us from the student mobility 'matrix'. We had no choice but to close down completely. And we did, going into voluntary administration and then liquidation early in 2021.

The story, though, is not over. An association of 'Friends of AFS Australia' has formed, and when the time is right, AFS will fan the embers with new energy and almost certainly new types of program. Here, too, the pandemic brings destruction but opens the way to new growth.

The end of neo-liberalism

Neo-liberalism in western thought and policy practice is fast losing its hold. The stories and recollections show me putting a distinct Janus-like face on this. My early political education opposed the incursion of market mechanisms into the workings of the state, such as the outsourcing of public services, the sale of government entities and market-led displacement in working class suburbs.

Then, I became neo-liberalism's unconscious agent. Convinced of the merits of good technocratic urban management, I worked to replace prescriptive older forms of land use control and bureaucratic organisation with flexible strategic planning and engagement with markets. I was driven by the belief that a smart combination of private and public operators would modernise the way we develop and run our cities, and that there were good ideas from the private sector that government agencies could take up. The radicalism of student years and my Californian time gave way to wearing suits and being moderate.

I believed urban policy—whether national urban policy in the Australian government, or urban growth management in NSW—was capable of making fundamental changes to cities and how they were run. I was proud of the methods we used, often government-wide instruments of 'implicit' urban policy, not just putting land use plans on maps and hoping one day development will fill in the zones.

But later, from the 1980s, when economic growth in the west faced cyclical crisis again, the 'new governance', pursued by Ronald Reagan, Jimmy Carter, Margaret Thatcher and Milton Friedman and his Chicago cronies, led to a 'hollowing out of the state'. Those new instruments I had worked on lost much of their effectiveness. In NSW this was abetted by incompetence, and regrettably overseen for part of that by premier Bob Carr, once my planning minister whom I admired so much at the time.

Now, with the hindsight shown in the previous chapter, I see that my faith in urban management methods was in part misplaced. Recourse to the private sector in city development and aping the market within corporatised government entities have made cities much harder to plan and manage, and weakened the electorate's power to guide their growth in the public interest. Institutional amnesia, lack of political will, ignorance of the agency that many decision-makers really have, and widespread belief that state structures are immutable—all have worked to weaken the sophisticated policies, strategic plans and coordination systems in which I believed.

As a university leader, too, I carried a 'managerialist' agenda to corporatise the higher education institutions, and later work with international clients to open up private education. Through experience with public–private partnerships as a project developer and a transaction adviser, I saw their merits, despite misuse across in the urban sector through corrupt deals and distorted government priorities away from 'social' PPPs to easier projects like toll roads. Likewise, I came to support an active role for private education, and for-profit providers like SABIS and Laureate with whom I worked, in a world where government provision is often inadequate in quality and scale, especially for very poor communities.[2]

In other words, my reflections on practice in urban planning and education are different. Cities would be better planned and managed if we had a deeper understanding of the state and a commitment to urban governance, whatever the technocratic methods that underlie professional practice. Here, neo-liberalism has failed us. But in education, including international education and intercultural learning, we can usefully keep some of its legacy, including private provision and well-designed public–private partnerships.

The planner who didn't plan

Despite being a planner, I have not been one to set long-term goals and pursue them. Perhaps that is a privilege of the post-war generation, where for me, one opportunity has led to another. I have seen for later generations that it is not so possible in a more fragile, atomised and disrupted economy.

I wasn't born of just a baby boom but an economic boom. I am lucky to have lived through the longest period of continuous growth on record, growing up in the 'golden age'. By contrast, the Great Depression and Second World War marked my parents' years. My father was away in the Middle East, New Guinea and Borneo, never talking much about the war years, and losing his partnership as a private civil engineer on return. Both suffered from enforced separation over four war years. It is only in 2021 that my sisters and I wrote a book on my father's life. We regretted not asking him more about his life when he was alive. No wonder my parents' generation was cautious and frugal, values my friends and I rejected so noisily during the 1960s.

But a lack of lifelong goals—apart from that teenage dream of making my inner life and outward actions self-consistent—does not mean that this career was aimless. Through most of it I have been driven by equity and social justice, letting those values set what I chose to do in the many jobs and countless projects taken on.

My early scholarly bent turned me to research and evidence-based policy—a technocrat in the making. But my mentors, especially George Clarke and Pat Troy, and involvement in urban social movements, biased me towards action. My further education was 'learning by doing', often in positions where I was out of my depth, with no time to wait for complete solutions. The lesson is to dive in if the direction is right, even if you feel unprepared. This meant that I sometimes failed—witness the RMIT Penang campus—but out of that destruction came learning and new approaches. The lesson is to learn from failures. By all means take risks—how can we progress otherwise?—but know the stakes and keep your exits open.

The stories recounted are mainly about my professional life. But that is not the half of it, even for a self-confessed workaholic. One's personal life is more important, not that I cover that subject in any depth in my narrative. Work-life balance matters, which I failed to achieve, as does the love and support of others who have sustained me, like Lori does now. Of course, that is true for any generation.

It was my fascination with how cities worked and how they might be changed for the better that drove the early part of my career, working in a planning office in Sydney, getting involved in urban politics. I shared that passion with Jill; work and our love were tied together. That period of economic and population growth opened up jobs in the urban sector easily, and I thought this would go on forever. The way got bumpier as I moved into higher education and international education, but each job still led into another, while raising a family with Vivian. Even work as a consultant after RMIT came as a flow of personal referrals rather than through a business plan or marketing. For younger professionals, that career free-flow has gone, a new economy and society rising from the destruction of the pandemic and facing urgent climate change action.

In some ways I haven't wanted to grow up—no career plan, a tendency to be the ingénue, the 'wise fool' and not the cynic, attraction to risky behaviour, a sense of mischief. Luck has favoured me, reinforcing my optimism, which can be unrealistic at times. The convergence on urban planning of my father's career and mine was unintentional—he as a city engineer, me as an urban planner—but may have grown from the seeds of the examples he planted when I was young.

With the same luck I have been favoured with partners, family and friends, who mostly put up with my 'marriage to the job' in whatever positions I've had, including my children, who were too young in many of the Melbourne years to know the difference or resent their neglect. Love from those others sustained me, and still does, as the cycle of creative destruction keeps turning.

ACKNOWLEDGEMENTS

Many contributed to this book, some without knowing. I am grateful to Regina Lane, the publisher, and Liz Harrington of Laneway Press; Rebecca Wylie, the editor; and Luke Harris, the book designer—all for their friendly, frank and unfailing advice.

I thank Peter Spearritt, a friend and seasoned author, who gave me good advice as I set out on the trail of publishing, with contacts and encouragement, as did Nick Melchior of Springer Australia.

Rob Freestone also gave me advice and encouragement, especially with our conversations about George Clarke and the City of Sydney strategic plan. The late Patrick Troy encouraged me to write about the history of national urban policy in Australia for a joint book which we started, and my chapter on DURD relies much on his extensive record.

Ann Markusen kindly read the chapter on California years and corrected errors. Mark Weiss provided a good anecdote from those same years.

For the chapter on RMIT I am grateful for David Beanland's and Ruth Dunkin's unique anecdotes and commentaries, and Robert Glass, who saved the work of a prodigiously researched but unfinished history of RMIT 1980–2000 by placing it in the State Library of Victoria.

For advice, stories, information and photos about RMIT's Penang campus I am grateful to Mal Rowe and Brian Stoddart.

For his history of RMIT Vietnam, and comments and information on the chapter on RMIT Vietnam, I thank Nguyen Xuan Thu, as well as great anecdotes and corrections from Michael Mann and Kenn Crompton.

From the beginning to the end of work on this book, my friend through most of those years written about, Wendy Sarkissian, gave me frank and fearless advice, detailed edits and constant support.

Lori Mooren also provided detailed feedback on drafts and loving support through the whole process, putting up uncomplainingly with my seclusion at the desk and the clutter in our house made by boxes of documents, now, mercifully, going to archives and recycle bins.

ACRONYMS

ADB	Asian Development Bank
AFS	AFS Intercultural Programs, previously American Field Service
AIPF	Asia Injury Prevention Foundation
AIT	Adorna Institute of Technology Sdn. Bhd.
AIUS	Australian Institute of Urban Studies
ALP	Australian Labor Party
AMS	Academic management system
ANU	Australian National University
ARC	Australian Research Council
AUQA	Australian Universities Quality Agency
AusAID	Australian Agency for International Development
Austrade	Australian Trade and Investment Commission
BHP	BHP-Billiton, previously Broken Hill Propriety Company Ltd
BIUST	Botswana International University of Science and Technology
CAAC	Civil Aviation Administration of China
CAE	College of Advanced Education
CCID	Community Colleges for International Development
CPD	NSW DEP Central Policy Division
CPUSA	Communist Party USA
CQAHE	Committee for Quality Assurance in Higher Education
CSIRO	Commonwealth Scientific and Industrial Research Organisation
DEP	NSW Department of Environment and Planning
DSE	Victorian Department of Sustainability and Environment
DURD	Australian Department of Urban and Regional Development
FIT	Footscray Institute of Technology
HCC	NSW Housing Committee of Cabinet
HUD	US Department of Housing and Development

ICT	Information and communication technology
IFC	International Finance Corporation
INQAAHE	International Network for Quality Assurance Agencies in Higher Education
INTI	INTI International Universities and Colleges
ISO	International Standards Organisation
JV	Joint Venture
LCI	Learning Cities International Pty Ltd
LEP	Local Environmental Plan
LRC	Learning Resource Centre
MASD	Management Authority for Saigon South Development
MFP	Multifunction Polis
MIT	Massachusetts Institute of Technology
MITI	Japan Ministry of International Trade and Industry
MMBW	Melbourne Metropolitan Board of Works
MOET	Vietnam Ministry of Education and Training
NCA	Northern California Alliance
NCDC	National Capital Development Authority
NTEU	National Tertiary Education Union
NUPC	National Urban Policy Collective
NURDA	National Urban and Regional Development Authority
OECD	Organisation for Economic Cooperation and Development
PIT	Phillip Institute of Technology
PNGSDP	Papua New Guinea Sustainable Development Programme
PPP	Public–private partnership
PRC	Australian Government Priority Review Committee
PRMDP	Philippines Regional Municipal Development Project
PSB	Commonwealth Public Service Board
QUT	Queensland University of Technology
RAAF	Royal Australian Air Force
RAND	RAND Corporation, named after 'Research And Development'
RCHI	Royal Children's Hospital International, Melbourne
RCSD	Regional Council for Social Development
REP	Regional Environmental Plan
RMIT	Royal Melbourne Institute of Technology
ROC	Regional Organisation of Councils
RSL	Returned and Services League of Australia
SATS	Sydney Area Transportation Study

SCATS	Sydney Coordinated Adaptive Traffic System
SEPP	State Environmental Planning Policy
SIDCURD	Standing Interdepartmental Committee on Urban and Regional Development
SPA	NSW State Planning Authority
SROP	Sydney Region Outline Plan
SSA	Second Sydney airport
TAFE	Technical and Further Education
TNT	TNT Limited, previously Thomas Nationwide Transport
TVET	Technical and vocational education and training
UC	University of California
UCC	NSW Urban Consolidation Committee
UDP	NSW Urban Development Program
UN	United Nations
UNSW	University of New South Wales
UOIP	University Office of International Programs
UPNG	University of Papua New Guinea
USSR	Union of Soviet Socialists Republics
VIC	Victorian Institute of Colleges
VNU	Vietnam National University
VPSEC	Victorian Post-Secondary Education Commission
VUT	Victoria University of Technology
WSROC	Western Sydney Region Organisation of Councils
WTO	World Trade Organization

ENDNOTES

INTRODUCTION: INVITATION TO ADVENTURE

1   The term is from Schumpeter, Joseph A. (1994) *Capitalism, Socialism and Democracy*. London: Routledge and has been widely applied by the thought of political economists and urban analysts relied upon in this book.

CHAPTER 1: QUEENSLAND ROOTS AND BRANCHING OUT

1   Lang, Kylie (2021) 'Bombshell Churchie lawsuit claim: I was drugged, tied to a bed and raped by my teacher' *Courier Mail* 5 June 2021. https://www.thechronicle.com.au/news/queensland/man-sues-church-claims-he-was-gangraped-by-teacher-cop/news-story/e0b99bf7ab83da0408c6e18d1f6a7554. Accessed 30 June 2021.

2   See Caro, Robert (1974) The Power Broker: Robert Moses and the Fall of New York. New York: Knopf.

3   See especially Jacobs, Jane (1961) *The Death and Life of Great American Cities*. New York: Random House.

4   Turmelle, Luther (2018) 'More adult sexual misconduct uncovered at Choate, according to new report' *New Haven Register*, 12 October. https://www.nhregister.com/news/article/More-adult-sexual-misconduct-uncovered-at-Choate-13303828.php. Accessed 16 June 2011.

5   Wilmoth, David (1967) 'Resort development on Hayman Island', *Capricornia* 4: 121–128. https://www.researchgate.net/publication/352497793_Resort_development_on_Hayman_Island. Accessed 19 June 2021.

6   Wilmoth, David (1970) 'Consumer accessibility and shopping centre location on the Gold Coast' in Nicholas Clark (ed.), *Analysis of Urban Development*. Melbourne: Department of Civil Engineering, University of Melbourne: 3.96-3.101. https://www.researchgate.net/publication/352523893_Shopping_centre_location_Gold_Coast. Accessed 19 June 2021.

7   *Australian Financial Review* (1967) 'Priority for cities urged', Editorial, 2 August.

8   Gold Coast City Council (1969) *Gold Coast Urban Region - Strategic Plan - 1970–1990*. Southport: Council of the City of Gold Coast.

9   See: https://www.queensland.com/en-ca/attraction/pine-ridge-conservation-park. Accessed 19 June 2021.

CHAPTER 2: URBAN LIFE IN SYDNEY

1   Stretton, Hugh (1970) *Ideas for Australian Cities*. Adelaide: An Orphan Book; Harvey, David (1973) *Social Justice and the City*. London: Edward Arnold and Baltimore: The Johns Hopkins University Press; Lloyd, Clem and Troy, Patrick (1981) *Innovation and Reaction: The Life and Death of the Federal Department of Urban and Regional Development*. Sydney: George Allen and Unwin: 27.

2   Wilmoth, David (1972a) 'The Heads' tales', *Royal Australian Planning Institute Journal* 102: 87–91. http://www.tandfonline.com/doi/abs/10.1080/00049999.1972.9656370. Accessed 16 June 2011.

3   Powell, Tony (1974) Producing planners: discussion points. Royal Australian Planning Institute ACT Division, 30 March.

4   Haig, Robert Murray and McCrae, Roswell C. (1927) Major Economic Factors in Metropolitan Growth and Arrangement; a Study of Trends and Tendencies in the Economic Activities within the Region of New York and its Environs. Regional Survey of New York and its Environs, volume 1. New York: Regional Plan Association.

5   Kenzotaki, D. (1969) 'Intersex' *AD (Architectural Design)*, 7: 471–472. For Masters and Johnson work see Masters, W. H. and Johnson V. E. (1966). *Human Sexual Response.* Toronto and New York: Bantam Books

6   Meier, Richard (1962) *A Communications Theory of Urban Growth.* Cambridge MA: MIT Press.

7   Wilmoth, David (1972b) 'Communication in the urban system', *Proceedings of the Ecological Society of Australia* 7: 211–230 and Wilmoth, David (1972c) 'Communication technology and the future city', *The Human Consequences of Technological Change.* Sydney: University of Sydney, Volume II, reprinted in *Archetype* (1972) 3, 1: 26–33. https://www.researchgate.net/publication/352524196_Communication_technology_and_the_future_city. Accessed 19 June 2021.

8   Wilmoth, David (2003) Information infrastructure and the connected city. Paper presented to State of Australian Cities National Conference, Parramatta, 3–5 December. https://apo.org.au/sites/default/files/resource-files/apo-nid309592.pdf. Accessed 18 June 2021.

9   Colman, James (2016) *The House that Jack Built. Jack Mundey, Green Bans Hero.* Kensington: New South Publishing.

10   Llewelyn-Smith, Michael (2012) 'Planning in Sydney and the work of George Clark', chapter 5 in Michael Llewelyn-Smith, *The Politics of Planning Adelaide.* Adelaide: University of Adelaide Press: 133–153.

11   Farrelly, Elizabeth (2021) *Killing Sydney: The Fight for a City's Soul.* Sydney: Picador: 130.

12   Llewelyn-Smith: 137.

13   City of Sydney (1971) *City of Sydney Strategic Plan.* Sydney: Council of the City of Sydney. As examples see *Sydney Morning Herald* (1971) 'No mean city' (editorial), 21 July; or, in Punter's words, 'Its political astuteness, policy sophistication, analytical depth, comprehensiveness and detail were on a far higher level than any previous city planning document in Australia, let alone Sydney': Punter J. (2005) 'Urban design in central Sydney 1945–2002: Laissez-Faire and discretionary traditions in the accidental city', *Progress in Planning* 63: 47. https://www.researchgate.net/publication/27649473_Urban_Design_in_Central_Sydney_1945-2002_Laissez_faire_and_discretionary_traditions_in_the_accidental_city. Accessed 19 June 2021. For a 50-year review see Freestone, Rob (2021) 'Jubilee celebration for Sydney's first foray into "people" planning' *Sydney Morning Herald* 7–8 August: News Review 23. https://www.watoday.com.au/national/nsw/city-plan-was-sydney-s-first-foray-into-a-strategy-designed-for-the-people-20210803-p58fk6.html?ref=rss&utm_medium=rss&utm_source=rss_feed. Accessed 10 August 2021.

14   Llewelyn-Smith: 153.

15   Stretton, Hugh (1971) Seminar presentation. Adelaide, 27 July. MS.

CHAPTER 3: THE SHORT FLOWERING OF NATIONAL URBAN POLICY

1   For a good overview of the build-up of urban problems see Troy, Patrick (1992) Loves Labor Lost: Whitlam and Urban and Regional Development. Paper presented to Conference: Whitlam Revisited, Graduate School of Management, Public Sector Management Institute, Monash University, 3–4 April.

2   Self, Peter (1992) 'Socialism' in Goodin, Robert E., Pettit, Philip and Pogge, Thomas (eds.) (1993) *A Companion to Contemporary Political Philosophy.* Oxford: Blackwell: 334–51.

3   Whitlam, Gough (1972) ALP campaign speech, Blacktown 13 November. https://electionspeeches.moadoph.gov.au/speeches/1972-gough-whitlam.

4   For Tom's story see Uren, Tom (1994) *Straight Left.* Milsons Point: Random House.

5   Australia (1972) *Report of the Commonwealth-State Officials on Decentralisation.* Canberra: Australian Government Publishing Service.

6   Australia, House of Representatives (1972) *Hansard* 10 October, 27th Parliament, 2nd Session http://historichansard.net/hofreps/1972/19721010_reps_27_hor81/#debate-22. Accessed 16 June 2011.

7   Walsh, Maximillian (1972) 'PM turns to the city' *Australian Financial Review*, 20 September: 1, 8.
8   Australia, Prime Minister (1972) Speech by the Prime Minister, the R. Hon William McMahon, CH, MP, in the House of Representatives, Canberra. National Urban and Regional Development Authority Bill, 11 October: 4.
9   See especially Lloyd and Troy (1981).
10   Whitlam, Gough (1985) *The Whitlam Government 1972–1975*. Ringwood: Viking: 381.
11   Lloyd and Troy: 33.
12   Stein, Harry (1994) *A Glance over an Old Left Shoulder*. Sydney: Hale & Iremonger: 186.
13   Troy, P. N. (1976) 'Federalism and urban affairs 1972–75', *Royal Australian Planning Institute Journal* 14, 1–2: 15.
14   Lloyd and Troy: 36; Troy (1992): 22.
15   Lloyd and Troy: xi.
16   Fisher, Norman (1974) DURD Memorandum 9 May.
17   To situate this conflict as one of the biggest, but not the only problem the government had with the PSB, see Kelly, Paul (1973) 'Growing pains', Series on Labor's Public Service, *The Australian*, 9 May: 11.
18   Lloyd and Troy: 86–87.
19   Juddery, Bruce (1973) 'Born to Tom Uren: DURD, a super-department – now see how it grows', *The National Times*, 2–7 July: 28–29.
20   Lloyd and Troy: 118.
21   Carey, Patrick Bernard (1986) *Administrative Jurisdiction and Coordination; the Case of the Department of Urban and Regional Development 1972–75*. PhD thesis, Department of Government and Public Administration, University of Sydney: 147.
22   Mant, John (1976) 'Peter Till memorial', *Royal Australian Planning Institute Journal* 14, 3–4, July/October: 51. https://www.tandfonline.com/doi/abs/10.1080/00049999 .1976.9657992. Accessed 19 June 2021. Also see Brown, Nicholas (2002) 'Till, Peter Leonard (1937–1976)', *Australian Dictionary of Biography*, Canberra: National Centre of Biography, Australian National University, http://adb.anu.edu.au/biography/till-peter-leonard-11862/text21237. Accessed 13 September 2017.
23   Stein: 186.
24   Ackland, Richard (1973) 'Public service "soviets" formed', *Australian Financial Review*: 1, 8.
25   For an example of the type of document that the visitors brought see Inner Sydney Resident Action Groups (1973) The People and the City: A Question of Survival. Working Paper in Discussions National Government Departments. MS.
26   Ackland: 1, 8.
27   For an instructive but discouraging chronology of Australian very fast train proposals of that era, see Williams, Paula (1988) *Australian Very Fast Trains-A Chronology*. Canberra: Parliamentary Library. April. https://www.aph.gov.au/About_Parliament/ Parliamentary_Departments/Parliamentary_Library/Publications_Archive/ Background_Papers/bp9798/98bp16. Accessed 16 June 2021.
28   Uren, Tom (1973) Letter to the Prime Minister. January. MS.
29   Coughlan, H. K. and Butler, W. P. (1973) Responsibilities of the Department of Urban and Regional Development and the Cities Commission. MS, DURD.
30   John Paterson Urban Systems (1973) A National Urban Framework. Canberra: Cities Commission, MS.
31   Lloyd and Troy: 98–100.
32   Cities Commission (1974) *Urban and Regional Development Overseas Experts' Reports 1973*. Canberra: Australian Government Publishing Service.
33   Alonso, W. (1971) 'Problems, purposes and implicit policies for a national strategy of urbanization', *Working Paper 158*, National Commission on Population Growth and the American Future. Washington DC. See also Alonso, William (1974) 'A report on Australian urban development issues' in Cities Commission (1974): 1–21.
34   Wilson, R. K. (1978) 'Urban and regional policy', Chapter 6 in Scotton, R. B. and Ferber, Helen (eds.) *Public Expenditure and Social Policy in Australia. Volume I: The Whitlam Years, 1972–75*. Melbourne: Longman Cheshire: 196.
35   Lloyd and Troy: 197.
36   Commoner, Barry (1971) The Closing Circle: Nature, Man, and Technology. New York: Knopf.

37   Powell, A. J. (1973) National Urban Strategy. Paper presented to the Royal Australian Planning Institute Summer School, Terrigal, written 3 December.
38   Lloyd and Troy: 194.
39   Australia, Department of Urban and Regional Development (1974a) Settlement Policy. Urban Policy Weekend paper no. 2, 23–24 February, MS.
40   Wilmoth, David (1974) Current Issues in the Formulation of a National Strategy for Urban and Regional Development. Paper presented at Urban Research Unit Seminar, Australian National University, 22 April.
41   Australia, Department of Urban and Regional Development (1974b) *A National Program for Urban and Regional Development*. Canberra: DURD.
42   Australia, Department of Urban and Regional Development (1974b).
43   Lloyd and Troy: 194.
44   Wilson: 179.
45   Australia, Minister for Urban and Regional Development (1974) *Urban and Regional Development 1974/75 Budget*. Canberra: Australian Government Publishing Service.
46   Logan M. I. (1974) Towards an Action Program. 21 February. MS, DURD.
47   Lloyd and Troy: 26.
48   Neilson, Lyndsay (1974) 'The new cities programme', *Royal Australian Planning Institute Journal* 12, 1: 14–20.
49   Australia, Commonwealth Cabinet (1974) Decision no. 2795, 17 September. Canberra: National Archives of Australia.
50   *Australian Financial Review* (1971) 'Australia needs nine more Canberras', 29 April. Also see Neutze, Max (1973) *The Case for New Cities*. Canberra: Australian Population and the Future Commissioned Paper no. 11.
51   Alonso, William (1970) 'What are new towns for?' *Urban Studies* 7, 1, February: 37–65. https://www.jstor.org/stable/43081140. Accessed 19 June 2021.
52   Australia, Commission of Inquiry into Land Tenures (1973) *First Report of the Commission of Inquiry into Land Tenures*. Canberra: Commission of Inquiry into Land Tenures, subsequently published at Canberra: Australian Government Publishing Service (1974).
53   See Bachrach, Peter and Baratz, Morton S. (1962) 'Two faces of power', *The American Political Science Review* 56, 4 December: 947–952. https://www.jstor.org/stable/1952796. Accessed 19 June 2021.
54   Whitlam, E. G. (1970) Remarks to a meeting of the Institute of Municipal Administration, Canberra. Late May. Reported in *Canberra Times* 'Mr Whitlam urges new Australian "structure"'.
55   Wood, Michael (1977) 'The "new federalisms" of Whitlam and Fraser and their impact on local government', *Politics*, 12, 2: 105. https://www.tandfonline.com/doi/abs/10.1080/00323267708401621. Accessed 19 June 2021.
56   *Western Australian* (1973) 17 December, quoted in Wood (1977).
57   Australia, Productivity Commission (2017) *Horizontal Fiscal Equalisation, Draft Report*, Canberra: Australian Government Publishing Service: 2. https://www.pc.gov.au/inquiries/current/horizontal-fiscal-equalisation/draft/horizontal-fiscal-equalisation-draft.pdf. Accessed 16 June 2021.
58   Whitlam, E. G. (1971) 'A new federalism', *Australian Quarterly* 43, 3: 6–17. https://www.jstor.org/stable/20634451. Accessed 19 June 2021.
59   Australia, Department of Urban and Regional Development (1973a) The role of regions in current Australian government programmes. DURD memo, undated.
60   Australia, Department of Urban and Regional Development (1974c): 14.
61   Troy, P. N. (1976) 'Federalism and urban affairs 1972–75', *Royal Australian Planning Institute Journal*, 14, 1–2: 17. https://www.tandfonline.com/doi/abs/10.1080/00049999.1976.9656482. Accessed 19 June 2021.
62   Australia, Prime Minister (1973) Letter to The Hon. L.H. Barnard, M.P., Minister for Defence, 14 November.
63   Work was under way for Telecom 2000, which did not report in draft until 1975 as Australian Telecommunications Commission (1976) *Telecom 2000. An Exploration of the Long-term Development of Telecommunications in Australia*. Melbourne: ATC; Australian Post Office Commission of Enquiry (1974) *Report of the Commission of Inquiry into the Australian Post Office*. Canberra: Australian Government Publishing Service (Vernon Report). Also see Abbott, Malcolm (2013) 'Microeconomic reform and the Whitlam

Government: the case of telecommunications and post', *Journal of Australian Studies* 37, 4: 503–519. https://www.researchgate.net/publication/271938302_Microeconomic_ reform_and_the_Whitlam_Government_the_case_of_telecommunications_and_post. Accessed 19 June 2021. My interest in a possible PhD thesis topic at Berkeley was in network analysis of communication flows *within* metropolitan areas.

64 Australia, Department of Urban and Regional Development (1973b) Submission by the Department of Urban and Regional Development to the Australian Post Office Committee of Inquiry. Media release 17 August.

65 Wilmoth, David (1973) *Communications and Urban Structure*. Master of Town and Country Planning thesis, Department of Town and Country Planning, University of Sydney.

66 Ecological Society of Australia (1972) *The City as a Life System?* Special Conference Issue of the Journal of the Ecological Society of Australia.

67 Laut, P., Margules, C. and Nix, H. A. (1975) *Australian Biophysical Regions*. Canberra: Australian Government Publishing Service. The first, cruder, physiographic regions were defined in 1951 (Pain, Colin, Gregory, Linda, Wilson, Peter and McKenzie, Neil (2011) *The Physiographic Regions of Australia. Explanatory Notes*. Canberra: Australian Collaborative Land Evaluation Program and National Committee on Soil and Terrain).

68 Australia, Department of Post-war Reconstruction Regional Development Division and National Mapping Office (1949) *Australia, Showing Regions for Development and Decentralisation*. Canberra: Department of Post-war Reconstruction.

69 Australia, Department of Urban and Regional Development (1973c) *Regions. Suggested Delimitation of Regions for the Purposes of Section 17, Grants Commission Act 1973*. Canberra: Australian Government Publishing Service.

70 Special Minister of State (1973). Financial Assistance for Local Governing Bodies: Objectives, Criteria, Information Requirements and Conditions. Canberra: Australian Government Publishing Service.

71 Whitlam, E. G. (1975) cited in 'The debate on regionalism', *Community*, 2, 4: 4.

72 Australia, Prime Minister (1973).

73 Carey: 159, and Butler, W. P. (1974) Notes on the 1974 Programme for Standing IDC on Urban and Regional Development, MS, December.

74 Australia, Department of Urban and Regional Development (1975) *Australian Government Regional Boundaries*. Canberra: Australian Government Publishing Service.

75 Australia, Department of Urban and Regional Development, Secretary (1974) Memo, 3 April.

76 Enfield, John (1974) Comments on Integrated Regional Action Program. Interdepartmental memo, MS.

77 Australia, Department of Urban and Regional Development (1974d) *Australian Government Assistance to Local Government Projects*. Canberra: Australian Government Publishing Service.

78 Carey: 166. Also see Painter, Martin (1979) 'Urban government, urban politics and the fabrication of urban issues: the impossibility of urban policy', *Australian Journal of Public Administration* 38, 4: 335–346. https://www.researchgate.net/publication/229931382_ URBAN_GOVERNMENT_URBAN_POLITICS_AND_THE_FABRICATION_ OF_URBAN_ISSUES_THE_IMPOSSIBILITY_OF_URBAN_POLICY. Accessed 19 June 2021.

79 Carey: 176.

80 Australia, Minister for Urban and Regional Development (1975) Report of the Interdepartmental Committee on Overlap in Australian Government Grants to Local Bodies. Canberra, March. MS. See also Lloyd and Troy: 125.

81 The officers' committee supporting the ministers had on it the key players, chaired by John Enfield of Prime Minister and Cabinet, and including Marie Coleman of Social Welfare Commission, Bill Butler and Michael Keating of DURD and A. R. G. Prowse of Treasury. See Department of Urban and Regional Development (1974) Report of the IDC on Overlap. MS.

82 Whitlam E. G. (1972) *Labor Party Policy Speech 1972*. 13 November, Blacktown Civic Centre, Sydney. https://whitlamdismissal.com/1972/11/13/whitlam-1972-election-policy-speech.html. Accessed 16 June 2021.

83 See Bunker, Raymond (1972) *Town and Country or City and Region?* Parkville: Melbourne University Press.

84 Bunker, Ray (2007) Don Dunstan Oral History Project. Don Dunstan Foundation https://dspace2.flinders.edu.au/xmlui/bitstream/handle/2328/3219/BUNKER_Ray_Cleared.pdf?sequence=2. Accessed 16 June 2021.

85 Australia, National Population Enquiry (1975).

86 Australia, Department of Urban and Regional Development, Strategy Division (1975a). Sydney Metropolitan Strategy. MS, January.

87 Australia, Department of Urban and Regional Development, Strategy Division (1975b) Metropolitan Development. Strategy Division Working Paper 3, Canberra: DURD, November.

88 Purdon R. L. and Wilmoth, G. D. (1972) Submission to the Parliamentary Standing Committee on Public Works. Department of Town and Country Planning, University of Sydney, 25 July.

89 Hawker, G. (1975) Public Administration as a Vehicle for Decentralisation. Urbanisation Seminar on Restructuring Employment Opportunities. Department of Geography, Research School of Pacific Studies, Australian National University, Canberra, 5–6 December.

90 Interdepartmental Committee on Office Location (1973) Australian Government Office Location. Report of the Interdepartmental Committee on Office Location. MS.

91 Australia, Commonwealth Cabinet (1973) Submission no. 786. Australian Government Office Location. Cabinet decision no. 1819, 17 December.

92 Lloyd and Troy: 196.

93 Gourley, Paddy (2017) 'Past government pushes to the bush flopped ... except for the move to Canberra', Canberra Times, 1 May. http://www.canberratimes.com.au/national/public-service/past-government-pushes-to-the-bush-flopped--except-for-the-move-to-canberra-20170426-gvssll.html. Accessed 16 June 2021.

94 Australia, Prime Minister (1975) Speech by the Prime Minister, the Hon. E. G. Whitlam, QC, MP at the Opening of the Meeting of the Capital City Lord Mayors, 27 June 1975, at the Town Hall, City of Sydney. http://pmtranscripts.pmc.gov.au/sites/default/files/original/00003802.pdf. Accessed 16 June 2021.

95 Williams, Paula (1998) Second Sydney Airport – A Chronology. Commonwealth Parliamentary Library Background Paper 20, 1997–98. Canberra: Parliament of Australia 29 June.

96 Hoban, Des (1973) DURD's professionalism and the Galston airport decision. DURD memo to Mr G. Craig: 3.

97 Uren (1994): 303.

98 See Hocking, Jenny (2020) The Palace Letters: The Queen, the Governor-General, and the Plot to Dismiss Gough Whitlam. Melbourne and London: Scribe.

99 Australia, Commonwealth Cabinet (1975) Urban and regional development agreements and progress. Decision no. 19, 19 November. Series A12908, document 7426190. Canberra: National Archives of Australia. The state of play of urban and regional development programs as at July 1975 is well set out in a 'Comprehensive background to urban & regional development ministry programs for the information of ministers in their budget deliberations', Australia, Commonwealth Cabinet (1975) Decision no. 3768, 23 July. Series A5915., document 7500619. Canberra: National Archives of Australia. https://recordsearch.naa.gov.au/SearchNRetrieve/Interface/ViewImage.aspx?B=7500619. Accessed 19 June 2021.

100 For a review locating differing views of DURD's legacy in the broad currents of ideology, see Orchard, Lionel (1999a) 'Shifting visions in national urban and regional policy 1', Australian Planner 36, 1: 20–25 and Orchard, Lionel (1999b) 'Shifting visions in national urban and regional policy 2', Australian Planner 36, 4: 200–209. http://dx.doi.org/10.1080/07293682.1999.9665717. Accessed 16 June 2021, and http://dx.doi.org/10.1080/07293682.1999.9665761. Accessed 16 June 2021.

101 Troy, P. (1993) 'Loves Labor Lost: Whitlam and Urban and Regional Development' in Emy, H., Hughes, O. and Mathews R. (eds) Whitlam Revisited: Policy Development, Policies and Outcomes. Leichhardt: Pluto Press.

102 Wilmoth D., Purdon, R., Strickland, A. and Logan, M. I. (1976) 'Towards a national strategy for urban and regional development', in McMaster, J. and Webb, J. (eds.) Australian Urban Economics. Sydney: Australia and New Zealand Book Company: 7–50.

103 Troy, Patrick (1980) Report to the Development Coordinating Committee of Cabinet, 1980, unpublished NSW government report.

104 Albury–Wodonga developed only 6000 residential lots, some industrial sites and other facilities, before the lands acquired were sold off and the Albury Wodonga Development Corporation wound up in 2014, 41 years later (Mulcahy, Mark and Kotsios, Natalie (2014) 'Axe falls on Albury-Wodonga Corporation' *The Newcastle Herald*. 12 May. http://www.theherald.com.au/story/2275008/axe-falls-on-albury-wodonga-corpora-tion/). Accessed 16 June 2021.

105 Orchard (1999a).

106 Orchard (1999a).

107 For more of the story of the program see Troy, Patrick N. (1978) *A Fair Price*. Sydney: Hale and Iremonger.

108 McPhail, Ian (1978) 'Local government' in Troy, Patrick N. (ed.) *Federal Power in Australia's Cities*. Sydney: Hale and Iremonger: 111.

109 For a detailed review of this particular legacy see Kelly, Andrew H., Dollery, Brian and Grant, Bligh (2009) 'Regional development and local government: three generations of federal intervention', *Australasian Journal of Regional Studies* 15, 2: 171–193. https://ro.uow.edu.au/cgi/viewcontent.cgi?article=1268&context=scipapers. Accessed 21 June 2021.

110 Troy (1992): 23.

111 Australia, Parliament. House of Representatives Standing Committee on Infrastructure, Transport and Cities (2018) *Building Up & Moving Out: Inquiry Into the Australian Government's Role in the Development of Cities*. September. https://parlinfo.aph.gov.au/parlInfo/download/committees/reportrep/024151/toc_pdf/BuildingUp&MovingOut.pdf;fileType=application%2Fpdf. Accessed 1 December 2019. Also see Prime Minister, Minister for Cities, Urban Infrastructure and Population, Minister for Immigration Citizenship and Multicultural Affairs, Minister for Regional Services, Sport, Local Government and Decentralisation, Minister for Education (2019) A Plan for Australia's Future Population. Media Release, 20 Mar 2019. https://www.pm.gov.au/media/plan-australias-future-population. Accessed 1 December 2019.

1   NSW Department of Environment and Planning (1988b) Murray River Regional Environmental Plan No. 1 – Murray River Riparian Land. Sydney: DEP.

2   Very Fast Train Joint Venture (1988) *VFT: Concept Report*. Canberra: Very Fast Train Joint Venture.

CHAPTER 4: DRIFTING IN ASIA

1   *The Straits Times* (1975) 'Bomb terror at Games' *The Straits Times*, 10 December: 1.

2   Thompson, Thomas (1979) *Serpentine*. New York: Carroll & Graf Publishers.

3   Australian Federated Press (2010) 'Sobhraj fails to overturn murder ruling' *Sydney Morning Herald*, 31 July; https://www.smh.com.au/world/sobhraj-fails-to-overturn-murder-ruling-20100730-10zq8.html. Accessed 16 June 2021.

4   Neville, Richard and Clarke, Julie (1979) *The Life and Crimes of Charles Sobhraj*. New York: Macmillan.

5   Murdoch, Lindsay (2010) 'Australian traveller reveals his chilling close encounter', *Sydney Morning Herald*, 31 July. http://www.smh.com.au/world/australian-traveller-reveals-his-chilling-close-encounter-20100730-1101o.html. Accessed 16 June 2021.

6   Indo-Asian News Service (2010) 'Sobhraj braces for battle of books' 20 March.

7   See for example, Murdoch (2010) and *Sobhraj, or How to Be Friends with a Serial Killer*, documentary film produced by Wellmann, Jan and Goel, Anil. London: Faction Films, December 2004.

8   A good introduction to Zen is Watts Alan W. (1957) *The Way of Zen*. New York: Pantheon.

CHAPTER 5: CALIFORNIAN POLITICS AND US NATIONAL URBAN POLICY

1   See, e.g. Markusen, Ann (1979) 'Regionalism and the capitalist state: the case of the United States', *Kapitalistate* 7, Winter: 39–62. Reprinted in revised form in Clavel, P., Goldsmith, W. and Forester, J. (eds.) (1980) *Urban and Regional Planning in an Age of Austerity*, New York: Pergamon Press.

2   See, e.g., Castells, Manuel (1980) *The Economic Crisis and US Society*. Princeton: Princeton University Press.

3 Markusen, Ann and Wilmoth, David (1982) 'The political economy of national urban policy in the USA: 1976–81', *Canadian Journal of Regional Science* V, 1, Spring: 125–144. http://cjrs-rcsr.org/archives/5-1/Markusen.pdf. Accessed 16 June 2021.

4 See https://www.marxists.org/history/usa/pubs/kapitalstate/index.htm. Accessed 16 June 2021.

5 Wilmoth, David (1980) 'US national urban policy and a state theory of policy formation', *Kapitalistate* 8: 164–167.

6 Marcuse, Herbert (1964) *One-Dimensional Man: Studies in the Ideology of Advanced Industrial Society*. London: Routledge & Kegan Paul; Miliband, Ralph (1969) *The State in Capitalist Society*. New York: Basic Books; Mollenkopf, John (1983) *The Contested City*. Princeton: Princeton University Press; Poulantzas, Nicos (1978) *Political Power and Social Classes* (translated from 1975 edition, Timothy O'Hagen). London: Verso Editions.

7 National Urban Policy Collective (1978) *President Carter's National Urban Policy: A Critical Analysis*. Berkeley CA: University of California, Berkeley; US Department of Housing and Urban Development (1978) *The President's National Urban Policy Report*, Washington DC: USGPO.

8 Weiss, Marc A. and Schoenberger, Erica (2015) 'Peter Hall and the Western Urban and Regional Collective at the University of California, Berkeley', *Built Environment* 41, 1: 63–77. https://www.ingentaconnect.com/content/alex/benv/2015/00000041/00000001/art00007;jsessionid=1shzwur8xkj4k.x-ic-live-01#. Accessed 21 June 2021.

9 Hartman, Chester W. (1974) *Yerba Buena: Land Grab and Community Resistance in San Francisco*. San Francisco: Glide Publications.

10 Clavel, Pierre, Forester, John and Goldsmith, William (1980) *Urban and Regional Planning in an Age of Austerity*. New York: Pergamon Press.

11 Bluestone, Barry and Harrison, Bennett (1982) *The Deindustrialization of America*. New York: Basic Books.

12 On some days when I felt like skiing, I hopped on a plane from Oakland to Denver for Winter Park and came back the same night, the flight for free!

13 I'm grateful to Mark Weiss for this anecdote.

14 US White House (1978) New Partnership to Conserve America's Communities: a Status Report on the President's Urban Policy. Washington DC: White House, June: 13.

15 US White House: 13.

16 Giddens, A. (1984) The Constitution of Society: Outline of the Theory of Structuration. Cambridge: Polity Press; Wilmoth, David (1986a) 'Structure and agency in the formation of national urban policy in the USA 1976–1980', *Progress in Planning* 25, 2, 1986: 84–130. http://www.sciencedirect.com/science/journal/03059006/25/part/P2. Accessed 16 June 2021.

17 Jantsch, Erich (1967) *Technological Forecasting in Perspective*. Paris: OECD. http://en.laprospective.fr/dyn/anglais/memoire/prevtechen.pdf. Accessed 16 June 2021.

18 Alcaly, Roger E. and Mermelstein, David (eds.) (1977) *The Fiscal Crisis of American Cities*. New York: Vintage Books.

19 Weiss, Marc (2020) Personal communication.

20 See Elbaum, Max (2002) Revolution in the Air: Sixties Radicals Turn to Lenin, Mao and Che. London and New York: Verso, and, by a SFSU colleague, DeLeon, Richard Edward (1992) Left Coast City: Progressive Politics in San Francisco, 1975–1991. Lawrence: University of Kansas Press.

21 Anonymous (1977) An Urban Perspective for the Northern California Alliance. MS.

22 Anonymous (1977) A Critique of the Northern California Alliance. *Encyclopaedia of Anti-Revisionism On-Line*. https://www.marxists.org/history/erol/ncm-6/nca-critique.htm. Accessed 16 June 2021.

23 We used Cornforth, Maurice Campbell (1960) *Materialism and the Dialectical Method*. New York: International Publishers, a good exposition.

24 Bundy, McGeorge (1977) 'The issue before the court: who gets ahead in America?', *The Atlantic*, 240, 5: 41–54.

25 Elbaum: 243.

26 Wilmoth, David (1977) 'Our man in Cuba', *Concrete* 1, 4, October 1977: 1, 5.

27 For an account of urban policy in the years before see Acosta, Maruja and Hardoy, Jorge E. (1991) *Urban Reform in Revolutionary Cuba*. New Haven: Antilles Research Program, Yale University.

28 Eckstein, Susan (1977) 'The debourgeoisement of Cuban cities', in Horowitz, Irving L. (ed.) *Cuban Communism*. New Brunswick: Transaction: 443–474.

29 Lawrence, Peter (1964) Road Belong Cargo: A Study of the Cargo Movement in the Southern Madang District, New Guinea. Manchester: Manchester University Press: 8.

CHAPTER 6: THE ROUGH AND TUMBLE OF SYDNEY'S PLANNING

1 Jay, Christopher (1982) 'As the resources boom ebbs Wran tightens NSW's belt', *Australian Financial Review*, 11 June: 12–13.

2 Gleeson, Gerald (1982) Annotation on Letter Advising Ministers of Infrastructure Financing Policy, MS, 26 February.

3 See Raymond Bunker (1983) *Urban Consolidation: the Experience of Sydney, Melbourne and Adelaide*, publication 111. Canberra: Australian Institute of Urban Studies.

4 Bedford, Hon E. L. (1981) 'A programme for urban consolidation', Speech to Local Government Association Conference, 26 October.

5 e.g. NSW Department of Environment and Planning (1984) *Planning Issues in the Sydney Region: Urban Consolidation*. Sydney: DEP.

6 Bedford: 2.

7 NSW Cabinet Decision (1981). Government Initiatives in Relation to Multi-unit Dwellings in the Sydney Region. MS.

8 e.g. see *Sydney Morning Herald* (1981) 'Red brick myths'. Editorial, 14 November: 12.

9 Reid, Helen, Jones, Janet and Wilmoth, David (1983) The development of urban consolidation policies in Sydney. Paper presented to ANZAAS Congress, Perth, 18 May.

10 Wilmoth, David (1982a) Urban Consolidation Policy and Social Equity. Paper presented to a Conference on Urban Consolidation and Equity, Centre for Urban and Environmental Studies, Macquarie University, 8 November.

11 Glascott, Joseph (1982) 'State plan for town houses, villas', *Sydney Morning Herald*, 25 October 1982: 1.

12 Municipality of North Sydney Town Clerk (1982) 'Re: N.S.W. Government's Urban Consolidation Programme. Further Recommendations from the Central Policy Division – Department of Environment and Planning.' Letter to the Town/Shire Clerk, Maitland City Council. 24 September.

13 NSW Department of Environment and Planning (1982a) *Draft State Environmental Planning Policy – Medium Density Housing*. Circular no. 40, 19 October.

14 NSW Department of Environment and Planning (1982b) *Draft State Environmental Planning Policy – Medium Density Housing*. Circular no. 43, 15 November. See Coultan, Mark (1982) 'Bedford in bid to defuse housing row' *Sydney Morning Herald*, 11 December.

15 Manidis Roberts (1982) Urban Consolidation: Concrete Development Opportunities. Consultant report. Sydney: Manidis Roberts Pty Ltd.

16 e.g. Reid *et al*.

17 See Reid *et al* and consultant reports, including Pratt, Iain (1986) *A review of Demand for Multi-unit Housing in the Sydney Region*. Sydney: DEP, March.

18 Hickie, David (1983) 'Goodbye to the quarter-acre dream', *The National Times*, 16–22 Jan: 21–22.

19 Troy, Patrick (1996) *The Perils of Urban Consolidation*. Sydney: The Federation Press: 129.

20 See Troy (1996): 160; Troy, Patrick (2013) 'Consolidation policy and its effects on the city', in Ruming, Kristian, Randolph, Bill and Gurran, Nicole (eds.) *State of Australian Cities Conference 2013*. Sydney: State of Australian Cities: 15; Newman, P. and Kenworthy, J. (1999) *Sustainability and Cities: Overcoming Automobile Dependence*, Washington DC: Island Press. For a transcript of one Troy versus Newman debate on ABC Radio National see http://www.sos.org.au/new_newsletters/March_2006_troy. htm. Accessed 16 June 2021.

21 Wilmoth, David (2004a) 'The 1980s: new directions for planning', in Toon, John and Falk, Jonathan (eds.) *Sydney: Planning or Politics: Town Planning for Sydney Region since 1945*. Sydney: Planning Research Centre, University of Sydney: 111–134.

22   New South Wales Department of Planning, Industry & Environment (2020) *Greater Sydney Regional Housing Activity* https://data.nsw.gov.au/data/dataset/sydney-region-dwellings/resource/058e4f0b-06b8-4ab0-a444-6fe65c23e4f6. Accessed 21 June 2021. See Searle, Glen (1995) Fiscal and Environmental Crisis versus Ideology and Local Amenity: Urban Consolidation Policy in Sydney, Paper presented to Annual Conference of the Association of Collegiate Schools of Planning, Detroit, October.

23   Troy (1980); Paterson, John (1982) Thumb nail history of metropolitan planning. NSW Department of Environment and Planning MS; NSW State Planning Authority (1968) *Sydney Region Outline Plan*. Sydney: State Planning Authority.

24   Paterson, John (1982) Urban Policy Review, Newcastle – Sydney – Wollongong Urban Region, Content and Work Plan, DEP MS, 3 February.

25   Meyer, Bob (2005) 'Sidney Luker Memorial Lecture 2005: Fifty years of Sydney's planning,' *New Planner* 67: 10–1; Spearritt, Peter and DeMarco, Christina (1988) *Planning Sydney's Future*. Sydney: Allen & Unwin.

26   NSW Planning and Environment Commission (1980) *Review: Sydney Region Outline Plan*. Sydney: NSW Government Printer.

27   Transport Strategy Advisory Committee (1982) *Sydney Urban Expansion Study – First Cut*. Report to the NSW Urban Development Committee, September. These expert groups have disappeared from most state governments now. In NSW and Victoria they were outsourced to academic centres that had to survive by begging subscription fees from state agencies, which after a time were not forthcoming.

28   Sydney Area Transportation Study (1974) *Sydney Area Transportation Study*, Sydney: NSW Ministry of Transport.

29   Wilmoth, David (1982b) Sydney Urban Expansion – First Cut. DEP Memo to Director DEP, 17 September.

30   NSW Department of Environment and Planning (1983) Towards a Metropolitan Strategy for Sydney, Parts I and II. DEP report for the Urban Development Committee, December.

31   Kacirek, J. P. F. (1983) *South Macarthur*. Macarthur Development Board Report. 4 May.

32   Wilmoth, David (1984a) Consultations on the Metropolitan Strategy Progress Report, Report to the UDC, CPD DEP report, 19 March and Stone, Carolyn (1984) Metropolitan Strategy. Report on Consultation to Date. DEP CPD memo, March.

33   Self, Peter (1984) Report on the Development of a Metropolitan Strategy for the Sydney Region, Annexure to Progress Report on Metropolitan Strategy, Head, CPD, DEP, 6 April.

34   NSW Department of Environment and Planning (1988a) *Sydney Into Its Third Century: Metropolitan Strategy for the Sydney Region*. Sydney: Department of Environment and Planning; also see Meyer, Bob (1993) 'Metropolitan strategies for the Sydney Region' in Freestone, R. (ed.) *Spirited Cities*. Sydney: The Federation Press: 209–224.

35   See e.g. Wilmoth, David (1988a) 'The urban impact of population growth' in Day, Lincoln H. and Rowland, D. T. (eds.): *How Many More Australians? The Resource and Environmental Conflicts*. Melbourne: Longman Cheshire: 109–120 and Wilmoth, David (1983) Population issues and metropolitan planning in Sydney. Paper presented to Seminar on Australian Population Issues, Research School of Social Sciences, ANU and Department of Immigration and Ethnic Affairs, Canberra, 15 September. I also taught a course on migration and cities at UNSW in 1987.

36   Murphy, Jason (2011) 'Sydney's slide puts brakes on economy' *Australian Financial Review*, 19 December https://www.afr.com/politics/federal/sydney-s-slide-puts-brakes-on-economy-20111219-i44v9. Accessed 16 June 2021.

37   See Wilmoth, David (1987) 'Metropolitan planning for Sydney' in Hamnett, Stephen and Bunker, Raymond (eds): *Urban Australia: Planning Issues and Policies*, Melbourne: Mansell: 158–188.

38   NSW Department of Environment and Planning (1989) *Sydney Into Its Third Century: Metropolitan Strategy for the Sydney Region 1989 Update*. Sydney: NSW Department of Environment and Planning.

39   For a good analysis of Sydney's transport infrastructure issues of this period see Searle, Glen (1999): 'New roads, new rail lines, new profits: privatisation and Sydney's recent transport development', *Urban Policy and Research* 17, 2: 111–121. https://www.tandfonline.com/doi/abs/10.1080/08111149908727797. Accessed 21 June 2021.

40 e.g. NSW State Transport Study Group (1985) *Sydney Urban Expansion Studies: Long Term Issues Study*. Sydney: State Transport Study Group.

41 For an overview of Sydney's planning in the 1980s see Wilmoth (2004).

42 For more details see Wilmoth, David (1988b) District Centres Policy and Practice in Sydney, paper presented to 21st Congress of the Royal Australian Planning Institute Melbourne, 29 August.

43 NSW Department of Environment and Planning (1984a) *A Centres Policy for the Sydney Region: Discussion Paper*. Sydney: Department of Environment and Planning.

44 See Wilmoth, David (1988b).

45 NSW Department of Environment and Planning (1984b) *Draft Sydney Regional Environmental Plan (Commercial Centres)*. Sydney: DEP, June. Retailing was a distinctive metropolitan planning arena not covered in this story. See Wilmoth, David and Sommerville, Ross (1984b) Towards a Retail Policy for Metropolitan Sydney. Paper presented to Australian Institute of Urban Studies Workshop on Assessing Economic Impact of Retail Centres Development, Sydney, 23–24 May.

46 *Sydney Morning Herald* (1982) 'Go-west orders for Govt departments', *Sydney Morning Herald*, 23 July: 1.

47 NSW Development Coordinating Committee of Cabinet (1982) Meeting Report, 12 May; NSW Public Service Board (1984) 'Relocation of government departments to the suburbs' *Public Service Notices*. 10 October: 1. Also see Searle, Glen (1997) 'Ideology and New South Wales State Government Head Office Relocation', *Regional Policy and Practice* 6, 1: 13–19.

48 For a later recounting of efficiency problems see Iffland, Katrina (1988) 'Exodus – or how 5,000 Govt staff left the city', *Sydney Morning Herald*. 30 August. NSW Department of Environment and Planning and NSW Public Service Board (2015) *Review of the Suburban Office Relocation Programme*. Sydney: Department of Environment and Planning, June.

49 Plant Location International (Australia) Pty Ltd (1986) *Private Office Suburbanisation in Sydney*. NSW Division Occasional Paper, Australian Institute of Urban Studies.

50 Morris, Mike (1987) 'Change of plans on relocation program', *Liverpool Champion*, 25 February; NSW Public Service Board (1988) 'Relocation of government departments to the suburbs' *Public Service Notices*. 30 March: 3.

51 Wilmoth, David (1984b) 'Urban impacts of foreign and local investment in Australia: directions for further research' in Adrian, Colin (ed.): *Urban Impacts of Foreign and Local Investment in Australia*. Canberra: Australian Institute of Urban Studies: 277–289.

52 For example, see Amalgamated Metals, Foundry and Shipwrights Union (1984) *Jobs and Manufacturing Prospects for Western Sydney*, Sydney: Amalgamated Metals, Foundry and Shipwrights Union; Horinek, Josef (1983) *Youth and Employment Prospects in Western Sydney*. Blacktown: Western Sydney Region Organisation of Councils; and, later, Blakely, Edward J. and Fagan, Robert H. (1988) *Metropolitan Strategy in Sydney: Employment Distribution and Policy Issues*. Monograph 36, Institute of Urban and Regional Development, University of California, April.

53 Larcombe, Graham and Blakely, Edward (1983) *Prospects for Employment Generation in the Illawarra*, Sydney: Department of Environment and Planning.

54 Mee, Kathleen (1994) 'Dressing up the suburbs: representations of western Sydney' in Gibson, Katherine and Watson, Sophie (eds.): *Metropolis Now: Planning and the Urban in Contemporary Australia*. Leichhardt: Pluto Press Australia: 60–77.

55 Troy, Patrick (1980).

56 Wilmoth, David (1992) 'Managing urban expansion: Sydney's urban development programme', *Urban Policy and Research* 5, 4: 156–166. https://www.tandfonline.com/doi/abs/10.1080/08111148708551313?journalCode=cupr20. Accessed 16 June 2021.

57 Parliament of NSW, Public Accounts Committee of the Forty-eighth Parliament (1985) *Eighteenth Report. Economic Urban Development. Inquiry Concerning the Operations of the Land Commission of New South Wales*. Sydney: NSW Public Accounts Committee : 15–17.

58 Wilmoth, David (2005) Urban Infrastructure and Metropolitan Planning: Connection and Disconnection. Paper presented to State of Australian Cities Conference, Griffith University, Brisbane, 30 November–2 December. https://apo.org.au/sites/default/files/resource-files/2005-12/apo-nid60399.pdf. Accessed 16 June 2021.

59   e.g. Schmidt, William (1985) 'American private developers baulk at paying for commu-
      nity services', *Financial Review* 11 November.
60   e.g. NSW Department of Environment and Planning (1984c) *Draft Circular, Guidelines
      on Section 94 Contributions Relating to Residential Zones in New South Wales*, Sydney:
      DEP; Grealy, Michael (1986) 'Mr Carr's levy plan may cost the councils', *Sydney
      Morning Herald*, 1 April: 17.
61   NSW Department of Environment and Planning (1986). *Illawarra Regional
      Environmental Plan No. 1.* Sydney: DEP.
62   Glen Searle reminded me of this.
63   NSW Department of Environment and Planning (1988b) Murray River Regional
      Environmental Plan No. 1 – Murray River Riparian Land. Sydney: DEP.
64   Very Fast Train Joint Venture (1988) *VFT: Concept Report.* Canberra: Very Fast Train
      Joint Venture.
65   Wilmoth, David (1986b) 'Planning in China: report of the 1984 AIUS delegation',
      Australian Urban Studies 13, 4 February: 26–28.
66   Kanaley, David and Reffell, Gillian (1986) Planning and Development Prospects in
      Sanshui County. New South Wales Contribution to the Sanshui Planning Experiment.
      Sydney: NSW Department of Environment and Planning.
67   Whitlamdismissal.com (1977) 'Did The Earth Move For You Too, Dear...' 30
      November. See http://whitlamdismissal.com/1977/11/30/did-the-earth-move-nichol-
      son.html. Accessed 21 June 2021.
68   Wilmoth, David and Forbes, Dean (1988a) 'Urban opportunities in Tianjin', *Australian
      Urban Studies* 15, 4, February: 16–17. https://doi.org/10.1080/07293682.1988.9657399.
      Accessed 19 June 2021; Wilmoth, David and Forbes, Dean (1988b) 'Opportunities for
      urban planning in Tianjin, China', *Australian Planner* 26, 4: 19–33; http://dx.doi.org/10.
      1080/07293682.1988.9657399. Accessed 16 June 2021.
69   Wilmoth, David and Forbes, Dean (1990) 'The spatial development of Tianjin' in
      Forbes, Dean and Linge, Godfrey (eds.): *China's Spatial Economy: Recent Development
      and Reform.* Hong Kong: Oxford University Press: 160–180.
70   Wilmoth, David (2004b) Tianjin's Capacity for Urban Planning and Development.
      Report from Tianjin visit 27–28 November. China Development Bank and World Bank
      Institute International Symposium on City Planning, 24–29 November.
71   Wilmoth and Forbes (1988b): 30.
72   See Li Xiaoxi, Duan Ruijun, and Zhang Huanzhao (2010) 'A case study of Tianjin
      Economic-Technological Development Area' in Zeng, Douglas Zhihua (ed.) *Building
      Engines for Growth and Competitiveness in China: Experience with Special Economic Zones
      and Industrial Clusters*, Chapter 3. Washington DC: The World Bank: 87–121.
73   Preen, Mark (2018) 'The Beijing-Tianjin-Hebei Integration Plan', *China Briefing.* 26
      April. https://www.china-briefing.com/news/the-beijing-tianjin-hebei-integration-plan/.
      Accessed 21 June 2021.
74   Alexander, Nathan and Rushman, Gordon (eds.) (1994) *Tianjin Urban Heritage
      Conservation Strategy.* Melbourne: Australian Institute of Urban Studies, Victorian
      Division.

CHAPTER 7: HELPING BUILD A UNIVERSITY

1   Murray-Smith, Stephen and Dare, Anthony John (1987) *The Tech: A Centenary History
      of the Royal Melbourne Institute of Technology.* Melbourne: Hyland House; RMIT
      Centenary Commission. 1997. *Report of the Centenary Commission.* Melbourne: RMIT.
      23 November.
2   Dare, Tony (undated) A brief history of RMIT. Adapted by Richard Peterson with
      additional text by Peter Y. Navaretti and Margaret L. Ruwoldt. http://www.rmit.edu.
      au/heritage/history.htm (no longer posted online).
3   Glass, Robert (2005) *RMIT 1980–2000.* Melbourne: RMIT University: 245. I am
      indebted to Bob for his encyclopaedic coverage of these years of RMIT's history, used
      in these pages extensively. He makes the point (p. 245) that Chris Ryan influenced the
      commonwealth ministers at the time as they wanted to burnish their environmental
      image as the Tasmanian Greens had just won seats there.
4   Wilmoth, David with Victoria, Department of Planning and Housing (1990) *Urban
      Development in Victoria: A Discussion Paper.* Melbourne: Department of Planning and
      Housing.

5   Eccles, Des, O'Connor, Kevin and Wilmoth, David (1989) *Melbourne's Future Growth: Issues and Concerns*. Report prepared for Municipal Association of Victoria, Urban and Development Institute of Australia and Housing Industry Association, Melbourne, September.

6   This was expressed in Victorian Post-Secondary Education Commission (1992) *Strategic Planning Issues for Higher Education in Victoria*. Melbourne: Victorian Post-Secondary Education Commission, March and Victoria, Office of Higher Education (1992) *Strategic Plan for Higher Education in Victoria*. Melbourne: Office of Higher Education, August.

7   Beanland, David, Bangay, Bob, Gwynne, Gabrielle and Milton-Smith, John (1988) Report of the Integrated Task Force on Some Changes Related to the Creation of an Integrated University of Technology. Director's Advisory Committee Report, RMIT. August.

8   Australia, Department of Employment, Education and Training and Dawkins, John [(1987) *Higher Education: a Policy Discussion Paper*. Canberra: Australian Government Publishing Service, December; Australia, Department of Employment, Education and Training and Dawkins, John (1988) *Higher Education: a Policy Statement*. Canberra: Australian Government Publishing Service. May.

9   Brett, André (2018) 'The Victorian College of Pharmacy: a case study of amalgamation failure and success in Australian higher education', *History of Education* 47, 5, 644–662. https://www.tandfonline.com/doi/full/10.1080/0046760X.2018.1459877. Accessed 21 June 2021.

10   Victorian Post-Secondary Education Commission (1988) *Options for the Development of Higher Education in Victoria*. Melbourne: Victorian Post-Secondary Education Commission.

11   Glass (2005): 73.

12   Commonwealth-State Joint Working Party on University Education in the Western Suburbs of Melbourne (1989) *University education in the western suburbs of Melbourne*. Melbourne: Interim Report of the Commonwealth-State Joint Working Party.

13   Much later, in 2009 when Melbourne's east–west job imbalance had worsened, I was hired by the state government to help map out a university-led advanced economy cluster.

14   Glass (2005): 179.

15   Beanland, David (2021) Personal communication, 2 June.

16   Glass (2005): 179.

17   Glass (2005): 182.

18   Glass (2005): 180.

19   Wilmoth, David (1990a) Acting Director Comments to the Hon Peter Hall MLC for Gippsland Province, 8 May, cited in Glass (2005): 183.

20   Glass (2005): 183.

21   *The Age* (1991) 'The high price of stubborn pride', *The Age*, 27 March: 13.

22   Glass (2005): 189.

23   Now some parts of universities do have a Royal Charter e.g. Royal Holloway within the University of London.

24   Glass (2005): 190.

25   Parliament of Victoria (1992) *Royal Melbourne Institute of Technology Act, no. 42 of 1992*. http://www.austlii.edu.au/au/legis/vic/hist_act/rmiota1992444.pdf.

26   Beanland, David (1992) 'RMIT: 105 years of excellence', *Australian Campus Review Weekly*, 22–28 October: 12.

27   Sweetnam Godfrey and Ord (1993) *RMIT Strategic Facilities Plan*. Melbourne: Sweetnam Godfrey and Ord Pty Ltd.

28   UNESCO defines a learning city as a city that: effectively mobilizes its resources in every sector to promote inclusive learning from basic to higher education; revitalizes learning in families and communities; facilitates learning for and in the workplace; extends the use of modern learning technologies; enhances quality and excellence in learning; and fosters a culture of learning throughout life.' UNESCO Global Network of Learning Cities, https://uil.unesco.org/lifelong-learning/learning-cities#:~:text=UNESCO%20defines%20a%20learning%20city,learning%20in%20 families%20and%20communities%3B&text=enhances%20quality%20and%20ex-cellence%20in,culture%20of%20learning%20throughout%20life. Accessed 16 June 2021.

29   See https://uil.unesco.org/lifelong-learning/learning-cities.
30   Elliot, Peter (2003) City Campus Urban Spaces Framework 2003. RMIT MS. Also see Durance, Paula Christine (2016) Bringing the World to Melbourne: Transnationalism, Agency and Contributions of International Students to Making a City, 2000–2010. PhD Thesis, The University of Queensland, School of Education: 164. https://espace. library.uq.edu.au/view/UQ:415136. Accessed 16 June 2021.
31   See https://www.rmit.edu.au/maps/melbourne-city-campus/building-20. Accessed 16 June 2021.
32   See Wilmoth, David (1994) Information Technology Services and Local Economic Development: the Case of Pacific Central. Paper presented to International Workshop on Information Technology and Regional Development, Ogaki, Japan, 27–29 November.
33   KPMG Real Estate Group (2003) *RMIT University Strategic Property Review*. October. MS.
34   Newman, John Henry Cardinal (1910) *The Idea of a University. Defined and Illustrated*. London: Longmans, Green and Co.
35   Boyer, Ernest L. (1990) *Scholarship Reconsidered: Priorities of the Professoriate*. New York: Carnegie Foundation for the Advancement of Teaching.
36   The Melbourne College of Decoration and Design in 1993, the Melbourne College of Printing and Graphic Arts in 1995, and the Melbourne Institute of Textiles in 1999.
37   RMIT (1992) *Annual Report 1991*. See Glass (2005): 351 free following for a fuller account.
38   Australia, Higher Education Council (1992) *Higher Education: Achieving Quality*. Canberra: Australian Government Publishing Service; Australia, Committee for Quality Assurance in Higher Education (1995) *Report on 1994 Quality Reviews*. December. Canberra: Australian Government Publishing Service. Australia, Committee for Quality Assurance in Higher Education (1996) *Report on 1995 Quality Reviews*. Canberra: Australian Government Publishing Service.
39   RMIT (1993) Quality at RMIT: Portfolio Submitted to Committee for Quality Assurance in Higher Education. Melbourne: RMIT, 3 vols.
40   Australia, Committee for Quality Assurance in Higher Education (1994) *Report on 1993 Quality Review*, Canberra: Australian Government Publishing Service.
41   Beanland, David (1993) 'Quality: a message from the Vice-Chancellor', *RMIT Openline. The University Newspaper*, 8 December.
42   Australia, Committee for Quality Assurance in Higher Education (1995).
43   McMullen, Denis (1996) 'The Committee for Quality Assurance in Higher Education: A Critical Review', *Student Essay*. https://search.informit.org/doi/abs/10.3316/ aeipt.127111. Accessed 16 June 2021.
44   Parratt, Elisabeth and Holian, Rosalie (1999) ISO 9000 Certification: Is it Worth it? *RMIT School of Management Working Paper* No. WP 2/99, July.
45   Maslen, Geoff (1999) 'Senior staff upheavals batter RMIT', *Campus Review*, 27 January: 5.
46   RMIT (2002) Report of the RMIT Refugee Support Task Force. October. Melbourne: RMIT.
47   Davy, Gillian (2003) 'RMIT pledges support for refugees', *Green Left*. 26 February, Issue 527. https://www.greenleft.org.au/content/rmit-pledges-support-refugees. Accessed 21 June 2021.
48   Dunkin, Ruth (2003) 'Message from the Vice-Chancellor' in GS@RMIT. Invitation: Founding Partnerships. RMIT: 5.
49   Samson, Katelyn (2004) *Universities and the Sustainability Saga: A Case Study of the Rhetoric and Reality of Sustainability at RMIT University*. Thesis submitted for the degree of Bachelor of Social Science (Environment) (Hons), School of Social Science and Planning, RMIT University, November: 51.
50   Association of University Leaders for a Sustainable Future (1990) *The Talloires Declaration. 10 Point Action Plan*. https://www.iau-hesd.net/sites/default/files/docu- ments/talloire.pdf. Accessed 16 June 2021.
51   Samson: 45.
52   RMIT (2021) *RMIT Annual Report 2020*. Melbourne: RMIT: 50. https://www.rmit. edu.au/about/governance-management/annual-reports. Accessed 30 June 2021.
53   Del Rio, Victor (2007) *High-Profile Crisis Management in Australian and New Zealand Organisations*. Doctor of Philosophy thesis, Faculty of Economics and Commerce,

The University of Melbourne. October. https://minerva-access.unimelb.edu.au/bitstream/handle/11343/39399/67745_00004245_01_HPCM_Final_01052008.pdf?sequence=1&isAllowed=y. Accessed 21 June 2021.

54   Later the two systems became products of the same merged company.

55   A Gartner report for The University of Melbourne listed contributing technical factors as the decision to use Windows 2000 for servers despite the PeopleSoft system more commonly running on Unix, RMIT being insufficiently experienced with Windows 2000; concurrent use of two versions of PeopleSoft; use of undersized application servers. The system was on Windows NT 4.0, then was moved to Windows 2000 without regard for the extra resources needed; a hardware and job-scheduling set-up in which the Cobol-heavy PeopleSoft tended to slow down other work; use of too basic a level of Windows 2000; RMIT use of the Advanced Server platform, not the more scalable Datacentre Server; a fragile interface to SAP's R/3 record system; RMIT going to the software vendors only when "the internal resources exhausted their capabilities"; and, because RMIT chose to run the system on Windows 2000, a relatively new platform, having trouble finding sufficiently skilled staff.

56   See Hammer, M. and Champy, J. (1993) *Reengineering the Corporation: A Manifesto for Business Revolution*. New York: HarperBusiness, revised updated edition, HarperCollins, 2004.

57   Victorian Auditor-General (2003a) *Report on Public Sector Agencies. Results of Special Reviews and Financial Statement Audits*. 30 June 2002. Melbourne: Government Printer for the State of Victoria. February 2003: 58–88. https://www.parliament.vic.gov.au/papers/govpub/VPARL2003-06No4.pdf. Accessed 16 June 2021.

58   I am grateful to Ruth Dunkin for this point.

59   *The Age* (2002) 'Fix computer problem now, RMIT ordered', *The Age*, 28 June; Victorian Auditor-General (2003b) *Report of the Auditor-General on RMIT's Finances*. Melbourne: Government Printer for the State of Victoria. June. https://www.parliament.vic.gov.au/papers/govpub/VPARL2003-06No22.pdf. Accessed 16 June 2021.

60   Victorian Auditor-General (2003b): 20; Victoria. Auditor-General of Victoria (2003a): 64, 6.1

61   RMIT (2004a) 'Operating result from ordinary activities before income tax' in Summary of Performance for the Years 1999 to 2003' *RMIT Annual Report 2003*: 55. https://www.rmit.edu.au/content/dam/rmit/documents/about/Governance-and-management/annual-reports/2003-financial-annual-report.pdf. Accessed 16 June 2021.

62   Victorian Auditor-General (2003a): 66.

63   Ketchell, Misha (2003) 'RMIT to scrap $47m software system', *The Age*, 28 February. https://www.theage.com.au/education/rmit-to-scrap-47m-software-system-20030228-gdvart.html. Accessed 21 June 2021.

64   *Crikey.com.au* (2003a) 'Exposed: the Ruth Dunkin PhD' 29 June and *Crikey.com.au*. (2003b) 'RMIT's deficit worsens, bonuses rise' 23 October.

65   For that new structure see RMIT (2002) *Annual Report 2001*. Melbourne: RMIT: 28.

66   Button, James and Ketchell, Misha (2003) 'The woman who offers leadership without easy answers', *The Age*. 8 February 2003. http://www.theage.com.au/articles/2003/02/07/1044579934946.html. Accessed 16 June 2021.

67   Buckell, Jim (2003) '"If I'm guilty, why doesn't someone sack me?"', *The Australian*, 11 June: 29.

68   See Button and Ketchell.

69   See Dunkin, Ruth (2000) From Entrepreneurial University to Innovative University. Inaugural Address. 30 October. Melbourne: RMIT Corporate Affairs.

70   Button and Ketchell.

71   Hamilton, Stuart (2002) *Review of University Governance*. Melbourne: Knowledge and Skills Victoria.

72   The arguments for RMIT Council are set out in Wilmoth, D. (2003) The Governance of RMIT's Controlled Entities: Notes for Council Discussion, Paper prepared for RMIT Council Retreat 1–2 August.

73   See Campbell A., Goold, M. and Alexander, M. (1995) 'The quest for parenting advantage', *Harvard Business Review*, March–April: 120–130 and FitzGerald, McCann (2017) 'Managing subsidiaries: a balancing act', *Lexology*, 7 March. https://www.lexology.com/library/detail.aspx?g=2c0c7957-f6b1-43e2-b715-899d4a188ee1. Accessed 1 June 2018.

74   Rood, David and Guy, Roslyn (2004) 'Head resigns from troubled RMIT', *The Age*, 28 August, 2004. https://www.theage.com.au/national/head-resigns-from-troubled-rmit-20040828-gdyjep.html. Accessed 16 June 2021.

75   Rood and Guy.

76   Maslen, Geoff (2004) 'RMIT's problems have not gone away', *Campus Review*, 8 September.

77   For example, *The Age* (2004) 'Turnaround keeps RMIT head at the top', 17 April. https://www.theage.com.au/national/turnaround-keeps-rmit-head-at-the-top-20040417-gdxoyn.html. Accessed 16 June 2021.

78   *The Age* (2005) 'RMIT's new chief one of a vice-chancellor pair', *The Age*, 22 January, 2005. https://www.theage.com.au/national/rmits-new-chief-one-of-a-vice-chancellor-pair-20050122-gdzeyy.html. Accessed 16 June 2021.

79   Gardner, Margaret (2005) Vice-Chancellor's Inaugural Address: A Tale of Two Cities. RMIT. 23 May. MS.

80   Drucker, Peter (2001) 'The second half of your life', chapter 21 in Drucker, Peter F. *The Essential Drucker*. Oxford: Butterworth; and Drucker, Peter F. (1999) 'Managing oneself,' *Harvard Business Review* 77, 2: 64–74.

81   Fang Po-Ching https://www.aic-iac.org/wp-content/uploads/Po-Ching-Fang_CV%EF%BC%8BStatement.pdf. Accessed 16 June 2021.

82   See Mintzberg, Henry (1993) 'The pitfalls of strategic planning', *California Management Review* 36, 1, Fall: 36–47. http://www1.ximb.ac.in/users/fac/DPdash/dpdash.nsf/0/7ff4b4eba439d790e52568b2001830ff?OpenDocument. Accessed 21 June 2021.

83   Ancona, Deborah, Malone, Thomas W., Orlikowski, Wanda J. and Senge, Peter M. (2007) 'In praise of the incomplete leader', *Harvard Business Review* 85, 2: 92–100, 156. https://pubmed.ncbi.nlm.nih.gov/17345683/. Accessed 21 June 2021.

CHAPTER 8: INTERNATIONALISING THE 'WORKING MAN'S COLLEGE'

1   Glass, Robert (2001) *RMIT as an International Education Provider*. Discussion Paper no. 1. Analysis of the Development of the Royal Melbourne Institute of Technology 1980–2000. 31 August. MS.

2   Australia (1984) *Report of the Committee to Review the Australian Overseas Aid Program*. Canberra: Australian Government Publishing Service: 90–93, cited in Glass (2001).

3   Australian Government (1984) *Mutual Advantage: Report of the Committee of Review of Private Overseas Student Policy* (The Goldring report). Canberra: Australian Government Publishing Service, cited in Durance: 5.

4   Glass (2001): 5.

5   RMIT (1995) *Annual Report 1994*. Melbourne: RMIT: 13.

6   RMIT (2021): 27.

7   RMIT (1994) RMIT International Strategy. RMIT, December

8   e.g. RMIT University Office of International Programs (1994) Administrative Procedures for International Programs and Projects. 4 January.

9   RMIT (1995): 30.

10   RMIT (1994).

11   RMIT (1994).

12   See Knight, Jane (2006) Higher Education Crossing Borders: A Guide to the Implications of the General Agreement on Trade in Services (GATS) for Cross-border Education. A Report Prepared for the Commonwealth of Learning and UNESCO. Vancouver and Paris: Commonwealth of Learning and UNESCO. https://unesdoc.unesco.org/ark:/48223/pf0000147363. Accessed 16 June 2021. For the theory of trade and investment see Hirsch, Seev (1976) 'An international trade and investment theory of the firm', Oxford Economic Papers, New Series, 28, 2, July: 258–270. https://www.jstor.org/stable/2662697. Accessed 21 June 2021.

13   RMIT (2019): 19.

14   Australian Business Monthly (1993) September, quoted in Le Vin, Carmelle and Adams, Tony (1993) Royal Melbourne Institute of Technology (RMIT) History of Offshore Programs. An Interpretation. RMIT. MS. July: 6.

15   Le Vin and Adams: 37.

16   City of Melbourne (2010) Student and Education Profile of Melbourne Local Government Area. Melbourne: City of Melbourne.

17 Lawler, Geoff and Wilmoth, David (2005) The Role of Education in the Regeneration and Cohesion of the City of Melbourne. Paper presented to World Conference on Urban Education: Knowledge Capitals? Education in the Cities for the 21st Century, Manchester, 28 November–1 December: 13. https://www.researchgate.net/publication/352467234_The_Role_of_Education_in_the_Regeneration_and_Cohesion_of_the_City_of_Melbourne. Accessed 21 June 2021.

18 Durance.

19 Durance: 167.

20 Fincher, R. and Shaw, K. (2009) 'The unintended segregation of transnational students in central Melbourne', *Environment and Planning A*, 41, 8: 1884–1902. https://journals.sagepub.com/doi/10.1068/a41126. Accessed 21 June 2021.

21 RMIT (2004b) *RMIT Annual Report 2003*. Melbourne: RMIT: 34.

22 Nadarajah, Y. (2005) 'Origins of the local-global project in the Hamilton region'. *Local-Global* 1: 1. RMIT Globalism Institute: 11.

23 Le Vin and Adams (1993).

24 RMIT (1994): 31.

25 Bowden, John and Patrick, Kate (1994) 'Internationalising the curriculum', in RMIT (1994): 40.

26 Wilmoth, David (1997) Interuniversity Cooperation – the Case of the Disappearing Universities? Paper presented to International Conference on Interuniversity Cooperation and Exchanges, Beijing 19–22 August: 4. https://www.researchgate.net/publication/352472710_Inter-university_Cooperation_-_the_Case_of_the_Disappearing_Universities. Accessed 21 June 2021.

27 Patrick, Kate (1997) Internationalising the University: Implications for Teaching and Learning at RMIT. A Report on the 1996 Commonwealth Staff Development Fund Internationalisation Project Conducted by RMIT. Melbourne: Educational Program Improvement Group, RMIT. February.

28 Maslen (1999): 10.

29 Rizvi, Fazal (undated) Internationalisation of Curriculum. RMIT MS. For his thoughtful reflections on RMIT's internationalisation of the curriculum after his time at RMIT, see Rizvi, Fazal and Walsh, Lucas (1998) 'Difference, globalisation and the internationalisation of curriculum', *Australian Universities' Review* 41, 2: 8–11. https://files.eric.ed.gov/fulltext/EJ584086.pdf. Accessed 21 June 2021.

30 RMIT Business Advisory Service (1992) *RMIT Campus Development Options for Asia. A Policy Discussion Paper*. MS. RMIT Resources Division, Business Advisory Service, 2 June. Tom Yardley, Principal Consultant.

31 Sullivan, John and Silver, Alan (1995) The RMIT Wuhan Project. Paper presented at the Fourth International Symposium on the Role of Universities in Developing Areas, RMIT, Melbourne, 11–14 July.

32 In hindsight this administrative autonomy seems in stark contrast with today's Xinjiang, another of China's 'autonomous' regions.

33 RMIT (1994) RMIT International Strategy. Country Action Plans. RMIT: 5.

34 e.g. 'Audit had found that accountability structures and mechanisms relating to the International Student Program at RMIT are comprehensive and range across all activities of RMIT. The Office of International Programs provides central policy direction and accountability which ensures that international activities are adequately planned and monitored.' Victorian Office of the Auditor-General (1993) *The International Student Program at Royal Melbourne Institute of Technology*. Melbourne: Victorian Office of the Auditor-General: 11.

35 Adams, Tony (1997) *The Internationalisation of the Royal Melbourne Institute of Technology (RMIT): a Case Study*. Melbourne: RMIT Faculty of Education, Language and Community Services Dean's Paper, July.

36 1998 Inaugural Australian Export Award for Education, Governor of Victoria Export Award for Education and the International Business Asia Newsmagazine Award for Best Australian Small to Medium Business in Asia.

37 Dunkin, Ruth (1992) RMIT's Strategic Options in Asia: Some Preliminary Views Based on Malaysia Visit. DVC (Resources) Report, MS, February.

38 Dunkin (1992).

39 RMIT International University Malaysia (1997) Branch Campus Proposal. MS. RMIT, June.

40   Government of Penang (1992) *Penang Into the 21st Century*. Penang: Kerajaan Negeri Pulau Penang. October.

41   See University of Sydney (1991) 'Agreement for Penang centre', *The University of Sydney News*, 23, 35: 286. 17 December. http://sydney.edu.au/arms/archives/uninews/630_ The%20University%20of%20Sydney%20News%20Vol%2023%20No%2035%20 December%2017%201991.pdf. Accessed 16 June 2021.

42   The name *INTI* is derived from the Sanskrit word meaning 'Essence'. The college is now part of the Laureate group of companies, with which I have since been active. https:// newinti.edu.my/campuses/inti-international-college-penang/

43   Adorna Group of Companies (1997) *Adorna Company Profile*. Penang: Adorna Group of Companies.

44   I am grateful to Brian Stoddart for this point.

45   I am grateful to Mal Rowe and Brian Stoddart for these points. Brian reminds us that the property developments were integral to all Adorna projects, including the campus, as financing for most new projects was leveraged off the previous project.

46   Malaysia (1996) Private Higher Educational Institutions Act 1996. Laws of Malaysia Act 555.

47   Stoddart, Brian (1997) Adorna Institute of Technology. Planning Schedule 1997–2000 Draft. Paper prepared for Malaysia Campus Workshop, Melbourne, MS, 14 February.

48   I am grateful for Mal Rowe for this information.

49   I am grateful to Mal Rowe for reminding me of this story.

50   Here, too, I am grateful to Mal Rowe for this recollection.

51   This information is from Mal Rowe.

52   Mal Rowe re-identified the site and provided photographs and other reminiscences.

53   Pro Vice-Chancellor International, RMIT University (2002) 'Response provided by Pro Vice-Chancellor International, RMIT University' *Report on Public Sector Agencies* June 2002. Part 2: Education and Training: 44.

54   Wilmoth, David (1999) Learning from Penang. Paper to Major Initiatives and Projects Committee of Council, RMIT. 9 June.

55   The difficulties of a minority position in a joint venture, and one with multiple principals over the agent, AIT, are analysed by Sakamoto, Robin and Chapman, David W. (2010) *Cross-border Partnerships in Higher Education: Strategies and Issues*. New York: Routledge, especially Lane, Jason 'Joint ventures in cross-border higher education', chapter 4.

CHAPTER 9: VIETNAM'S FIRST INTERNATIONAL UNIVERSITY

1   Thu, Nguyen Xuan (2016) *Journey from a Village School to the RMIT International University Vietnam*. Westminster, California: Nguoi Books; Beanland, David (2011) The Birth of RMIT International University Vietnam, Speech to RMIT Vietnam Tenth Anniversary Dinner, Ho Chi Minh City, 25 December, reprinted in Thu (2016): 213–222.

2   I am grateful to David Beanland for reminding me of this.

3   RMIT (1996) A proposal for the establishment of the RMIT International University in Ho Chi Minh City, Vietnam. MS. July.

4   Thu.

5   Government of Vietnam (2000) Decree of the Government on Foreign Co-operation and Investment in the Areas of Medical Examination and Treatment, Education and Training, and Scientific Research. No. 06/2000/ND-CP, 6 March.

6   Government of Vietnam (2000); Government of Vietnam (2012) *Decree on Foreign Cooperation and Investment in Education*, 73/2012/NDCP Hanoi, 26. September; Government of Vietnam (2018) *Regulations on Foreign Cooperation and Investment in Education*, 86/2018/ND-CP. Hanoi, 6 June.

7   RMIT International (1998) RMIT International University Ho Chi Minh City, Vietnam. Preliminary Feasibility Study. Melbourne: RMIT International.

8   RMIT (1999) RMIT International University Vietnam. Feasibility Study. Melbourne: RMIT. August.

9   Victorian Auditor-General (2002) 'Case studies of selected associated entities and joint ventures of Victorian universities', *Report on Victorian Public Sector Agencies*, Melbourne: VAGO, June: 22.

10   The Victorian Auditor-General found, in a review of four offshore campus arrange-
      ments, that only RMIT Vietnam avoided 'original estimates [that] were overly
      optimistic': Victorian Auditor-General (2002) *Report on Public Sector Agencies, Part 2:
      Education and Training* 'Case Studies of Selected Associated Entities and Joint Ventures
      of Victorian Universities' Melbourne: Victorian Auditor-General's Office: 22.

11   Wilmoth, David (1990b) 'Urban infrastructure financing in Australia: a review in the
      context of international experience', *Urban Policy and Research* 8, 4, December: 159–168,
      https://www.tandfonline.com/doi/pdf/10.1080/08111149008551441. Accessed 19 June
      2021; Wilmoth, David (1990c) Urban infrastructure financing in Australia. Keynote
      paper presented to Joint NSW Government / University of NSW Conference on
      Financing Urban Infrastructure, Sydney, 24 August.

12   Wilmoth, David (2001) 'ADB private sector financing for RMIT International
      University Vietnam: an investor's perspective', Paper presented at Seminar on Private
      Sector Development Strategy: The Strategy in Action – an Investor's Perspective, Asian
      Development Bank Annual General Meeting, Honolulu, 8 May. https://www.scribd.
      com/document/27821082/ADB-Private-Sector-Financing-for-RMIT-International.
      Accessed 18 June 2021.

13   O'Clery, Conor (2007) The Billionaire Who Wasn't: How Chuck Feeney Secretly Made
      and Gave Away a Fortune. New York: Public Affairs.

14   The Atlantic Philanthropies (2014) *Laying Foundations for Change: Capital Investments
      of The Atlantic Philanthropies*. Vol 2, Compendium. New York: Magnum Foundation:
      45. https://layingfoundationsforchange.org/LayingFoundationsForChange_Book.pdf.
      Accessed 21 June 2021.

15   Gutteridge Haskins and Davey (2001) *RMIT International University Vietnam:
      Resettlement Action Plan*. Washington DC and Manila: International Finance
      Corporation and Asian Development Bank. April. Also see Asian Development Bank
      (1998) *Handbook on Resettlement A Guide to Good Practice*. Manila: Asian Development
      Bank (https://www.adb.org/sites/default/files/institutional-document/32259/
      handbook-resettlement.pdf. Accessed 21 June 2021); Asian Development Bank
      (1994) *Handbook for Incorporation of Social Dimensions in Projects*. Manila: ADB
      (https://think-asia.org/bitstream/handle/11540/6061/Handbook%20for%20
      incorporation%20of%20social%20dimensions%20in%20projects%20May94.
      pdf?sequence=1. Accessed 21 June 2021); and International Finance Corporation
      (1990) 'Policy on involuntary resettlement', *Operating Procedure* 4.30, June. Washington
      DC: International Finance Corporation (https://www.ifc.org/wps/wcm/connect/
      c41b5296-4485-43e3-a1d5-0876c39b1b19/OD430_InvoluntaryResettlement.
      pdf?MOD=AJPERES&CVID=jqeB1iA. Accessed 21 June 2021). I am grateful for
      Michael Mann for recalling the overnight ducks.

16   I am grateful to Michael Mann and Kenn Crompton for this information.

17   Phuong, Le Nhan (2014) quoted in The Atlantic Foundation. *Laying Foundations
      for Change: Capital Investments of The Atlantic Foundation*. New York: The Magnum
      Foundation: 213.

18   Wilmoth, David (2002) Learning Resource Centres in Vietnamese Cities and Regions.
      Paper presented to OECD Conference on Learning Cities and Regions, Melbourne,
      14–15 October. https://www.researchgate.net/publication/242162307_Learning_
      Resource_Centres_in_Vietnamese_Cities_and_Regions. Accessed 16 June 2021.

19   The Atlantic Philanthropies: 40.

20   Hoang, Lien (2018) *The Atlantic Philanthropies Viet Nam*. The Atlantic Philanthropies:
      43. https://www.atlanticphilanthropies.org/wp-content/uploads/2018/03/AP-Viet-
      Nam-Country-Book.pdf. Accessed 16 June 2021.

21   The Atlantic Philanthropies: 40–42.

22   Wilmoth, David (2004c) 'Rats in the labyrinth: A sustainability story from Vietnam', in
      Sarah Holdsworth and Tricia Caswell (eds.) *Protecting the Future: Stories of Sustainability
      from RMIT University*. Collingwood: CSIRO Publishing: 159–175. https://
      researchrepository.rmit.edu.au/esploro/outputs/bookChapter/Rats-in-the-labyrinth-a-
      sustainability-story-from-Vietnam/9921858690701341. Accessed 18 June 2021.

23   The Atlantic Philanthropies: 47.

24   I am grateful for Michael Mann for this recollection.

25   The Atlantic Philanthropies: 48.

26   The Atlantic Philanthropies: 40.

27 See Robinson, Michael and Stueart, Robert D. (eds.) (2001) *Systems and Standards for Libraries in Vietnam: Proceedings and Outcomes of a Workshop.* Melbourne: RMIT International University Vietnam.
28 Shaw, Christopher (2001) E-learning in Higher Education: Possibilities for Vietnam: Presentation to Videoconference on Connectivity, Knowledge and Tertiary Education, Vietnam Development Information Center, 15 August 2001.
29 See Hoang: 107.
30 https://www.aip-foundation.org/what-we-do/where-we-work/. Accessed 21 June 2021.
31 Wilmoth, David (2006a) Building New Campuses in Foreign Markets: Starting up RMIT Vietnam, https://www.researchgate.net/publication/352472416_Building_new_campuses_in_foreign_markets_Starting_up_RMIT_Vietnam. Accessed 19 June 2021; Mann, Michael (2006) Building New Campuses in Foreign Markets: RMIT University in Vietnam – Before (the Case for Development) and After (the Reality – What Happened). Papers presented to International Investment Forum for Private Higher Education, International Finance Corporation Headquarters, Washington DC, 1–3 February.
32 Pham, Anh (2018) 'Employers' perspectives on Vietnamese returnee students' Chapter 11 in Ly Thi Tran and Simon Marginson (eds.) *Internationalisation in Vietnamese Higher Education.* New York: Springer: 201–215. https://www.researchgate.net/publication/325657735_Employers'_Perspectives_on_Vietnamese_Returnee_Students. Accessed 19 June 2021.
33 Lawton, William and Katsomitros, Alex (2012) International Branch Campuses: Data and Developments. The Observatory on Borderless Education. Also see https://www.researchgate.net/figure/Top-15-IBCs-in-student-numbers-2010-11_tbl1_225083589. Accessed 16 June 2016.

CHAPTER 10: LEARNING CITIES

1 https://uil.unesco.org/lifelong-learning/learning-cities.
2 Kate Shaw's 2010 article in *The Age* was subtitled 'Celebratory claims of being a 'knowledge city' are more often about marketing the right images than creating opportunities and space for creativity to flourish' ('Thinking outside city limits', 13 November: Insight: 7). https://www.theage.com.au/national/victoria/thinking-outside-city-limits-20101112-17r90.html. Accessed 19 June 2021.
3 Hamilton, Walter (1991) Serendipity city: Australia, Japan and the Multifunction Polis. Crow's Nest, NSW: ABC Books.
4 Chan, Gabrielle (2018) 'Cabinet papers reveal confusion over 'vague' plan to build futuristic Japanese city in Australia', *The Guardian*, 1 January. https://www.theguardian.com/australia-news/2015/jan/01/cabinet-papers-reveal-confusion-over-vague-plan-to-build-futuristic-japanese-city-in-australia. Accessed 16 June 2021.
5 The Future North Queensland Syndicate (1990) *The North Queensland Multifunction Polis (NQMFP).* Townsville: NQMFP.
6 Australia, Commonwealth Cabinet (1987) Cabinet Submission 5463 - Multifunction Polis (MFP) - Decision 10590. National Archives NAA: A14039, 5463: 10. https://recordsearch.naa.gov.au/SearchNRetrieve/Interface/DetailsReports/ItemDetail.aspx?Barcode=31750674&isAv=N. Accessed 21 June 2021.
7 Australia, Commonwealth Cabinet (1989) Cabinet Submission 6409 - Multifunction Polis (MFP) - progress report - Decisions 12567/SA and 12600, Attachment E: 34. https://recordsearch.naa.gov.au/SearchNRetrieve/Interface/ViewImage.aspx?B=31430641. Accessed 21 June 2021.
8 Andersen Consulting and Kinhill (1989) *Multifunction Polis Joint Feasibility Study. Consultancy Final Report*, December, Section 3: 19–20.
9 Australia, Commonwealth Cabinet (1990) Cabinet Submission 7293 - Consideration of the report of the Joint Steering Committee (JSC) on the Multifunction Polis (MFP) feasibility study and future project management - Decisions 14055/ER, 14161/ER and 14277: Attachment E: 4–5. https://recordsearch.naa.gov.au/SearchNRetrieve/Interface/ViewImage.aspx?B=31429377. Accessed 22 September 2021.
10 MFP Adelaide Community Consultation Panel (1991) *Report.* Volume 1. Canberra: Australian Government Publishing Service: 4–5.
11 MFP-Adelaide Management Board (1991) *MFP-Adelaide Management Board Report on the Feasibility of MFP-Adelaide.* Adelaide: MFP-Adelaide Management Board, May.

12 Joint Steering Committee to the Australian and Japanese Governments (1990) *Multifunction Polis Feasibility Study*. Also see Andersen Consulting and Kinhill (1989).

13 This dropped to 50,000. Brinkworth, Jenny (1991) 'Landmark symbol urged for MFP', *The Advertiser*, 4 June: 13.

14 Della-Giacoma, Jim and Cribb, Julian (1991) 'Japan "left out" of MFP plans', *The Australian*, 28 May: 8.

15 Yencken, David (1989) *Multifunction Polis: Social Issues Study. Report for the Department of Industry, Technology and Commerce*. Canberra: Department of Industry, Technology and Commerce. For me, notable contributions were McCormack, Gavan (ed.) (1991) *Bonsai Australia Bansai*. Sydney: Pluto Press; Inkster, Ian (1991) *The Clever City: Japan, Australia and the Multifunction Polis*. South Melbourne: Sydney University Press; Hamilton, Walter (1991) *Serendipity City: Japan, Australia and the Multifunction Polis*. Sydney: ABC Publications; Mouer, Ross E. (ed.) (1990) *The MFP Debate: A Background Reader*. Bundoora, Victoria: La Trobe University Press and James, Paul (1990) *Technocratic Dreaming: Very Fast Trains and Japanese Designer Cities*. Melbourne: Melbourne Left Book Club and Heinemann.

16 Lewis, Rosie (2015) 'Cabinet papers 1988–89: Backing for Multifunction Polis in Adelaide', *The Australian*, 1 January http://www.theaustralian.com.au/in-depth/cabinet-papers/cabinet-papers-1988-89/cabinet-papers-198889-backing-for-multifunction-polis-in-adelaide/news-story/8b3045ac6b05b4afab2d11646c6a1eb7. Accessed 16 June 2021.

17 Sugimoto, Yoshio (1989) *Five Concerns About the MFP Project*. Discussion Paper for Advanced Information City Workshop, 11 October 1989, the University of Melbourne. http://mailstar.net/sugimoto.html. Accessed 21 June 2021.

18 MFP Community Consultation Panel (1990) *Progress Report*. Canberra: Department of Industry, Technology and Commerce, December.

19 *Canberra Times* (1991) 'Multi-function polis is given the green light', *Canberra Times*, 1 August.

20 McCormack.

21 MFP Adelaide Community Consultation Panel (1991): 17.

22 Arnstein, Sherry R. (1969) 'A ladder of citizen participation', *Journal of the American Institute of Planners* 35, 4: 216–224. http://www.tandfonline.com/doi/abs/10.1080/01944366908977225. Accessed 16 June 2021.

23 Parker, Paul (1998) 'The Multi-Function Polis 1987–97: an international failure or innovative local project?', *Pacific Economic Paper* No. 283. Canberra: Australia-Japan Research Centre, Research School of Pacific and Asian Studies, The Australian National University, September; and Smith, J. (1990) *Australia – Going, Going, Gone? A Critique of the Multifunction Polis Project*. Bedford Park, South Australia: The Flinders Press; Harwood, John (1991) 'A quiet night in Port Adelaide', *Australian Society*, May: 30–31.

24 See Parker: 8 for a summary and review.

25 Australia. Bureau of Industry Economics (1994) *Evaluation of Commonwealth Support for the Multifunction Polis*. Research Report 58. April.

26 Australian Government (2016) *Smart Cities Plan*. Canberra: Department of Prime Minister and Cabinet. https://cities.dpmc.gov.au/smart-cities-plan.

27 Struben, Hein W. 1989. International Workshop on the Information City. Reportage deel I. (trans. Goold, Sheridan) MSS, April; Japan Association of Planning Administration. 1989. The 2nd International Workshop of the Information City. Urban Development and Design in the Age of the Advanced Information Society. Tokyo: JAPA; JAPA. 1989. Ogaki International Symposium. 'Yume Okoshi' Linking the World and Nishi-Mino. Tokyo: JAPA.

28 Melbourne Vice-Chancellors' Forum (2007) Melbourne, Australia's Knowledge Capital: The Contributions of Melbourne's Universities to the City's Economic, Cultural and Community Development. Melbourne: Howard Partners. https://www.howardpartners.com.au/assets/melbourne-australia-s-knowledge-capital.pdf. Accessed 16 June 2021; Lawler, Geoff and Wilmoth, David (2005) The Role of Education in the Regeneration and Cohesion of the City of Melbourne, Paper presented to World Conference on Urban Education: Knowledge Capitals? Education in the Cities for the 21st Century, Manchester, 28 November – 1 December, https://www.researchgate.net/publication/352467234_The_Role_of_Education_in_the_Regeneration_and_

Cohesion_of_the_City_of_Melbourne. Accessed 20 June 2021. For a full account of RMIT's community engagement in the city see Durance, Paula Christine (2016) Bringing The World To Melbourne: Transnationalism, Agency and Contributions of International Students to Making a City, 2000–2010. Brisbane: School of Education, The University of Queensland. Thesis submitted for the degree of Doctor of Philosophy: 132. https://espace.library.uq.edu.au/view/UQ:415136. Accessed 16 June 2021.

29 John, Bridget Poppy, Mokopakgosi, Brian and Wilmoth, David (2013) 'Botswana Country Hub: Africa's first education hub', in Knight, Jane (ed.) International Education Hubs: Student, Talent, Knowledge-Innovation Models. Dordrecht: Springer Science: 145–164. https://link.springer.com/chapter/10.1007/978-94-007-7025-6_9. Accessed 19 June 2021.

30 Wilmoth, David (2008) 'Innovation in Private Higher Education: the Botswana International University of Science and Technology', Paper and Presentation to International Finance Corporation International Investment Forum on Private Education, Washington DC, 14–16 May, 2008. https://docplayer. net/3135963-Innovation-in-private-higher-education-the-botswana-international-university-of-science-and-technology.html. Accessed 18 June 2021.

31 John et al: 162.

32 Knight, Jane (2018) 'International education hubs', chapter 21 in P. Meusburger et al. (eds), Geographies of the University, Knowledge and Space, 12: 637–655. https://doi. org/10.1007/978-3-319-75593-9_21. Accessed 16 June 2021.

33 Wilmoth, David (2012) Empowering Liberian Youth through Technical and Vocational Education and Training: International Case Studies for Stakeholders' Consultative Forum Monrovia. Ministry of Youth and Sports, Liberia. https://www.researchgate. net/publication/352532429_Empowering_Liberian_Youth_through_Technical_and_ Vocational_Education_and_Training_International_Case_Studies. Accessed 19 June 2021.

34 University of Central Asia. https://www.ucentralasia.org/. Accessed 16 June 2021.

CHAPTER 11: GOVERNING CITIES

1 Machiavelli, Niccolò (1981) The Prince. Harmondsworth and New York: Penguin Books; Micklethwait, John (2011) 'Taming Leviathan' The Economist, Special Supplement, 19 March. https://www.economist.com/special-report/2011-03-19. Accessed 22 June 2021.

2 RMIT Faculty of Engineering (1996) Report of the RMIT delegation to China for the purpose of determining potential commercial opportunities for the faculty of engineering. MS. April.

3 Australia-China Review (1997) 'RMIT China aviation coup' Australia-China Review 11, May: 7–8.

4 Department of Housing and Regional Development (1995) Australian Urban Export Strategy. Canberra: Department of Housing and Regional Development.

5 Moodie, Rob et al (2008) Melbourne 2030 Audit Expert Group Report. Melbourne: Department of Planning and Community Development, September.

6 Victoria, Department of Infrastructure (2002) Melbourne 2030. Melbourne: Department of Infrastructure.

7 Metropolis Association (2008) Report for Commission 5: Metropolitan Performance Measurement, 2007–2008. Barcelona: Metropolis Commission.

8 Wilmoth, David (2006b) 'Activating Urban Indicators: Fables for Our Time', Keynote address and Rapporteur's Report to the World Urban Forum III Activating Urban Indicators at Metropolis Workshop in Vancouver, 18 June 2006. https://www.semantic-scholar.org/paper/Activating-Urban-Indicators%3A-Fables-for-Our-Time-Wilmoth/571 8eb6256661d4d6d2e06e96a64bd0320719287. Accessed 18 June 2021.

9 Aliakbar, Anabestani, Anabestani, Zahra and Heydari, Akbar (2013) 'Analysis [of] the satisfaction of the residents of Golbahar new town with the living conditions and its effects on Mashhad metropolis', International Journal of Management Sciences and Business Research 2, 11: 1–13. http://www.ijmsbr.com/Volume%202,%20Issue%20 11%20paper%201.pdf. Accessed 16 June 2021.

10   Wylie, John (2013) 'Can a town reinvent itself before its economic engine disappears?' *Yale Insights*, Yale School of Management. https://insights.som.yale.edu/insights/can-town-reinvent-itself-before-its-economic-engine-disappears. Accessed 16 June 2021.

11   Papua New Guinea Sustainable Development Programme (2012) *Western Province Business and Investment Guide*. Papua New Guinea Sustainable Development Programme. https://issuu.com/businessadvantage/docs/png_westernprovince_lr. Accessed 16 June 2021.

12   Howes, Stephen and Kwa, Eric (2011) *Papua New Guinea Sustainable Development Programme Review*. Papua New Guinea Sustainable Development Programme, 29 December. This article has been taken down since change of leadership of PNGSDP. For general information on PNGSDP see https://www.pngsdp.org/. Accessed 16 June 2021.

13   Shaw, Brad Damie (2017) Reframing Technical Vocational Education and Training in Papua New Guinea: An Autoethnographic Investigation into the Commercialisation of a Mining Town Technical College. PhD thesis, Faculty of Education, Monash University. https://bridges.monash.edu/articles/thesis/REFRAMING_TECHNICAL_VOCATIONAL_EDUCATION_AND_TRAINING_IN_PAPUA_NEW_GUINEA_An_Autoethnographic_Investigation_into_the_Commercialisation_of_a_Mining_Town_Technical_College/5146666. Accessed 22 June 2021.

14   I have been particularly influenced by Fukuda-Parr, Sakiko, Lopes, Carlos and Malik, Khalid (eds.) (2002) *Capacity for Development: New Solutions to Old Problems*. London: Earthscan Publications. http://sakikofukudaparr.net/wp-content/uploads/2013/01/CapacityForDevelopmentBook2002.pdf. Accessed 1 July 2021.

15   Schumpeter (1994).

CHAPTER 12: CREATIVE DESTRUCTION

1   For global connectedness see Altman, Stephen A. and Bastian, Phillip (2019) *DHL Global Connectedness Index. Mapping the Current State of Global Flows. 2019 Update.* https://www.dhl.com/content/dam/dhl/global/core/documents/pdf/g0-en-gci-2019-update-complete-study.pdf. Accessed 16 June 2021.

2   The equity case for private education in poor countries is well made in Tooley, James (2012) *From Village School to Global Brand: Changing the World through Education*. London: Profile Books.

INDEX

www.ingramcontent.com/pod-product-compliance
Lightning Source LLC
Chambersburg PA
CBHW060645150426
42811CB00085B/2429/J